PETER STOREY

I BEG TO DIFFER

ministry amid the teargas

Tafelberg

ALSO BY PETER STOREY

With God in the Crucible – Preaching Costly Discipleship,
Abingdon Press, Nashville, 2002.

Listening at Golgotha – Jesus' Words from the Cross,
Upper Room Books, Nashville, 2004.

And Are We Yet Alive? – Revisioning our Wesleyan Heritage in the New Southern Africa, Methodist Publishing House, Cape Town, 2004.

Tafelberg, an imprint of NB Publishers,
a division of Media24 Books Pty (Ltd),
40 Heerengracht, Cape Town, South Africa
www.tafelberg.com

Copyright © Peter Storey

All rights reserved.
No part of this book may be reproduced or transmitted in any form or by any electronic or mechanical means, including photocopying and recording, or by any other information storage or retrieval system, without written permission from the publisher.

Set in 11 on 16 pt Sabon
Cover by scartletstudio.net
Cover pictures by Brenda Veldtman, ANA Pictures
Book design by Melanie Kriel
Edited by Alison Lowry
Proof read by Kathleen Sutton
Index by Mirie van Rooyen
Commissioning editor: Gill Moodie

Printed and bound by Creda Communications
First edition, first impression 2018

ISBN: 978-0-624-0-7968-2
Epub: 978-0-624-0-7969-9
Mobi: 978-0-624-0-7970-5

FOR ELIZABETH,
the sons and daughters she loved,
the grandchildren she cherished,
and
Sophie Elizabeth
who bears her name.

A candle-light is a protest at midnight,
It is a non-conformist.
It says to the darkness,
'I beg to differ.'

Samuel Rayan
Your Will be Done (Singapore: CCA, 1984)

Contents

Introduction: The Train to Koedoespoort 11

1. The South African English 15
2. Homes and Schools 26
3. Kilnerton 35
4. Then There Was Elizabeth 45
5. The Sea 56
6. The God Thing 66
7. Reluctant Scholar 80
8. Stumbling into Ministry 93
9. The Island 107
10. Life Line in the Lucky Country 119
11. District Six 133
12. The Ocean in a Single Drop 143
13. Then Came the Bulldozers 152
14. Amateur Journo 159
15. Young Church 175
16. Spreading Wings 186
17. No Soft Landing 198
18. Broken Open Church 210
19. Ministry with a Whiff of Teargas 226
20. Encounters in the Public Square 241
21. Shadows of War 259
22. A Blow Falls 275
23. Perfect Storm 287
24. Bearing Witness 295
25. Trial by Friendship 304
26. National Leadership 311
27. Among God's People 323
28. Stress Fractures 338
29. Hostage Crisis 347
30. Confronting Expediency 364
31. Soul Wounds 371
32. The Thin Orange Line 384
33. Taking on the Guns 396
34. Days of Grace 408
35. Search for Healing 423
36. Something New 430
37. Professor at Large 440
38. A Last Task 446

Epilogue 457
Endnotes 468
Author's Notes and Acknowledgements 484
Index 486
About the Author 496

Introduction

The Train to Koedoespoort

The boy loved the train.

He loved the enormous Class 23 locomotive with its six powerful driving wheels, burnished copper tubing and swishing pistons, all producing an exhilarating mixture of belching smoke, roaring noise and hissing steam. Sometimes, when the load being hauled to or from Lourenco Marques was heavier than usual, an even bigger, four-eight-two configured Class 15E would do the job.

The train was important in his life. None of his classmates rode a steam train to school. Each morning he would wait – on the cinders, never on the platform – and when the train pulled in, his three friends would open the door and he would climb the vertical steps to join them. They were English-speaking kids from Cullinan diamond mine, fifteen miles further up the track. The heavy wooden door would close with a satisfying 'thunk' when he came on board. It was always one of the 2nd Class compartments, a world of dark varnished wood and upright green leather South African Railways seats, with chrome luggage racks, and faded sepia photographs of the Blue Train roaring across the Karoo or the Orange Express climbing a Drakensberg pass.

Twice each day this was their world.

They would like to have been closer to the smoke-belching locomotive, but that was not possible. The 2nd Class coaches were in the middle of the train, neatly sandwiched between 3rd Class, nearest the front, and 1st Class, furthest away from the cinders and grime. Important people sat in 1st Class, and 3rd Class was where the natives sat. They knew that.

There were other schoolchildren on the train. They also rode in 2nd Class, but never with the boy and his friends. They wore a different coloured school blazer and tie, and spoke Afrikaans, a language he and his friends struggled with for one class each day under the eye of their least favourite teacher – and then forgot. The Afrikaners went to a different school and were part of a different world that the boy and his friends had no interest in exploring. They were not aware of any overt hostility, just indifference. Sealed in their safe compartment, looking out through the familiar Springbok emblems etched on the windows, they and the Afrikaner strangers and the special people who sat in 1st Class were carried in a rush of noise and steam and smoke across the dry brown veld.

The natives were on the train too. Unlike his friends from Cullinan, the boy had been taught to call the natives by another name; he called them 'Africans'. His friends usually used other names too, words like 'kaffer' and 'munt', but were careful not to do so around him. They were a little awed by his father being a church minister and amazed that the boy and his family lived among the natives. The boy played on their respect, of course, and also the superior knowledge he had about the natives. Above all, he enjoyed them knowing that his father was not just an ordinary clergyman, but a 'Governor'. His title was Governor of Kilnerton Institution, where hundreds of Africans lived. They came from all over the Transvaal and further afield to be educated by his father and other good and wise people.

The boy's journey was always too brief. He envied his friends' longer ride to Cullinan. Their dads worked on the diamond mine there. Travelling home, he was the only one to get off at Koedoespoort station, again dropping down to the cinders on the opposite side from the station platform. He would stand right there, alongside the creaking bogeys as the locomotive took the strain and the coaches stretched and complained their way into motion. Then he would begin his walk home. It was the same every day.

THE TRAIN TO KOEDOESPOORT

But not on this day ...

This day, from the time they boarded the train in Pretoria things had been different. As they steamed through its eastern suburbs, the boy and his friends could hear the singing and shouting of the Afrikaner youths. Muffled though the sound was by the compartment walls, it was louder and more raucous than anything they remembered. Although it was early in the season, perhaps Afrikaans Hoërskool had won an important rugby match? Perhaps that explained their excitement.

This day, when the boy got down alongside to the tracks, he stood as usual to watch and feel and hear the train pull out. As it began to move, and the coaches slowly passed him, the shouting he had heard earlier became an ugly jeering. When he looked up it seemed that all the Afrikaner youths were leaning out of their carriage. They were waving little flags he didn't recognise, and they all seemed to be shouting at him and the words came thick and fast, *"Kaffer-boetie! Kaffer-kind! Nasional wen! Malan wen! Apartheid kom!"* The boy was still looking up in shock when someone hawked, and spittle began to fly. It seemed that the whole train was spitting on him. He stood, covered in their spittle, transfixed by confusion and shame, until the clickety-clack of the guard's van faded into the hot autumn silence. Then, fighting back tears, he ran home through the tall yellow grass, desperate to know what wrong he had done to deserve such derision.

Later on this day, the boy's father told him that a change had come in the land. From this day, there would be a new government consisting entirely of Afrikaners with no love for English speakers and a different way of treating people, especially the Africans. There had been an election; people called 'Nationalists' had won, and they resented those who worked for the welfare of the Africans. "It's because you got off at this station, son. That's what made the difference. They know that only people involved with Africans get off here."

The boy didn't understand much, but he knew that his world had changed; it had been invaded by a new and dark foreboding. The happy rides encapsulated in that safe and familiar compartment would never be the same. He had got off at Koedoespoort station – that's what he had done wrong. That's what made the difference.

It was May 1948 and the boy was nine years old.

1

The South African English

People like me are usually called English-speaking South Africans, but my generation was more accurately the last of the South African English. We were born in Africa and our ancestors of the last 200 years lie buried in African soil, but we never totally belonged here. The haunting beauty of our birthland – bold brass skies and scudding cumulus, dusty, gold-grey veld and dry brown sandstone, thorn trees and the smell of dust after rain – all these may have crept into our hearts, but they were not indigenous to our souls. Our inward beings were formed less by the geography of our birth than by the heritage, values, and rituals of a small island in the mists of the Northern hemisphere. We were proud South Africans, but to be South African was to be in most important ways, British. When I measure the strongest influences on my young life I have to acknowledge that those things I can identify as essentially African are outweighed by this other identity. Compatriots of my generation, though surprised by the question, have most often grudgingly agreed. They also agree that our children are different from us, making us the last of the South African English.

Post-colonial sensitivities require that this be a matter for interrogation rather than pride. The apartheid decades that occupied centre stage between 1948 and 1994 tended to overshadow the ravages of Dutch and British colonialism that preceded them and we South African English liked to cast the blame entirely on the Afrikaners. We downplayed our own forbears' role in the systematic conquest, humiliation and subjugation of the land. Since 1994 we have been held more rigorously to account – and rightly so. But these things are never simple and nor can I make them so. I have to confront those parts of my story stained with colonial wrongs and I know there will be more to uncover and repent of. Yet, as in all cultures, there are deep contradictions. My guilt has to be accompanied by gratitude, because without this heritage I would be culturally rootless and deeply impoverished. Ironically, the sharpest moral tools I use to critique the wrongs of my own people were forged in me by the same heritage. That is the paradox of my culture: the story of my people and their influence all around the world is one in which high moral codes that produce fine Christian character co-existed with exploitative colonial practices, and too often the one was used to justify the other. I, like my first South African ancestors, am both marred and ennobled by the influence of that faraway island.

On 15 May 1820, three long months after leaving Gravesend in the naval transport *Aurora*, my great-great-great-grandfather John Oates and his family were ferried through the surf onto the beach of Algoa Bay where the city of Port Elizabeth now stands. The 3 700 settlers who arrived that year consisted mostly of people adversely affected by Britain's economic woes following the Napoleonic wars. They were grateful to take their government's offer of 100-acre farming plots in faraway South Africa. They sailed in groups gathered by different leaders, one of whom was Hezekiah Sephton, a London carpenter and devout Methodist. Sephton's party consisted of more than one hundred co-religionists willing to make the journey. They knew they were to be pioneers, but were less aware of the political role envisaged for them by the Colonial Office, which was to form a stabilising 'buffer' on the dangerous, contested frontier between the Cape Colony and the Xhosa people. The Xhosa had already been significantly dispossessed and would make a number of failed attempts to forcibly win back their land from the white interlopers.

John Oates and his spouse Elizabeth were settled in the Assegai Bush River area with other members of the Sephton party in a valley which they named Salem. Today, nearly 200 years later, the little Methodist chapel with its cluster of surrounding dwellings shows little change, but its quiet loveliness belies the struggles it has witnessed.

The story of the Settlers' first years of farming is one of unrelenting hardship and near starvation. Most of them had been small traders or artisans – Oates himself was a shoemaker – and wresting a desperate living from the unforgiving *zuurveld* was an enormous and unfamiliar challenge. Some of the Dutch farmers in the region helped them and slowly they learned to be frontier folk – to plough, hunt, fight, ride and trek with the same skill as their new compatriots – but this did not alter their essential Englishness. The Dutch over time became Afrikaners, cutting ties with their origins and chafing under what they saw as foreign colonial governance, but my ancestors had no difficulty seeing themselves as being both rooted in the soil of South Africa *and* subjects of the British Empire. How could it be otherwise? The language they spoke, the books they read, the poets and sages who touched their souls, the customs they followed, the way they worshipped, all remained essentially British. When they clashed with colonial authority – over the issue of press freedom, for instance, or political representation – it was to the higher principles of their British heritage that they appealed. The land they had settled might be wild, cruel and unpredictable, but it was now a proud province of the Empire.

The belief that this was the natural order of things persisted until my generation. It was strengthened, if anything, by the call to arms in three British wars. At the turn of the twentieth century both my grandfathers fought against the Boers in what was a kind of civil war – the South African War, identifying with the British Crown against the Transvaal and Free State republicans. World War 1 claimed the life of a great-uncle in the slaughter of the Somme and the Second World War saw another relative killed training to be a fighter pilot. I was born nine months before this conflict began, and it had an enormous

– perhaps disproportionate – impact on me. My early childhood was lived in the shadow of seemingly permanent crisis. 'The War' dominated everything. Most of my male relatives were first known to me only in photographs, wearing khaki uniform. I was told that they were 'up North', the mysterious, catch-all destination for South African troops, all of them volunteers, who spent six years fighting Fascism in Abyssinia, then the Western Desert and Italian campaigns. It may have been far away and I may have been very small, but as the most brutal conflict of all history unfolded, I inhaled its contagion. A gargantuan struggle – somehow critical for my life – was afoot. It seemed to be about a good or evil future and my earliest impressions were of fears that it would go badly. I recall my parents crouching over the scratchy radio, straining to hear Winston Churchill's words of defiance on the BBC. I can even remember at three and a half years being in the car as my father drove from farm to farm in the Ermelo and Carolina districts of the Transvaal bringing news to scattered families that a husband or son had been captured or killed at a place called Tobruk. The heaviness of it all must have struck hard into my child's mind for the image to be with me still. Later the tide turned and names like El Alamein, Stalingrad, Malta, Palermo and Salerno, Monte Cassino, Normandy and the rest lodged in my memory.

The war ended for a wide-eyed seven-year-old on the lawns of the Union Buildings in Pretoria where a great thanksgiving service was held. My father, then minister at the central Methodist church in the city, helped lead the service. 'Oom Jannie' Smuts was there in his Field Marshall's uniform, the British Commonwealth had triumphed, good had conquered evil, and thanking God seemed the most appropriate response in the world.

In the immediate post-war years I learned for the first time what normality was for the South African English: food rationing ended and Dad could put away the wood and muslin sieve he had fashioned to refine flour – albeit illegally – in the war years. My mother put away her Red Cross uniform. Genuine butter was once more available but I was by then a peanut butter addict. For the first time Christmas gifts were newly bought and not hand-me-downs from older, 'pre-war' cousins. Steamship schedules between Southampton and Cape Town resumed, and the reading material my sister Valmai and I devoured – the *Boys' Own* and *Hobbies Magazine*, and her *Girls' Crystal* – arrived each week by Union Castle liner, as did the *Women's Weekly* that guided thousands of mothers' knitting habits. We were Wolf Cubs and Scouts, or Brownies and Girl Guides. All our story-books came from England, and my imagine-world was inhabited by the knights of Arthur's Camelot and past tales of derring-do by Britishers in distant outposts like the Khyber Pass, Khartoum, and on the seas off St Vincent and Trafalgar. Biggles and Bulldog Drummond sorted out the more contemporary villains who wished us ill. I pored over every page of Arthur Mee's ten-volume *Children's Encyclopaedia*, absorbing worlds of knowledge through the filter of an unapologetic imperialism, with its uniquely British amalgam of chivalry and Christian piety that sanctified the sword so long as it was wielded by good men. My heroes took it for granted that duty, service and sacrifice were paramount, and that failure was not the worst that could happen, so long as it was in a noble cause and integrity preserved. Thus, the selflessness of Scott's failure in the Antarctic was a more inspiring model than Amundsen's mere success and left an indelible mark on me. The saga of the motley Dunkirk rescue fleet covered a military rout with glory. Our heroes eschewed bombast and despised self-advertisement, yet their qualities of modesty and understatement concealed a steely, unquestioned confidence that the Empire we belonged to was a divinely ordered force for good in the world.

Something else about us, not easily understood by others, was that one's politics made little difference to these loyalties and values. My dad favoured the socialism of the British Labour Party, influenced as it was by the Methodist movement. He admired leaders like Ramsay

MacDonald, the first ever Labour Prime Minister, brilliant Christian radical Sir Stafford Cripps and fiery Aneurin Bevan, founder of the National Health Service. Churchill was honoured for his inspirational war leadership, but would always be a Tory rogue. Yet none of this leftish sympathy diluted respect and affection for the Royal Family, nor was there any question about being proud citizens of both South Africa and the British Empire. The South African English were sure that they rejoiced in the best of both worlds.

This sense of privilege reached its apogee during the Royal Visit of 1947. We stood for hours in our Wolf Cub uniforms to watch the glistening White Train whoosh by, rewarded by the tiniest glimpse of their Majesties. We listened entranced as a shy Princess Elizabeth, newly turned 21, broadcast from Cape Town that: "… my whole life whether it be long or short shall be devoted to your service and the service of our great imperial family to which we all belong … God help me to make good my vow." When she said, "I am six thousand miles from the country where I was born, but I am certainly not six thousand miles from home," she summed it up for the South African English.

My mother's forbears were also of 1820 Settler stock. The names Thorne, Kidger and Stretton on her mother's side figured large in the Eastern Cape. Jack Wood, my maternal grandfather – a fastidious and grumpy old gentleman who used to carefully note the time of sunset so that he could switch on the lights of his Vauxhall exactly thirty minutes after – rose to be Postmaster of East London. He had fought in what we called the 'Boer War' as a mounted trooper with the famed Driscoll's Scouts. Because he and Granny Mabel lived by the sea we made our annual holiday trek there from Pretoria in the 1938 Chevrolet, much of it on muddy dirt roads. Whenever we visited, I was awed by the cavalry sabre perched in the umbrella stand along with his brolly and walking sticks, wondering how many Boers he had stuck with it, but never daring to ask. I recall no conversations with him; I don't think he spoke to small boys.

My paternal grandfather John Storey was a cabinet-maker from the English Lake District who had sailed to South Africa in the 1880s to enter the Methodist ministry. That didn't work out as planned and he settled in Kimberley and went back to his craft. Widowed once, he then married grandmother Ivy Oates, granddaughter of the settler John Oates. He died long before I was born, but I like to think that some dexterity with my hands might be evidence of his DNA. My father had only one photograph of him, showing a very handsome man with gentle eyes and I think I felt a wistful closeness. It was easier to relate to the person in the picture than to my living grandfather. In later life, there was a moment when I felt John Storey did come close to me: I was preparing to clean a graceful display cabinet he had made. More than a century of polish had blackened the Burmese teak and I wanted to uncover its original golden glow. With one of his wooden-handled screwdrivers, passed down through my father, in hand, I started to remove the cast-iron hinges. The screws came free smoothly – that is the nature of teak – and right then it struck me that the last person to turn those screws, possibly with this very screwdriver, had been Grandfather John. It was a moment of connection and he and I finally met. Artisan he may have been, but he was a cultured man, known for his mastery of the English language and its poets. His volumes of Wordsworth, Shelley, Keats, Browning and Pope line my bookshelves still, together with biographies of his political heroes, William Gladstone and Abraham Lincoln. He was also a respected lay preacher and Sunday School superintendent. During the siege of Kimberley he joined the Town Guard manning the perimeter trenches, while I'm told that Granny Ivy was known to sit a horse with regal grace undeterred by the odd Boer cannon shell. Nearly 6 000 Boer shells fell on the town, killing 155 people, with hunger and disease claiming 1 500 more, mostly among the black and coloured population.

I was born only 28 years after the Act of Union, designed to heal the bitter aftermath of that war. In 1910 Boer and Briton had buried the hatchet to build a nation together, with the former colonies and Boer republics now forming the Union of South Africa. The fact that up to the 1930s every prime minister of this new self-governing British dominion was a former Boer general, and the readiness of two of them – Louis Botha and Jan Smuts – to rally to Britain's aid in the wars of 1914 and 1939 seemed to underline this spirit of reconciliation, but the reality was more complicated. Afrikaner bitterness and English condescension were not an easy mix, and lurking behind both was the fact of white racial hegemony: "We ought not to forget," said British Prime Minister Asquith in 1910, "that besides Briton and Boer, South Africa contains a vast population of His Majesty's coloured subjects, and we may feel the strongest confidence that the same wide liberality of treatment which has made Union possible will be as promptly shown to these coloured races."[1] That was not to be: the 'coloured subjects' were, of course, both forgotten and betrayed. Their struggle would continue for 84 more years. Meanwhile, unity between the two white tribes tended to rely more on the expediencies required for racial domination than any real warmth.

Thus, the cultural narrative that shaped me majored in British values and virtues, but was largely silent about the ugly, dark fault-lines running through the history of my people. That had to wait for new understandings to dawn. It was much later when the opportunity came to travel to the United Kingdom and I made my first visit to Westminster Abbey, the high temple and repository of all that was British. Confronting me there were the stark contradictions of my heritage. I was deeply moved by the modest tablets and plaques honouring the poets, writers and Christian saints whose work had honoured God and transformed society for the better, shaping one of the more humane and tolerant of nations anywhere, as well as enriching my mind and touching my soul. But the larger more triumphalist statuary seemed to be reserved for the admirals and generals of Empire. Standing among them I suddenly found myself weeping, overwhelmed by an unfamiliar shame. Here, cast in bronze or carved in stone, were gathered the warriors of my tribe, the instruments of centuries of colonial conquest and bloodletting in every corner of the world, including my own. Here was the ugly subtext to what I knew was noble and good in my culture. There was no way of calculating the measure of suffering and dispossession they had meted out and I had to face the reality that for every Shakespeare, Milton, Browning or Wordsworth, every Shaftesbury, Nightingale or Wilberforce, every Scott or Shackleton, every Tyndale, Whitefield or Wesley, there were plenty of representatives of this other face of my heritage.

This, of course, was a perspective my Afrikaner compatriots would gladly have shared with me had we ever talked to each other, but most of the South African English had little relationship with Afrikaners and even less awareness of the complexities of their politics. Beyond our Afrikaner heroes – those who the English saw as having fought a good fight, and then wisely embraced the imperial project of their conquerors – was a deep, unhealed anger. British scorched-earth policy during the South African War had left wounds which many determined to keep open until vengeance could be exacted. The burning of Boer farms and the desperate suffering of their women and children in concentration camps were seen as war crimes. Their loss of independence and having to bow once more to the Union Jack rankled deeply. The domination of the economy by English speakers and their ill-disguised attitude of superiority were further cause for resentment. To these Afrikaner nationalists, my kind of South African was not wanted; to them we were still *uitlanders* with our loyalty given to a faraway British monarch, and no rooted patriotism for the soil of Africa. If things got bad, they said, we could pick up our marbles and go to any number of English-speaking destinations around the world. Much of this was true, and as it happened, when things did get bad, many English speakers did just that. The surprise was that a time came when many Afrikaners did too, but that was long into the future.

Those of us who had waved flags as the royal Daimlers swept past in 1947 didn't know that the visit marked not only the apogee but the beginning of the end of South Africa's Englishness. Prime Minister Jan Smuts, though a colossus on the world stage, had lost popularity at home. Thousands of World War Two veterans were struggling to find jobs in the post-war economy and were blaming him. With an election in the offing, Smuts had calculated that a visit by the Royal family would boost his chances, but the opposition National Party, who had scarcely disguised their Nazi sympathies in the War, had a trump card of their own. Central to Afrikaner mythology was the 'Great Trek', the saga of their nineteenth-century migration away from British domination into the interior. Its centenary in 1938 had been re-enacted by thousands of bearded 'trekkers', and as their covered wagons trundled through towns and villages all over the nation, they fanned the flames of Afrikaner identity and republicanism, converging on Pretoria to lay the cornerstone of a massive monument. Then, during the War they used the absence of both English and Afrikaner Smuts loyalists 'up North' to build their political strength. The trekker exercise was repeated in preparation for the Voortrekker Monument's dedication. By the time 250 000 of them gathered on the hillside below the monument in 1949, Dr DF Malan's National Party, in an alliance with the smaller Afrikaner Party, had defeated Smuts, carrying the country with a slim majority, and had been in power for a year. Afrikaner men again grew 'trekker' beards – not a fashionable accessory at the time – to identify with the event.

The new reality would take some time to sink in. Our elders had been shocked by the election result but I'm not sure they saw it as anything but temporary, and beyond my nasty experience on the train tracks after the election, I had much to learn about how fundamentally things had changed. During the monument celebrations I remember joining older friends on our bikes, baiting the bearded men in their corduroys and *velskoens*, mocking their *bokbaards*[2] with rude, bleating noises, then tearing off before they could catch us.

We should have taken their monument much more seriously. To non-Afrikaners, exploring the Voortrekker monument is a chilling experience but it offers the best clue to the nationalistic racial fervour gripping post-war Afrikanerdom. The architecture is 'Nazi kitsch', designed to overwhelm with massive scale and impregnability. Inside the vast gloom, marble friezes recount battles between brave Boers and primitive savages, climaxing with the Afrikaners' own version of manifest destiny: like the Israelites of old, the trekkers are seen on the eve of the Battle of Blood River, making their solemn vow to a God who would seal their conquest over the Zulu in exchange for a promise of perpetual piety. Here, too, as in Westminster, ideology is baptised by theology, but unlike Westminster, no gentler, more altruistic forms of heroism offer any relief. If Westminster presents the British Empire as one on which the sun would never set, the Voortrekker monument, through a strategically placed aperture in its roof, ensures that on every anniversary of Blood River all the sun's brightness would be focused in a narrow shaft falling on a sarcophagus representing the Afrikaner people alone.

The fragile 38-year experiment of white unity in partnership with the British Commonwealth of nations had tended to favour the South African English and now it was about to unravel. In his 1948 victory speech, Nationalist Prime Minister DF Malan proudly reversed the words of the young Elizabeth: "In the past we felt like strangers in our own country," he said, "but today South Africa belongs to us once more. For the first time since Union, South Africa is our own." The 1910 arrangement had also favoured South Africa's two white tribes to the exclusion of millions of blacks, but the 'us' Malan now referred to meant Afrikaners only. On that May afternoon in 1948 the jeering youths who rained spittle on me as the train pulled out of Koedoespoort station had reason to celebrate. Their day of vengeance had come. The South African English had been brushed aside and for the first time South Africa would be ruled by their people alone.

2

Homes and Schools

Number 570 Schoeman Street in Pretoria wasn't my first home, but it is the first that I recall with clarity. I had been born at 25 Muir Avenue in a town called Brakpan, where my dad was involved in building the new Methodist church. He was good at that sort of thing, and actually used our back yard to cast the rose window that would dominate the sanctuary. My birth at 3.30 am on a Sunday was apparently a difficult one and my mother often reminded me that I had been lucky to emerge alive, having been dragged out of her womb with a pair of callipers. She said it took a nurse and doctor 45 minutes to 'bring me round'. These reminders often coincided with bad behaviour on my part. Her logic seemed to be that I owed her both gratitude for surviving birth and contrition for the tough time I had given her. Looking back I think Mom's family were rather hard people and I'm not sure she was very good at showing affection – although, as is sometimes the case, I'm told that the primary school children she taught for many years experienced her quite differently. Dad was differently made. He was a gentle and sensitive soul whose heart had been softened first by the beauty of the Lake District poets and then captured by the servant-spirit of Jesus. I don't recall him teaching me much in a direct way, but I watched his life and knew it was deeply good. In his leisure hours he was a craftsman of sorts, having inherited wood-working skills from his father. I never tired of watching him work the stubborn kiaat he used to make bedroom furniture and lounge stools. No mechanical tools in the 1940s and 50s – everything cut, shaped, planed and sanded by hand. He also loved to work with metal, and built an 'O' gauge scale model Class 23 locomotive, soldering the intricate bits out of odds and ends and filing pistons and drive rods out of nails. He had to wait until a couple of years after the war to power the loco with an electric motor from Britain. The train it pulled was modelled on the Orange Express, which used to ply between Joburg and Durban – altogether a remarkable work.

There lay between father and son a very 'English' reserve which meant that I probably learned more about Dad from his sermons than any conversation. It was in the pulpit that he could speak eloquently of the things that mattered most. Words like 'Grace' and 'Love', 'Nobility' and 'Truth' were the ones he most often used, and it was evident from his life that these virtues had taken up residence long since within. For him they were inextricably bound up with the experience of knowing Jesus. But there was another tributary too, from which a unique beauty had flowed into his soul: in one of his last letters he urged me to read the English poets. "Try Wordsworth's *Excursion*," he wrote. "It holds all the great spiritual values that have made our English tradition, which we dare not let die in South Africa without handing ourselves over to an inhuman authoritarianism." He had been re-reading *The Excursion* and said he "knew again how our blessed tradition has moulded and sustained my thoughts of freedom and human dignity – in other words, why I think the things I do." These may seem unfashionable words in our days of post-colonial revisionism, when the ugly underside of Anglo-empire is rightly exposed and trashed, but it is important that we do not forget the virtues he spoke about. They too are part of our bequest and over centuries those virtues have inspired many a determined resistance against tyranny. South Africa may be free, but freedom is not enough: the brutalities of the past survive under new guises and they have left us callous, uncouth and uncaring of human life. In our speech and in our actions, we are a violent people who have to relearn the virtues before we can become a kinder, gentler South Africa.

Brakpan was a grimy mining town on the East Rand, later claiming dubious fame for also being the birthplace of BJ Vorster, one of South Africa's toughest apartheid prime ministers who came to power after the assassination of Hendrik Verwoerd. Many years later I was to have a brief encounter with him, one with a friend's life at stake.

Methodist ministers are committed to itinerancy, promising to go where the Annual Conference sends them, and when I was two years old Dad was transferred to Ermelo. There are snapshots only of life there. I have mentioned the impact of World War Two and the fall of Tobruk. It was in Ermelo that I made my first friend, Michael Russell. Michael fell out of Dad's Chev one day as it went around a corner: one moment he was there, the next not. Luckily he landed in a sandbank but carried a long scar on his forehead all his life. Our family, consisting of my parents, my older sister Valmai, our Airedale dog and I, lived in a church manse[3] with a large field as our back yard and I recall thorny bramble bushes and two cows. I have a fairly clear mind-picture of the Methodist church where Dad preached, and a ministers' concert at which the famous Reverend JB Webb conjured sweet music using a violinist's bow on a carpenter's saw gripped between his knees. It was when Dr Webb was suddenly moved to the prestigious Methodist Central Hall in Johannesburg, that Dad succeeded him at the main Methodist church in Pretoria and we took up residence in Schoeman Street.

The house had a big palm tree on the front lawn and a tennis court in the back yard. Methodist manses were social centres in those days so our home was constantly frequented by members of the congregation. Church youth and young adults used the tennis court on summer evenings and weekends. We also housed our 'farm cousin' Hector Thorne from Warmbaths, some 70 miles to the north, so that he could attend Pretoria Boys' High. He got my bedroom and Dad built in a portion of the veranda for me. With just a quarter inch of hardboard between me and Pretoria's bitter winters, I learned to deal with cold early in life.

My first school was Miss Mickey's Kindergarten just up the road in Arcadia. There is a vague memory of getting into trouble for kissing a girl, but I cannot swear to it. Then on to Arcadia Primary School until Dad was transferred to Kilnerton Training Institution outside of Pretoria in 1948. Kilnerton demands a chapter all to itself, but in terms of schooling it meant that I was moved to Hatfield Primary on the eastern edge of Pretoria, nearer our new home. Both schools offered me a strong learning foundation. Memories of the classroom are minimal though and it seems that apart from the brief flirtation at Miss Mickey's, I kept out of trouble. A scary exception was when, exploring a store-room in the rambling Kilnerton Mission House I found a small bottle of deadly strychnine poison and took it to school, proudly showing it off to my schoolfriends and then carelessly leaving it in a desk. My parents were summoned and had to witness me being dressed down by the school principal. He was pale with what I thought was rage, but in retrospect it was probably shock. No doubt he was imagining little bodies lying all over his school – a scenario that could well have been actualised. My most vivid memories have nothing to do with learning really: special assemblies on the day the war ended, with all of us singing *Now Thank We All Our God,* the visit of Field Marshal Bernard Montgomery soon thereafter, who arrived in his famous Desert Rats camouflaged open Humber car and talked down to us in clipped, superior tones, then gave us all a half-holiday. There was another when the new Union Castle liner *Pretoria Castle* came into service on the Southampton–Cape Town run; we felt we had launched her ourselves. My strongest subjects were English, History and Art and I did reasonably well in the others – except for Arithmetic. From very early on I developed an aversion to numbers and mathematical symbols, which still leaves me disadvantaged.

The insularity of a white English-speaking child's life in the South

Africa of the 1940s and 50s, not only in relation to the other 'white tribe', but more so when it came to black people, was almost absolute. My memories of early childhood carry only two black images: one was Mita Gongo, the Xhosa domestic worker in our Pretoria home, whose kind, lined face remains quite clear to this day; the other was roving bands of young black men, some of them playing mouth-organs, who were seen walking down Schoeman Street on Sunday afternoons. They were no doubt mostly employed in white homes and gardens, enjoying their only day off, but Mita Gongo called them '*Amaleitas*' and there was something vaguely threatening about them, possibly because Mita didn't like them. Other black persons touched my life in a tangential way, like the old man who drove the horse-drawn ice-cream cart down Schoeman Street, selling wafers for a tickey – threepence – but there is little other recollection of them, such was their place in our universe. My childhood memory is a parable of the general white experience. Black persons impinged on our lives only in a marginal and subservient role and things would have remained so had the Methodist Church not later intervened with the move to Kilnerton, taking our family out of its white bubble and locating us in the middle of a large black college campus.

Methodist ministers were paid very little, so outings and school holidays were severely limited, but we did venture occasionally to Johannesburg, 30 miles away, for a shopping day and maybe lunch at John Orr's department store. En route we usually stopped on the side of the tree-lined road to pick mushrooms in the fields. Joburg had trams – red and cream behemoths that rumbled on tracks down the middle of the city streets. Every so often the spring-loaded arm that connected one of them to the powerlines above would jump loose, the tram would screech to a halt and the conductor would fish out a long pole from its tubular hiding place and juggle the arm back into contact – all in a shower of crackling sparks to entertain us.

Dad would sometimes swop pulpits with JB Webb and would

preach in the Central Hall in Pritchard Street, the church where, in the 1920s he had first experienced the call to be a minister. The organist then was the famous Rupert Stoutt, who unbelievably would still be there when I entered that pulpit some 50 years later.

School holidays were usually spent with relatives, sometimes with Hector's family on their farm near Warmbaths. The farm was a poor investment that never repaid their back-breaking work. Their humble farmhouse had rocks weighting the tin roof to hold it down. Cattle and peanuts or sunflowers were what they farmed and their life was hard. There was the heartbreak of one holiday, when anthrax struck Uncle Strett's herd. Hector struggled to hold back his tears as he shot the doomed beasts and we retched with the stench of burning cattle carcasses. Uncle Stretton Thorne was a hard-bitten, pipe-smoking '*bloedsap*' United Party supporter. The next farm belonged to the Tromp family, with old man Tromp a passionate Afrikaner Nationalist, full of bombast now that his party was in power. At night I used to lie on the carpet next to the crackling fire listening to the two of them almost coming to blows as they argued. However, the Tromp/Thorne feud was as much about pride as politics: whenever Tromp decided to plant sunflowers Strett would stubbornly plant peanuts, and vice versa – and Tromp seemed always to be right. He became more prosperous as Uncle Strett and Aunt Muriel sank deeper into debt. Those farm holidays taught me a deep respect for the farmers of our land, not to mention politics 101. I also learned something else: anxious to prove my manhood, I nagged Hector to take me hunting. He finally agreed and we set off with me proudly hefting the .303 rifle. It was a long, burning hike before we crossed some spoor. "You're in luck," Hector said, "that looks like kudu." Sure enough, after another 30 minutes, there the beast stood in the bush: a magnificent bull, at the shoulders as tall as me, with long horns spiralling majestically skywards. The day was dying and the animal was silhouetted darkly, all except for the pink glow of his soft translucent ears against the setting sun. He seemed to be looking straight at us. "He's yours," Hector whispered, and then added, "if you want to kill him." I was transfixed. I never even raised the rifle. I knew I could never kill something of such grace and beauty. The moment when that great animal won my heart stayed with me and I have never wanted to hunt again.

Another holiday venue I enjoyed was being packed off to my dad's sister Beattie and her spouse Harry in Germiston. They had chosen a road less travelled by my Methodist family: Harry liked his whiskey, and Beattie was, well, very sexy. The house had some slightly risqué pictures and one or two charming art deco nude statuettes, all of great fascination to a pubescent boy. They also had the latest audio technology called a radiogram, combining a radio and gramophone in one piece of furniture. Cousin John's latest vinyl record with Roy Rogers singing *Don't Fence Me In* would play on the one side, until Uncle Harry walked in, flipped a switch, and immediately the radio took over on the other. Their home was so full of *things*.

Most of my wartime Christmas hand-me-downs – 1930s-era *Hobbies Annuals*, Dinky Toy cars, puzzles – had once been owned by John, and he had a Lionel train set which I loved to lay out and operate. Harry was an inveterate tinkerer and accomplished radio ham. I used to sit next to him as, with a whiskey in his left hand, with his right he delicately manipulated the glowing dials to pick up voices from thousands of miles away. His garage was filled with technical junk that provided an endless treasure-trove for me, and wonder of wonders, on the back lawn stood a full-size radar aerial discarded from one of the navy's World War Two frigates. How this massive piece of hardware travelled the thousand miles from Simon's Town to Germiston and into Harry's yard remains a mystery.

It was while staying with Uncle Harry and Aunty Bea that I met Field Marshal Smuts. They took me to a United Party fête in the grounds of Victoria Lake, and there he was, in full khaki uniform with red cap band and tabs, medal ribbons from three wars, Sam

Browne belt, and swagger-stick tucked under his arm. I clearly remember him leaning down to shake my hand, his kind, lined face with its white goatee beard close to mine. "How do you do, young man?" he asked courteously. I have no idea what I replied but my aunt preened with pride. And then, on Victoria Lake I fell in love for the first time with boats and boating, but the story of that romance belongs in another chapter.

When I entered Pretoria Boys' High School (PBHS) in 1951 the impact of the National Party regime elected in 1948 had already been felt there. Before their more infamous legislation against black South Africans, they attacked those of their own kind whom they saw as anglophiles. PBHS was a favourite school for Afrikaans-speaking farmers who sent their sons to learn English and receive a more liberal education. The new regime put pressure on such families to end this practice and by the time I arrived, the hostels had been gutted of many stalwart Afrikaner boarders – often the backbone of the school's *gees* (spirit) and its rugby prowess. They were transferred to Afrikaans Hoërskool across the railroad tracks. PBHS was weakened, its discipline became poor and my time there did not serve me well. Had I stayed, I think I might have ended up a problem to society. I was an inconsistent scholar, excelling only at English, History, Geography and Art, the last mentioned subject taught by the great and gloriously eccentric Walter Battis. I tried other languages but gave up uselessly on both Latin and German, settling finally on Geography as an escape. I had a handful of good school friends but because Kilnerton was so far from the Pretoria suburbs where they lived, I saw little of them after school.

The year 1952 saw the tercentenary of the landing at the Cape of Jan van Riebeeck and the first Dutch East India Company settlers and a handful of boys from PBHS would be selected to travel to Cape Town for the celebrations to be held on the new Foreshore, the reclaimed land outside of Van Riebeeck's Kasteel de Goede Hoop.

The Nationalist government planned to use the commemorations to emphasise the civilising role of whites among the 'backward' indigenous people. Living at Kilnerton my parents were not impressed, but I hoped very much to be chosen because I'd never seen the Mother City. I believed it to be a place of great beauty – and it was a seaport, and that was where I would find ships. Sadly, I wasn't selected. Cape Town had to wait.

3

Kilnerton

Heading east from Pretoria on the road to Witbank, much of the undeveloped land between the city's edge and Silverton four miles on belonged to the Methodist Church. A rugged koppie flanked the road and back then Andy's Cash Store was the landmark where a left turn took you through the stone gate-posts of Kilnerton Training Institution, or KTI, as the students called it. A graceful red-roofed stone chapel crowned the koppie, with the campus clustered below its northern slopes facing the winter sun. Church land ran north a long way across the veld to a second ridge of low hills. The vast property was bisected by the railroad from Pretoria to Cullinan Diamond Mine and the Witbank coalfields and Portuguese East Africa (now Mozambique). This was the railroad used by a young Winston Churchill after he escaped from prison during the South African War – and by me for my more mundane commute to school.

Kilnerton was one of the campuses born through the genius of nineteenth century Methodist missionary strategy. The Reverend William Shaw, chaplain to the 1820 settler Sephton party, was not satisfied to minister only to the settlers and he turned his attention to the indigenous people of the Eastern Cape. Befriending Xhosa chiefs, he was able to build a chain of missions stretching 400 miles from Grahamstown to what is now Durban. Everywhere he linked spiritual work with education, gaining increasing acceptance for the Gospel among the amaXhosa. His strategy was taken up by fellow missionaries and bore rich fruit among other ethnic groups too, and names like Healdtown and Clarkebury in the Eastern Cape, Moroka at Thaba'Nchu in the Free State, Boichoko on the plains of the Western Transvaal, and Indaleni in Natal, became watchwords of Methodist missionary education. Kilnerton was opened in 1885, a full twelve years before any government school for blacks anywhere in South Africa, and at a time when even white education was very limited. By 1906, for instance, in the Orange Free State, of the 37 000 white children in the province, only 17 000 received any schooling at all. Kilnerton was one of the standouts in a Methodist network that at its height was educating 27.3% of black scholars across the land – excluding their many night schools. They were not alone in this enterprise; until their work was ruthlessly dismantled by the apartheid government the Christian churches together were educating the majority of black schoolchildren in South Africa.[4]

Dad now had responsibility for the leadership and administration of this famous institution with its 1 600 students. The 'Normal College' had 230 teachers in training while 600 students attended the high school. A primary or 'Practising School' – so named because this is where student teachers cut their teeth – had 700 children. The multi-racial teaching staff numbered 56 and additional administrative staff managed the boarding residences and what had originally been 2 400 hectares of land.[5] Students also tended extensive vegetable gardens where food for the dining-halls was grown. Like the streets of Pretoria Kilnerton's campus was planted with jacaranda trees and around September shimmered in a translucent mauve haze.

Methodists of that era had a high view of their missionary vocation and its potential impact on the fraught issues of race in South Africa. In a 1950 letter to a tutor at his Alma Mater, Richmond College, my dad wrote:

> You are all aware that, in this multi-racial land, issues are at stake which involve the dignity and destiny of millions of black men and women. To many, the way here may seem confused, but our own path

is quite clear and we have never wavered in our faith that in Christ, all personality finds its dignity and worth and that true education must be grounded in the Christian view of God, Man (sic) and the World. Here at Kilnerton, racial cooperation is on a high level and many young Africans are learning how the Spirit of Christ banishes the devils of racial prejudice and intolerance, and go out to be teachers and potential leaders of their fellow Africans. I believe that the Christian character of our students is the final answer to the doubts and fears of the European minority in this land. In the meantime have no fear: Methodism will be true to her great missionary tradition.

However, with the apartheid government beginning to flex its racist muscles after two years in power, he was far from sanguine about the future:

In the days just ahead, we may have to face a challenge which will test the deepest faith of our Church and we will find strength in the knowledge that you are praying that what was begun in faith by our fathers in Christ, will be continued in faith to the end.[6]

When we moved into the sprawling old Mission House on the campus, apart from the sound of passing steam trains, there was no hint of the nation's busy capital nearby. Kilnerton's lands once embraced parts of Pretoria East, including what are now the suburbs of Hatfield, Colbyn and Queenswood, and Mahlamba Ndlopfu, the current residence of the State President, but they had long-since been much reduced. However, for a ten-year-old kid with his first bicycle and a tendency to solitariness, they were the biggest back yard in the world. The campus buildings occupied only a small fraction of the land and it was the surrounding veld that drew me: head-high grass to lose myself in, cool bluegum forests to build hideouts and plan military campaigns, the rocky sandstone koppie with its thorn trees, scrub, lizards and snakes to discover or keep clear of, and thick reed beds where small streams trickled, waiting to be dammed up with mud. Like any rural kid, black or white, I became fairly deadly with a *kleilat* – a springy willow branch with a lump of clay moulded to its extremity to be delivered with velocity and accuracy. The trick of course, was the getaway afterward. With an imagination populated by all the adventurers and heroes of my book world there was not a moment that I felt alone, or lacked for ways of filling my time. A lifelong habit of solitariness was probably born in these years.

Around me the rhythms of the Kilnerton seasons brought their own stimuli. Every year held its athletic championships around the 440-yard running track which was also my bike's dirt track when I could get away with it. Boxing against St Peter's College students from Johannesburg had Methodist pride on the line and hopes of Anglican blood in the ring. My first sporting heroes were Kilnertonians; cricket, netball, tennis and soccer produced stars for us to idolise and the staff-student cricket match had much more at stake than a simple result: back in the dormitories he who had bowled the Governor out could afford to swagger.

Worship was a command performance, with women and men students singing gloriously as they climbed the koppie from their separate hostels to converge on the chapel. They sat divided by the aisle while staff members, ever watchful, sat on cross-pews in front. The Governor preached in English in the mornings and the Chaplain – delightfully named Reverend Tranquil Bam – led the evening vernacular language services. We did not attend in the evenings but the sound of the singing rolled down the slopes of the koppie and into our home. The students responded well to Dad's easy and intimate style of preaching. Morley Nkosi recalls that he "had a strong influence on many of us myself included. Listening to him conduct a service was enlightening and exhilarating. His sermons dealt with social issues that I could relate to even though they were based on interpretations of biblical texts.

They were accompanied by beautiful joyful singing of hymns he had chosen for every sermon."[7]

Winter evenings brought drama productions and choir concerts: Shakespeare plays, excerpts from *Pilgrim's Progress* and the works of other masters of English literature received polished and enthusiastic attention. But for a little white kid the moments of deeper fascination were when the roughly printed programme indicated a 'vernacular' item. Here students offered their own productions, mainly in Sotho or Tswana, often focusing on their village culture. As some tribal or domestic drama unfolded most of the whites were left guessing but the black audience was suddenly more electric and alive. The students were clearly in a more comfortable zone, and for a little while the power equation altered: this was their world, with most of the whites temporarily shut out. In a small way we were put into the place of disadvantage these black youth occupied almost all the time. It never occurred to my parents to have me learn either of the dominant languages of the region, and there is no mystery why: in those days the cultural current flowed altogether away from what was indigenous toward what was English and the possible value of engaging a black language fell outside the white imagination.

Important events at Kilnerton always ended with the singing of the haunting *Nkosi Sikelel' iAfrika*, the hymn written by a Methodist school teacher named Enoch Sontonga. We all learned the words but I'm not sure whites had much sense of their political resonance. Later – much later – it became South Africa's national anthem, but for the students it already held that status. South Africa was about to enter a defining struggle and youth at places like Kilnerton were becoming politicised, and there were reasons right there to make them chafe. Apartheid in its harsh institutional form may not have yet arrived but we had our own polite brand and even 'enlightened' institutions like Kilnerton were shot through with colonial attitudes. The culture was often paternalistic and segregation was practised in some quite unapologetic ways. The staff of 56 was divided roughly down the middle between white and black teachers who worked closely with one another on the job but retired to separate staff lounges for tea breaks. Salaries differed significantly too. I was too young to engage meaningfully with South Africa's tortured politics of race, but my whiteness nevertheless brought external advantages and internal consequences. Not only was I white but I was the Governor's son and assumptions of superiority found fertile root in a context where deference was often shown me on those grounds alone. Even at Kilnerton being white was good for privilege and bad for the soul.

With the subtext of South Africa's racism intruding in these ways into the life of the institution, tensions were sometimes tangible. When they broke the surface they were most often about living conditions and food quality – what today might be called 'service delivery'. My mother's duties included supervision of the dining-hall kitchens and the on-site bakery and soon after arrival we were shown how quickly things could go bad. With Dad away one afternoon, the Mission House was surrounded by angry students pelting our windows with stale bread. Someone in the bakery had got the mix wrong and the blame came Mom's way. Food protests were not new: later we found out that the first at KTI had been led by JB Marks[8] in 1917. I soon learned how rudimentary the dormitory accommodations were: discovering that I could make some extra pocket-money on my bike by delivering love letters between the men's dormitories and the women's hostel a half-mile away, I had gained access to both. For each student, a bed, some shelves and a metal trunk were more or less all there was. Ablution facilities were also spartan. Kilnerton was providing education and hostel accommodation for a mere £28 per year (around R1 500 today) and there were no luxuries.

Examination season typically brought heaviness and dread. High school principal Charles Jackson, who, it was said, could spot a student with his hands in his pockets a mile off, demanded the highest standards but the best that most of his products could hope for was to go on to the Kilnerton 'Normal College' to be trained as teachers under another legendary character, Kenneth Hartshorne. Among the exceptions was Nthato Motlana, who became the first black medical student at the University of the Witwatersrand and a significant community leader in the struggle that lay ahead. Another was Mary Xakane, the first black woman to become a doctor in South Africa. The second president of the SA Native National Congress, later to be renamed the African National Congress (ANC), Reverend Sefako Mapogo Makgatho, was one of the founding teaching staff of KTI; he taught there for 19 years before branching out as a church and political leader. He was renowned for his campaigns against discrimination and for his presidential address of 6 May 1919, in which he declared, "We ask for no special favours from the government. This is the land of our fathers." Other famous 'Old Kilnertonians' were struggle stalwarts Lillian Ngoyi, one of the leaders of the 1956 protest march by 20 000 women on the Union Buildings, and Barney Ngakane, Transvaal president of the ANC, singer Miriam Makeba, and the Robben Island veteran Dikgang Moseneke, who became Deputy Chief Justice in democratic South Africa.

I had to go to school of course, and here the power of custom once more had its way: for a white child to attend Kilnerton would have been unthinkable. So every morning I would walk through the long grass, away from a perfectly good school, to wait for the steam train that would take us to school in Hatfield, the nearest Pretoria suburb five miles away. Two years later, when I transitioned to Pretoria Boys' High, I swopped the train for a six-mile bike ride in the long hot summers and bitter winters – well worth it for the independence it gave me and the detours past a certain girl's house on my way home. I was, after all, beginning to explore adolescence.

With the election of the National Party and its policy of specially designed 'Bantu Education', places like Kilnerton were doomed: they educated black people too well. It took a while and by the time the axe fell in 1955, my father had been appointed elsewhere, but the intimidation began right after the election. Land had already been expropriated for the massive Koedoespoort railway works across the line and Kilnerton was now described officially as a 'black spot in a white area'. At night fires were set in our fields by white vigilantes and shots were fired into the mission property. As the first apartheid legislation began to take shape Dad began to confront it in his preaching and in other ways, but he was spared the indignities that came to his successor, Reverend Deryck Dugmore, when the government intervened directly in the institution. Dr Stanley Mogoba[9] recalls the day when the Bantu Education inspector came and assembled the entire staff: "The *kafferboetie* (kaffer-brother) days are over now," he announced, and began to list a number of draconian changes in the way Kilnerton was to be administered. The response of the students was an immediate strike and for a time the campus was virtually ungovernable, but in the end the state won and KTI's life as an institution of integrity was over. Curriculum and rules would now be dictated by the apartheid government.

We left in December 1952 for Cape Town, so were gone by the time the takeover happened, but I recall picking up some of the agonised discussions about whether to close KTI entirely rather than hand any part of it to the apartheid administration. My father was of this mind, but the issue was finally decided by the Methodist Conference in response to the pleas of black parents. Their cry was, 'better half an education than none'. The fact that the church could still offer chaplaincy and supervise the residential, social and spiritual life of the students was a sop that eased the decision, but in reality KTI was gutted. Its tragedy was multiplied all over South Africa as the suffocating hand of Bantu Education fell upon one great mission campus after another. KTI's life finally ended in 1962.

Almost all of the Kilnerton lands were sold to finance the church's response to yet another brutal government policy: the forced removal of hundreds of thousands of black people into vast new 'townships' outside the cities – places like Mamelodi outside Pretoria and South Western Townships (Soweto) south of Johannesburg. The money was used to build scores of churches for these displaced people in their new, harsh environment, while some funds were husbanded in a trust that continues to resource mission and educational endeavours.

It is impossible to measure the destruction caused by this deliberate dumbing down of black education. Trade union leader Cyril Ramaphosa bluntly expressed the sentiments of millions of black South Africans when he said, "We can learn to forgive many of the terrible things apartheid did to our people, but the worst by far was the Bantu Education Act. It did more long-term damage than anything else. That we cannot forgive." But while the immediate future was now held to ransom by the apartheid ideologues, they could not undo the past, and because of the Christian mission campuses, a crucial generation of brilliant and increasingly politicised students had already slipped through their grasp. Leaders like Luthuli, Tambo, Mandela, Tutu, Sisulu, Sobukwe and a host of others all owed their school education to the churches. It would show in the quality of their leadership.

A young white lad had also been introduced to black South Africans in a way open to only a tiny fraction of my contemporaries. Instead of encounters always being of a master-servant nature, I was in daily contact with black persons whom I naturally looked up to. However distorted by the customs of the day, the five years on the Kilnerton campus changed my outlook forever and drew an invisible, but real line between myself and other whites of my age.

If you head east these days on the road from Pretoria to Witbank you will find that urban sprawl has obliterated most of the Kilnerton campus. The koppie is built over with pricey white homes, but on the ridge, if you look very carefully, you will see that the stone chapel is there, and alongside the widened road, hidden in tall grass, the stone gate-posts still stand as mute witnesses to an era when fine education and Christian character-building produced the generation who would one day liberate South Africa. And Bantu Education? This iniquitous strategy to retain white supremacy by stunting black development produced its own bitter fruit for South Africa's white rulers. In 1976 burning resentment over this issue, particularly with the added insult of forcing Afrikaans language instruction upon black scholars, finally exploded. A younger generation, fearless and confident and ready to die, marched out of the Bantu Education schools into history.

4

Then There Was Elizabeth

In 1953 Dad was transferred from Kilnerton to Rosebank Methodist Church in Cape Town, a steepled gothic sanctuary nestled on the old Main Road below Cape Town University. My sister Valmai stayed on as a boarder at Pretoria Girls' High to complete her matriculation but I was enrolled for my last three years of schooling at Rondebosch Boys' High School (RBHS). I was fortunate to get in because admission to this fine school was at a premium; RBHS probably saved me from uselessness. The ethos of the school was different than I had known. It was a community where, without fuss, ethical values were lifted up and expected of all of us and where, for the sake of the school, I think we found ourselves wanting to be more decent human beings. Part of this ethos came from a very strong Christian Union, regularly attended by up to 200 of the 500 boys, and some of the boarders attended Dad's church each Sunday too. But there was more to it. In a quiet and totally unassuming way headmaster 'Nobby' Clarke simply expected it of us – and mainly got what he expected.

I found myself growing in new ways, in confidence and in exploring friendships. I played school sport for the first time – travel and distance having made that impossible at PBHS. I loved cross-country running and while never reaching first team standards, revelled in rugby and cricket, the former played as it was meant to be – in the mud and slush of a Cape winter, and the latter on school fields that imitated the village greens where the game was born. I was almost useless with a cricket bat but made up for it by being a reasonably good fast bowler. Dad had been a fine rugby player and I wished I could do better to impress him, but playing flank for the 4th rugby team one Saturday morning, I was upside down in a loose maul when someone leapt on it and my neck gave way with an ominous crack. Stretchered off the field, I was found to have fractured one of my neck vertebrae and that put paid to rugby for some time. The game obsessed us: as schoolboys we camped all night outside Newlands Rugby Stadium to watch our Springbok heroes play the British Lions, or the All Blacks. Even then, the occupants of the 'Malay Stand' – reserved for people of colour – tended not to share our enthusiasm for the home team: they cheered the visitors. But life for us boys was simple and uncomplicated by the nation's pathologies. None of us thought it strange that every Springbok in the team was lily white.

While never a brilliant scholar, I must have done some work and was invited into the prestigious Twelve Club. At each monthly meeting one of the twelve would have to produce a paper on a challenging subject. Mine was on the 'Development and Techniques of Plastic Surgery', still a relatively new speciality. It was my first experience of being regarded as 'bright', and I felt somewhat fraudulent about it.

Something else was happening too. In 1953 I met the girl who was to become the love of my life and my wife for 54 years. Elizabeth Hardie was the daughter of an Old Mutual Insurance manager. Tom Hardie had married into the Tonkin clan – a family deeply embedded in the mayoral history of Cape Town and of Rosebank Methodist Church. Elizabeth was an only girl with three brothers, one of whom (Allan) became over the years the nearest thing to a brother to me. Elizabeth was a year older than me, but in the equivalent Standard 8 (Grade 10) class at our sister institution, Rustenburg Girls' High School. Her cousin Megan invited her to play badminton in the church hall with the new minister's son. It was a less than romantic meeting, with Elizabeth commenting afterward that I was 'a very rude boy'. But everything has to have a beginning, and when later that year both our families holidayed at Knysna, 300 miles up the coast, there was time to get beyond cheekiness. Like most teenage relationships, there were ups and downs, but a die seems to have been cast. Apart from her rosy Scottish complexion, ready smile and bright blue eyes, what most attracted me to Elizabeth Hardie was her steadfast, principled goodness and her quiet, unruffled, honest handling of anything that came at her, including me. In all our life together, that never changed.

There was one complication: her family was deeply involved in Moral Rearmament (MRA), a movement that had evolved out of the Oxford Group led by Dr Frank Buchman. In some ways MRA emulated the eighteenth century Wesleyan Class Meetings, where people bared their souls and confessed their failings to one another. The practice of listening for personal guidance from God was emphasised and major decisions taken on the basis of this 'guidance', especially if it came via Buchman himself. In itself, MRA spirituality could be helpful, although definitely scary to someone like me who was anything but ready to spill out my insides to a group of strangers. The real problem, however, was the political ideology that Buchman had grafted onto what was essentially a pietist spiritual movement. Like John Wesley, Buchman was convinced that the inward spiritual journey needed to express itself in transformational action in the world, but that is where the similarity ended. Wesley saw Christian activism as a journey downward to the poor of the earth and became more and more committed to social justice; Buchman's 'guidance' drew MRA into the anti-communist paranoia of the 1950s. Its simple beginnings tended to be displaced by an obsession with the world ideological struggle, focusing upward on people of power and beginning to look like a religious version of McCarthyism. Anything vaguely left of centre was suspect, and it was apparent to me that in the eyes of MRA people like my dad, who was increasingly vocal in his opposition to the government's apartheid policy, were 'unwitting tools of the communists', a notion that chimed much too cosily with the official line of the apartheid regime. It disqualified MRA as far as I was concerned.

This was sad because, in their zeal to guide people to a deeper spiritual life, MRA members crossed South Africa's racial barriers sooner and more whole-heartedly than most white South Africans.

I wanted Elizabeth, but I didn't want the right-leaning ideology of MRA and when our relationship got serious this led to some strains between Tom Hardie and myself. Elizabeth's mother Flo, deep as she was into the MRA ethos, kept her own council. She secretly liked me. Fortunately, as the climate within the movement grew more suffocating, some, including Elizabeth, rebelled. Under the preaching and spiritual mentorship of my father, she had come to an increasingly mature and clear sense of her relationship with God and had been troubled by some of the obsessions in the MRA 'sharing groups'. She decided that she had grown beyond this. Even then, her rebellion was very Elizabethan: it consisted simply of a quiet, non-judgemental withdrawal and typically, though having left the movement, she faithfully retained the friendships she had made within it.

We both approached matriculation with Elizabeth consistently outshining me academically. Not that we were in competition: she was disciplined and persistent in her studies; I tended to sit on my bike outside her house and whistle at her as she beavered away at her desk. I was doing just that when a wood truck came roaring up the road and a small log flew off it, hitting me in the face and knocking me out. It was a parable of our different approaches to study but she did rush out and I woke up in her arms. Elizabeth earned a first-class matriculation and won the school music prize for pianoforte; I managed a university pass and won nothing. I could argue that I didn't see much point in academics because my secret ambition was to go to sea, but the more likely reason was a simple procrastination and aversion to work. All the more astonishing then, that at the RBHS Centenary in 1997, I found myself listed as one of the school's eight distinguished alumni.[10] Whatever they saw in me four decades after leaving school was not linked to any academic prowess while there.

Yet, the 1950s being what they were and despite her excellent performance at school, instead of moving on to university Elizabeth enrolled at Cape Town's Technical College to be trained in shorthand and typing. Increasing numbers of young women were breaking the bonds of old custom, but I'm not sure Elizabeth's school achievements were sufficiently affirmed at home for her to imagine herself at university. She did want to be a nurse but an early visit to a casualty ward put paid to that. All her life she would struggle with her self-worth and underestimate her intellectual abilities. For her and thousands of others, secretarial work was still seen as the norm. So she began a career of quiet service, which peculiarly matched her temperament but which never explored her full intellectual potential. Over the years she nevertheless read voraciously and her capacity to absorb and apply the deep wisdoms she found in her books was beautiful to see. It would take 40 years before, in a lovely irony, she first sat in a university lecture room among students one third of her age, who all worshipped her and hung on her wisdom.

Elizabeth always said that she loved me from 1953 and that was that. For me it was not that simple. I needed to do some exploring, but she took my wanderings in her stride and waited them out. There was another fellow around who was persistent if not successful. He liked birds and photography and they went out together often. I'm glad to say he didn't win her heart, but his hovering presence was a warning that I shouldn't take anything for granted and had better get my head straight; she was not going to wait forever. I finally saw sense in the middle of my seminary training at Rhodes University. By then I knew I could love no other and we conducted the kind of long-distance romance completely beyond the comprehension of today's generation: twice-weekly long letters written on tissue-thin blue 'airmail' paper, and one three-minute telephone conversation each week. The only telephone in my university residence was located under the stairs and our conversations often had to take place with a couple of other lovelorn students waiting for me to hang up. Every three minutes the local operator butted in asking for more coins. We knew that he listened in and we sometimes profited when he got so interested that he forgot to cut us off. Once when I was dead broke, I asked him for a couple more minutes and he graciously consented. During our courtship Elizabeth was working first for John Dickinson stationery company, then at the Motor Union insurance. When we married she left the workplace for twelve years, giving birth to our four boys and anchoring them through their early lives, often in my absence.

This chapter is not meant to pre-empt the altogether 62 years of our relationship, but to make sense of them. Wherever Elizabeth may appear in the coming chapters, it will always be less prominently than she deserves, because whatever public contribution I may have been permitted to make could not, and would not have happened without her.

Our marriage spanned 54 years. Marriages are both public and private affairs. Falling in love and the joys and challenges of exploring that love in a lifelong relationship are deeply personal, but the decision to spend the rest of your life together has public consequences, which is why marriage officers may not conduct weddings behind closed doors. When two people make those vows of love to each other it may be an exercise of private choice, but they are also doing something of import for wider society. For better or worse, the quality and permanence of our relationships touch circles wider than we are aware of. In Elizabeth's and my case, over the years we found ourselves *in loco parentis* to numbers of younger couples who said they found strength in our marriage. This had little to do with me; it was rather because of time they spent with my remarkable spouse. Times without number, when we travelled together for me to engage in some high-profile public commitment, it was Elizabeth's quiet contribution to a conversation that was remembered afterward more than my speech. She was the 'great encourager'.

Her diary was full of the names of people who had shared some burden with her and to whom she regularly wrote, and for whom she prayed. She could empathise with people in all sorts of circumstance and they knew instinctively that this person's concern was utterly genuine and could be trusted. It came naturally out of a soul that had been to school with the greatest of all soul-lovers.[11] Her secret was a simple one: she spent her life seeking to imitate Jesus in a way that was completely authentic. I never heard a pious platitude from Elizabeth. When she spoke – always thinking deeply before doing so – her words were shared in ways that encouraged, or enriched, or gently reproved – but always loved – whoever she was speaking to. In the years of training Life Line counsellors, I used to lift up psychologist Carl Rogers' 'non-directive' counselling method as a best practice model. Rogers described the most healing attitude to others as 'unconditional positive regard', and this is how Elizabeth saw other people. She never tired of quoting one of her bosses, Desmond Tutu, saying, "When we meet a stranger we should genuflect, because in every person we meet the *Imago Dei* – the Image of God."

No marriage is without struggles; the law of self-disclosure makes it impossible to hide our self-truths no matter how adept we think we are at disguising them. But much depends on whether the frailties thus exposed are grasped as opportunities to find 'a more perfect union' or as reasons to cut and run. I won't traverse the sore places which I, more than she created, except to stand in awe of how much more ready she was to learn and grow from them. The most consistent beneficiary of Elizabeth's wisdom and patient love was of course myself. It was an inestimable gift, of unwavering reliability.

As a mom she was wise and selfless – but often anxious about whether she was doing the job right. She grew up with three brothers and quite naturally regretted not having enjoyed a sister or daughter, yet this never affected her love for each of our sons, John, Christopher, David and Alan. Sometimes reserved in the showing of affection, she nevertheless had an instinctive grasp of what each needed in the way of parenting. When one of them stumbled or ran into trouble, she sometimes took it too much to heart and worried more than was helpful, but she was a patient listener to each one, and above all she prayed for them – a phrase that may sound pious to some ears. But Elizabeth understood that prayer for others is more than tossing some names at God. Real prayer is to carry somebody's need intimately, patiently and painfully in one's heart, holding them in love and lifting them tenderly and consistently into the light of God's grace. Real prayer costs and Elizabeth was willing to pay its price.

During the years when she was not working money was spread very thin. She tried not to let me see it, but the boys knew that she worried deeply about making ends meet. The only meal we might ever have out was the odd trip to Pan-Burgers, the local drive-in eatery. In charge of our meagre budget, she often went without, always putting me and the boys ahead of herself. The Methodist Church of Southern Africa (MCSA) was attempting to achieve a measure of income equity for its ministers, but stipends were not only racially skewed, they also left inner-city ministers like me far behind those appointed to the more salubrious suburbs. When we were unable to match what some of their school friends enjoyed, the boys used to hear for the umpteenth time that I didn't receive a salary, but a stipend – 'an allowance for living, not payment for services rendered'. The lack of money was not fatal, but we did regret having to see our sons sometimes missing out, even though they now look back with some sense of pride that they could handle it. It was also hard not being able to reciprocate when taken out by friends for a dinner or movie. When Elizabeth did go back to work her salary outstripped my stipend even when I was a Bishop and the extras making the difference to our lives came from her income.

There was another kind of scarcity too: to my shame, especially through the boys' teen years, Elizabeth carried far too much of the parenting burden. Even in normal times, a minister's routine is the reverse of most, tending to be busiest when the rest of the world is off duty. Evening meetings, Saturday weddings and Sunday services all conspire to make for a different-shaped family week. But our times were not 'normal' and, as we shall see, nor were my commitments. As the political struggle ramped up and extra burdens came my way I was frequently an absentee husband and parent. I would come home late and often tired or too distracted to share Elizabeth's day or have time for the boys. For me duty meant that when a school rugby match clashed with a mass funeral in some township, it was the boys' game that lost out. Elizabeth seldom complained but she was often lonely and no matter how much the boys might have 'understood' there was part of them that felt the loss keenly, as did I the guilt. Worse still, I found difficulty switching off when I was at home. As one of them put it, "Even when you were home, Dad, you weren't here." He was right: I was often not fully present, unable to let go of the stuff churning in my head. So, while we may now cherish the times of closeness we did have, nothing – no justifying of the circumstances – can bring back opportunities lost. It did mean perhaps that each of our sons learned earlier than most how to cope, make decisions and accept consequences, and remarkably it seems that each one seems to have found in his own way a balancing out between their sense of resentment and a genuine pride in their parents.

Returning to the workplace in 1972, Elizabeth went on to build an impressive record with two of the most influential institutional players in the South African struggle for justice and equity, first as personal assistant to three different General Secretaries of the South African Council of Churches (SACC),[12] and then in a similar role at Independent Mediation Service of South Africa (IMSSA). The latter included a period of secondment to the Wits-Vaal Peace Accord office.[13] But far more important was the sense of value and vocation she found for herself in her work positions: her lifelong struggle with self-worth was requited by the knowledge that she was doing work that made a difference in the nation. Whether by enabling Bishop Tutu to be the nation's prophet in chief, or facilitating the massive difference Charles Nupen and IMSSA made to trade unionism and labour relations, or ensuring that peace monitors were in place in the midst of the pre-election strife of the 1990s, she oiled the wheels and ensured that they never lacked for the right resources. She also provided moral wisdom when needed. No matter who the boss – including Desmond Tutu – if some decision or action fell short in that department Elizabeth had a quiet, unthreatening way of questioning it and suggesting a worthier alternative. This latter quality formed a strong compass for me all through our marriage. Elizabeth kept me honest. When she worried that I was cutting ethical corners or being over hasty, a strategic question or two would bring me up short. I would maybe argue the case for a while but most often I would change course in the end.

Perhaps her greatest achievement was an internal one: the overcoming of fear. Most people did not know how frightened she was. Ever since childhood she had been nervous and afraid, of the war, of the dark, of strangers, of failing, of being left alone, of public speaking, of violence, of the future. All the more amazing, then, were her acts of courage, especially during the 'struggle' years: facing the jeers and catcalls from passing cars as she stood holding an anti-war placard on Jan Smuts Avenue, being arrested in Pretoria for marching on the Union Buildings, venturing into conflict-ridden townships to help set up peace committees, or standing between threatening thugs and Desmond Tutu's office door, refusing them entry. Then, having to watch family members go into harm's way for the 'cause'. About the risks Desmond Tutu was subjected to, she wrote, "I cannot save him but I can walk with him," and what she believed to be right trumped even a mother's fears. In later years when I sat listening to her speaking to a crowded roomful of people in strong, confident tones, I often wondered if they had any idea how much courage she had to summon to do it.

You don't get to be like that without inner reinforcement. Cynics who dismiss faith as a mere crutch for dysfunctional people haven't encountered the real thing. Authentic faith takes us on a journey in which we invite Jesus and his teaching to interrogate every part of our lives, seeking both the desire and resources for transformation. Lived faithfully, this journey enables deep inner overcoming in those places where we need to be different. It also makes life different by placing the turmoils of the moment into God's 'big picture' perspective, replacing our fears with serenity. It lifts up changeless virtues to inform our actions, shaping us toward integrity. It reminds us that because our lives are already given, they are therefore impossible to lose, freeing us from fear.

All her life, Elizabeth was on this journey and that is why she populates each chapter of this book.

5

The Sea

I have sometimes thought that I only made one real sacrifice in my life, which I suppose is not true, but if there were others, they all seem to have flowed from the decision to end a naval career before it really began. My yearning to go to sea was born the first time I sat in a boat of any kind, around age five. It was small sailboat on Germiston's Victoria Lake hundreds of miles from the ocean, but from then on I never doubted what I wanted. Further, of all the dramas during World War Two, the grinding attrition of the Battle of the Atlantic had most captured my imagination. I was awed by the grey ships of the Royal Navy, the men who sailed in them, and the six long years they had fought a hidden human enemy as well as the fury of nature itself. Unsurprisingly, there had grown in me a single-minded, uncomplicated intention to become a naval officer and spend my life at sea.

I blame God entirely for the frustration of this ambition.

I signed up in the South African Navy fresh out of school in 1956. As I boarded the bus for the 120-mile journey to the training base at Saldanha Bay, I was joining others who would spend a year at the Naval Gymnasium, young men from whom the Navy would select its next batch of officers and personnel. There were no women in those days, and certainly no black South Africans, but this was to be my first experience up close with Afrikaners. My initial encounter was a telling one in terms of the changing power dynamics in the military. Seated beside me in the bus was a pleasant young Afrikaner who, discovering that I was fairly well informed on matters naval, plied me with questions about life in the service. I was surprised that someone could sign up with so little knowledge of what he was getting into, yet a couple of days later this same person was kitted out as a commissioned officer and I found myself obliged to salute him. I was going to compete with 350 others to earn the Queen's Commission, but he and some other Afrikaners on the bus that day were the first of the *blitzoffisiers* – 'lightning officers' – created overnight by the Nationalist government to dilute the solidly English-speaking character of the Navy and to infiltrate political support for the new regime. Seasoned officers with WWII records understandably resented these untested political appointees.

At the time, however, such issues hardly touched my life. Given my memories of 1948, I was relieved to find myself relatively at ease with my Afrikaner compatriots. Politics was taboo in the mess-decks, the English and Afrikaans languages were used on alternate days and we simply had no time to reflect on our cultural divides. Life at SAS *Saldanha* was both brutal and stimulating. We were knocked into shape by some leathery old salts who had seen decades of service in the Royal Navy and carried the scars to prove it. They were jealous custodians of naval tradition going back to the days of Nelson, and they knew how to deal with uppity recruits. Most feared were the GIs – Gunnery Instructors – who thought nothing of drilling us until we dropped. Rock 'n roll was bursting onto the music scene at the time, and our first acquaintance with its beat was not on a dance-floor, but through the PA system while polishing floors on our knees before sunrise. Morning PT was followed by parade drill and classes, and in the afternoons we practised rope-work, knots and splices, rowing and small-boat work, sailing the Navy's traditional whalers and cutters across the bright waters of the bay. A 70ft, WWII launch challenged our skills at pilotage, picking up mooring buoys and coming alongside. We ate well and played hard in inter-divisional sports competitions and boat-pulling regattas. Our prize for surviving the first three months was a bumpy truck-ride south to a weekend shore-leave in

Cape Town. The wild alcohol-fuelled drive back on the Sunday evening might have been the riskiest part of being in the Navy.

We all wanted real sea-time and I was fortunate to get some earlier than most. In April 1956 the frigate SAS *Transvaal* had a mishap on a replenishment mission to the South African weather station on Marion Island, deep in the Southern Ocean. Her motor boat had capsized while offloading stores through the notorious surf around the island and a Petty Officer drowned in the incident. She also had a number of men ashore at the time and was obliged to steam back the 1 200 nautical miles to pick up another boat and some temporary crew. I was excited to be among the dozen chosen, issued with a hammock and cold weather gear, and flown in an Air Force Dakota to Cape Town. Our first sight of the ship was depressing: she had battled home in the teeth of a 117mph gale and had taken a severe battering. Most of the gear on the upper deck had been swept away. There was no time to waste, the ship was still loaded with most of the stores needed at Marion, and as soon as essential repairs had been completed, we steamed out of Simon's Town, heading for the Southern Ocean.

My first assignment at sea in a warship was less than romantic: the Petty Officers' bathroom below decks was a tiled space lined with stainless steel washbasins, urinals and toilets. I was told that the 'brightwork' needed polishing, and the deck swabbed. I was also told to 'look lively' about it. Swabbing the deck required flooding the space with some sea water, then mopping it toward a single drain-hole – or 'scupper' – in the corner. This would have been simple if the entire space was not rising, falling and rolling from port to starboard and back in a gut-wrenching, corkscrew motion. Looking through the closed scuttles, I could see the grey mountains near Cape Point one moment and the next, nothing but green ocean sluicing past the glass. No sooner had I swabbed the water toward the scupper than it ran back at me, gurgling contemptuously at my efforts. My head began to spin and my breakfast left me. It had taken me less than 30 minutes to succumb to the sailor's nemesis and things were not looking good. One doesn't vomit in the Petty Officers' bathroom.

There are no words for the sheer misery of seasickness. Those immune to it are born lucky; the rest of us have to bear it for longer or shorter periods before the 'sea-legs' come. Forty-eight hours of wanting to die usually dealt with mine but a fellow cadet on that first voyage was so ill that we thought him lost overboard. He was found hidden behind some coils of rope in a dark storage space, grasping his stomach, dry-retching and semi-conscious. He never went to sea again. The navy, of course, refused to recognise the illness. Officers watched with cold eyes as you mumbled an excuse and ran from your post to deposit another meal over the side. As long as you chose the leeward side of the ship they pretended nothing had happened.

Marion Island is well into the 'Roaring Forties' in the treacherous Southern Ocean. Howling gales bludgeon it all year round, so delivering stores to the weather station required taking swift advantage of the limited windows of good weather between. Our passage south had been almost as rough as the vessel's earlier ill-fated one, with the gale this time reaching 90 miles per hour. More or less over my seasickness, I exulted in lookout duty on the bridge-wing of the frigate as she smashed into the massive seas, burying her bows deep into solid water and then, with a shudder through her hull, heaving high into the night, tossing the spray back into our faces, readying for the next assault. I was in awe of the fact that nothing stood between me and the chaotic black depths but the thin hull of this vessel, creaking and groaning as she took on the worst the Southern Ocean could hurl at her. Ships are living things and the bond between them and the souls aboard is something only sailors understand. It was also very cold. The Loch Class frigates had open bridges and as we plunged further south, the icy wind could whip scalding cocoa or 'chai' out of the mug in your gloved hands, freeze it in mid-air and send the solid pellets clattering against the bridge house. Off watch below, life was sodden.

These ships, built hurriedly for wartime convoy duty, had no luxuries. Amidst the violent motion, when I did sleep, it was in a canvas hammock slung over a large generator that hummed and buzzed on and off all the time.

The only landing stage at Marion was a platform suspended by cables from a cliff. Everything we carried had to be ferried from the anchored ship by motor launch and hoisted to the cliff top. Then a long slope up the soggy, lichen-covered surface led to the cluster of wooden huts that constituted the 1950s-era weather station. I came to know that slope. For 22 hours non-stop I hefted 4-gallon jerry-cans of diesel fuel, one in each hand, to the dump behind the huts. We needed to get the job done before the weather closed in. The ground was covered in wire netting to prevent us from sinking in, but it was very heavy going. Over our ordinary seaman's clothing we wore kapok flying suits, duffle coats, thick gloves, sea-boots and balaclavas, but when we paused to rest, our drying sweat chilled us to the bone. We even brought a piano ashore, somewhat dismantled, but still ungainly enough to make for a very risky passage in the launch. Apart from our marooned shipmates we were the first outsiders the weather people had seen for six months, but you would not have thought it. They looked on while we sweated and seemed quite relieved when we were on our way again. Presumably a preference for isolation is why they chose the job.

There were other sea-going opportunities. Simon's Town was still the headquarters of the British South Atlantic fleet in those days and in the dead of winter, when the Cape of Good Hope transformed into the Cape of Storms, the annual NATO Capex exercises had South African ships working in heavy seas with a Royal Naval squadron 'hunting' a British submarine. I had chosen the anti-submarine branch so spent time in the 'asdic'[14] hut abaft the bridge, juggling what looked like a little car steering wheel, directing the sonar pulses beaming out underwater. It was all WWII vintage weaponry and some of the officers and senior hands had vivid memories of the Battle of the Atlantic. They remembered when all of this was life and death, and however staged the exercises were, when the dreary, repetitive '*pingggg*' suddenly became '*pinggg-guh*' hearts stopped momentarily and the hunt was on. During these exercises there was a moment when things did threaten to get real. When Egypt's President Nasser nationalised the Suez Canal, we were ordered into port to fully ammunition our ships because there was a chance we could be sucked in to a looming conflict. It was then that I saw the older hands on board become very serious, but the Suez crisis dragged on for months until the disastrous British, French and Israeli attacks on the Canal Zone. After the canal closure South Africa's only task was coping with the massive increase in shipping rounding the Cape.

I was loving every minute of it and looked forward to the day when I would be gazetted as a midshipman. During the entire year there was only one moment of doubt: some of us had been sent to Salisbury Island, Durban to familiarise ourselves with Torpedo and Anti-Submarine (TAS) weaponry and I recall us crowding round a dismantled 21-inch torpedo while our instructor showed us how it functioned. I marvelled at the technology that drove this weapon through the water at 45 knots, and the guidance system that led it to its target. Yet I also remember the beginnings of a nagging question: all this clever science to blast human beings to smithereens? I know now that on that day the seeds of a different attitude to war and peace were planted in me – seeds that would germinate nearly a decade later.

I would love to claim that the decision at the end of 1956 to enter the Christian ministry was motivated by faith and vision, but it was more like being kidnapped.

The call – I can give it no other name – came at a most inconvenient time. During the year, some 20 of us had been selected as

'Upper-Yardsmen', a term from the days of sail that set us aside as potential officers. Some had already dropped by the wayside and the time had now arrived for final selection as Midshipmen. It was the moment we had worked for.

Enter the Reverend Arthur Attwell, childhood hero and at that time Methodist Chaplain in the SA Navy. Arthur had been a Royal Naval officer in WWII, in the 'little ships' in the Mediterranean and Adriatic, where a stealthy war was fought supplying Tito's partisans from the sea or dropping commandos to support them. His war had been a desperately dangerous one and beneath his kind exterior, like so many veterans, he carried some deep emotional wounds. Meeting him as a child and being shown the tattered White Ensign from his last command sealed my determination even then to become a career naval officer. Arthur was now a deeply respected padre in the Navy and had been invited to SAS *Saldanha* to help in the officer selection process. Commander 'Flam' Johnson, later to become Chief of the Navy, but at that time CO of the training establishment, asked Attwell to have a chat with me to confirm my intentions.

Meanwhile, I had been thrown into confusion by what I can only call an 'inner encounter'. That same day, alone on the cliffs above the small boat harbour, I experienced a clear and unexpected conviction that cut across everything I had wanted and worked for. Something spoke inside me, saying, "You will be a minister." It was as simple as that and almost as matter of fact as if a passing officer had barked an order, yet it came with more authority than anyone in the Navy could muster. I'll leave it to the psychologists to wring from it what they will; all I know is that it was as real an experience as any I have known and it shook me to my boots. This was not what I wanted. I admired my dad, whose preaching had always moved me, but while I wished I could emulate his fine character and moral example there was no conscious desire to follow his vocation. Furthermore, he had never once hinted that he would like to see me in the ministry. This was an ambush. Having listened since to scores of stories from young candidates for ordination, I know beyond doubt that God 'calls' people in every generation to serve in this way, but unlike most of them, I was anything but pleased and remain mystified about why it landed on me.

Later that day Padre Attwell invited me to sit down alongside the sports fields for a chat. I had no idea of his mission, but I needed very much to tell someone what had happened to me. Arthur enjoyed recounting what happened afterwards: in the wardroom that evening Commander Johnson enquired, "Well, Padre, do we have our man?" Attwell's response was, "Yes, sir, in a manner of speaking we do, but not quite in the way you expected. He's signing up in my outfit instead."

In the end I was gazetted as a midshipman. I had passed out well, with my most prized award being one in practical seamanship. The Orator's Cup also came my way, whether as a piquant nod to my new future, I don't know. Our passing out parade was a proud one, but it was hard to ignore the new political realities: we received our awards from the hands of Defence Minister FC Erasmus, an ex-Nazi sympathiser who was steadily forcing his nationalist ideology onto the armed services. Perhaps such factors were only passing shadows for an ambitious young man preoccupied with a career crisis, but I like to believe that a wider providence was tipping me in a new direction. Someone seemed to be clear that it was time to go.

Untangling from the navy was a little complicated and I asked God to please understand if it took me a while. I was placed in the reserve with links to the SAN base at Port Elizabeth. My future seminary at Rhodes University, Grahamstown, was 80 miles inland from there but one of the schools in the college town had a naval cadet detachment and I was also attached there as an instructor. The deal was that I would report for sea duty during university vacations.

One of these stints was during the Christmas vacation of 1957/58. I was attached to the fast frigate SAS *Vrystaat* under one the SAN's legendary captains, 'Tackers' Terry-Lloyd, when we received orders to proceed at speed to a surprising destination. Margate was the premier holiday resort on the Natal south coast and in a real-life precursor of the movie *Jaws*, the area had suffered nine shark attacks in quick succession, six of them fatal. There were no shark nets in those days and 'Black December', as it became known, caused panicked vacationers in their hundreds to pack up and trek back inland, emptying most hotels and holiday accommodation. Margate and the surrounding resorts faced a serious economic crisis. Whoever had the idea that the navy could do anything about this I wouldn't know, but it led to us using our anti-submarine weapons in anger for the first time. On 6 January 1958 the citizens of Margate packed the headlands to watch the fearsome sight of SAS *Vrystaat* racing toward the beach with a fine bone in her teeth, then executing a tight turn to starboard to bring her parallel. Speeding across the bay to ensure that our stern was not blown off by the explosions, we depth-charged the sea-bottom, causing spectacular bangs and masses of water to plume into the air behind us. Then, with the rocks of the northern headland looming perilously close, another tight turn took us out into deep water. The genesis of all this spectacular action was some mad scientist's theory that in addition to any sharks we might kill, if we could sufficiently distort the shape of the bottom of the bay, the predators would stay away. We therefore went about redesigning the bottom of Margate Bay with a will, repeating the exercise. I modestly recall that all of us showed courage and determination in the face of the foe, but some massive explosions later we had accounted for only eight enemy casualties while hundreds of dead fish unfortunately had to be classified as collateral damage. We made a final, much slower sweep with a squad of riflemen in the bows, despatching any enemy wounded while other crew members with scoop nets ensured a decent disposal of as many of the edible fish as could be handled in the ship's galley. We had no hope of picking them all up and the mad scientist had apparently not anticipated the attraction that multiple dead fish might have for even more sharks than before. Perhaps that is why I'm still waiting for my Battle of Margate Bay campaign medal.

Ultimately – except for a six-month stint as chaplain that I tell of elsewhere – even this limited connection with the navy had to end. By the close of 1959 I was about to be appointed to my first church and had to hand in my papers. My longing to be at sea has never left me and I still feel more at home on the water than I ever did on land. One of my sons – Christopher – understands. He has the same gene and no speech is needed when we sail together.

There my spirit is always at peace.

6

The God Thing

Where does one start with God? I'm not sure that arguing about God's existence is a helpful use of energy. We may be influenced one way or another – especially during childhood and youth – by familial or other external factors, but ultimately the choice is ours: we either build our lives around faith or we don't.

I choose to believe.

If one makes that choice, however, a critical question is what kind of God we're talking about. In the name of Christianity alone, a lot of different models are peddled out there, and most I wouldn't spend the time of day with. Today's televangelists, prosperity preachers and religious hucksters give God a bad press. Whether exploiting people's fears of divine wrath or commodifying God into a cross between a therapist and a stockbroker, their poor theology and ill-disguised greed are persuasive arguments for atheism. But the genuine article is worth another look.

I chose faith because of the beauty of the God I grew up with.

I suppose my first sense of the numinous was linked with church-going in the early 1940s. At Sunday School before church I got filled in on most of the better-known Bible stories but it was when sitting in the pews with the grown-ups that I felt it. They seemed to be engaging with an invisible presence among and around them. My childish curiosity needed to locate this presence and I decided that 'he' must reside behind the ornate organ pipes in the old Wesley Methodist Church in central Pretoria. They made loud noises and looked impressive enough to conceal whoever everyone called 'God'. Much of the service was spent staring at the pipes, hoping for an appearance.

More meaningful, however, was the influence of our home life on my child-soul. A quiet acknowledgement of God permeated our home. It was understated in a typically English way, with little push and a minimum of outward ritual. In grace before our meals and prayers before we slept, God was honoured as our authority, provider and guide. It was comforting to feel that there was this 'Somebody' above and beyond us who watched over us. But the most powerful God-moment in my early childhood had to do with Dad. One day I blundered into his study and found him at prayer. I can still see him now, on one knee, an elbow on the old horse-hair armchair next to his desk, one hand supporting his bowed head. It stopped me dead. Dad was the ultimate strength and security in my young life, yet here he was, kneeling in submission to some authority beyond himself. He wasn't angered by my interruption, neither did he show embarrassment. If there was any impression at all, it was that he had been in deep conversation with someone and wasn't quite ready to come away – that I had broken in on a special friendship. It was a profound parable and the impact on me was enormous.

I began to listen much more carefully to his sermons, and was increasingly drawn to the God he spoke about with such intimacy. His sharing about God included the entire biblical saga of a desert people's fortunes and sorrows through slavery and liberation, conquest and exile, but it was his focus on the life, teaching and example of Jesus of Nazareth that captivated me most. This young Jew's nobility of character and utter selflessness seemed to be the ultimate in human goodness, the Everest of what humanity could aspire to. More than that, it seemed that God was embodied – *incarnated* – in a unique way in his life, so that looking at him, one saw beyond the human and encountered the divine. Religious faith therefore, was not so much an attachment to dogma or ritual or creed as it was a *friendship* with Jesus. Religion was a *relationship with him*, and through him, with God. The heart of this relationship was discovering that one was loved, cherished, welcomed and embraced by a God whose essence was Love itself. Dad's preaching was the beginning of my discovering that this was true for me too. More important than my knowing about God was that *I was known*. God knew my name.

Therefore the *Sturm und Drang* of hell-fire religion had no place in my upbringing. Anyway I was a stubborn little fellow and I doubt that the terror of hell would have been much of a motivator. Fear of betraying *a great love* was another matter. If you spend time in the company of Jesus and of people whose lives have begun to look like his, you don't need legalistic threats of damnation to know that there are things in your life that need sorting. In the presence of real goodness my character blemishes showed up unbidden and my sense of alienation, of somehow falling short of the best I could be, was real. The most beaten up, abused word in the Bible is 'sin', which is sad, because the condition it refers to is real and should not be trivialised by religious legalists. Ever since humanity's first stirrings of God-consciousness, we have had one or other form of soul-police obsessed with listing and codifying our 'sins', presumably to be able to tick all the boxes to their God's satisfaction, but also to expose and exploit the guilt of others. This obsession with 'sins' is possibly the primary sin of religion itself. It was widespread in the time of Jesus and his refusal to buy into it was one of the things that got him into fatal trouble.

During my teenage days I had a brush with legalistic, fundamentalist Christianity. When we moved to Cape Town I sometimes attended a fellowship meeting in Rondebosch where a mix of peer pressure and loads of cream cakes brought some 30 or 40 of us schoolboys within preaching-range on Sunday afternoons. The recipe was simple and not much different from that used by televangelists today: first use every possible Bible text to convince us of our guilt before God, then offer Jesus as the Saviour sent by God to step in and take our punishment, thus rescuing us from eternal damnation. If we turned to Jesus and invited him into our hearts we would be 'saved'. If not ... well, we'd been warned. Woe betide us if a bus were to run over us when we left the meeting. This is not the place to engage this mechanistic dumbing down of the mystery of salvation but it is important to say that while parts of Scripture may appear to lend themselves to this narrative, there is a troubling disconnect between it and the kind of God Jesus reveals. What brutal Deity would plan that for a beloved son? What anthropomorphic God is so bound by human constructs of crime and punishment? And what puny God allows the work of salvation to be frustrated by a No 10 bus? This scenario reduces Jesus to a robotic pawn – a sacrificial offering sentenced beforehand to a violent death because of a pre-destined 'salvation plan'.

The dissonances are deafening.

Don't get me wrong. I believe that at Calvary something was happening that changed the divine/human equation forever, but in a very different way. The point about sin is that it goes deeper than a dirty deed or a forgotten ritual. The word *sin* means 'to miss the mark', to be less than I am meant to be. If I am created supremely for *relationship* with God, then sin is much more than the breaking of some impersonal law; it is the breaking of a lover's heart – God's heart. It alienates me from the relationship that completes me as a truly human being. A whole raft of destructive actions may flow from this alienation, but the fundamental need remains the mending of the relationship.

I still remember my dad telling of the one-sentence sermon that Japanese Christian Toyohiko Kagawa[15] used to preach over and over again on street corners in his native Kobe: "God is love – love like Jesus." It was as if no more need be said. God was, in the Apostle Paul's words: "... in Christ, reconciling the world to Godself."[16] If this is so, then on Calvary Jesus, far from being a robotic substitute slaking an angry God's need for retribution, was instead revealing God's real heart to the world – a heart of vulnerable love. The Calvary event was God, present in Jesus, suffering in Jesus, forgiving in Jesus and loving to the end in Jesus. What happened in that place, at that time, is timeless: it exposes what we do to God everywhere and always; it also reveals how far God will go for us everywhere and always. If this is so, then once I truly comprehend what my – and all humankind's – 'missing the mark' does to infinite love, and see God's willingness to suffer rather than stop loving, I find myself overwhelmed with gratitude and wanting to respond. "Love so amazing, so divine, demands my soul, my life, my all."[17]

It was this kind of God who won me, a divine lover whose belief in me was infinitely more significant than my failing efforts at faith in (him), a God who would never give up on me or the world (he) so loved, a God who wooed rather than threatened, whose vulnerability was more winsome than (his) omnipotence, and who transformed me not through fear, but by the "expulsive power of a new affection."[18] And yes, this God came to me in the story of Jesus, who lived and died in exactly that way. His resurrection is a mystery I cannot fathom, but I do know that it was God saying a resounding "No!" to the power of death and an even more resounding "Yes!" to the Jesus kind of life. Nothing we humans are capable of can succeed in killing it off. It rises again and again and his Spirit continues to confront us with its 'unutterable beauty'.[19]

It was the Methodist Church that nurtured me on this faith-journey. There is really no such thing as a 'no name brand' Christian. For better or worse, we find ourselves in communities with unique histories and traditions a little distinct from the others and emphasising slightly different dimensions of the faith. The Methodist Church has as many warts as any other, but I will always be grateful for certain of its emphases that were crucial in forming my faith priorities. It was born out of a spiritual renewal led by Reverend John Wesley and his brother Charles in the mid-eighteenth century. Loyal Church of England priests of considerable intellect and passion,[20] they chafed under the dry hand of an institution in serious decline at the time. Too many clergy were lost in the shallow distractions of English classism and had lost touch with the poor masses. By contrast the Wesleys, with John as leader, were searching for a truly holy life and at Oxford University they joined a group of serious-minded seekers known as the 'Holy Club'. Members held each other accountable for spiritual disciplines such as prayer, searching the Scriptures, regular attendance at worship and Holy Communion. However, the Holy Club differed from other such 'pietist' groups because of its equally rigorous practice of 'works of mercy'. England's poorest classes at the time lived in utter wretchedness and degradation and it was to these hurting people that Wesley and his comrades went, feeding the hungry, visiting debtors and condemned criminals in prison and aiding the sick and homeless. At Oxford their strict, methodical ways earned them the scornful nickname 'Methodists', and the name stuck. Methodism might have remained a fairly obscure movement had it not been for a powerful spiritual encounter which both John and Charles experienced within days of each other in May 1738. John's famous phrase "I felt my heart strangely warmed within me" described an overwhelming sense of the grace and love of God flooding his life, accompanied by a deepened faith in Christ and a new attitude of forgiving love toward "those who had despitefully used me".[21] His experience in that London meeting house in Aldersgate Street set him free from the constraints of self-obsession and ignited a passionate concern to share this 'awakening' with others. His first attempts to do so in the comfortable confines of Oxford Christianity were underwhelming: he was accused of 'enthusiasm', something not to be tolerated by the cynical religious establishment of the day. He was marginalised by them but this rejection didn't trouble him over much, because he was already becoming increasingly conscious of the call to focus on England's poor.

He responded to that call with unparalleled passion. Within a year he was preaching in the open air and reaching great numbers of desperately poor people. We are able to follow the fortunes of the movement in detail because of his careful journaling. In the 53 years between the Aldersgate experience in 1738 and his death, Wesley preached an average of two or three times each day, the first being usually at 5 am. His travels on horseback through the British Isles totalled the equivalent of nine times around the world. He wrote 230 books and pamphlets and established hundreds of new 'societies' – groups of new Christians – and personally appointed some 10 000 'Class Leaders' to watch over their growth. While remaining a renewal movement within the Church of England, the Methodists became a formidable spiritual force in the land. The break came around 1784 over the matter of ordaining preachers for the newly independent American colonies. Wesley had fine volunteers but couldn't find a bishop willing to ordain them, so he did it himself and there was no going back. There are today some 70 million Methodists around the world.

They arrived in South Africa with a touch of civil disobedience. During the second British occupation of the Cape, some Methodist soldiers in the colonial garrison requested spiritual oversight and a Reverend Barnabas Shaw was sent from England in response. On his arrival in Cape Town in 1816 he was forbidden to preach by the British Governor but he went ahead anyway and the first Methodist or 'Wesleyan' chapels and churches began to be built. Large numbers of the 1820 Settlers were Methodists too, swelling the ranks of what was to ultimately become the Methodist Church of Southern Africa (MCSA). The remarkable mission work of its first 150 years made it the largest multi-racial church in Southern Africa, 80% of its members being black. Certain Wesleyan emphases were to be crucial in developing the MCSA's role in the South African story.

First was the *all-ness* of God's grace. In Wesley's day various forms of the Calvinist doctrine of predestination were rampant, claiming that a sovereign God had pre-determined people's station in this life and their fate in the next, and there was nothing to be done about it.

Wesley fought this tenaciously, insisting that "prevenient grace" – a primal memory of God as our soul's true home – operated in all people. All could freely respond to the offer of wholeness in Christ and none, no matter how degraded, was excluded. There were often emotional scenes as he declared this message in the fields and marketplaces of England. The poor of the land could scarcely believe that they, too, were embraced by God's love. This powerful word '*all*' also had significant political implications in a class-ridden English society that believed the brutish status of the poor was divinely ordained. The ruling classes sensed the threat and often paid drunken mobs to attack Wesley and break up his meetings, but he would not be deterred. In his *La Democratie*, the continental political writer Ostrogorski spoke of the humanising influence of the leaders of England's Evangelical Revival: "They appeal always and everywhere from the miserable reality to the human conscience. They make one see the man in the criminal, the brother in the negro." They had "introduced a new personage into the social and political world of aristocratic England – *the fellow man.*" That fellow man, Ostrogorski predicted, "never more will leave the stage."[22] Indeed, this new honouring of all men and women, valuing human dignity above position and property, would ultimately flower in both the trades union movement and the British Labour Party,[23] and 200 years later Wesleyan convictions about an *all*-including God would have similar implications in an apartheid society shaped by Calvinist exclusionism.

A second consequence of Wesley's relocation was the practical empowerment of the poor. The early Methodists started free schools and economic co-operatives, the first free dispensary and building societies. Wesley's Benevolent Loan Fund was designed to "stimulate the expression of initiative and independence on the part of the underprivileged" and the Strangers' Friend Society with branches in every major city in the country was unique in that it operated "wholly for the relief *not* of our society but of poor, sick, friendless strangers."

Each of the great humanising social reformers who followed: William Wilberforce, Robert Raikes, Florence Nightingale, the Earl of Shaftesbury, John Howard and Elizabeth Fry had their faith roots in the eighteenth century evangelical renewal. Thus the emancipation of the slaves in the British Empire, the beginnings of popular education, the transformation of hospitals and nursing care, the ending of sweated labour in the factories and child labour in the mines, as well as prison reform – are all part of the legacy of Wesley's prodigious compassionate efforts. With this heritage, and given the deeply degrading circumstances in which so many South Africans are still forced to live, I don't believe any church congregation in our land can call itself Christian unless it is placing itself alongside the poor in practical, respectful, empowering ways.

Third, Wesley never consciously set out to be a social prophet, but like those we now call 'liberation theologians' he reflected on his theology in the light of his daily experience and what he found led him on a journey from *piety*, through *charity*, to *justice*. He found himself calling for social as well as personal transformation. Ever since the Holy Club days he had been committed to "works of mercy" among the poor, but now, in the process of regularly sharing their humble homes, their meagre crust, their heavy burdens and terrible degradations, he became increasingly aware of the *systemic* nature of economic deprivation. He scorned attempts by the rich to explain poverty away: "So wickedly false, so devilishly false, is the common objection: 'they are poor only because they are idle'," he declared.[24] Thus, while his primary passion was preaching people into the Kingdom of God, he increasingly campaigned to bring English society into conformity with that kingdom, seeking the conversion of *systems* as well as individuals. He promoted campaigns for justice and protested infringements of it. He attacked slavery as "that execrable sum of all the villainies", proclaiming liberty to be "the right of every human creature as soon as he breathes the vital air".[25] He protested the legal system and denounced war as the foulest curse he knew, "a horrid reproach to the Christian name". The liquor traffic, political corruption, persecution of Catholics in Ireland – all received his attention. He used the press, the pulpit, the pamphlet and the private letter. He believed that if God could make individuals Christian, God could make a Christian England. One common thread ran through all of Wesley's activism: he believed that every single person carried God's holy image and mattered infinitely to God. Therefore any infringement of human dignity was a spiritual, not merely socio-political matter. This remains true: however complicated or fraught the social problems we wrestle with today, the fundamental Christian question we must ask in judging them and seeking solutions is simple: does this do honour or violence to the image of God in those whom it impacts? Any political policy – like apartheid – that does such violence is an affront to God. Therefore when the church engages such issues, far from "interfering in politics" it is declaring that there is no area of life beyond God's moral authority.

Fourth, while he was convinced that no nation could be reformed without a spiritual awakening, Wesley was also persuaded that it would not happen without a radically different approach to wealth, property and poverty. At a personal level he saw money as a loan from God to be used for "first supplying thine own reasonable wants, together with those of your family; then restoring the remainder to God *through the poor*".[26] Wesley was seeking a "Gospel-shaped" economy rooted in compassion and equity and he was clear that those who strove to "corner" the fruits of the earth were "not only robbing God, but grinding the faces of the poor". If we leap 250 years to today's South Africa, who would deny that our nation stands in an uncannily similar place? Whatever we think of his belief that greater equity could come about through spiritual renewal, we cannot deny that achieving that equity for the South African nation is becoming literally the difference between its life or death.

I find that I can never read the story of my spiritual forbears without a sense of excitement. It leaves me with some idea of what being a Christian might look like. I have tried to put it into words thus …

> One who grows from the discovery of being loved and accepted by God into a life of disciplined love for God and neighbour, expressed in acts of devotion and worship, compassion and justice, who is willing to be held accountable to this by one's fellows, and has made an intentional option to stand with Jesus in solidarity with the poor and marginalised of society, against the powers that hold all such in bondage.[27]

I never ever had any singular 'warmed heart' experience, though there have been many moments of strong 'presence' or when some powerful spiritual truth has broken in on my consciousness. People speak of two kinds of 'conversion'. One is as if someone comes into one's darkened bedroom, flinging the curtains open, letting in the blinding light of day; the other is more like the slow awakening that dawn brings as it creeps gently through opened curtains into the room. Mine has been the second. I do speak in the next chapter about the day an 'assurance' about how I was meant to spend my life settled on my soul, but for the rest it has been a journey filled with small steps in the adventure of being a Jesus-follower.

One liberating truth for me has been that in following Jesus I am not asked to be superhuman. Episcopal priest and writer Barbara Brown Taylor writes: "I thought that being faithful was about becoming someone other than who I was … and it was not until this project failed that I began to wonder if my human wholeness might be more useful to God than my exhausting goodness." She goes on: "Committing myself to the task of becoming fully human is saving my life now." She believes that there is more than one way to do this, but because she is a Christian she says, "I do it by imitating Christ."[28]

I like that.

Another freeing discovery is that following Jesus is not about earning brownie points to 'get to heaven' – whatever that means. The whole point of his life was to remind us that this is God's world, to stand in solidarity with this world, to offer fullness of life[29] in this world, and to invite us into God's dream for this world and all of creation. In the Sermon on the Mount[30] he painted a picture of the kind of world our lover-God dreams for us, a world of love and justice, peace and joy. And in the words we call the Beatitudes[31] he described the kind of truly-human beings who could make that world a reality. Such people, he said, will be the yeast in the loaf and lights on the hill.

Heaven is not our priority. It can wait.

A tougher discovery is that following Jesus always involves other people who we have no hand in choosing. If we do invite him into our lives, Jesus asks the uncomfortable question: "Can I bring my friends?" And we look at the motley crowd clustered round him and see people of different colours and cultures and habits we were taught not to like, the unwanted and unwashed ... and we plead, "Do I really have to have them too?" And Jesus answers simply, "Love me, love my friends." The prayer "Lord, I've tried loving my neighbour, now can I please have your next ridiculous suggestion?" comes to mind. Yet if we can't make that leap, we miss everything because you can't privatise Jesus. In Daniel Erlander's *Manna and Mercy*[32] there is a passage that simply describes what happened every day when Jesus was around. It challenges every prejudice we ever had, and bursts with glorious promise of a new world:

> "Lepers, prostitutes, tax-collectors, sinners, poor people, discarded ones, blind people, debtors, outcasts, children, women, men, elderly people, sick people, Gentiles, Samaritans, Jews, demon-possessed people, outsiders, heretics, Pharisees, lawyers, and even rich people and big deals were ...

Invited, included, affirmed, loved, touched, liberated, healed, cleansed, given dignity, fed, forgiven, made whole, called, reborn, given hope, received, honoured, freed ..."

Now that is what *church* should look like: not meeting up with people who look and sound just like us, but working out how to practise the 'ridiculous' notion of loving people who are very different. The world is full of clubs where like-minded people gather, but *church* ... church should be an exciting laboratory of human relations surprises. It should fly in the face of our addictive prejudices and be the place where we find clues to humankind's most enduring dilemma – how to get on with each other. The Book of Acts is the story of how the first churches, led by the Spirit of Jesus, put up one barrier after another to try and stay safely in their religious, cultural, national and racial comfort zones, and how the Spirit knocked over their walls one by one. Simon Peter the Jewish chauvinist put it well when he cried out in amazement, "I now see how true it is that God has no favourites ..."[33]

God is still in the business of knocking over walls and invites us to share in the task. At the place where I worship these days, we end the service by clasping each other's hands and praying this prayer:

> May God bless us with discomfort at easy answers, half-truths and superficial relationships, so that we may live from deep within our hearts.
> May God bless us with anger at injustice, oppression and exploitation of people, so that we may work for justice, freedom and peace.
> May God bless us with tears to shed for those who suffer with pain, rejection, starvation and war, so that we may reach out our hand to comfort them and turn their pain to joy.
> And ...
> May God bless us with enough foolishness to believe that we can make a difference in this world, so that we can do what others claim cannot

be done: to bring justice and kindness to all our children and the poor.
In God's great grace, we say Amen – so be it.[34]

That prayer sends us out each week into a great unfinished adventure. It invites us realistically to live against the odds. I have never once regretted taking this path, although on myriad occasions I have had to confess failures in faithfulness. It remains the most exciting thing I can do with my life. I have also been asked what I would do if I was proved wrong – that the whole God thing was a nonsense. My slightly absurd answer would be that I think I would rather be wrong with Jesus than right with the rest of the world.

7

Reluctant Scholar

The first steps in the journey from the navy to the ministry took me to Grahamstown, and the Divinity Department at Rhodes University.

For those with a case against colonialism, Grahamstown makes an excellent target. Certainly, the nineteenth century Xhosa warriors resisting Boer and British settlement thought so; they attacked the town more than once and were repulsed with great difficulty. The sleepy 'City of Saints', so named for its many churches, is dominated by the Settlers Monument, a squat architectural reminder of the British interlopers – including both Elizabeth's and my forbears – who began arriving in 1820. This is the town that many of the settlers, more at ease with trading than farming, built as soon as they could. Grahamstown became the commercial and cultural heart of 'Settler Country'.

Nestling below the memorial is the campus of Rhodes University with its white stucco buildings and red tile roofs. In the 1950s, it was the smallest of South Africa's universities. The campus was an intimate, self-contained village of lecture halls, faculty offices, playing fields and residences tucked behind the old Drostdy wall at the upper western edge of Grahamstown. The wall drew a line between town and gown, the High Street being the bridge. Among the shops and businesses stood three monuments to early settler faith, the Anglican Cathedral of St Michael and St George, Trinity Presbyterian Church and Commemoration Methodist Church, built to mark the 20th anniversary of the settlers' landing. At the eastern end of the town the old main road climbed sharply as it exited toward East London, and cluttered across that hill was the black township of Joza, one of the poorest and most ramshackle in the land. In the 100 years since this seething frontier saw the last of its wars between Cape colony and Xhosa hinterland, little had disturbed the way the conquerors ordered matters of race and class. Black and white, poor and rich, lived in separate, desperately different worlds.

After WWII, the Methodist, Presbyterian and Congregational denominations struck a deal with Rhodes to train their candidates for ordained ministry. A Divinity Department was established and a dedicated residence – Livingstone House – was built. Between 60 and 70 theology students were to be found on campus each year, with Methodists outnumbering the students from the two smaller churches. As an ecumenical venture, it was ahead of its time and a resounding success, but as a response to South Africa's original sin it never got to first base. We were all white, with our black counterparts housed 60 miles away in a small town called Alice, where the Federal Theological Seminary rose alongside the blacks-only Fort Hare University. Thus our first steps toward being Christian ministers were taken in a segregated bubble and the sadness is how little it seemed to bother many of us. The thought that women of any race might possibly be called to the ordained ministry was of course even further from possibility. It would remain a female-free zone for some time yet.

My first year at Rhodes was an uneasy one. I had been an enthusiastic volunteer for the Navy, but here I was an unwilling conscript. I counted myself fortunate at first not to be housed with the '*Tokkelokke*' or 'Theologs' in Livingstone House, but rather in an ex-women's residence named Olive Schreiner, on the edge of the female campus. The ground floor had been turned into lecture rooms and offices and eleven male students who were not straight out of school occupied the rooms upstairs. The absence of urinals in the communal bathroom was a mild nuisance, but there were ample compensations: out of our windows on nice days we had the pleasant distraction of our near neighbours sunning themselves on their lawns.

My mind, however, was mainly elsewhere. Eighty miles away in Port Elizabeth was a Naval Reserve Base, to which I was now officially attached while working my way out of the service. There were boats to play with there, so I hitch-hiked down whenever I could. I was still deeply torn, giving little attention to my studies. My heart simply wasn't there. I felt myself a poor fit with the ministry and wished I could be as confident in my vocation as my fellows. There is of course something gloriously random and counter-intuitive about the call to ministry, resulting in many unlikely recruits. Those entering the Divinity School with me included a typewriter mechanic, an architect, an engineer, a travelling salesman, an Irish auctioneer and a London policeman. Yet, in spite of their widely differing backgrounds, I was conscious of a further, invisible gulf: they seemed to want to be there and I didn't. This tension tore at me for a full eighteen months before God seemed to take pity on me. Sometime in my second year I had to conduct worship and preach in a small congregation that suffered the efforts of many student preachers. For some reason I settled on a Scripture passage that seemed to mock my own condition; it was all about *knowing* and *being sure*. The Apostle Paul was claiming two certainties: "I know him in whom I have believed," he said, "and am persuaded that he is able to keep that which I have committed to him …"[35] The sermon that emerged was titled *I am persuaded …* and it was in the preaching of it that it began to become true for me. John Wesley was once told to "preach faith until you have it …" and it seemed I was doing the same. I remember coming back to my room, sitting on the side of my bed and saying to myself, "I do belong. I'm meant to be here," and to God, "You called me, so you're going to have to put up with me now, for the rest of my life." Something was settled that night. I was persuaded! Methodists would call it the gift of 'assurance'.

With that, an enormous load of uncertainty and resistance was lifted, but there were other battles to fight. I still struggled with what was to be a lifelong anxiety about academics. While I had no problem engaging with the lectures or grasping the content of set-books by simply skimming them, I battled to retain what I had read. I could hold an intellectual argument with the best, but could quote no authorities to back it up because my memory had already mislaid them. Also, my difficulty with languages other than my own still haunted me. Theologs were expected to major in Systematic Theology and Biblical Studies, New Testament Greek being cast-iron requirement for the Biblical major. After a few weeks of Greek I panicked and cast about desperately for an alternative. The dean of the faculty finally suggested that I replace Biblical Studies with Philosophy. "You'll escape Greek," he said, "but you'll sweat like you've never sweated before." All theologs had to do Phil I and it didn't seem so bad. Our professor was a delightful gentleman named Barret who had been gassed in the trenches of WWI. His lectures were held in Olive Schreiner at 8 am, a challenging time to be awake, so I often met my colleagues coming out of the lecture while I was fetching shaving water from the bathroom. When I ran into the professor taking tea one day in the students' union he invited me to join him. "Haven't I met you before, young man?" he asked. I confessed that I was one of his first year students, but that I was not very good at attending his lectures. Unfazed, the former Oxford don said, "Well, if you can pass without attending my lectures, you're the kind of gentleman we need. Now, do you take milk and sugar?" I loved him for that.

In Philosophy II, Professor Barrett was succeeded by someone who was to become specially beloved. Daantjie Oosthuizen was small in stature and big of heart. His humility co-existed with massive intelligence and a gentle but incisive humour. He offered his students genuine respect but no intellectual quarter. He was an Afrikaner unafraid to question apartheid and this made him an early target of the Security Police. The Philosophy Department was not known for sympathy to religion but Daantjie was an unapologetic Christian. A colleague once confronted him, wondering why someone of his obvious intellect should bother to follow Jesus. Daantjie thought for a moment, then squinting at him through his thick spectacles, said, "Who else would you recommend?" He was a Christ-like man absent of all religiosity and I will always be grateful for the two years spent with him. It was as tough as my dean had promised. There were three students in the second year, and only two of us survived to Phil III. No more slipping into the back of the lecture theatre, nor escaping rigorous intellectual engagement. I would not have survived had it not been for Daantjie's kindness. He recognised the struggles, but also the potential in me, and seemed to think me worth nursing. It was in his classes that I learned how to think, and to lean into the tough questions without fear when they threatened my faith. In fact, quite the opposite happened: Jesus seemed to manage quite well without my dubious assistance and engaging with the great minds and spirits of human thought confirmed for me the pre-eminence of this Jewish carpenter.

Mixing with students beyond Divinity's church-conditioned community kept my feet on the ground. We are told that Jesus was heard gladly by common people but theologians and the religious have done their best to reverse that. To this day I still have no time for religiosity, nor for what William Sangster used to call the 'language of Canaan' – the arcane code-words that the religious use to communicate with each other. I also enjoyed a brief foray into Sociology, another required subject. Professor Irving, burdened with too many theologs in his class, felt the need to remind us that: "You 'gentlemen of divinity' focus on what *ought* to be; here we study what *actually is*," another warning about the way faith and the church could lose touch with the real world.

The other subjects – including two years of Biblical Studies and Church History and three of Systematics – were all more or less easily managed and began to be fun. Our teachers, we discovered, could be fun too. When fellow student Ken Carstens used his 'crit' sermon to lambast South Africa's whites with the vivid image of "two million white plutocrats being rowed by fifteen million sweating black slaves up the economic stream," Professor Hewson responded with just one remark: "Kenneth," he said, "it must have been some boat!" When I critiqued theologian WR Matthew's Christology, saying that he was "barking up the wrong tree", Professor Maxwell returned my essay, remarking in the margin: "Comparing the Dean of St Paul's to an over-enthusiastic and misguided puppy is an impertinence – unless it is indeed the wrong tree." The generous mark he gave me indicated that we agreed about trees. All too late in the day I had begun to thrive and though I was to struggle with reading and memory retention for the rest of my ministry, for the latter half of my three-year sojourn at Rhodes, the classroom became a place of pleasure instead of pain.

There was also time for fun – probably too much of it. I had moved into Livingstone House in my second year and occasional cross-town raids on St Paul's Anglican college were returned in force. Livingstone House had to be defended, sometimes with water hoses, and when the battle was over we were to be found on our knees, like kids with a jigsaw puzzle, trying to refit the parquet flooring blocks that had floated away in the fray.

First year students were known as 'Inkettes'. One of them – whom I liked very much – was trying to raise Rag funds with her Phelps House associates by offering male students coffee for a shilling, plus a kiss for two shillings. They were still falling short of their target so she and I looked for a stronger incentive. In those days – disgustingly colonial as it may seem in the more enlightened present – students could leave their shoes outside their rooms for polishing, so in the small hours of one morning I crept down the Livingstone hallways stealing the left shoe of each pair. I delivered a boxful of left shoes to my Inkette friend and a notice soon appeared in Livingstone House announcing that anyone wanting their shoes back should go to Phelps bearing one more shilling. As streams of Livingstone men rummaged through the big box for their missing shoes the Inkettes raked in more money with their 'coffee and kiss' trade. However, when they finally closed the door on the last Livingstonian and began to clear up, they discovered that most of their teaspoons were missing. Next day a notice appeared in Phelps House announcing: "Teaspoons available at Livingstone House for 6d an item."

While I was at Rhodes, Dad became the leader of the Methodist Church in Southern Africa. In those days we followed the British pattern of electing a 'President of the Conference' each year, which had the disadvantage of inconsistent leadership, but did prevent leaders from getting too big for their boots. The President's year began with the Annual Conference in October, over which he presided, and then consisted of visitations to all the Districts, offering inspiration and leadership. All this happened without any let-up in his local church responsibilities. Dad's Conference was to be at East London, so I hitch-hiked the 100 miles to hear his Presidential Addresses dealing with the national spiritual and political landscape. I was incredibly proud of him of course, while trying not to show it. He had become steadily more trenchant in his critique of the government, describing apartheid as slavery in another form and morally indefensible. He now confronted it head on. Apartheid, he said, when pushed to logical conclusions, ran into theological conclusions. It was a sin against God: "The government's view is that while one white man (sic) and one black man are friends, apartheid will have failed; the Church's view is that so long as one white man and one black man are not friends, the Church will have failed." The Church, he declared, was therefore on a collision course with the regime. It would disobey certain laws and government pressure to conform: "We will not place the Church at the disposal of the State."

I came away from East London quietly thrilled with Dad's clear witness, but also shocked by the reaction of some of his colleagues.

While black Methodists warmly welcomed it, many white clergy were either lukewarm or openly hostile. I was thinking that my father would not have an easy year in leadership, but it turned out that he would not have the year at all. A longstanding heart problem wore him down and halfway through his Presidential year he was forced to hand over the reins and sail to England for one of the early open-heart surgeries pioneered at Guy's Hospital. What he had achieved, however, was to lay the ground for South African Methodism's most critical decision, taken a year later. During the 1950s some conservative white church leaders, encouraged by the government, argued that the MCSA should accept the new apartheid realities and, much like the Dutch Reformed Church, break into racially defined segments. There was a real danger that this view might prevail. My father, together with some others, saw a very different vision: after meeting with top black Methodists Seth Mokitimi, Ezekiel Mahabane, Gabriel Setiloane and Jotham Mvusi, he urged instead "frank and free discussions about the appointment of an African President". Presaging the debate that would dominate the following Conference, he roundly rejected any separatism: "Let our motto be, 'Let us go on *together* in the name of the Lord,'" he declared, "'and in the name of the Lord, let us *stay together*.'" He was too ill to be present at that Conference, but was thrilled when it pronounced its conviction that, "it is the will of God that the Methodist Church remain one and undivided."[36]

My own first act of public protest was in 1959. Rhodes faculty and students in academic regalia marched through Drostdy Arch and down the High Street protesting the Extension of University Education Act, which meant exactly the opposite. The act banned black students from registering at 'white' universities. That year I also wrote to the Minister of Justice, Mr CR Swart, and organised a group of Divinity students to join me as signatories registering our "vehement protest" at his treatment of ex-Chief Albert Luthuli. The Nobel Peace Laureate and President of the ANC had been banned for five years in 1954 and now a further five years had been slapped on him. My concern had a personal dimension because I had met Luthuli in our home in Cape Town when Dad was organising the Defence and Aid Fund.[37] I was in awe of this bluff Zulu giant, who exuded warmth, strength and conviction. It seemed absurd that such an obviously good person should be treated thus. In his reply the minister decided to do Bible study with us, suggesting that seeing we "had already delivered judgement on the poor misguided sinner, the Minister of Justice, it would perhaps be wise of [us] to read and digest the parable of the Pharisee and the Publican ..."[38]

There was also a foray into student politics, beginning with something of a necessary humiliation. Elections for the Students' Representative Council (SRC) were beginning to reflect national politics and becoming increasingly bitter. A crisis split the SRC and forced the resignation of some of the incumbents and in the ensuing rough and tumble I joined the name-calling, labelling one of the candidates named Rudolph Gruber a "megalomaniac and a Nat" which, given the state of politics today, might seem fairly tame, but not so in 1959, when we still referred to fellow students publicly as 'Mr' or 'Miss'. Whatever I felt about Mr Gruber, I had no proof whatever for what I had said. My conscience gnawed at me over the weekend and at a mass student meeting on the Monday, having already written to him personally, I offered a public apology to him and for being one of those who had contributed to the chaos. I then pleaded that we all reject the hate and malice that remarks like my own had stoked and rather focus on facts and principles instead. This seemed to have a positive effect on the rowdy meeting. In the election that followed some students put my name forward and I found myself on the SRC. Mr Gruber went on to become prominent in the South African Foundation, an organisation established to promote SA interests overseas. I do not know whether he was a Nat after all, but he wasn't a megalomaniac and we kept up a friendly contact over many years. My shame at having so easily smeared another person in the heat of the moment led me to decide that whatever fights lay in the future, I would not descend to that sort of behaviour again. I have tried not to.

At some point, I also became an assistant editor of the student newspaper, *Rhodeo*. The editor was Hugh Lewin, son of an Anglican priest and a courageous and principled person who was later to serve seven years as a political prisoner and record his experiences in the powerful book *Bandiet*. Our claim to fame as *Rhodeo*'s editorial team was to print an issue carrying big blank spaces denoting the stories that government censorship had forbidden. Soon, in the humourless logic of our rulers, it became illegal to leave blank spaces in newspapers.

SRC membership also thrust an entirely different duty upon me, that of organising the traditional Casbah evening during Rag Week of 1959. Casbah was a fête, with various stalls, games and competitions to raise Rag funds. I decided that this year would be bigger and better than anything before and we moved the whole event out of the safety of a university hall onto the Rhodes Great Field. As evening came, the field was a fairyland of coloured lights with students and townsfolk milling happily around the stalls. Our centrepiece was a floodlit ring where a boxing display would climax the evening. My fellow *tokkelok* Ken Eddie and I sat in the commentator's box in the grandstand, taking in the tranches of cash delivered to us from the stall-holders, and all was well until the Graham Hotel downtown closed and male students in the later stages of inebriation arrived on the field. For some reason the brightly lit boxing ring attracted them and it was soon filled with drunks – far too many of them – swinging wildly at each other. The structure itself began to teeter and sway drunkenly, the poles and floodlights above it describing ever-widening arcs through the night sky. When the end came it was impressive: the ring collapsed, drunks were flung in all directions, sparks hissed and crackled and a large portion of Grahamstown was plunged into inky blackness. We had tapped into the town's power grid to light the Great Field and our impromptu boxing exhibition had blown it. On the field, darkness and chaos reigned and Casbah was no more. By the glow of Ken's cigarette lighter we scraped all the takings into one bag. Ken grabbed some bottles of wine donated as prizes, and we slipped out of the box and down to his old black MG parked behind the grandstand. We got to it without being seen and before anybody could miss us we were back behind a locked door in Ken's room in Livingstone House, wondering how we could wriggle out of this disaster. Running out of ideas, we got quietly tipsy – a first for both of us – and waited for the morning.

The following day an outraged Vice-Chancellor demanded that the entire Rag Committee appear before him, together with the SRC. Things were worse even than we thought. It turned out that not only had we ruined Casbah and subjected half of Grahamstown to a blackout, but unknown to us a student couple had been exploring their very close relationship under the boxing ring when it collapsed and had been fortunate to escape with their lives, if not their dignity. Vice-Chancellor Tom Alty tore into us and announced that he was cancelling Rag, and considering the facts, his parting words were memorable: "Next year, maybe you should get the theologs to organise Casbah, so it ends up half decent." I made myself as small as I could while SRC chair John Benyon loyally failed to mention that Alty's suggestion had already been tried and found spectacularly wanting. Professor Hewson, responsible for Methodist students, a thoroughly gracious person and a close friend of my father, was furious. "You could be sent down for this," he hissed when I stood before him, "we have all been shamed." My misery deepened as I waited for the axe to fall, but was saved by the liveliness of the student body. They poured into a protest meeting that sent a suitably servile resolution to Dr Alty, pleading for the restoration of Rag in return for a ban on any future Casbahs. Alty relented, the Rag procession went ahead, and I survived. Also, my policy of ensuring regular deliveries of cash takings to the commentary box meant that we could chalk up a record Casbah income in spite of the disaster. It had indeed been a very different – but final – Casbah.

On 21 August 1959, just as we were bracing ourselves to prepare for our final examinations, my world fell in. In the small hours of that morning a hand on my shoulder shook me gently awake. It was Prof Hewson telling me that my father had died. The person I most loved and admired was gone. In something of a daze I got myself ready for the drive to Port Elizabeth, and then onto a Vickers Viscount – my first flight on a commercial aircraft – to Cape Town. I found my mother and sister at the home of friends, Mom lying in a darkened room, silent and stricken. Dad was only 58 when he died and being ten years younger than he, a long life of loneliness lay ahead of her. At the funeral in Rosebank Methodist Church, my sister and I sat on each side of her, listening as good people spoke, but I recall little of what they said. I had slipped into the church an hour before the service. The coffin was already in place and I had spent a little time beside it, thinking and saying what I needed to, and regretting all the things left unsaid between us. My recollection of that moment is of a strange counterpoint of pain and certainty: pain that he and I would now never break through our mutual reserve into the closeness and comradeship of an adult father-son relationship, and the certainty that whatever now occupied that coffin, it was no longer my dad. "He's not here," I whispered to myself. "That's no longer him in there." In the desolation of it all, and without much mature faith to turn to, the gift of that moment was an existential one – another moment of 'being persuaded', a deep assurance of Resurrection life.

The return to my last couple of months at Rhodes wasn't easy, though my fellow students were very kind. I wrote my exams robotically, my only anxiety being that I had not mastered enough of Ryle's *Concept of Mind* and Kant's *Critique of Pure Reason* to get through

Phil III. In the end I got the degree, not very well, but probably better than I deserved.

I left Rhodes at the end of 1959 with a fairly good theological and biblical grounding, but I'm not sure how confident I was about the work that lay ahead. We had received limited instruction in the actual practices of ministry, so the work of 'caring for souls' would have to be learned on the job. Nor, frankly, had there been enough emphasis on nurturing our own inner spiritual lives; that too, it would seem, was a DIY matter. But we had at least become a cohort of colleagues: the three-year journey had bonded us, and in my case, a couple of closer friendships had begun to penetrate my habitual solitariness. Yet I doubt any of us realised how poorly we were equipped for the 'secular 60s' that were almost upon us. We were about to enter a decade when confidence in religious belief would sink to its lowest ebb in 200 years. It was represented most sensationally by *Time* magazine's famous April 1966 cover: large red letters on a solid black background, asking, "Is God Dead?" In ten years, the graduating class photograph we proudly posed for would be a bit like that of a World War I infantry company entering the trenches: half of those smiling young men would be gone from ministry, casualties of a seemingly unassailable assault on their faith foundations.

Meanwhile, a telegram from the Methodist Conference which had my life in its hands informed me that I was now the Probationer Minister appointed to Bellville Methodist Church, Cape Town.

8

Stumbling into Ministry

Probationer Ministers are Methodism's apprentice clergy – partly cooked. Probation lasted six years, three at seminary and three in-service. The ministry was exclusively male in those days, and when entering we had to be single, assuring the Conference in the quaintly absurd language of the Church that we had no 'secular encumbrances', that is, wives. Probationers were also completely at the mercy of the Conference Stationing Committee and could be sent anywhere in Southern Africa. When Conference met in October, the number of senior students slipping into the Livingstone House chapel for earnest prayer increased. I recall one of them, James Polley, praying aloud, "Anywhere, Lord, anywhere – except Otjiwarongo!" But the Stationing Committee was not without compassion; they appointed me to be near my newly widowed mom and the rest of my probation would be spent in Cape Town – at Bellville for one year and then in Camps Bay and Milnerton.

As I hoisted down my suitcase onto the platform at Bellville railway station, a small man with a big smile strode toward me, hand stretched out in greeting. Rob Raven was one of the lay leaders and he loaded me into his car and took me home to lunch where his spouse Margaret had prepared a meal of welcome. I immediately warmed to this homely couple and their children and would find refuge there many times. After lunch we headed for the church. In 1960, Bellville Methodist Church consisted of a multi-purpose hall utilised during the week as a youth club, Scout hall, group meeting place, badminton court and whatever else came up. On Sundays it was converted for worship by introducing a pulpit and Communion table. The congregation was only ten years old and I was to discover that such communities are often a lot more fun than old established ones.

After inspecting the premises, we went off to get the key to my new digs at 10 Boston Street. A single room served as both bedroom and office. Squeezed into the small space were a bed, wardrobe, dresser, desk and chair. The bathroom was down the passage and I would eat around the corner at the landlady's place. Other tenants were a newly wed Afrikaans couple and an engineering student who had a back room. He and I soon struck up a friendship over the old MG sports car that he tinkered with and sometimes got to go. Our landlady's claim to fame was that she had been a Jehovah's Witness. The JWs don't give up their own without a fight, so she was something of a celebrity among the Baptists to whom she had defected. She would drop bits of her stock talk, "I was a Jehovah's Witness," into table conversation. "When I was a JW," she said as she dished up our not very appetising supper, "I would have called you a goat because when we knocked on a door and got a hostile response, we would tick the 'Goat' box." To earn 'Sheep' grade in her visitation book, people had to offer a warmer welcome. Her spouse was a quiet little man, who only came into his own when saying grace in sonorous High Dutch. For me the unusual thing was that it followed, rather than preceded the meal, which made total sense: depending on how edible the food was, I could opt in or out of thanking God.

Our third destination was a garage to pick up a battered maroon Puch motor scooter, which was to be my official mode of transport. After taking possession I went off somewhere quiet to learn how to ride it.

Although I had spent years just thirteen miles away in Rosebank, I had never visited Bellville. Cape Town's snootily English Southern Suburbs tended to be divided from the Northern Suburbs by a '*boerewors* curtain' beyond which Afrikaans and a more working-class culture dominated. I soon found that my Youth Guild took a dim view of their new minister courting a girl from 'the other side' but once Elizabeth trusted me and the Puch enough to cross the curtain on my pillion they got to know her and made an exception.

After church on my second Sunday evening the youth leader named Alfie Schnehage told me that the group had arranged a welcome party at one of their homes. All I had to do was follow their cars, so I nodded and mounted the Puch while they packed into three 1930s-vintage Austin 7s and some other jalopies. It was drizzling, but having ridden the scooter for a few days, and been tested and licensed, I felt no concern; all I had to do was stick behind them. They had other ideas of course, mapping out a diabolical route with so many twists and turns that I was soon hopelessly lost. Things got worse when they veered off across a couple of wet fields, with me hanging on grimly, peering through mud-spattered goggles to make out the faint red of their tail-lights. I realised that this was a test I simply had to pass, so I gripped the handlebars, sliding and praying and skidding my way through – and back onto the paved road. When I finally arrived among the laughing youngsters I was mud from head to toe, but I was now one of them. Some remain firm friends to this day.

I had little training in church administration but Rob Raven and the other lay leaders helped me along. The congregation was used to junior probationers, "not broken in yet," as ex-serviceman Alec Pawson used to say. They showed wonderful forbearance as I stumbled my way into ministry and into their completely unearned trust. Rough-hewn and straightforward, they were some of the finest people I have known. Their faith was simple – it was about living decent lives, working honestly, doing right by their families and trying to take God seriously. Factory foremen, fitters, train drivers, traffic cops – I found that I could move comfortably among them and enjoy the friendship they readily offered.

The year 1960 was of course one of massive political import in South

Africa. It was the year of Harold Macmillan's 'Wind of Change' speech in the South African Parliament, of the rise of Poqo, the Pan-Africanist Congress (PAC), and the anti-pass-book campaigns climaxing in the March 21 Sharpeville massacre. Just nine days after Sharpeville, in Cape Town a 24-year-old Methodist lay preacher and PAC activist named Philip Kgosana led a march of 30 000 men from the township of Langa to Caledon Square police station in the heart of the city. That day Elizabeth was attending the Technical College in the same street that the marchers converged upon and she called me later to share her amazing experience: to get to her train she had to walk through the serried ranks of men besieging the police station and filling the adjoining streets. "I was really scared," she said, "but the marchers were so disciplined. They stood in silence, and quietly made way for those of us trying to pass through. Not a single man touched me." I silently thanked God for their dignity and also her courage. Kgosana was deceived by a promise that he and other leaders would be given an interview by FC Erasmus, now Minister of Justice, and on the strength of that he ordered his followers to disband. Amazingly, the 30 000 men left the city as quietly as they had come. The government then struck with lightning speed, declaring a State of Emergency the same day. Hundreds, including Kgosana, were arrested and the ANC and PAC were banned.

Langa and Nyanga townships were cordoned off by the military and some of my navy friends were now camped out with units surrounding the townships. I went to visit them, relying on my clerical collar and the Puch to get me through. It was troubling to see good friends and their men being used in this way. "This is not what I joined the navy for," confided one sub-lieutenant, unfamiliar pistol on his hip. He was right. There was a sharp awareness in me that – but for the intervention of my calling – I could have been right there with him, sent to crush political protest. I came away beginning to understand that God's call on the cliffs of Saldanha Bay had rescued me from being on the wrong side of my nation's darkening history. Arrests continued and by May 18 000 people, including Nelson Mandela and PAC leader Robert Sobukwe, had been detained. South Africa's slide into a deadly cycle of confrontation, repression, uprising and more repression, was beginning to take shape.

However, for a young probationer serving his first church, all this was tangential to my vocational exploration. Life was a series of 'firsts'. I was learning to come up with a sermon every week. Preparation was a long, painful business and required discipline, patience and prayer, but I found an excitement in quarrying into a passage of Scripture and extracting its relevance for my people's lives. Seeing I was experiencing the joys and sorrows of courtship too, my first marriage preparation classes were probably longer on empathy than wisdom. Baptisms – which are God's wonderful way of declaring God's love and acceptance even when we don't know it – were a trial until a learned colleague advised me that I should always take the baby's thigh in a vice-grip. "They are shocked into silence just long enough," he said. "Then if they planned to cry it only happens when you hand them back to their parents." My first home visitations were approached with much trepidation, but I was surprised by the readiness with which people revealed their deep selves to this inexperienced pastor. Even more astounding was that in spite of my newness to the task, they would sometimes tell me that my counsel had helped them.

My first encounter with bereavement would have tested much better pastors than me. Five Bellville men in one family had gone out fishing in a blustery False Bay and their ski-boat had overturned. Three of them, two brothers and a brother-in-law, drowned. They came from a low-income Afrikaans background, and one of them had been linked with our church. When I arrived at their home, his widow sat in shock while people came and went. The next hours taught me much about pastoring grief-stricken people, the most important lesson being that presence trumps pontificating every time. I listened as a solemn dominee stood before this new widow and launched into a pious lecture about how her husband and brothers had gone to be with God, and that it was not for us to question "the Lord's will", and more of the clichés unthinking religious people offer at times like these. As for me, I wouldn't be interested in a God whose 'will' included a wholesale family drowning. I watched her stricken face, and when she looked toward me pleadingly, I got up and said, "Enough! That's not the kind of God we believe in," and escorted him out. A little while later, another visitor arrived, this time a woman who had a fairly racy reputation around the town. When she entered the room, there were no words; she simply walked across to the young widow, took her in her arms and they wept together for a long time. Then, still saying nothing, she went into the kitchen and began to do the kind of stuff people do in kitchens. Of the two visitors, I knew which one was sent by God. I know that some Christian traditions differ theologically, but I sometimes wonder whether we don't have quite different Gods.

There were the inevitable bloopers too. Later that year I stood in the parking lot at Maitland Crematorium commiserating with a grieving family. Looking down the long path to the crematorium itself, I saw the undertaker signalling me. Without a second's thought I said, "Excuse me, I must go and see what's cooking down there." It was only after two or three steps that it hit me; sweat burst from my pores and ran down my backbone, but there was nothing I could do, I simply had to keep walking.

Meanwhile Elizabeth and I were planning our marriage for the end of 1960. We were excited and quite undaunted by our shaky economic situation. My monthly stipend was £11.15s, and the insurance company where Elizabeth worked had recently raised her salary to £20 a month. Neither of us had any worldly goods to speak of. With timber scavenged from a Bellville factory I spent my days off fashioning an upholstered headboard and side cabinets for our first bed – my wedding present to her. Hers to me, given in advance for obvious reasons, was a Black & Decker drill/sander to which I could attach a small circular sawblade. It was my first power tool and must have been sufficient for the task because the finished headboard lasted us 42 years before we promoted ourselves to a queen-size bed.

Prime Minister HF Verwoerd had announced a Referendum for October 1960 to determine whether South Africa should become a republic. I recall preaching a vaguely 'political' sermon on the Sunday before the vote, reminding the congregation of the importance of "belonging to something bigger than our nation alone," and the dangers for South Africa's voteless millions if we cut off ties with the Commonwealth of Nations. Only whites could vote, of course, and 52% of them said Yes to becoming the Republic of South Africa. Afrikaner nationalism had prevailed once more. It was the first time I saw the newlyweds in in our boarding house become animated; they were clearly overjoyed. The ex-servicemen in my congregation felt very differently. It was as if their six years of sacrifice 'up North' in WWII had been for naught.

Our wedding was on 31 December 1960. I had told Elizabeth for some time that I would still have to conduct the Watch-Night service[39] at Bellville on our wedding night. She later claimed that she had only pretended to believe me. The wedding was in the family church at Rosebank on a bright breezy morning, with a reception in her family's garden. Tom Hardie's roses were in bloom with Elizabeth the loveliest rose of them all. The Bellville youth group had offered their most presentable vehicle, an Austin A30, so we could drive off in something more dignified than the Puch and we decamped to the usual good wishes and confetti. Our happy honeymoon at the Hout Bay Hotel and then in Hermanus was enlivened by a mouse in our room on the first night and coming upon a homeless and hurting old man lying on the beach the next day. It took some hours to see to his needs and in later years Elizabeth pointed to that moment as the one when she realised that in marrying me she had married the Church.

Bellville could not house a married minister so we came back from honeymoon, suntanned and happy, to move into a new home. The people of Bellville had done a good job breaking me in, and while they prepared to welcome their next greenhorn I was now given responsibility for Camps Bay and Milnerton. Our tiny house in Camps Bay was attached to the church premises in Farquhar Road, only a couple of hundred yards from what is now one of the most expensive beachfronts in the world. In 1961, however, Camps Bay was a still a sleepy village, not quite aware that a great city lay over Kloof Nek. There was a small shopping centre, some sports fields adjacent to the Rotunda Hotel and a few hundred homes set on the slopes below Table Mountain's western buttresses known as the Twelve Apostles. Until we arrived, my new congregation had been an autonomous 'Interdenominational' church. Having fallen into difficulties, they had voted to join the MCSA and my job was to shepherd them into Methodist ways. I soon found that while the word 'interdenominational' sounded admirably inclusive, it was really code for a more fundamentalist-leaning Christianity and they might have been happier with the Baptists than with the theologically liberal and socially conscious MCSA. They also found that there was a world of difference between the autonomy they had enjoyed and the highly organised and integrated Methodist Circuit system. We had inherited a group of conscripts rather than volunteers, and if they were not feeling too comfortable about the change, neither was I.

Milnerton, on the other hand, was an encouraging contrast: the suburb was in its infancy and the Methodist congregation still very new. Sunday services were held in the local pub, with an early morning team airing the place, clearing out the empties and arranging the chairs. Young families were moving into the suburb in numbers and on the days I was there I simply had to watch for removal vans, drop in to welcome them and invite the new arrivals to our Sunday 'Pub Service'. It was a different era, of course, with most of them keen to have their children in a Sunday School – these days I'm not sure that would be most people's priority. During my four years there we grew rapidly, requiring two moves, first to the tennis club and then to the primary school hall, by which time plans were afoot to build our own church. Like Camps Bay, many of our new members knew little about Methodist ways, but there the similarity ended. They were wonderfully open to newness and some of my most enjoyable times were spent in discussion groups in people's homes, turning over all sorts of questions, debating issues of faith and life.

It was during the Camps Bay/Milnerton years that our first two sons, John and Christopher, were born. Elizabeth was a natural when it came to mothering, both before and after birthing the boys. Both pregnancies went off without problems and the boys were born in the Mowbray Maternity Home, each for the princely sum of R6.50.[40] The rules had recently changed, allowing expectant fathers to be present during their baby's birth and I will always be deeply thankful for the experience. I was horrified at the level of pain involved and still recall my feelings of utter impotence, unable to do anything for Elizabeth's agony except hold her hand. The birth-struggle and first breaths and cries announcing new life were astounding, sacred moments. Far from being the text-book proud father, I felt myself in the presence of the Life-force itself and humbled beyond measure. The moments following – between a heroic mother now at rest and a dad seized by wonder – were indescribable. With our firstborn, John, safely in Elizabeth's arms I blinked back tears of joy and looked round to thank the doctor, only to find him as tearful as me. All choked up, he said, "It was my first too." The 'Mowbray' was of course a teaching hospital and I breathed a prayer of thanks for the steady hand of Sister Townsend, who had supervised the whole process. Christopher's turn came only 20 months later in August 1963, and with the same sense of miracle, but Chris didn't want to wait. On the hectic ride we were stopped for speeding on De Waal Drive, but the ruddy-faced traffic cop quickly paled when he realised what was happening. He became our speedy escort to the hospital and looked much relieved to hand us over to the same doughty sister.

The work at Milnerton continued to expand rapidly, and though I struggled with the conservative-leaning leadership at Camps Bay, that congregation also grew. The growth there, especially among young adults and couples, tended to send my more rigid critics underground but never completely silenced them. I tried my hand at a more public approach and held services a couple of times in the famous Rotunda. Good crowds turned up and I enjoyed engaging with less 'churched' people, some of whom decided to join our regular services. Younger members responded to my more open theology and found it refreshing. Elizabeth and I formed some special friendships among them. With occasional bumps in the road, Camps Bay and Milnerton were pleasant and undisturbed places in which to spend our early marriage and learn how to be young parents ourselves.

Then two things happened to change our lives.

The first was my appointment as part-time chaplain to Robben Island Prison, and the second was the decision by my Circuit to invite a controversial Australian evangelist, Alan Walker, to come and preach to the people of Cape Town.

Robben Island came into my life in 1962. At the weekly staff meeting of ministers in the Cape Town Circuit we were told that a new prison was being established there and the church needed to provide chaplaincy. Were there any volunteers? None of us was looking for extra work, but the sailor in me saw a chance to get on the water again, so I put up my hand. That started the formalities to arrange my security clearance for monthly visits. What none of us knew was that Robben Island was destined to become South Africa's notorious political prison and one of the ugliest symbols of apartheid's cruelty. The story of my 30-month chaplaincy to the prisoners there is told in Chapter 9, but the almost obscene contrast between dreamy Camps Bay, modern Milnerton and the conditions I found on the

Island evoked a deep disconnect. Like the Kilnerton experience of my schooldays, my visits there took me into a separate world – this time a starkly alienating one. It was a wake-up call reminding me that I was ministering in one of the most unequal and unjust societies in the world.

My first meeting with Australian Dr Alan Walker was in September 1963, when he arrived to lead a controversial preaching mission among us. The ministers in our Circuit had read his book *The Whole Gospel for the Whole World*[41] and we had invited him because he was an evangelist with a difference. We were used to American evangelists preaching a pietist message about personal sin while completely ignoring the besetting social sin of our land – apartheid. Walker was different: he was not so much interested in getting people to heaven as seeing God's kingdom of love and justice established on earth by transformed people. While all of his packed evening services in Sydney ended with a simple altar call, he was also a resounding voice for social justice in his country, a trenchant opponent of the 'White Australia' policy and of militarism world-wide. It was said that the first question Australian Prime Minister Robert Menzies asked on a Monday morning was, "What did Walker have to say yesterday?" We felt that this man would shake up not only the Methodist Church, which had gone uncomfortably quiet, but the nation itself, and we were soon proved right.

The Alan Walker Mission of 1963 was nothing if not controversial. Even before he arrived, National Party politicians and media were calling for him to be refused entry. He had criticised apartheid from afar and clashed with apartheid propagandists in Australia. On his arrival at Cape Town airport he strode purposely to one side of the barrier separating white and 'coloured' welcomers, reaching out to shake coloured hands first. His press interviews were uncompromisingly anti-apartheid. On the special trains we hired to take people to Goodwood Stadium, people ignored the colour bar and the South

African Railways encountered integration for the first time. Evening rallies in the stadium attracted about 8 000 people each night and Walker waded into the issues, never failing to attack racism and segregation. Yet, shot through each sermon was a winsome appeal to consider not only the challenge of Jesus' social ethic, but the intimate offer of new life through God's forgiveness and acceptance. For me this personal-social balance was Wesleyan theology at its best. On the closing night I stood next to Bert Pfhul, one of Cape Town's better-known conservative Methodist lay preachers. "I can't believe it," he said. "This man has just preached a political sermon on apartheid and hundreds of people are walking forward to offer their lives to Jesus."

Our campaign was a joint venture with Pretoria Methodists, so Walker's mission addressed the two capitals of the nation. The most provocative moments were lunch hours in the Cape Town City Hall and Pretoria's Church Square, where Walker's *I Challenge the Minister* format consisted of a brief, punchy address, followed by questions from the public. Typical of those encounters was when a man shouted, "Who the hell are you to come lecture us? What do you know about South Africa?" and Walker's sharp riposte: "I don't know everything about South Africa, but I do know something about the Kingdom of God and there is no apartheid at the gates of heaven, so you shouldn't have it here."

For some months I had been involved with Theo Kotze[42] in publicity and communication and, with some prescience perhaps, had been tasked with editing a newspaper to promote the Mission. Knowing little except the *Rhodeo* experience, but keen to have a go, I asked cub reporter Tony Heard to help me. He was a member of my Camps Bay church and did know something about journalism, rising later to be perhaps the best-known editor of the *Cape Times*. Together with my friend John Gardener, we put together *Christian Impact*, a successful, if brief, venture. Its main legacy for me was a 'feel' for journalism that opened me to later opportunities.

Meanwhile, a conviction was forming in my mind. As I read and heard about Walker's home church in Sydney I yearned to experience what seemed to be the most effective city church anywhere in the world. Suburban ministry, serving people who looked alike, lived the same comfortable lives and all seemed to visit the same hairdresser, had never truly grabbed me. I preached and pastored as conscientiously as I could but something was missing. On the other hand, the inner city, with its robust pace, its myriad needs, its polyglot populace, and its grit and grime, always stirred me. We had large city churches, of course, but no specially trained city ministers. Our downtown congregations consisted largely of suburbanites who drove into town to hear the 'big' preachers and consequently their programmes offered little genuine engagement with the needs and cries of the city. They were suburban churches in the wrong place. By contrast, in the 1960s Sydney's Central Methodist Mission (CMM) was deeply immersed in the struggles of big-city life and was pioneering new ways of communicating with, and pastoring, mass society. I so wanted to see Walker's CMM in action that for the only time in my ministry, I initiated a conversation about my future. Securing an interview with Walker in his hotel room, I haltingly spoke of a growing call to city ministry. Was there any hope of spending perhaps a year with the CMM team, testing that call and learning from them? To my surprise he was wide open to the idea and promised to follow it up when he returned to Australia.

During our time in Camps Bay my probation had ended and I had been ordained. The last lap had not been easy. Before my final exams I had woken one morning to find the right side of my face paralysed. I couldn't close my staring right eye or blink at all and when I tried to speak only the left side of my mouth worked and my words sounded like a gobbling turkey. I had been struck by Bell's Palsy and it was a devastating blow, especially for someone in a vocation requiring regular public speaking. There is no known cure other than the passage of time, but one of my congregation was determined to act. Jacques Marais was a specialist at Groote Schuur Hospital and within hours he had me there receiving electric massage treatment, repeating this daily for some time. I believe his intervention made the crucial difference and over the next six months some 80% of function was restored. Most importantly, even if I would go through life with a slightly lopsided face, months of word exercises paid off and normal speech returned. The final rituals before Ordination required us to bear witness to our call and undergo an oral examination before the assembled Synod of ministers. Still sounding very turkey-like, I found this to be an ordeal, and was immensely relieved when the Synod voted for me to proceed.

There is something overwhelming about Ordination. It is a moment made holy by its reminders of call and commitment, of love and service, of duty and sacrifice. Stern words are spoken, vows are made, prayers are prayed and hands laid upon your head. You rise from your knees knowing that you have joined a two-millennial-old Order – the 'Ministry of Word and Sacrament' – and are wedded to it for the rest of your life. Moments in the service still live powerfully with me: the sense of panic when the congregation replied to the question about our worthiness to be ordained with a full-throated, "They are worthy!" How did they know? If only they knew …! And then, feeling the crushing pressure of seven pairs of hands on my head: this was not a gentle benediction. It was a heavy, heavy transmission of gift and task. I specially missed my dad that day. He had been ordained exactly 30 years previously and his had been a sadly truncated ministry. I knew that he had kept faith with his vows. Would I? In the moment of my Ordination when the Presiding Bishop prayed, "Father, send the Holy Spirit upon Peter …" it was very much as if those pressing their hands upon me were urging a new measure of God into my frail soul.

9

The Island

It lies there like the just-visible hump of a submerged leviathan, barnacled with a sprinkling of ugly buildings and smelling of kelp and sea-growth. Just seven miles from the mainland city of Cape Town, it might as well be in the middle of the South Atlantic.

Robben Island.

There is nothing beautiful about this place. Exposed to driving Atlantic gales in winter and the hot summer South Easters, the island is ringed by treacherous black rock shoals and thundering surf. Apart from a few gum trees its vegetation consists mainly of the rapacious Port Jackson willow which has triumphed over the indigenous *fynbos*. It is traversed by old military roads made of a blinding mixture of crushed shells and white limestone. A rutted landing strip is located at one end. At the other a small harbour provides the only safe approach from the sea.

Ever since Europeans came to the Cape of Good Hope, the island has symbolised white domination and been chaptered with human suffering. Variously a leper colony, a place of exile, a mental asylum, naval garrison and prison, it has always offered cold comfort. It has been a graveyard for unwary shipping and for the hopes of those transported there. When I set foot on its shores in 1962 I was not the first Methodist minister to preach to prisoners there. Some 140 years before, the great Methodist pioneer Reverend Barnabas Shaw visited the Island, "preaching on Captain Peddar's veranda to such as understood English, and afterwards in the prison to the convicts in Dutch."[43]

Among the 1963 arrivals there was Nelson Mandela, who most people do not realise had two introductions to the Island. His first had been via the degrading route that introduced most Robben Island prisoners to their new home, the prison launch *Dias*. Seasick and desperately trying to keep their balance while shackled to one another in the stinking, rolling hold of the launch, prisoners often endured white prison guards returning from the mainland urinating on them through the skylight above. Mandela's first stay was short; within months he was taken back to Pretoria to join the rest of the Rivonia treason trialists, so called because they had been netted by a Security Police swoop on the secret headquarters of the African National Congress in the Johannesburg suburb of Rivonia. Those captured were, in Mandela's words, "the entire High Command of Umkhonto we Sizwe",[44] the fledgeling armed wing of the ANC. The long trial that ensued, the guilty verdict and the sentence of life imprisonment, is now part of the lore of the liberation struggle. The day after their sentencing in mid-1964, Mandela and his colleagues were secretly flown from Pretoria to the Island airstrip to begin the incarceration that was to make the Island notorious throughout the world. They had narrowly escaped the hangman's noose and when they asked what their sentence of life imprisonment actually meant the answer was, "You will be here until you die."

The previous year had already seen the arrival of Robert Sobukwe, leader of the banned Pan-Africanist Congress, whom Justice Minister John Vorster liked to call "public enemy number one". It would be a while before I could make his acquaintance.

As the first Methodist chaplain there, I was also the first minister to visit them. That exposure was to have a huge impact on me. It dramatised the great gulf between white and black realities in our land. Each crossing in the prison boat transported me between worlds that could not have been more different. My congregation of white Camps Bay families expected me to preach to them, to teach them and to minister to their needs within the context of a comfortable faith. The adults worked in banks, insurance companies and other 'normal' businesses just over Kloof Nek in Cape Town and their children spent the carefree after-school hours surfing the breakers that rolled in from the west. A few miles out into that same ocean was a different universe, a bleak and hellish prison-house prepared for those who dared to challenge the status quo upon which Camps Bay and every other comfortable white suburb was founded.

When I first arrived, the new maximum security cell block was being completed by common law prisoners and this is where the Rivonia trialists ended up, becoming the most prominent of thousands of political prisoners to experience the horrors of the Island over the next thirty years. Looking back, it seems absurd – even irresponsible – that someone as inexperienced as I should have been entrusted with the sensitive responsibility of being their minister. What could a kid in his twenties do for people of this calibre, and in such straits?

The fact is that the full weight of what was happening on Robben Island had not begun to dawn upon my superiors, nor myself. It would be good to be able to claim that the Methodist Church had the foresight to ensure the best possible pastoral care to these incarcerated men who were obviously leaders of the future, but that would be less than truthful. In what was then a largely white-run denomination, the national significance of people like Robert Sobukwe, Nelson Mandela, Walter Sisulu and the others had yet to become evident; it was sufficient that a very junior, recently ordained minister could do the chaplaincy job.

The journey in the prison launch *Dias* lasted forty minutes – longer in bad weather. As it wallowed through the swells, I travelled on the upper deck with returning warders and their families, experiencing a huge sense of alienation. There was a bizarre disconnect between their bantering chatter and our cruel destination. I learned later that many prisoners who had never seen the ocean before had also to struggle with the terror of this alien element. Ex-prisoners still recall their fear on hearing the mournful hooting of the Mouille Point foghorn for the first time, and their hatred of the gulls' mocking cries.

On my first visit I was met at the small dock by a warrant officer in a pick-up truck and driven through the entrance archway crudely painted with the Prisons Service crest and motto, 'We Serve with Pride'. I wondered if this officer or his fellow guards saw the similarity to another arched gateway in Poland, where the mocking words '*Arbeit macht frei*'[45] greeted the train-loads of victims herded there by other claimants to a master-race ideology.

The white limestone road led to the Church of the Good Shepherd, also known as the Leper Church. Built in the leper colony days and designed by famed architect Herbert Baker, it is a church of beautiful proportions, but its lovely stone exterior belied the emptiness within. It had been stripped of altar, font and pulpit, as if not one single symbol of the grace of God should be permitted to penetrate the lives of the inmates. Nor were there any pews: the groups of common law prisoners, together with some of the less prominent 'politicals' marched from their nearby cells, had to sit on the cold floor. The absence of service books was less of a problem because in those days Christian hymns in Xhosa, Tswana, Sotho and Zulu were widely known by black South Africans, learned by heart when they were children. My own memory of years of vernacular worship in the Kilnerton chapel helped too. The singing was soulful and the sermons simple. I tried to offer homilies on the love of God for these men, and God's care for their faraway families. In spite of my inadequacies the words were always received with appreciation and with many sighs and exclamations, as if this strange young white man, this hour of rough and ready worship and the words spoken in God's name offered a tiny crack of light into their shadowed lives.

It was at such a service late in 1964 that one man approached me with a request for Holy Communion. He was wearing the crude prison-issue canvas tunic and the short trousers black prisoners had to wear in both summer and winter, and on his feet were sandals roughly cut from motor car tyres. I had neither bread nor communion wine with me, so all I could do was assure him that next time I came, we would celebrate the Eucharist. His name was Mutlanyane Stanley Mogoba, a young PAC activist who had both studied and taught at Kilnerton Training Institution. I was not to know that he had suffered whippings and unspeakable humiliations on the Island for leading a prisoners' strike. While he was in solitary confinement, another prisoner, Dennis Brutus, had slipped him a religious book to read, and alone in his cell Mogoba experienced a deep encounter with God and a clear call to the ordained ministry. He would one day be elected Presiding Bishop of the Methodist Church, becoming my friend and ultimately my immediate superior. Much to my regret, as it turned out I was not permitted to keep my promise to him.

But that was all in the future.

On that first day, between morning and afternoon services, I was offered lunch in the mess-hall used by the Afrikaner warders. It was an even more isolating experience than the boat ride. Their remarks about the prisoners were crudely racist and I was stung and shamed by their assumption that because I was white, I would share their prejudices. Their world had no space for whites with a different view. It was frightening to see how unquestioningly they assumed superiority over their charges, and the way they relished the power conferred on them by this brutal job. Our conversation soon stumbled. I didn't have the courage to take them on alone so I shrank into a cocoon of silence, seeking inner distance from them. I determined never to eat there again and after that day Elizabeth provided sandwiches for my lunch. Between services I would trek up one of the island roads to an enormous concrete and steel defensive emplacement dating back to World War II. There I consumed my lunch in the shadow of a 9.2-inch gun turret and in the company of some of the sluggish and harmless black mole-snakes that infested the island. I remember musing at the idea of the prisoners taking over the gun, training it on Parliament a mere seven or eight miles away across the water and turning the tables on their captors. In its operational years, the gun could easily have done the job; I vaguely recalled a movie with a similar theme.

Each visit over the next two years was a deeply lonely affair, but I was given one early gift. The warrant officer driver had pointed out a small, south-facing wooden bungalow. It was there that Robert Mangaliso Sobukwe, the charismatic leader of the Pan-Africanist Congress, had begun his lonely exile.[46] He had just completed a three-year prison sentence for leading the pass-burning campaign that climaxed in the Sharpeville massacre, and instead of being released at the end of 1963, he remained incarcerated by parliamentary decree, utterly isolated for as long as the apartheid regime chose to keep him there. None but his guards was ever permitted near him, and they were not supposed to speak to him. Sobukwe had been a Methodist lay preacher, so I asked to see him. I was refused at first, but some persistence revealed that the authorities were legally obliged to give me access. For every visit, however, I had first to get written authority from the Chief Magistrate of Cape Town.

By the time I visited him, Robert Sobukwe had already earned the grudging respect of his gaolers. My driver, a tough non-commissioned officer in his fifties, remarked that none of the baiting by bored young guards around the perimeter had succeeded in evoking a reaction from him. "Every morning, this man comes out of his house dressed as if he is going off to work," he said. "He is very dignified."

As we approached the weathered hut, I wondered what kind of welcome I would receive. The SABC and the press had portrayed Sobukwe as a dangerous black nationalist with a hatred of whites. Would he want to see me – a young white minister?

Sobukwe met me on the steps of his bungalow. I was immediately struck by his handsomely chiselled features and patrician bearing.

Tall and wiry and dressed in neat slacks and a white shirt and tie, he offered me a guarded but polite welcome, inviting me inside as if this was his own home and I was a guest coming for tea. The room we entered served as both bedroom and living space, with a neatly made bed, a simple bedside cabinet, a table and chair, and a small bookcase. It was spartan but adequate. Sobukwe gestured to the only chair and sat on the edge of the bed. Conversation was desultory at first. I knew he was sizing me up and didn't blame him. I said that many Methodists would be excited to know that one of our ministers had got to see him. We swopped names of mutual acquaintances and stories of Healdtown, the Methodist college both he and Nelson Mandela had attended. It was the year that Reverend Seth Mokitimi was about to be elected the first black President of MCSA, and he spoke admiringly of Mokitimi's influence as a chaplain and housemaster at Healdtown.

Our conversation soon warmed, and after that, each time I came to the island we were able to have about thirty minutes together. He had a consistent aura of calm about him, sucking contentedly on his pipe while we talked. He chose his words carefully, spoke quietly and had a gentle sense of humour. Our discussions were perforce circumscribed, always in the presence of the guard, who stood near the door, pretending to be uninterested. Even so, it was possible to engage something of the depth and breadth of his thinking. His Christian faith was informed by wide reading and it was quite clear that he saw his political activism as an extension of his spirituality. He was excited by Alan Walker's 1963 preaching campaign in our country, and the furore around Walker's challenge to the apartheid state. This was the kind of witness he expected of his own church leaders, only to be frequently disappointed. He was impressed when I told him I was hoping to go and work under Walker for a year. I was later permitted to bring him a few theological books, and included all of Walker's writings. Both of us being pipe-smokers, I could also bring his favourite tobacco and we used to chuckle that both this Methodist minister and lay preacher had a taste for Three Nuns blend.

Robert Sobukwe impacted me very powerfully. For all my contact with black South Africans, here, for the first time, I was engaging with somebody risking all for the liberation of his people. The calibre of this man, the cruel waste of his gifts, and the silence of most South African Christians around his incarceration, touched me to anger. On his part, he always expressed genuine appreciation of our times together, but even though I was one of the only people, apart from his captors, ever permitted to see him, I sensed that he would never put too much trust in these visits. Why should he place faith in this white man, any more than any other? I always came away angered and ashamed. Once, when leaving him, I expressed my shame that I could depart the island so freely, leaving him a prisoner. His response was quick. Gesturing toward Cape Town, with its Houses of Parliament occupied by his tormentors, he said, "I'm not the prisoner, Peter – they are."

Every visit made it more evident to me why the apartheid government feared Robert Sobukwe so much, but the years of virtual solitary confinement later began to break even this man. Benjamin Pogrund, biographer and close friend of Sobukwe, tells that by 1969 he was near a breakdown. "The government took fright and hastily sent him off the island, to banishment in Kimberley, which included house arrest and bannings." Sobukwe qualified as an attorney and practised law in Kimberley, enjoying the admiration of the local people there. Activist Joe Seremane spoke with wonder about the "Prof's" magnanimity, telling of how, when passing a police van with a flat wheel, Sobukwe stopped to help the white cops fit a spare.[47] In October 1975, twelve years after our first meeting on the island, I had a last visit with him in his Kimberley home. A security police car was parked outside as usual, indicating that he was still being watched. With John Rees, then General Secretary of the South African Council of Churches, who had helped support Sobukwe's family for a number of years, I had an hour with him. The flame still burned within him, perhaps with an even brighter incandescence. We prayed together and parted. Two years later Robert Mangaliso Sobukwe was diagnosed with lung cancer and died in 1978 at the age of 54.

Spiritually, Robert had travelled a bumpy journey. After I left the Island, the chaplaincy was taken over by the Reverend Theo Kotze, who was later to become Beyers Naudé's right-hand man in the Christian Institute. Theo was a seasoned minister, and could offer far more to this remarkable man than I. After Theo, however, there was an encounter with a very different, legalistic religious approach, which put Robert off chaplains for good. I believe that he refused further ministry.

I was also the first chaplain to Nelson Mandela and his fellow Rivonia trialists. When they arrived in mid-1964, they entered a period of extreme hardship and very tough manual labour in the island's lime quarry. I of course saw nothing of this, because Sunday was the one day of rest granted them. They were incarcerated in the squat, Maximum Security B Section, with its ugly watchtowers, cold grey passages and grey-painted barred doors. The whole place had a makeshift look about it, as if thrown together in a hurry, using the cheapest materials – all except, that is, for the frontage, built of finely pointed stone. It was a hateful place, and it struck me just how little it cost to oppress people. Stone walls, crude iron bars and doors, a mix of concrete and barbed wire and a few miles of icy ocean was all that was needed. Robben Island terrorised not only its inmates, but was a bleak warning to all considering defiance of the apartheid state.

Services of worship for Mandela's group were an exercise in ingenuity. I was not permitted into their cells and in those early days of their incarceration they were not allowed out of them, even for church. Each cell in the now famous narrow hallway in B Section had two doors: an inner iron grille, which was kept locked, and a wooden door, left open. I had to lead worship walking up and down the long passage, pausing at each door to make eye contact with the prisoner within. I was touched by the way each returned my glance very intentionally, and by the friendliness on most of their faces. At each end of the passage stood a stony-eyed warder who preferred to fix his gaze on the middle distance until I turned around to retrace my steps. The young Nelson Mandela was in the prime of his life, strong and robust, with a feisty look in his eye, and a ready twinkle too. In those days he gave the impression of a coiled spring – much more the prize-fighter than the father figure who later became beloved around the world. Walter Sisulu was the studious-looking one, helped by his heavy spectacles and the kindest of faces. I recall the gnome-like, not-so-friendly features of Govan Mbeki, Communist Party ideologue, who I'm sure critiqued my ideological impurities after I was gone. Eddie Daniels was the only non-ANC person[48] as well as being the only representative of the Cape coloured community, and had an impish smile. The other person I recall especially is Ahmed Kathrada, the only Muslim among the Rivonia group. I was struck by his quiet dignity and the respect he showed an alien faith.

Obviously this was a poor substitute for community worship. While we got the singing of hymns right very quickly, and the harmonies were as good as any, the reading of Scripture and the preaching had to come piecemeal to each person as I passed. This led to my developing a series of 'sound-bites' (the phrase had not been invented yet) to leave with each one, a style that may have become part of my preaching.

I began to agitate for a better deal, demanding that the Rivonia group be given the same minimal privileges of worship as others on the Island. My requests fell on deaf ears until, on one particularly cold day, I pleaded with the senior warder for the service to at least be held in a sunny corner of the exercise yard adjacent to the cells. To my surprise he agreed and we all crowded into that one warm spot, using a couple of wooden benches for pews. The singing was hearty, the smiles much in evidence, and I couldn't resist choosing an appropriate text from John's Gospel, 'If the Son sets you free, you shall be free indeed'.[49] As they basked in the welcome sunshine, Mandela and the group had no difficulty seeing the pun, and it added to the high spirits of the moment. I was struck by the poise and strength of these men. Being their first years there, my time visiting the Island coincided with the worst and most degrading cruelties they were to suffer, yet they had a collective energy about them, an obvious solidarity with each other and, yes, a *confidence* that was remarkable.

There can be few instances in the world where such a remarkable group, of such moral stature, have been gathered in one place of shared suffering. Here were leaders of their people and future leaders of us all, in short trousers, canvas jackets, sleeping in those early years with nothing but thin floor mats between their bodies and cold concrete, and regularly subjected to dreadful indignities. None of them was permitted more than two letters and two family visits each year. The story of their victory over these humiliating circumstances has been told and retold as a triumph of the human spirit.

Robben Island introduced me to the most remarkable of South Africa's future leaders, but it also stamped on me a deep aversion for the apparatchiks of apartheid and a lifelong inability to make polite small-talk with fellow whites who supported this system. It affected my preaching in the comfortable white enclaves of Camps Bay and Milnerton and would distance Elizabeth and me from some friends and family too. Like most whites they preferred not to hear about such unpleasant things, while I found it impossible to be silent about my experiences. It was not something I could control. It was a reaction to the grotesque contrast between life for those prisoners and the life that went on for the rest of us just a few miles over the water. I remember conducting a family wedding around that time and struggling to get through it because a prominent National Party member was present. For me there could be no easy conversations with the kind of people who needed a Robben Island to support their civilisation, yet there was also the uneasy awareness that I and 'my people' were complicit too.

I was never able to bring Holy Communion to Stanley Mogoba. Later in 1964 a letter arrived from the Prisons Department indicating that my security clearance had been withdrawn, and that I could no longer visit the Island. No reasons were given.

I did not realise just how deeply the pain of that place had seared my own psyche until the turn of the century, when I found myself escorting two American friends on what is now an obligatory pilgrimage for visitors to Cape Town. It was my first return to the Island in 37 years and I had not prepared myself for this sudden encounter with long-buried memories and emotions. In the tourist bus I suffered an unexpected and embarrassing breakdown. It happened outside Robert Sobukwe's house, where I was able to share some extra information about him. The guide was overwhelmed at meeting somebody who had actually been with Sobukwe, and she and the driver, who I recognised as an ex-prisoner from those dreadful years, both joined me in a flood of tears. When we got to the lime quarry, the three of us had to walk off some distance to have our weep, with a busload of bemused foreign tourists looking on and probably wondering whether people bawling on each other's shoulders was *de rigueur* for such visits. Fortunately this is not the case; the Island is today a shining example of reconciliation, with former prisoners and former guards sharing responsibility for its management. Nevertheless, as another well-known former inmate, Archbishop Njongonkulu Ndungane, says, "Don't romanticise the Island. It was a hellhole."

10

Life Line in the Lucky Country

At the end of 1964 Elizabeth, our two small boys and I found ourselves crammed into a small cabin in the bowels of the Shaw Savill liner *Northern Star* for the six-week passage to Sydney, Australia. The conversation with Dr Alan Walker during his 1963 preaching mission in Cape Town had brought an invitation to join the CMM staff in 1965 – preferably for two years. I would need to secure permission for study leave from MCSA, of course, and we would have to find money for the steamship fares. This latter happened in an unexpected and somewhat sad way. In early 1964 my Navy chaplain friend Arthur Attwell was driving to Saldanha when he fell asleep at the wheel. The car rolled and he was thrown out, breaking his back. In the small hours of the Sunday morning I met the ambulance bringing him in to the Military Hospital in Cape Town. Barely conscious, he asked if I would take over his services, so after being assured that he was going to pull through, I drove off to preach in his place. The upshot was that I was appointed acting Naval Chaplain at Simon's Town, Saldanha and the Air Force base at Langebaanweg for the months that Arthur was out of action. It was my last service to the Navy and I was grateful to do it as a chaplain this time and for a man who had been a mentor and friend. The irony is that this income from the military not only took our family to Australia, but enabled me to work under one of the world's most militant pacifists.

After a six-week passage from Cape Town, stopping at Durban, Freemantle and Melbourne, we gathered on deck with the rest of the ship's passengers for the unforgettable entry to Sydney Harbour. We made our stately way through the heads and up the miles of water with green suburbs and sparkling coves on either side, passing the beginnings of the new Opera House and tying up right below the famous 'coat-hanger' bridge. Alan Walker and a couple of associates were waiting to greet us.

Sydney's Central Methodist Mission (CMM) was a very different kind of church, with evening services held in a theatre, and a cluster of more than 20 homes and hospitals for homeless persons, children, women at risk and the elderly. To my knowledge it was the only church that ran its own psychiatric hospital and Walker had just opened the first telephone-based counselling and crisis intervention service in the world, called Life Line.

The Life Line Centre was a bold new attempt to engage the pain and problems of a great city of three million people. Its inspiration could be traced back to both a personal tragedy and one of Australia's most venerable success stories. One Saturday night, Alan Walker received a call from a man named Roy. Desperately lonely and in debt, Roy was threatening suicide. Walker pleaded with him to come in to CMM and talk about it in person. After a second call, Roy agreed to see Walker on the Tuesday, but just a few minutes before he was due, a call came instead from the police. They had found the body of a man named Roy Brown in a gas-filled room in seedy Kings Cross. On his chest was a letter addressed to Walker. After speaking of his fear of dying, Roy wrote, "I'm leaving the world unwanted, unloved and without hope."[50]

Alan Walker was wrenched by this experience, made worse by the knowledge that Roy was just one of too many who reached this kind of *extremis* in the uncaring city. Wrestling with how to respond, he recalled how a uniquely Australian need had been met by imaginative compassion. The bleak isolation of Australia's outback farm stations had given birth to the Flying Doctor Service, which had been established by a missionary named John Flynn. To call up the airborne doctors in emergencies Flynn invented the 'pedal bicycle radio' – a stationary bike attached to a battery charger and radio transmitter. Re-reading the story of Flynn, Walker was struck by one powerful phrase: Flynn had cast a "mantle of safety" over the outback. Recalling that Roy had reached for a telephone, Walker began to put the two together and an idea began to crystallise: could not the network of telephone lines covering Sydney become a different kind of safety mantle, one uniquely appropriate to the city?

Life Line was no small venture. By the time the first centre opened in March 1963 a headquarters had been prepared and a professional staff of thirteen employed. The heart and soul of Life Line, however, was the team of 150 lay volunteers who had been trained for nine months as telephone counsellors to service the phones in shifts 24 hours per day. Nobody had done this anywhere in the world, although something similar was soon to be launched in the United Kingdom under the name Samaritans. The volunteers had been attending classes for some months and would soon take their places in the telephone counselling room. As opening day approached, Walker and his team were still searching for a name, but it was the *Sydney Morning Herald* that provided the needed inspiration: referring to the project in a headline as a "telephone life line", and the name stuck. Still, after many months and an investment of many thousands of dollars, when the first counsellor took the first call on 16 March 1963 with the words, "This is Life Line. Can I help you?" nobody knew how the city would respond. They need not have feared: from the moment the switchboard opened, the calls came pouring in. By the time our little family arrived in Sydney at the start of 1965 the call rate was around 800 per month, covering every possible kind of human need.

What I didn't know was that Walker had me slated as the new director of the centre. The first director had just resigned citing ill health and I soon found out why. Alan Walker was not an easy task-master; he was extremely demanding and often a very difficult person to work for. My Life Line predecessor advised me, "When it's your week to report at staff meeting, take some Valium." But I had worse worries: I had arrived to observe city ministry from a safe position on the pastoral staff and now found myself thrown into directing CMM's flagship project – and apart from some rudimentary lectures in counselling and a mere five years' experience with the life problems of my parishioners, I was completely unqualified. It had happened with the Robben Island challenge and was happening again. Was this going to be the story of my life? I felt utterly exposed.

I must have been good at fooling people. I set myself a crash course in counselling theory and began to learn the language of the therapeutic world. I trained myself in the art of listening with head and heart, and in the Rogerian methodology[51] which was judged best for a lay-driven service. Little did most people know that the director was more of a layperson in the field than many of those he was tasked with leading. My staff were warmly supportive, however. They needed a strong person to act as buffer between them and the much feared Dr Walker, and strangely, though I was struggling to master the new world of crisis intervention, I found I could handle him better than most. We had an early collision over Elizabeth's role. Walker thought all senior staff spouses ought to participate fully in the life of CMM and he soon asked where she was. Elizabeth was struggling in a new land, a poorly provided home, with two small children and no transport or support. That's where she was. I told him that he had hired me, not my spouse, and that if he raised her name in that way again, we would be off back to South Africa. He looked at me in speechless surprise and then, to his credit, apologised. Things were fine from then on and the Valium was never required. Over the years I think we came as close as he would ever permit anyone to and I think he recognised that my resistance to his authoritarianism never compromised my loyalty to him, nor my admiration for the gifts he brought to his ministry. In fact, my ability to 'handle' him proved useful: at the international level I could lubricate his often gritty relationships, especially with British counterparts who found him arrogant and overbearing – which he often was – but it was the fact that he was so often right that I think irked them most of all.

Our two years in Sydney were enormously fulfilling and happy. We loved the city, the breathtaking harbour with its myriad sails on a Sunday afternoon, the ferries ploughing to Manly and the bluff and open people. There were only eleven million Australians at that time and while we were there, of that number, they celebrated the two millionth 'New Australian' since the end of WWII. If you were willing to work, you were welcome – unless, of course, you were not white. The migrants had all come from Britain and Europe, and they set about becoming 'fair dinkum Aussies' with a will. There was an energy and a youthfulness about the 'Lucky Country' that was infectious. Elizabeth soon found friends and slotted herself very happily into weekly volunteer work at Gateway, an emergency children's shelter – of her own free will, of course.

At Life Line, I soon found the confidence to lead and enjoyed a deeply satisfying relationship with my staff. They loved that I kept Alan Walker at bay and banned his habit of walking around the centre, popping into various offices and frightening the life out of them. I also found pastoring and guiding the more than 200 volunteer counsellors rewarding. Calls to the centre grew to 1 000 per month. On Sunday mornings I preached mostly to a congregation of homeless men who gathered in the Life Line chapel. Interestingly, a handful of women, rather than men, used to staff the service. We found that this was the only female contact most of these ragged men ever had and they deeply valued the maternal hospitality, fiercely protecting their 'angels' from any problematic behaviour.

My day began with reading all telephone counsellors' reports from the previous 24 hours, monitoring the counsellors' effectiveness and determining how to respond to the needs raised. Many calls were anonymous, with no follow-up possible. In other calls, contact details had been given, enabling a follow-up interview to be arranged. Problems covered the whole gambit of human need: unwanted pregnancies, debt, marital stress, homelessness, parental difficulties, child abuse, domestic violence, immigration problems, cultural adjustments etc., with much of our work involving liaison with other agencies specialising in one or other of these needs. I began to know the geography of Sydney's caring heart, the people and places where a helping hand was to be found. I also got to know the seamier side of that great port city and the darker terrain of hurt and despair to be found on its streets. The 30 or so threatened or attempted suicides we encountered each month required a special regimen. Life Line was equipped with radio-controlled cars (still something of a novelty in the 60s) and the 'Trouble Team', as we called it, was always on standby. Looking back, I wonder at the vulnerability of our TTs. A male/female team would be despatched to some dark alley where someone was trying to bleed himself to death, or where a deranged person was threatening harm; or I would find myself clinging precariously to the cliff-edge of the Gap[52] or the girders of the Sydney harbour bridge, talking down a frightened jumper. I recall once spending an hour listening to and seeking to calm a deeply disturbed man with a wild beard, who was brandishing a shot-gun deep in a suburban forest. The police were, of course, available as a last resort, but especially in cases involving domestic strife and suicide threats, they were happy for us to go in first. I was grateful and surprised to find myself untroubled by fear in such situations.

Life Line grew an enviable record of literally snatching people from death. The media was uniformly supportive and helped our fundraising with their stories. There was the tiny baby left on the steps of the Life Line Centre on Christmas Eve, who spent Christmas Day as Elizabeth's and my house guest. What could be more moving? Needless to say, our priority was the little child but I also learned how to milk a dramatic event like that to keep the work going. I was becoming an NGO professional!

There was also the opportunity to do pioneer work with compulsive gamblers. New South Wales was awash with poker machines and other opportunities to gamble on dog racing, the trotting track and the weekend horse races. The understanding of gambling as a compulsion akin in many ways to alcoholism was very new. Together with a skilled young psychologist I launched what we called the Gamblers' Liberty Group. In many ways we were exploring uncharted territory but after eighteen months, working with a group of 25 mainly men, each one trapped daily by an uncontrollable urge to gamble, we were satisfied that the parallels with alcoholism were overwhelming. While some physiological factors were obviously absent, the psychological patterns were uncannily similar. We found the most effective therapy to be a simple adaptation of the Alcoholics Anonymous twelve-step regime. I experienced a great deal of joy working with the tough, brutally honest programme and the wide spectrum of persons we were able to help. They ranged from the political secretary of a New South Wales cabinet minister to a grizzled ex-serviceman who still had nightmares about the Japanese soldier he had killed close up in WW II. It was deeply fulfilling to see these decent people begin to find some success in dealing with an insidious addiction.

The Australian experience gave me a number of important gifts:

First, it confirmed my call to the city. The city was where I belonged and the rest of my active ministry would be in downtown churches. What I had seen in Sydney gave me a boldness to launch new and experimental ways of engaging the city's needs and not to be afraid of failure. I became perhaps South Africa's most committed advocate for this specialised form of ministry. I would continue to love the city passionately and live my life to the rhythm of its beating heart. The sleepy suburbs would never again claim me.

Second, I learned more about preaching. My father had been a noble example of fine preaching and by a sort of involuntary osmosis I had possibly inherited some of his way of drawing his hearers into intimacy with God. I had also learned that Dad's denunciations of injustice, always informed by clear theological convictions, were part and parcel of faithful preaching. Now I was listening to another great preacher. For two years, in the packed evening worship service, I sat on the Lyceum stage and was transfixed. Despite all his prickliness with individuals, when given a platform, Alan Walker was the most incisive, persuasive, passionate and fearless preacher I have ever known. He would take on some great theme, making profound truth simple yet never trite. He unpacked the divine for our use on earth without ever losing its mystery. Spurning the fancy orator's flourishes, he would paint word pictures with simple but memorable Anglo-Saxon phrases, silhouetting the truths of the Gospel against the backdrop of our mid-1960s world. Always he helped us see how such truths applied not only to our personal lives, but to the life of society. I was in awe of his mastery of structure, often the secret of any great preaching. Each sermon hung on a carefully crafted outline, manageable chunks of truth bound together to make a seamless whole. It has become fashionable to mock such sermon structure, but I still recall some of Walker's sermons today, while the arty wandering through a Scripture passage that sometimes passes now for preaching strikes me as ephemeral by contrast. I determined that I would try to learn from him. While we were in Sydney he once said to me: "God has given you the gift of being able to move people deeply with words. See you use it well." I hope I have.

Third, I became a Christian pacifist. All the time I worked at Life Line a *Wizard of Id* cartoon on my office wall showed a soldier informing the king that there was a peace demonstration outside the palace. "Disperse them," orders the king, but the quaking soldier demurs: "Your Majesty, have you ever tried to mix it with a bunch of militant pacifists?" The irony about Alan Walker was that for all his aggressive personality, he was a pacifist. In 1938 he had been on a study tour of Europe and Britain. In Germany he had seen the Nazi menace up close, and he had also met Donald Soper,[53] famous British Methodist socialist and pacifist. On the steamship home to Australia, Walker had wrestled with issues of faith, war and peace, praying and agonising his way into a commitment to non-violence. Appointed to a tough coal-mining town where almost every household was giving men to fight in WWII, he paid a heavy price for that commitment, but never faltered in his conviction that, "Peace is no longer an option; it is a stark, absolute necessity."[54] By the time I came to be with him, he was leading the campaign against Australian involvement in the Vietnam War. In 1966 President Lyndon Johnson visited to pressure the Australian Prime Minister to send troops. Walker was having none of it. I found myself caught up in the bitter controversy and needed at last to wrestle with the tangle in my own mind. Not long before, Alan had devoted a full sermon to *Why I am a Christian Pacifist*. I found in his arguments an incontrovertible confirmation of the convictions firming in my own soul. "Any ultimate trust in force," he said, "is a denial of God … to stoop to … warfare because it is said that life's highest values cannot otherwise be safe is to commit the sin of idolatry." The real betrayal of life's finest values was when in supposed defence of them, we denied them. "I indict war because of what it does to human nature." He went on to demonstrate that war, far from achieving peace, always sowed the seeds of further conflict. Even the so-called "good war", WWII, had Korea, Hungary and Vietnam as consequences. "War as a policy has failed," he declared. Above all, there was the undeniable declaration that the teachings of Jesus allowed him no alternative. Lifting up the central lessons of Jesus' life and death, Walker said, "I can come to no other conclusion than that Jesus was the first Christian pacifist," and again, "No-one dare put Christ in uniform!" At the same time, he made it clear that Christian pacifism was not passivity, nor was it painless. It was a new way of sacrificing for justice and freedom and Gandhi and Dr Martin Luther King had shown how hard and dangerous the struggle could be, and how getting killed could be as much a possibility for the pacifist as for the soldier.

My nascent doubts dating all the way back to that menacing torpedo in naval training had now to be resolved. So when I finally stood with the peaceniks in front of the Canberra parliament, I had crossed a line. I was going to try and walk the road of Christian pacifism, not because it yet made total sense for me, but because I could no longer make any sense of war. Since then I have worked and prayed for a time when Christians will stand together, hand in hand across this planet and say, "We will not go to war. Kill us if you wish but we will not kill. No good end can be achieved by evil means."

Fourth, I found the LGBTQI[55] community. Numbers of persons calling Life Line were homosexual. In those days 'gay' was the last word they would use to describe themselves. The Stonewall riots in New York, widely regarded as the start of a new gay activism, were still in the future. In the mid-1960s, Sydney's gays and lesbians were people of fear, living deeply hidden lives, concealing their sexual orientation from friends, family and employers. Not to do so would mean almost certain shame and rejection. They called us, not for encouragement toward any kind of liberation, but because they wanted our help to become what others called 'normal'. They wanted their homosexuality not respected, but *removed*. And, God forgive us, we tried to help them achieve this. Homosexuality was still classified as a mental illness at that time. The Church, most parts of which are still untransformed today in this regard, offered no relief. Our psychiatric hospital experimented with a new 'wonder drug' called LSD in the hope of reorienting gay persons, but the most common treatment was so-called 'aversion therapy', using electric shock treatment. Heterosexual images were accompanied by pleasurable sensations, homosexual images with pain. In retrospect, the brutality of these well-meant efforts is hard to credit, but it is another chapter in the painful story of the heterosexual world's cruelty to LGBTQI persons. I was simply not well-informed enough to challenge these protocols, but I was often first responder to a suicide call from someone who could not live any longer with the 'stain' of his or her homosexuality, and later, in listening to the litany of desperate efforts to become 'normal', a conviction formed in me that this state of being was generally immovable and unchangeable. The notion that anyone would freely choose a life of such pain was untenable. I came away from my numerous engagements with gay and lesbian persons convinced that they could no more transform into heterosexuals than I could become homosexual – that they and I were fixed in who we were. These encounters marked my first hesitant steps away from ignorance and the prejudice that it bred.

Fifth, I think I caught some of Walker's intolerance and sharpness. I am ambivalent about its harmfulness because I believe that for both of us it was about taking seriously the job at hand. For me there was also much of the naval expectation of discipline. There is a view that Christians should be known for being 'nice' and later when I was in leadership there were staffers or clergy colleagues who took exception when I upbraided them for slipshod and half-baked work. Because we were Christians working in a Christian organisation they seemed to expect a wider margin of tolerance than any decent hardworking person in business would ever get away with. Given that in my view, the work we were doing was of greater importance, I could never understand this attitude. It seemed to me that a higher level of commitment should be taken for granted. Maybe it was a generational thing too. I recall a young probationer minister who turned up in the office persistently late. When I confronted him, he said, "I'm very much in touch with my need for sleep," at which point I indicated that if he didn't mend his ways he might find my foot very much in touch with a part of his anatomy. For most clergy the need to be loved tends to be high in our hierarchy of needs; I fear it was a little different with me and if I erred on the side of being too demanding, it's too late now. However, there is another side to this: I do believe that when any staffer shared a genuine problem with me, I could and did listen and sought to act with compassion. I also know that while I have always put my views strongly and in ways that perhaps intimidated some, when countered with a clearly better argument or shown to be mistaken, I've never had trouble acknowledging my error and moving in a different direction. I think some of my colleagues found this equally disconcerting.

Toward the end of our second year in Sydney, there came a time of choice. We were invited to stay and for me to join the Australian Methodist Church. It was a tempting offer. We were living in the 'Lucky Country' of youth, sea, surf and sand, I was in an exciting and strategic job, and our children would grow up free of South Africa's historic burdens and sins. To make it worse, our homeland was sliding further into darkness. Prime Minister Hendrik Verwoerd, the patronising supreme apologist for the apartheid policy who held the National Party in thrall, had just been stabbed to death at his seat in Parliament. His successor, Brakpan-born BJ Vorster, was a less intellectual, tougher character, iron-fisted and ruthless. What kind of future lay ahead?

In the end it was a no-brainer: we had to go home. I had promised to do so. Also, I was the very first Methodist minister who had been permitted this kind of hands-on – as distinct from academic – study leave and if I reneged, it was unlikely anyone else would get the same privilege. Above all, there was the inescapable feeling that we would be chickening out of the call to make some contribution, however small, to our nation's struggle. In making this decision I first saw the steely courage beneath Elizabeth's pacific exterior. By this time she was a happy Australian who had forged some deep friendships. She would ordinarily have seen no need to move back home but that was what we had promised and however dark the horizon back over the Indian Ocean, she agreed the decision to be right, raised no concerns, voiced no fears, and began to pack.

A couple of Sundays before leaving, I spoke at the CMM Public Issues platform, on the subject, *Which Way South Africa?*, suggesting that as our national crisis deepened a new kind of church would need to be born, a "confessing Church" similar to that which had been born in Nazi Germany. This too would need to be a church "under the Cross", willing to suffer. I also did something important for myself. Settling on the decision to return home, I had been asking myself what guidelines might help keep me faithful in apartheid South Africa. I have refined them since, but essentially they are the same today as they were spoken that day in 1964:

The first was to be a truth-teller, to proclaim the truth without fear and expose the lie of apartheid; the second was to bind up the broken, siding with the victims of injustice wherever I found them; the third was to try and "live the alternative", seeking to be a visible contradiction of the apartheid state's cruel segregation practices and offering a picture of God's alternative; the fourth was to work in non-violent, Christ-like ways to bring in a new dispensation of justice, equity and peace.

Of all the gifts I took home with me, these four principles were the most crucial to my future. Time and again they would be my personal Life Line, holding me fast when I feared I would lose my grip.

The road home was an indirect one. While Elizabeth and the two boys boarded Shaw Saville's *Northern Star* for the six-week passage to Southampton via Ceylon, Suez and the Mediterranean, I flew to the USA on a mission for the newly formed Life Line International. My brief was to tell the story in a chain of cities across the continent, seeking city church leaders willing to organise America's first Life Line centres. Apart from a suicide prevention line linked with a Los Angeles hospital and a spiritual advice line at Norman Vincent Peale's Marble

Collegiate Church in New York City, nothing like Life Line had been seen before. Telephone counselling was a brand new idea. I sowed the seed in a number of cities, and the first centres emerged later in Oakland, California and Dallas, Texas, while Marble Collegiate decided to ramp up their service into a fully operational counselling centre. A copyright issue prevented the use of the name Life Line in the USA, so on that continent it became Contact Teleministries.

This, my first trip to the USA, was another game changer: I took the opportunity to visit as many downtown ministries as I could – thirteen in all – learning much for what lay before me. There was a sense of excited anticipation because back home my first city church assignment was waiting.

11

District Six

The third Sunday in January 1967 …

I am standing for the first time in the mahogany pulpit of Buitenkant Street Methodist Church, looking out at my new congregation. This church on the edge of District Six was once a Dutch wine-store, converted for worship in 1883. Its gracious interior imitates England's nineteenth century Methodist chapels: in addition to seating 500 people in the nave, a U-shaped gallery supported by delicate cast-iron columns accommodates another 300. The pulpit is elevated, lifting me halfway between the people below and those in the gallery. Polished woodwork gleams softly in sunlight streaming through the golden north window.

Today the church is full. It is a hot Cape Town morning but everyone is in their Sunday best, men in suits, ties and burnished shoes, women in bright dresses with their heads covered either by hats or 'doeks' – headscarves. The only hatless woman in the church is Elizabeth. Children are everywhere, let off Sunday School to come and inspect the new minister. Our two little paleface kids on each side of Elizabeth are sizing up the situation with wide eyes.

I'm both nervous and excited. Excited because I'm back in what we Methodists call 'Circuit ministry' – preaching, teaching and pastoring in my first city church. I am also nervous because most of the people facing me know that under the government's Group Areas Act, they and the rest of the area's 60 000 mostly mixed-race inhabitants are to be ruthlessly cast out of the city and forced to live elsewhere.[56] The only reason given is that they are people of colour. Those making this decision needed no other authority than that they are white.

The question I'm struggling with is, why should this congregation, forced to face dislocation and heartbreak by people like me, have any regard for this white preacher – and what hope is there that I might win their trust?

While we were still in Sydney the leaders of what was then known as the 'Cape Town Coloured Circuit'[57] had invited me to become their Superintendent Minister. Their invitation helped our decision to return to South Africa because it meant that we would at least be serving people who were experiencing the pain, rather than the privileges of apartheid. With the congregation soon to be exiled to the bleak Cape Flats[58] my Bishop[59] warned that this would be an appointment without a future, but I had asked for just one assurance. "Promise me," I said, "that you won't entertain any moves to close it down, and I'll do the rest." He agreed.

District Six was a tightly packed community occupying the lower slopes of Devil's Peak and descending into the city. It was the most multi-racial piece of real estate in South Africa, where 'coloureds', Indians, Africans and whites had lived in harmony for a century. 'Coloured' – mixed race – people made up the majority, with Muslims and Christians more or less equally divided, the former descended mainly from the Dutch East India Company's slaves and the latter from Khoi[60] roots, or the many interracial unions of the Cape's earlier history. Higher up, Walmer Estate housed the better-off classes – teachers and business people. Much poorer people lived further down the slopes in tenement housing dating back to the late Dutch and early British occupations. Many homes, despite their occupants' limited means, were carefully tended, but half the tenements were owned by white slum-lords and were badly neglected, their exteriors unpainted, with crumbling masonry, rusting balconies and chipped steps.

Narrow cobbled streets were alive with bustling activity. Children darted everywhere, playing hopscotch or football, or some form of catch. With most menfolk at work, the streets were commanded by the women – no-nonsense matriarchs who chatted across washing lines or over vegetable peeling and other chores. All of them mothered all of the children around, equally quick to kiss a grazed knee or dish out a hefty clout. They were the cement in the community. Males were mainly artisans and labourers, and too many of them, rubbing up against the indignities of apartheid every day, relied on alcohol to dull their frustrations.

To outsiders District Six was a slum, and though houses were dilapidated and overcrowded, the interiors of most belied their ruinous facades. The house-proud matrons saw to that. Neat linoleum covered the floors. Living rooms had an Edwardian parlour feel about them, with lace curtains, sepia family portraits, old-fashioned furniture and a radiogram,[61] and often a fern in the corner. Kitchens were the family's usual gathering places, with the warm after-scent of curry and other spices hanging in the air. Shelves for the pots and pans were decorated with friezes neatly cut from newspaper. Bedrooms were small and it was unusual for a child to have a bed to him or herself. There were no bathrooms; family members utilised a tin bath in the kitchen and hot water from the kettle for their ablutions. The single outside toilet required a trek to the end of the narrow back yard.

Manners and customs had a period feel too, reminding me of my grandparents' era. Family discipline was firmly pre-Spock, with a cast-iron respect for elders and children expected to be available at all times to run errands. Few homes were equipped with telephones so barefoot kids were the prime means of local messaging, most often to the 'Babbie' store on the corner where the Jewish or Muslim shopkeeper was always ready to arrange short-term credit. As older youths moved into employment they were expected to 'work for their parents' for two years before thinking of courting or regarding their wages as their own. District Six had its own economy tailored to the needs of people living very close to poverty. There was the inevitable gang culture found on the mean streets of poor communities, yet the District was rich in cultural, religious and sporting activities: people banded together not only to survive, but to overcome their circumstances. A Cockney-type humour was the great prophylactic against hopelessness. Once, standing in the Albertus Street side-door of the church, I saw a man approaching on the sidewalk. He stopped suddenly, leaning slightly forward, eyes shut and face twisted into a grimace. Thinking I was witnessing a heart attack I made toward him: "Are you okay?" After a tense few seconds his face relaxed and he threw me a cherubic grin, "Fine thanks, Father," he said. "Just passing a wet wind." And off he swaggered.

I arrived brimming with ideas gained at the Sydney CMM about how to make a city church relevant not only to its traditional membership, but to the wider community and to the workers who poured into the city each weekday. But first Elizabeth and I needed to feel the heartbeat of the District Six people. She had no idea that by simply turning up with the children on Sundays, she was already breaking new ground. Among our predecessors the white minister's spouse and family had belonged to a 'white' congregation elsewhere. With two small boys on her hands and a third child on the way she had limited opportunity, but typically focused on building one-on-one relationships with individuals. The best way for me to get close to the people was to visit them in their homes, yet I found that the Circuit Superintendency carried an enormous administrative load. Apart from some 600 members at Buitenkant Street, there were three other congregations in 'coloured' communities around the city and one 50 miles away in the farming town of Darling. Each had day schools attached, with all the complications of teachers' appointments, staff disputes and – above all – toilets. I calculated that I now superintended over 100 ancient school toilets, with at least one or two springing a leak each day of the year.

Keeping afloat financially seemed to be the priority in this Circuit. At least two evenings a week found me sitting in the cramped vestry waiting for Class Leaders to see me. One of John Wesley's great innovations had been the Class Meeting – a dozen or so members, meeting each week for spiritual guidance, prayer and mutual encouragement. Each also brought a penny to support the general work and the poor. My congregations were still divided into classes but the spiritual function had long since faded. Class Leaders did little else than collect the 'church dues' which they then delivered to me. As we went through their Class books and I totted up the 25c monthly offerings of each person, they did update me about those who were sick or in trouble of any kind, to guide my visitation in the next week, but money ruled us. The books of all five congregations were my responsibility, as was the banking. My friend Don Slade from Camps Bay days generously helped me master basic bookkeeping, but each Monday was still spent laboriously counting hundreds of coins and the few banknotes that came in at Sunday services and banking them. I couldn't believe that trust levels were so low that these functions had to be kept in the hands of the white Superintendent. If real ministry was to happen, things had to change.

I put out the word asking for suggestions of a possible volunteer assistant. A school principal offered the name of a young teacher named Jane Abrahams. "You should ask Janie," he said. "She is very bright." Jane was 21 years old, the eighth in a family of nine children living in a tenement row in De Villiers Street. She volunteered to sit in the church and handle the monies, freeing me to discuss pastoral issues with the Class Leaders, who began to get the message that from now on ministry would be more important than money. I soon found that Jane had an encyclopaedic knowledge of the congregation, a love for people and a passion to see new things happen in this old church. I warmed to her sharp intelligence and feisty spirit and began to look for ways in which she could share the ministry and be my bridge into the community. After deductions, she was earning R78 per month in a school about to be shut down by the Coloured Education Department. If I could match that amount from somewhere, would she be willing to come on board rather than take another teaching post? When she said yes, I approached a generous Methodist who agreed to match her present salary for eighteen months – time enough for us to transform the financial picture. I had to think up a title for her because no appointment quite like this had happened before anywhere in MCSA. She became my Pastoral Assistant.

We faced daunting challenges. District Six should not be romanticised. Its people triumphed over much, but racial trauma, poverty and an unhealthy religiosity wove a destructive web in their lives. While the 'coloured' community may have had it somewhat better than Africans, they too had internalised the stigmata that racism inflicts on all people of colour. Those who argue that they lived only with 'petty' apartheid – separate schools, buses, beaches, amenities, entrances, elevators and the like – forget that 'petty' apartheid was not petty at all. Its indignities, beginning with race classification,[62] insinuated themselves into people's sense of humanness. Desmond Tutu has identified the worst thing about apartheid as "when they call you a non-European, a non-this, you might think it isn't working on you. But in fact it is corrosive of your self-image. You end up wondering if you are as human as those others. You wonder 'does God actually love me, black, as he loves a white child?'"[63]

I was first shocked into awareness of this at our Sunday School's annual presentation in front of the congregation. Looking out at the ranks of lovely children, something seemed amiss, until I realised that the lighter skinned, more straight-haired children were in the front rows, with all the dark-skinned, more crinkly-haired kids relegated to the back. The person in charge of them was a school principal by profession, proud of his education and university degree, yet when lining up these precious children he had unapologetically enthroned 'whiteness' as the measure of who should be more visible. The same racial criteria used by the Race Classification Board – examining people's head and body hair, complexion and facial features – had also become imprinted on his unconscious.[64]

Another heartbreaking example was when parents urged their more 'European'-looking children to 'try for white'. If they could convince the Race Classification Board that they were white in looks and complexion – or that they were 'generally accepted as a white person' even if 'not in appearance obviously a white person', the doors to a better life would open to them. But the price was high: it meant an end to contact with their darker parents and siblings. Sometimes, conducting the funeral of a parent or grandparent, I wanted to weep as I watched family members standing around the grave, united awkwardly in grief, but still constrained by years of separation from reaching out to each other. In all those years they had often never dared to even greet if they bumped into each other in a public place. Habit had made them guilty strangers.

Living under racism also turned people on each other. I was shaken when, in an early meeting, the doyen of our lay preachers, Mr PD Williams, launched a bitter attack on me for what seemed no reason at all. When I approached him asking what I had done to offend, his answer was, "Nothing, Reverend, nothing … but today I was pushed off a bus by one of you whites and I'm so angry. I had to take it out on someone." There were not many whites they could do that to, so resentments turned inward. The smallest slights led to destructive quarrels and I found myself refereeing absurd spats in which one family decided that they were 'not speaking' to another. All Christian teaching about forgiveness was forgotten until the approach of Easter or Christmas perhaps nudged them toward reconciliation.

Poverty was the second challenge. The poorer parts of District Six had families living from hand to mouth in often desperately crowded conditions. I once was called late at night to a home where an old man was 'very sick', only to find him already dead. To move his body we had first to wake the two children sleeping in the same bed. They had slept unknowing through his last hours.

White landlords neglected their properties but never brooked late payment of rent. When one of my lay leaders contracted tuberculosis, exacerbated because of the damp in his tenement house, the uncaring landlord turned out to be the same respected gynaecologist who had brought Elizabeth into the world in polite, white Mowbray in 1937. "The doctor who gave life to me," she said, "is making people sick here."

Poverty sucks the oxygen out of people's lives, but ironically there are few more rewarding places for a minister to be than with the poor. Perhaps I could do nothing about 'big picture' systemic poverty, but it took very little to change the circumstances of an individual family. I often found myself arranging last-minute rescues for people facing eviction until we were able to launch a small revolving credit scheme to help tide people over these crises. Wonderfully, there were no defaulters. No matter how long it took, the poorest of the poor were punctilious in repaying their loans. Even amid all the pain there was deep satisfaction in going to bed knowing that somebody's family had a roof over their heads and a meal in their stomachs because the Church was there for them.

Yet there was more to it than that. I was beginning to understand that if Jesus had a home address in this world, it was among the poor. The Jewish carpenter became much more real to me in District Six and it was people like Mr and Mrs May who did it. They lived in a tiny two-room cellar not far from the church. A paraplegic for 27 years, Mr May was wheeled down to Adderley Street each day to sell matches. When he was back in his bed, Mrs May, a tiny woman with a badly twisted spine, used a crutch to hop around as she cared for him. The first time I visited them I wrote, "A strange glow on a rainy day in that room." Their tender love for each other and the quiet gratitude with which they welcomed each day touched me deeply and I used to take Holy Communion to them more often than necessary, not for their sake but for mine. And they were not alone: I found I was being changed by the poorest of the people I had come to serve.

Conversely, the Christianity of the more well-off in District Six often had a different face. As I struggled through my first months there I found little of the beautiful joy and freedom Jesus declared. A Calvinistic religiosity held too many of my congregation in thrall. They lived as if faith was all about sin and retribution with the 'Reverend' the apparent arbiter. My first Leaders' Meeting[65] had an agenda item titled '*Straf*' – punishment. It seemed that this was when unmarried girls who had fallen pregnant were disciplined and suspended from membership. It was redolent of the most straight-laced nineteenth century legalism. This was not the liberating Methodism I knew and I announced that this item would never again appear on the agenda, but much more than that had to happen. The answer had to involve introducing the congregation to a different Jesus and a different God than the one they seemed to fear more than love. It also required a different kind of minister, who would be with, rather than over, the people. But how?

By happenstance, the 100-year-old Albertus Street Primary School behind our sanctuary was about to be closed, offering an opportunity to do something new and different with the property. In January 1968 I invited younger church members to join me each Saturday morning in transforming the two-floor former school. For six months we slaved away, sanding, sawing, remodelling and painting, until there emerged an attractive upstairs community centre and restaurant called the Carpenter's House. On the wall in the coffee bar was an impression of Jesus at his workbench with this prayer ...

O Master Carpenter of Nazareth,
Who at the last with wood and nails
purchased man's whole salvation,
Wield well Thy tools in this Thy workshop,
That we who come to Thy bench rough-hewn,
May be fashioned to a truer beauty by Thy hand.[66]

Downstairs second-hand partitions and old furniture from my brother-in-law Allan Hardie enabled us to provide an assembly hall and two offices, allowing me to locate in the community rather than working out of our manse.

But something more than reshaping a building was happening: we were beginning to also reshape the lives of a remarkable group of young adults. They had quickly bought into the Carpenter's House vision, but had also found themselves on level ground – hammer and nails in hand – with their minister. A deepening bond was being forged and as we worked they began to open up about their lives. We decided to meet on Friday evenings too, calling ourselves the Seekers. Soon we were exploring issues of faith and life together. We talked of the 'inner journey' of spiritual disciplines and the 'outward journey' of engagement with society. There emerged a deepening honesty among us. Elizabeth and I knew that we could expect no transformation unless we were willing to expose our own vulnerabilities. She played a crucial role especially among the young women in the group and there came a symbolic moment of liberation when they decided to dispense forever with their traditional 'doeks' and hats and to attend church with hair uncovered. Because of the role hair texture played in the racialisation and stratification of women in this community, it was a massive step toward self-acceptance. Acknowledging their lifelong discomfort when interacting with whites, the Seekers set up occasions when contact could not be avoided, and then analysed their behaviour and feelings afterwards, all the time growing confidence in their own self-worth.

12

The Ocean in a Single Drop

The Seekers changed everything. Soon they were challenging older members to get on board with the new directions we were moving in. After-church coffee in the Carpenter's House had Seekers at each table stimulating discussion of the evening's sermon. My sermons didn't fixate exclusively on political oppression but I made a point of showing that no matter the subject, the Gospel had both personal and social implications, and the consistent thread in all of them was this thing Christians call 'grace' – being loved for who we are as dignified children of God, and loving others unconditionally and without exception. One Sunday night the Seekers replaced the altar with a trestle-table loaded with food and proceeded outside to invite homeless people and passers-by to a sit-down meal upfront, while reminding the congregation about who Jesus regarded as most important. Church members were shocked out of their belief that faith was about being respectable and began to learn that it was about extravagant compassion and hospitality instead.

We launched a Youth Cabaret with more than 200 kids bopping and jiving to live bands on Saturday nights. It was a risky undertaking because of District Six's flourishing gang culture but Cabaret was so popular that tough teenagers seeking entrance meekly submitted to body searches when Jane and her team suspected they were carrying knives or drugs – which they often were. In the middle of Cabaret the kids, Christian and Muslim, would pause with remarkable attentiveness while the Seekers presented a simple re-enactment of a Jesus parable or I said a few words. Then the band would assault our eardrums once more. We had sanded off a fair bit of the gnarled floor they were dancing on and I had some anxious moments as it bounced up and down under 200 pairs of feet, but it held. Fifty years later I still meet people who loved Youth Cabaret, "where we could enjoy ourselves without getting into trouble".

During weekdays the Carpenter's House was a lunch club for workers. Simple meals were on sale for 15c, and billiards, darts and 'kerem'[67] boards were available; but more significant was that people of colour could sit down in dignity in a city where they were refused such service anywhere else. On Wednesdays we held a 40-minute 'Lunchtime Crossfire' in the church. Workers were invited to eat their sandwiches in the pews while I offered a brief Christian perspective on current affairs subjects and then took questions. Questioners were not slow in coming forward. Silenced people were finding their voice.

We deracialised the Circuit's name to the 'Inner City Mission' with the focus being on serving the community rather than simply pastoring a congregation. Word spread that sermons at Buitenkant Street were about real life and were not afraid to tackle political issues. One person likes to remind me still that as a teenager she used get hidings for sneaking out of her house on Sunday evenings to come to our services. Her Catholic parents beat her, not for listening to a non-Catholic, but to "that Communist". When a young sex worker began to worship with us and found a new purpose for her life, extracting her from the brothel where she worked with two or three other girls was not a simple matter. She wanted to break free from sex work, but her friends needed her contribution to food and rent, so we paid in the average amount she would normally have earned, and took our new convert onto our staff to pursue her real passion, which was working with little children. The arrangement worked. Her 'Queen Bess Club' was a hit, and few who were there will forget the nativity play they presented to a church packed with rowdy street children, especially when Joseph varied the script by clouting the grumpy innkeeper. Glorious chaos ensued.

When *Jesus Christ Superstar* took the music world by storm, it was unsurprisingly banned by South Africa's grim censors as 'blasphemous'. We felt that the rock opera had value as a contemporary portrayal of the Jesus message and that the ban was absurd, so we decided to use Holy Week to stage a 'Listen in'. Huge speakers were installed for the occasion and 800 people packed the darkened church while Andrew Lloyd Webber and Tim Rice's work held them enthralled. It was a gamble but I figured that the police would think twice before arresting me for playing music about Jesus in Holy Week.

The congregation's public profile grew. In June 1967 Ds Beyers Naudé came to promote his Christian Institute (CI) Bible Study groups in Cape Town. The first meeting was held in our home and Beyers preached in our pulpit. Another guest was Clarence Jordan, who had founded the multi-racial Koinonia community in Alabama, and authored *The Cotton Patch Version of Matthew and John*. His story of endurance in the face of Ku Klux Klan attacks and other intimidation inspired us. Veteran ANC activist Dr William Nkomo became the first black African to meet with the Seekers and encourage them in their interracial forays.

I had been profoundly moved by Dr Martin Luther King Jr's non-violent witness to racial justice and we had played banned recordings of his speeches at Seekers meetings. When he was assassinated in April 1967 we decided to hold a public memorial service to coincide with his funeral in Atlanta, Georgia five days later. It turned out to be the only one anywhere in South Africa. I was shocked when the American ambassador and his staff refused our invitation to attend but it seems that they were waiting for the White House to tell them whether King was to be ignored as a rabble-rouser or mourned as a martyr. The decision must have come through just a few hours before the service because I suddenly got a request to reserve a whole bunch of seats for the ambassador and his entourage.

The church was also venue to a number of protests against the

District Six removals and the 90-Day Detention Act with speakers like anti-apartheid parliamentarians Helen Suzman and Colin Eglin. In those days such meetings were fairly polite affairs, but some fifteen years after my time, under successors such as Revs Alan Brews and Charles Villa-Vicencio, the venerable old building was to house much more risky protests, this time facing teargas with armoured vehicles backed up against its doors to cut off escape. But that lay in the future. My priorities were trying to ameliorate immediate suffering caused by apartheid's cruelty. Because of the laws against interracial relationships and marriage,[68] any couple falling in love across the colour-line became criminals. If they wanted to stay together their only hope was emigration, and for this I needed international help. The Australian consul-general smoothed the way for a number of couples to obtain entry to his country where they could be together without fear of arrest.

In September 1969, Imam Abdullah Haron of the progressive Claremont Mosque was murdered in the cells of Maitland police station. The Security Police claimed that the human rights activist had "fallen down the staircase", but the wounds on his body told another story. For some reason, this particular death in detention touched Anglican priest Bernie Wrankmore to drastic action. Bernie was probably as apolitical as anybody could be, but he was so incensed by months of callous cover-up, that around the second anniversary of the murder he climbed Signal Hill, entered a well-known kramat,[69] and vowed to fast – drinking only Table Mountain water and orange juice – until Prime Minister BJ Vorster agreed to order a judicial inquiry. I decided to spend some time with him each day if possible and we became friends. I also met his spouse Valerie and their young children, and as he began to waste away, she became increasingly anxious. With Vorster ignoring him, Bernie announced that he would mark the 40th day of his fast by preaching a sermon. Hundreds of Capetonians climbed the hill to listen to what became known as Bernie's 'Sermon on the Mount'. We hoped he would announce that he was calling it off, but he had nothing of the sort in mind. In spite of his weakened state he preached for nearly an hour, mainly about his spiritual discoveries during the fast, then announced that he would continue until the Prime Minister relented. With Val's anxiety deepening, I determined to get her to see the Prime Minister. We approached the very staid Leader of the Opposition, Sir de Villiers Graaff, who had little sympathy with Bernie's stand but helped persuade the PM to open his door. On 4 October 1971 Val and I flew to Pretoria for the appointment at the Union Buildings. Vorster was courteous but stone-faced while Val pleaded for some action that might convince her spouse to end his fast. He was adamant that torture was not tolerated under his watch but promised nothing. He did indicate, however, that "his door was open" if Bernie himself wanted to see him. With this tiny shred of hope, we returned to Cape Town. Bernie did make a secret trip to Pretoria but never got to see Vorster. His fast continued for an incredible 67 days before he finally gave up and came down. We crowded into his little flat above the Missions to Seamen and watched as he sat down with a beatific smile and ate his first meal – a poached egg.

A sprinkling of white people began to appear in our pews on Sundays, offering new opportunities. As part of the 'Commission for the Renewal of the Church',[70] a number of us had been arguing that unless MCSA congregations became more inclusive, our challenge to the apartheid government would always lack credibility. A Presbyterian minister named Rob Robertson had launched an 'intentional' integrated congregation in East London, convinced that, "You can't talk people out of apartheid, you have to mix them out of it."[71] In 1969 I visited him to learn more and then wrote a critique of MCSA for conforming "to the 'South African way of life' which it officially condemns". Arguing that it would never happen "naturally" in the South African context, I laid out a three-year intentional integration plan for local congregations. Reversing apartheid on "the broad fronts of national life" might be the ultimate goal, I wrote, but "the mere existence of any inclusive group gives the lie to the basic premise of apartheid."[72]

Travelling to Renewal Commission meetings in the 1960s offered further experiences of the humiliations of apartheid. Tom Hanmer, the brilliant educationalist heading up the Wesley Teachers' Training College in Cape Town, joined me for a flight to East London. Tom was nervous because he had never flown before. When we got to the check-in desk, his boarding pass indicated the rear row of seats, while mine was somewhere toward the front. "There must be some mistake," I protested. "Mr Hanmer and I are travelling together." The check-in clerk looked at Tom coldly and said, "There is no mistake. This man is Coloured. You may not sit together." I was flushed with anger and shame but fortunately the plane was not full and as soon as we were airborne I could walk back and join Tom. There are no words for what he must have felt.

The Renewal Commission thanked me for my paper, and referred the matter to the next meeting, but at Buitenkant Street we were already testing my thesis. I had written that integration would come about, "not by pretending an absence of prejudice, but by consciously identifying and confronting our prejudice and wrestling with it every step of the way."[73] Thus the whites who wanted to join us had to be willing to move through a process called My Brother and Me.[74] This consisted of weekly interracial encounters in which participants unpacked the meaning of racism and privilege. Today 'diversity training' is common, but in the 1960s it was revolutionary. Beginning with a polite welcome and some theoretical input on prejudice, it soon moved into more robust exchanges and role-plays. By the third week, the well-meaning whites arrived to discover that they were to be treated as 'non-whites' for the evening. They could only look on and listen while people of colour discussed them – their opinion neither sought nor permitted. They were not allowed to use the usual toilets and at the break had to go into the street to get their coffee or tea served through a window. There were more bruising evenings with responses varying from defensiveness to deep anguish before signs of transformation emerged. For the whites, it was nothing less than a conversion in which they had to recognise and confess their deep-rooted racism – and the guilt that came with it – for the first time. Some quit, but those who stuck it out found themselves becoming much more humble and sensitised people and they were welcomed into their first multi-racial community. For the 'coloureds' there was challenge too: could they overcome their ingrained inferiorities, and in many cases, bitterness, sufficiently to both challenge and ultimately welcome white members? Typical was Kate Brown, who had spent her life in the master-servant world of a domestic worker, and who found it desperately difficult to address whites as equals. When she finally did so, she spoke of being set free from an internal prison she had lived in all her life. My Brother and Me was later to have a wider impact but at the time we were taking our first small steps. I fretted to an American Methodist visitor that this effort at racial reconciliation was a mere "drop in the ocean" but he expressed amazement to find something like this in South Africa. "Never forget," he said, "that the whole ocean is present in a single drop." Ever since, I've tried to remember that when we live out even the smallest manifestations of what Jesus envisioned, his new world of justice and peace is already amongst us.

One of the whites coming to worship – a young man named Rob Thomson – came to see me. He had recently qualified as an actuary and confessed embarrassment at the amount of money he was now earning each month. He was looking for a meaningful way to put his new wealth to work and I pointed him in the direction of Maitland Garden Village[75] where we had a church and school and where 1 600 inhabitants lived with all the social problems associated with poverty. "See if you can make a dent in that," I said. Anxious to avoid any kind of paternalism, Rob came up with a remarkable plan: using his high salary, he employed a social worker to get into the homes of the people and both research and engage with their needs. She and Rob then worked together seeking to meet those needs. Nobody ever knew that he was financing the project.

I had long been concerned at how few 'coloured' youth could afford to go beyond school to enrol in university. Following school-leaving they were expected to begin contributing to their parents' income. This being so, I believed that the church should at least be empowering young workers to be informed activists in the factories and other places where they worked. By this time Reverend James Leatt[76] had joined the team and was in charge at Windermere, the shabby predecessor to what is now the suburb of Kensington. The Windermere Methodist Primary School there was on its last legs, decrepit, lacking in amenities and like most other church schools, under the thumb of apartheid's Coloured Education Department. When it closed, there was once again opportunity for innovation and we decided to re-model the building to serve the community.[77] Jim was already gaining experience supervising an 'owner-build' church project at Darling, where the Group Areas Act had booted us out of our prime site in the town and exiled the congregation with all other 'coloured' inhabitants to the other side of the railroad tracks. He tackled the new challenge with a will. Soon cracked walls were repaired, sagging floors replaced, windows glazed and spaces reconfigured. The old school on the corner of Bunney Street emerged with two new functions. The first was a fine pre-school for local children, and the second carried our hopes to train youthful Christian activists. We named the pre-school Gateway. It opened with 90 children and a waiting list of 150. Kathleen Edwards – the quietest Seeker who had nevertheless been the first to dispense with her doek – became its principal, exercising a firm but gentle leadership.[78] The new Christian Leadership Centre (CLC) consisted of residential cubicles for twelve young people, lecture rooms and dining and ablution facilities. Under the leadership of Alec Gordon, another Seeker 'graduate', CLC would offer three-month courses for young workers. They would live in community for the duration, going to work by day and attending classes in the evenings. Typical courses taught were Biblical Interpretation, A Theology of Hope, Community Development, Effective Youth Leadership and The Church, and Black Consciousness.

Later Jane, who had meanwhile spent eighteen months in the USA gaining further experience of urban ministry, returned to become the second director of the CLC. Fired by the growing impatience of the civil rights movement, she injected a more militant activism into the training. She and fellow Seeker graduate Gilbert Lawrence had become engaged to be married. With the help of a Methodist scholarship Gilbert studied medicine at the University of Cape Town but despite its 'liberal' claims he and the small handful of other 'non-white' medical students did not escape discrimination there: when the time came to dissect cadavers they were not only forbidden to work on 'white' cadavers, but were segregated into a separate room so as not even to see them. He was now qualified and was preparing to serve at the Bethesda Methodist Mission Hospital in Ubombo, Natal. At their wedding in 1973 Jane and Gilbert left the church with a CLC guard of honour throwing the power salute with black-gloved fists. I conducted the wedding and Elizabeth proposed the toast to bride and groom. A deep friendship across lines of colour had been sealed between the four of us. It survived the worst apartheid could do and would persevere unbroken for more than 40 years until the night when we would hold hands around Elizabeth's hospital bed and Gilbert would say the last prayer she heard on earth.[79]

13

Then Came the Bulldozers

All the while, a single-minded regime was proceeding to tear the heart out of District Six. Every week more families would report visits by the 'GG' car.[80] If they owned their property they would also be told the meagre compensation they would receive. They would be given approximate eviction dates but only a rough idea of where they would end up on the vast Cape Flats.

The rituals of dispossession tended to be sadly similar but for me the picture of the Abrahams family's dread 'moving day' comes most painfully to mind. They gathered for the last time in the bare living room, with worn-out linoleums of long ago exposed once more. Ma Abrahams, sitting on an old box and asking in her gentle voice, "Why, Reverend Peter, what did we do wrong?" and me with no words – just hot tears of anger and shame. Then holding hands and praying, some crying, others standing in numb silence, remembering the generations for whom this humble tenement had been home. Then blessing the house for one last time, and the family filing through the front door to be met by a crowd of neighbours waiting to farewell them. Then Ma getting into the waiting car with her daughters and the men mounting the truck behind, loaded with their worldly goods. Ma giving a brave smile and a little wave and the sad procession of pain moving off down De Villiers Street while old friends waved handkerchiefs and dabbed their eyes.

This gut-wrenching ritual was repeated over and over, in street after street, closely followed by the government demolition teams. It was as if a brutal regime could not wait to wipe out every remembrance of this one community in all of South Africa whose existence proved their race phobias to be nonsense. Jane was in the USA when her family was moved and when she returned, her home no longer existed. The bulldozers had seen to that.

Nobody will ever measure the pain of District Six. My senior lay leader had just been relocated when we had an evening meeting at the church. I offered him a ride home. When we got out among the rows of matchbox houses perched on the sandy Cape Flats, he couldn't find it. We had to go to the railway station so he could retrace his daily walk back to what was now his home. In District Six he had paid R7 per month for two bedrooms, dining room, lounge and kitchen and walked to work each day. Now, for two rooms without ceilings or doors, a kitchen and a bathroom, his rent was almost exactly double. Train rides to town cost another R2.50 each month. They were now thirteen miles (21 km) from his work and the nearest shop was more than a mile (1.6 km) away. Another, more elderly member who landed on the Cape Flats came to me after less than a month there, asking me to bury his spouse. Tears streaming down his face, he said, "She died of a broken heart." A few weeks later, he too died. It was not only the loss of their homes, but the destruction of community solidarity that broke hearts. No attempt was made in the moves to keep friends and relatives together. "In District Six," said one victim, "Muslims and Christians used to wish each other well for their Holy days and share each other's feasts; our first Christmas on the Flats nobody knocked on our door to wish us. We were so sad." Donald Shriver says, "Aside from prison and official murders, few other apartheid strategies inflicted more radical damage on so many families."[81] The price for the dumping of people into Hanover Park, Manenberg and Bonteheuwel, Lavender Hill and the other apartheid ghettos, is still being paid. More than two decades into democracy, they are the most violent gang-ruled and drug-ridden localities in South Africa.

Out on the Cape Flats where the South Easter-blown sand found its way into every cranny in the matchbox houses, the church once more attempted to offer some small comfort to newcomers. My colleague Abel Hendricks and his spouse Freda were sent there to begin a ministry. They were told, "You will start with nothing – do what you can for the people." Like everyone else they lined up at the housing authority. Like everyone else they began life on the Flats in a matchbox house – in Kalksteenfontein – where Abel's only office was his car. They ultimately became a legend, responsible for founding the Cape Flats Methodist Mission and building churches and pre-schools across the Cape Flats. In a few short years they were caring for 5 000 people. After our arrival in District Six, we had soon come to know them as deep and dear friends. My bond with Abel was sealed in – of all places – New York City when he was on course there in 1969 and I was passing through. We arranged to meet and walked into a milkbar together. Suddenly realising what had happened, we both stopped, then broke down in tears and hugged each other and danced a small jig. It was the first time we had ever ordered a meal together in a public place. "There was liberation from years of conditioning, just in that small experience,"[82] Abel recalled. In a very real sense it was true for me too. Elizabeth and I drew some small comfort from the knowledge that when our dispossessed members got to their new dwellings, Abel and Freda were there to ease their arrival.

Sadly, our time in District Six was coming to an end. After five years Elizabeth and I felt a belonging among these remarkable people that we had never known before. Our lives had been changed by them in deep and indelible ways. Two more sons, David and Alan, had been born there just twelve months apart in 1967 and 1968, completing our family. Our children had the inestimable privilege of living their earliest years among South Africans of all shades. I felt that I had at least been able to touch the fringes of their pain, sufficient perhaps to witness to it with them.

But I was worn out.

Before I left Australia Life Line International had tasked me with establishing the movement in Southern Africa and this had consumed much spare energy. Just three months after returning home, I had met with Allan Hardie, Reverend Theo Kotze, Noel Wood and a small team to plan Africa's first Life Line centre in Cape Town, followed by meetings in Johannesburg with Beyers Naudé, Dr Bruckner de Villiers and Reverend Paul Welsh, Valmai's husband, in May 1967. Later in the year I got the ball rolling in Johannesburg by addressing a large promotional gathering there. The Cape Town centre opened in November 1968 with 500 calls received in the first three months. Life Line Witwatersrand followed in December 1969. That year, with help from Durban Rotary Club's Len Baumann and Reverend Alex Boraine, Life Line Durban was initiated, opening its telephone lines in December 1970. A centre was launched in Kimberley in 1969, followed by the East Rand in 1971, then Welkom and Pietermaritzburg. I even served as volunteer director of the Cape Town centre for a while, walking between my church and the Spin Street office each morning to check call reports and set duties for the day. Setting up the national body was stressful and time consuming.

Then in 1970 there was added the task of editing the MCSA's new monthly newspaper, *Dimension*.[83] It was too heavy a load and in mid-1971 my health broke down. The powers that be suggested I leave pastoral work altogether and take over the MCSA Publishing House, where I would administer the Methodist Bookshops across South Africa and be able to edit *Dimension* undisturbed. Feeling very low, I briefly accepted the idea but soon decided that to give up serving a congregation would deny my calling. Unsure what to do, I left things in the hands of God and the upcoming Methodist Conference, hoping that their thoughts might coincide. Driving to Durban for the Conference so I could cover its sessions for *Dimension*, I had to stop twice to get treatment for awful flu. By the time Elizabeth and I arrived in Durban, our fate had been sealed. Somebody asked me how I liked my new appointment: "What appointment?" I asked. "Sorry, I thought you knew. The Stationing Committee has moved you to Joburg." Though we often doubt it, Methodists have been encouraged to believe that the voice of the Conference can sometimes be the voice of God. Elizabeth wasn't at all convinced this time, but we went home to pack our bags.

The people of District Six deserved one final salute. The cruelty, sadness, faith and courage that we had seen needed to be memorialised and I felt that none should pass by our church in Buitenkant Street without being reminded of it. I wrote some words to that effect and asked the best-known engraving firm in Cape Town to inscribe them on a bronze plaque. They refused, citing fear of the Security Police. Other smaller firms also refused, until I finally had to get the plaque made in Johannesburg, promising not to reveal the engraver's name. It read ...

ALL WHO PASS BY
Remember with shame the many thousands
of people who lived for generations
in District Six and other parts of
this city and were forced by law to
leave their homes because of the
colour of their skins.
FATHER, FORGIVE US

On 21 November 1971 we dedicated the 'Plaque of Conscience' – the very first public memorial to the horrors of apartheid anywhere in South Africa – and then affixed it to the front wall of the church. Preaching that day I said, "We come in sadness and shame ... that compassion has been blinded ... and that the gods of racial purity can be more worshipped than the God who makes us all one family." Nothing could shut out the cry that a monstrous evil was being perpetrated and I warned that white Capetonians would pay a price in their souls: "As whites place those we hurt beyond our city walls where they are no longer visible, we are cutting ourselves off from our consciences and sealing ourselves into our own ghetto of indifference," and "Let none become comfortable in the presence of this terrible thing. Let none pretend it didn't happen. *All who pass by – remember with shame!*"

But there was need to speak also of hope: "We meet in pain and anger, but not in defeat. We meet here in confidence ... because God will not allow apartheid to live forever. The wall of partition being so cruelly built at this time will be broken down by our Christ. The tears that so many shed today will one day be wiped dry." I pleaded that whatever happened to the homes of the District, "let us commit ourselves to preserve this place. Let it stand as a shrine of hope, as one small part of District Six that none can take away from its people – and as a promise that they will return." Until then, I said, "Let this plaque be a judgement on those destroying this community and an offence to those who let it happen."

The plaque did stand, but not without a struggle. With police headquarters directly opposite the church that was to be expected. In the dead of night exactly one month after its unveiling, the plaque was crowbarred off the wall only to be replaced and once more ripped off. A smaller version was made and firmly cemented in place. Despite being defaced more than once, it survives to this day. Twenty-one years after we fixed it to the wall I was invited to preach again under the Plaque of Conscience, this time celebrating that the people of District Six could begin to return and rebuild. Now I could quote happier lines from a song about a different city ...

> The light of God was on its streets,
> The gates were open wide;
> And all who would might enter,
> And no one was denied.

No need for moon or stars by night,
Or sun to shine by day;
It was the New Jerusalem,
That would not pass away![84]

In the intervening years white Capetonians did feel shame. The bulldozed wasteland on the slopes above the city, set aside for their occupation, was prime land, yet apart from occupying a few renovated apartment blocks just below De Waal Drive, nobody seemed willing to buy. It was as if the wasteland that was District Six was hallowed ground. Only the government's new University of Technology and a couple of hotel chains were brash enough to desecrate it. The rest stood bare as mute testimony to inhuman cruelty and human pain – and as if waiting for its sons and daughters to return.

By the time freedom came, the remnants of the Buitenkant Street congregation, having refused in spite of much pressure and intimidation for 22 years to leave their church, had voted with incredible grace to join the ailing 'mother church' on Greenmarket Square, integrating that congregation by their presence and lending it new strength and leadership.[85] It is now known as the Central Methodist Mission and by one of God's strange 'coincidences' our youngest son Alan is Superintendent Minister. Buitenkant Street Church is now the District Six Museum, the most visited in Cape Town. The museum was launched by placing a great map of District Six on the floor of the old church, and inviting ex-residents to come and identify where they had lived and 'write themselves back' into the District by leaving messages on it. For the 60 000 people who lost their homes it is a guardian of both joyful nostalgia and painful memory. For those few who have begun to return it represents a promise fulfilled. For others yet waiting, it must remain a shrine of hope.

14

Amateur Journo

Despite a less than stellar academic record I have always loved English and had an ear for the rhythm of a good sentence. When I joined Hugh Lewin working on *Rhodeo* back in the 1950s, it didn't take long to get an idea of what a news story looked like and to slip into the required journalese. Then there was *Christian Impact*, the paper I edited with *Cape Times* reporter Tony Heard's help during Alan Walker's controversial preaching visit in 1963.

Five years later I was drawn more seriously into journalism. The context was a struggle for change within MCSA initiated in 1964 by a group of younger ministers – unoriginally dubbed the 'Young Turks'. We felt that our church's public witness had become inconsistent and timid, and that it needed to be much more robustly engaged in social issues. Its internal structures were still largely segregated and thoroughly out of date. Christianity world-wide seemed to be under siege, its theology out of touch, its ethics under question, and its practices increasingly irrelevant to the poor of the earth. In South Africa and the American South there was the added issue of entrenched, legalised racism, brazenly upheld by conservative Christians in both countries. We were losing young ministers who felt the church had no meaningful answer to the secular 60s.

Yet, in the midst of this depressing scenario were signs of new life. In the USA, churches were breaking out of their staid patterns and moving into experimental ministries in the inner cities. The civil rights movement, rooted firmly in the American black church and led by Baptist preacher Martin Luther King Jr, was demonstrating how relevant the church could be in confronting segregation. Among younger progressives in the MCSA was the belief that perhaps this creaking institution called 'church' might be ready to embrace a different future. In 1965 a Commission for the Renewal of the Church was set up under the leadership of Alex Boraine.[86]

The Renewal Commission set about its work with a will. We called on the church to rediscover its mission in the world, and presented a new structural architecture that looked outward rather than inward. Local congregations were to be governed by a much more participatory system and experimental multi-racial congregations were to be established in the inner cities. Methodist Circuits – largely segregated at the time – were to be replaced by geographic entities that disregarded race. We called for an end to the tradition of an all-male ministry[87] and to the racially segregated Synod sessions still held in some areas. In the face of complaints that structural change should wait until 'hearts were changed', we said that hearts were taking too long and needed a good shove in the right direction – that only when church members were made to change their behaviour would their hearts follow.

The commission also proposed a revamped communication strategy, replacing the venerable *Methodist Churchman* with a lively monthly newspaper. Being the only Young Turk with a smidgen of journalistic experience, this was where I came in. My name was put forward at the 1969 Methodist Conference to launch the paper. When traditionalists recognised that the tide was flowing against the old *Churchman*, they tried to keep the new paper in what they saw as more 'reliable' hands by nominating a redoubtable Methodist grandee, Reverend Dr C Edgar Wilkinson to oppose me. I was a 31-year-old upstart and had no doubt that Wilkinson would carry the day, but after a lively debate I was surprisingly elected, becoming the part-time, unpaid editor of an unborn and unnamed new Methodist newspaper.

It took a couple of months to navigate the closure of the *Churchman* and the absorption of three additional Methodist publications with their modest budgets and a tiny mailing list of 1 200 names and their subscriptions of 50c per annum. The new paper was still nameless when around a barbecue at our home, Alex's spouse Jenny suggested *Dimension* and it stuck.

A room attached to the garage of our home became my studio, with a light table and the crude pre-desktop publishing implements used back then. Hot-lead typesetting was still the norm. The resulting galley-proofs had to be cut into columns, passed through a messy hot-wax machine and fixed to dummy pages on the light table. I soon learned how to estimate word counts and space, but fell woefully short with the first issue. As the first rays of deadline day peeked into the studio, with all my copy used up and our first few adverts pasted down, I had filled only seven pages, leaving one empty page staring mockingly at me. Panic gripped me: it was too late to write anything and I needed to be at the printers, so desperate measures were called for. This first issue focused on Easter, so I grabbed a black marker pen and arched an enormous sweeping crucifix diagonally across the whole page, with the hanging figure of Christ in silhouette. Then I wrote in the shape of a cross, *My Dear Children, there was once, a long, long time ago, once upon a time, many, many, many years and months and hours ago – a man. Amen.* I titled it *The Death of a Man* and raced for the printers.

Reactions to the first issue were a parable of this strange creature called 'church'. Both the *Churchman*'s ex-editor and Dr Wilkinson, who had meanwhile become President-Elect of MCSA, thought their worst fears justified; they wrote scathing notes especially critical of *The Death of a Man*, hoping that this was not the blasphemous harbinger of low standards to come. But others enthused over it. Joburg minister Tom Parker even elevated it to philosophical greatness, saying it had evoked the "fantastically releasing theologies of Bonhoeffer, Kierkegaard and Tillich". About the rest of the first edition, battle lines were already beginning to be drawn. Some welcomed the mix of news, political and spiritual content; others protested coverage given to a twelve-point Election Manifesto signed by 70 ministers and laypersons. Most hoped the new paper would "steer clear of politics". Thus was the church divided, but either way, *Dimension* was on the map.

The second issue coincided with the 1970 general election and plunged directly into the public square. It carried a message from the MCSA President, calling for the [all white] voters to reject self-interest, love of power, race and class. A full page highlighted MCSA's history of opposition to apartheid reinforced by a cartoon showing a white voter casting his ballot while excluded blacks peer in through a window. Of course the paper carried plenty of in-house church news too. White Methodists enjoyed reading about their local churches and personalities but many were angered by *Dimension*'s forays into the political. Black readers welcomed our new engagement with public issues but being deeply conservative about how they ran their churches, were suspicious of some of the Renewal goals. An early editorial summed it up. Christians, it said, too often divided into "pietists" and "activists". The former thought the faith was all about personal salvation and the road to heaven, ignoring the need to transform the hells we made on earth. The latter tended to be so focused on bringing justice to the oppressed that they often neglected the inner spiritual life. *Dimension,* I wrote, stood for a marriage of the two – "the Gospel of personal salvation is supremely irrelevant unless it is preached from a platform of active social concern; the Gospel of social righteousness is utopian unless it is buttressed by the changed life." As far as I was concerned, this "double thrust" was why I was a Methodist – and why my readers should be too.[88] The coming years were to prove that many disagreed, but *Dimension* was to remain unshaken.

In its first couple of years, while circulation figures rose to 8 000, my only staff person was a part-time secretary managing circulation and accounts. I was editor, leader writer, sub-editor, cartoonist, illustrator and layout artist. My 'day' job, ministering to my District Six congregation and running the Inner City Mission Circuit, had not changed and on top of that was my extra-mural work establishing Life Line in Southern Africa.

To get *Dimension* out each month, I slipped into a routine that didn't change much over the next eight years despite significant changes in ministry appointments. Local church news – most of which was of the parish-pump variety – would flow in from a network of volunteer reporters each month, while I commissioned feature articles and comment from people who would help readers think. Other work was keeping abreast of hard news and any church-state developments, but the real slog occupied late nights – usually between 10 pm and 2 am – in the second and third weeks of each month. No matter how late I got home, the first task after supper was to wade through the incoming material, culling 'churchy' verbiage and doing rewrites on my old typewriter. Then all had to be marked up in type-sizes and column widths, pictures chosen and measured and headlines concocted. A couple of days' respite and the galley-proofs would come back and more late nights followed laying out the paper. An inevitable last-minute panic ensued, including writing the editorials, and at last – breathlessly – to the printer. *Dimension* was tiny in the world of publications, but I enjoyed the same exhausted satisfaction any editor would when watching the giant presses begin to turn, then reach blurring speed, finally spewing out neat bundles of the latest issue. If anyone has any doubt about the breathtaking advances in printing technology, it is worth noting that when we moved from the old ways to offset-litho printing in December 1973, production time at the printers was reduced from four days to 90 minutes.

Enormous support came from my old *Christian Impact* friend John Gardener, who authored a column called 'The Crucible' for many years with a deft literary touch. I asked Reverend Stanley Mogoba, ex-Robben Islander and now a faculty member at the Federal Theological Seminary, to be an assistant editor. His column, called 'Blackground', offered a black perspective on events in a church that still assumed a white Western character.

It didn't take long to discover the power of the Fourth Estate. The printed word, even in a newborn babe like *Dimension*, carried some clout. Our sixth issue front-paged a story about the food crisis in the new Transkei Bantustan, where four out of ten children were dying before they reached age ten. The SACC Inter-Church Aid was desperately trying to meet the need with no help from the Transkei government. When crusading editor Donald Woods took up our story in his *Daily Dispatch*, Chief Minister Kaiser Matanzima suddenly 'found' R360 000 earmarked for the purpose, which he said had been 'mislaid'. The money was released and children fed.

Then we covered the first of what became a non-stop catalogue of church-state crises. The World Council of Churches (WCC) announced large grants to liberation movements involved in 'armed struggle', including the ANC and PAC, and a firestorm followed. Prime Minister Vorster demanded that South African member churches denounce the WCC and resign from it. Town councils threatened to revoke member churches' rate-free status unless they did.[89] White church members fulminated about resigning. The crisis was a baptism of fire for 33-year-old Methodist layman John Rees, whose appointment as General Secretary of the SACC we had just reported. Emergency meetings called by the SACC brought forth a church response "dissociating" from the WCC's implied support of the use of violence but also refusing to leave the world body.

Dimension's editorial "regretted and challenged" the WCC decision but acknowledged the failure of SA churches to major in "Christian reconciliation and the overcoming of racism". I pointed out that if the WCC was to be condemned for implicitly supporting violence, the majority of white South Africans stood under a similar condemnation for supporting "... the daily acts of violence against human dignity carried out ... in the name of apartheid".

Black Methodists were significantly silent. They held their peace until the Methodist Annual Conference a month later. The debate began with white delegates fiercely denouncing the grants and demanding that MCSA leave the WCC. Some whites differed but the real shift came when the first black voice spoke. Dr William Nkomo, who had been our jovial medical doctor back in the Kilnerton days, stood to mete out bitter medicine to the Conference. He accused whites of "regarding black people in their hearts as less than men", reminding them that his people had to move apologetically through the country of their birth, being "daily subjected to intimidation, violence and terrorism far greater than anything the guerrillas had yet done". Even if the guerrillas were doing the wrong thing, he said, "I will pray for them until I die."

Nkomo's rebuke came with a confidence and conviction not heard from black delegates before and even though the final resolution was something of a compromise I knew I was witnessing the beginnings of a shift in the MCSA's centre of gravity. Conference decided to remain a member of the world body though its membership subscriptions would be held in suspense pending the outcome of consultations with the WCC leadership. More importantly, for the first time the Methodist Church confessed its "shortcomings in seeking a solution to the problems of racism", opening the door for a much more penetrating self-examination.

Dimension carried a blow-by-blow account and pictures of the Conference debate – but not without a fight. The all-powerful Secretary of the Conference, Dr Stanley Sudbury, who had clashed often with the Young Turks, told me that while "the press" were welcome at public events, they had never been allowed to cover actual debates, and nor would I. With hindsight the idea of an institution banning its own newspaper from its deliberations is absurd but we were still emerging from a very different era. Sudbury's prohibition made me all the more determined and after calling some sympathetic heavyweights to my aid, I finally got in on condition that I sat in one spot in the gallery and didn't move. I also secured agreement for the secular media to do the same. In spite of my enforced immobility I had scoured Joburg for an enormous long camera lens and managed to get candid pictures of delegates in debate – or in one case, asleep. Later I had to stifle a guffaw when, in the tense WCC debate, it was Sudbury who resisted a resolution to exclude the press: "The world should know that there is freedom of expression in the Methodist Church," he declared piously. Thus did press freedom finally come to the MCSA Conference.

In 1972, when I was moved to Johannesburg, *Dimension* went with me and we set up our 'newsroom and graphics department' in the basement of the old Clifton Methodist Church in Braamfontein. By this time circulation was up to 12 000 and apart from a new circulation manager I could afford to invite the indefatigable Helen Muller to be editorial assistant. Like me she did this in addition to her workload in the congregation and in the after-school care centres she directed. Her many gifts were indispensable in both the editorial and layout phases of the paper each month and I could focus more on content.

In the next few years the Renewal Commission was to discover just how stubborn and immovable a huge institution like MCSA could be. The 87 monthly *Dimensions* I edited show that some of the reforms mooted in the very first issue had only begun to take hold by the time I handed the job over eight years later. But other renewal objectives were achieved: Boraine had been elected President of the 1971 Conference at the age of 39, bringing a bold new activism to MCSA leadership. The WCC crisis had pressured member churches, including MCSA, into accelerating internal change. Countrywide 'Justice and Reconciliation' task groups had ensured that racial nomenclature was removed from Methodist structures and the last segregated Synods were abolished. Multi-racial in-service training courses for ministers became routine and, with the launch of an equalisation fund, inroads began to be made into our worst internal injustice – the inequality of ministers' stipends. The administration of local congregations was radically democratised. In 1976 the redoubtable Reverend Connie Oosthuizen became the first woman ordained into the Methodist ministry. In all these internal changes *Dimension* played a significant role in pushing the conversation forward.

But there was a bigger stage. Our little newspaper's story was being played out against a country-wide scenario of steadily increasing repression. What emerges from those early *Dimension* pages is the ruthless determination with which the government sought to bend the churches to its racial ideology. Confronting the state, often over objections from white readers, *Dimension* covered one crisis after another – all emanating from apartheid actions. Many of the battles were lost, some few were won, but each gave opportunity through the paper's reportage and trenchant editorials to witness to our deeply different understandings of right and wrong.

In March 1971 the regime deported American NYLTP workers Tammy and Reid Kramer.[90] MCSA churches with black or mixed congregations – many of them having existed for more than a century – were declared to be in 'white' Group Areas in dozens of towns like Stellenbosch and Darling in my own Circuit in the Cape. They had to abandon their churches and build anew in 'black or coloured areas'. By late 1972 Fort Hare University, now firmly in the hands of apartheid ideologues, was campaigning to rid itself of the 'subversive' liberal influence of neighbouring Federal Theological Seminary, the crown jewel of black theological education. It achieved this in 1975 by expropriating the whole FedSem campus, sending the seminary and its 112 trainee ministers into a long and painful exile. They camped in tents and caravans in Umtata, until Transkei's super-sensitive Chief Minister Matanzima forced them out once more, this time after they refused to expel two activist students who had offended him. They were then given shelter at Edendale Ecumenical Centre in Pietermaritzburg until a new campus could be built in Imbali township nearby. Nor was that the end of their troubles: a decade later, as President of MCSA I found myself in lengthy and frustrating telephone negotiations with Chief Minister Mangosuthu Buthelezi when an Inkatha-inspired impi[91] attacked the new campus because of some imagined political insult.

The secretive Schlebusch Commission investigated the Christian Institute, leading to criminal charges against Beyers Naudé and Methodists Theo Kotze and Brian Brown for refusing to testify. State agents harassed numbers of clergy and some Methodist prison chaplains were axed – as I had been in 1964 – without explanation. Informers were everywhere. One troubled black minister reported to me that he had just been dined by two security branch men at a posh Johannesburg hotel. They offered him R500 a month to inform on me. It was an enormous amount in those days and I jokingly advised him to take it – I had nothing to hide.

Dimension covered the beginnings of the Black Consciousness movement and the bannings of Steve Biko and one of our outstanding young ministers, Hamilton Qambela. In 1974 the Transkei 'homeland' government decided to grab ownership of historic Healdtown Institution and other famous Methodist educational campuses. Then it was the turn of our mission hospitals; the fact that the church could run them more economically because of highly motivated Christian staff who saw their work as vocation meant nothing. In a move described by Boraine as "an act of piracy", the state decided to take them too.

When 16 June 1976 broke upon the nation we led with the iconic picture of Mbuyisa Makhubu carrying the dying Hector Pieterson away from the killing ground and the issue was promptly banned, this in spite of our also carrying a remarkable story headlined 'The Slender Thread of Compassion', telling how the spouse of one of our black ministers in Soweto risked death to save the life of a terrified Afrikaans female social worker chased by angry youths.[92] Soon thereafter we were reporting Police Minister Jimmy Kruger's cold-blooded taunt, "If we use rubber bullets they will think we have rubber guns." As the mayhem spread, only one of our educational campuses now in the hands of the Transkei government was left intact; all the rest were torched by protesting students.

Time and again *Dimension* took on the apartheid beast while not neglecting parish-pump concerns. *Petty Apartheid Isn't ...* editorialised that if you were black, there was nothing petty about it because it carved deep wounds into the dignity of men and women. In the same issue I tackled whether ordained ministers should enter party politics and I encouraged Methodists to get involved in the coming "Year of Evangelism".[93] In April of 1974 my editorials dealt with the church's role in flood relief and with the South African Broadcasting Corporation's fostering of the right-wing Christian League.[94] That September *Dimension* denounced the Defence Further Amendment Bill as an attack on the freedom of religion that Christians would be "unable to obey ..." Alongside it was a call for MCSA to economise by using a single residential venue for Methodist Conferences. The editorials for October 1975 hit out at the Terrorism Act, accusing the authorities of taking powers "disallowed by any Christian understanding of government", and "sowing the seeds of tyranny". A second editorial bemoaned the fact that 73% of whites still believed it was "not our business as Church" to confront such evils.[95] As state violence and black rebellion spread across the land, *Dimension* called the government's massive firepower "a form of powerlessness" and called for the real power "that grows out of consultation and respect". The second editorial that month was about beerhalls in the townships that had been destroyed by the youth. "Let them stay that way," we opined.[96]

By the October Conference of 1976 feelings in MCSA were at boiling point. I had written:

"The focus of this time must inevitably be the wider situation of unrest in South Africa and its implications for the Church's witness and conduct. With many Methodists bereaved through police shootings and others detained in the giant security sweeps, with Black ministers caught helplessly in the conflict, deeply concerned as to their role, it is obvious that Methodism's response to this situation will be the priority."

But it took Black Methodist Consultation (BMC) leader Reverend Ernest Baartman to make sure it happened: he disrupted the opening session of Conference, demanding that the agenda be suspended to discuss the nation's crisis and threatening a black walk-out if this didn't happen. Wisdom prevailed and the agenda was set aside.

That December, speaking of the pall which events since June had cast over the Christmas season, I wrote that "Bethlehem may be a far cry from Soweto, but the cries of men [sic] have changed very little and Jesus whose life was saved only by being taken over the border into another country, would understand why many will observe this season in a spirit of pain." The same issue called 1976 a turning point for our land. I called on Prime Minister Vorster to withdraw riot police from the townships, release truthful casualty reports, provide counselling centres for the bereaved, offer a Christmas amnesty to all detained youths, allow them to sit their exams late, and set up a task force to deal with grievances. He should also sack cabinet ministers Treurnicht and MC Botha, with a mandate to their successors that "Bantu Education" be scrapped.[97]

Meanwhile our circulation had risen to 14 000 and our little church paper was quoted from time to time in the secular press in South Africa. I was excited when *Time* magazine and *The Washington Post* did the same.

After an ex-NYLTP delegate crashed through a sixth-floor window where he was being interrogated by the Security Police, *Dimension* took aim at deaths in detention: "… the detention system is barbaric because it is designed to break people. Any form of imprisonment which can ... lead to suicide is inhuman and abhorrent. If 'suicide' is a euphemism for something else then we are back in the law of the jungle." I said that if government leaders didn't like us calling South Africa a "police state" they could deal with it by the stroke of a pen, "simply by putting the power over people's lives back where it belongs, out in the open and under our judiciary".[98]

Just before the end of my time as editor a small news story in the 1977 Conference issue ignited the MCSA's biggest ever internal crisis. It carried the fairly harmless headline, *'No More Greetings'*,[99] but it resulted in Transkeian President Chief Minister Kaiser Matanzima declaring the Methodist Church of Southern Africa an 'undesirable organisation' and banning it from his Bantustan. The problem was an old MCSA tradition of sending a greeting to the head of state whenever the Conference convened. These greetings had become more acerbic as our relationship with the apartheid state deteriorated and at the 1977 Conference the whole practice was debated and abandoned altogether. During the debate some delegates had warned that continuing the practice would necessitate sending a similar message to the President of the new Bantustan, the 'Republic of the Transkei', thus implying MCSA recognition of this apartheid creation. In the end no message was sent to either, but when Matanzima – himself a member of MCSA – read our story he was so incensed by what he saw as a personal snub from his own church that he set about making MCSA illegal in his new 'republic'. The Undesirable Organisations Act was duly passed through his ersatz parliament and MCSA served with notice to leave.

One might dismiss this action as the bizarre hubris of a tinpot ruler, but to the 200 000 Methodists in Transkei it was only too real. Matanzima proceeded to establish a puppet 'Methodist Church of Transkei' led by close friend of the President, Reverend De Waal Mahlasela, and other opportunistic clergy, some of whom MCSA had disciplined in the past. Others were simply bullied, yielding to the intimidating pressure Matanzima and his police could exert. Seventeen brave ministers defied him and some of them were escorted at night to the Transkei border and 'deported'. MCSA President Abel Hendricks warned that the new church "created by pressure and action of the political state" had no chance of being recognised by world Methodism[100] – and it never was. The whole affair, however, brought a tragic disruption in a region where – because of more than 100 years of faithful witness – the majority of Christians were Methodists. This was not the kind of impact I had planned for my last but one issue of *Dimension* – but it made one heck of a story.

It took a military coup led by General Bantu Holomisa to restore MCSA to its traditional place in the Transkei. I was told that it didn't take the new ruler long. Apparently he asked: "Why was the MCSA banned?" and when no satisfactory answer came, said "Well, that was wrong" – and unbanned the church.[101] Ten years of exile from the region ended and rank and file members who had never lost their loyalty to their mother church brought their MCSA banners out of hiding and celebrated.

I had carried *Dimension* with me from Cape Town's District Six to Braamfontein and then, in 1976, on to Central Methodist Church, Johannesburg. I'd had eight years of working impossible hours and was now deputy to our District Bishop and a Vice-President of SACC. I was finding it difficult to report impartially on events that I was increasingly helping to shape.

It was time to go.

Putting my last issue to bed was a bitter-sweet experience. In a farewell article I said editing *Dimension* had been like having a baby every month. "All the classic stages of pregnancy have been there," I wrote, "without having nine months to negotiate them … and there were always complications at delivery."[102] I talked about the file I kept labelled, 'The Good, the Bad and the Ugly', which carried some of the more memorable bouquets and stinkbombs directed at us over the years – some quite unprintable in a church newspaper. "We have been accused of being unwitting tools of the Communists, the Progressive Party at prayer, and other epithets, some with accompanying threats to the health of the editor," I recalled.[103]

The unredeemed racism of many white Methodists had shamed me. Desmond Tutu was fond of saying that "the only people you can't wake up are those pretending to be asleep", and MCSA had a large dose of them. Our letter pages consistently carried vituperative complaints about *Dimension*'s political bias and motives and one wondered what these people had been hearing from our pulpits over the years. But at least there was a forum where Methodists could speak and listen to each other. They never stopped criticising the paper, but surprising numbers of them did read it. Some apparently bought it for other purposes, as evidenced by one letter asking, "Has anybody ever told you that your paper is most uninteresting. I find nothing in it that I can read. I am enclosing my subs all the same."[104]

Looking back at the monthly late-hour stints that got *Dimension* published, it was a miracle that we stayed clear of any major bloopers, but one typo raised a few eyebrows: we had Rupert Stoutt, the famous choirmaster of Joburg's Central Methodist Church stating with conviction that "the standard of sinning [in his choir] has been made possible by the dedicated sacrificial service of hosts of past and present choristers."[105]

The big argument of course was always about *Dimension*'s editorial stance. Although political content seldom reached more than 15% of each issue, we were told repeatedly that without it we would have won many more readers. That is surely true, but I was clear that we couldn't worship God and our circulation figures at the same time. I had no regrets and no repentance about *Dimension*'s unequivocal resistance to the philosophy and expression of apartheid and all its evil bedfellows. "Once allow this indefensible nostrum to find a place in your thinking," I wrote, "and all else becomes tainted with it … racism and the whole security system by which it is enforced, stinks in the nostrils of God and South Africa will never be clean until it becomes a forgotten memory."[106] As if to underline this conviction, my farewell article appeared alongside another story, a list of 44 names, headlined *Requiem: They Died in Custody*.[107]

To the oft-made charge that *Dimension* was not 'spiritual' enough, I replied that being spiritual was to illuminate everyday reality with the mind of Christ. That is what the Incarnation was all about; it was when we allowed our humanness to be touched by Christ's divinity that we were given a new citizenship by which all others had to be judged.[108] The Good News of Jesus will always come as bad news to the doers of evil, but to others it offers the breath of new life. As one editorial had indicated, "The glorious mission of the church is to bring people out of the limbo that lies between Good Friday and Easter morning, telling the joyful truth that humanity's verdict [death] has been overshadowed by God's."

The MCSA Conference has no system to honour its servants, apparently trusting such rewards to heaven, but occasionally it places a 'Special Resolution' in its minutes. After I presented *Dimension*'s report for the last time such a resolution was carried by standing vote. Among other things, it noted my "pioneering work in establishing a very high standard of Christian journalism", and the Conference gave thanks to God "for the pen of Peter Storey".[109]

What amateur journo could ask for more?

15

Young Church

We arrived in Joburg on a hot Saturday in January 1972, having driven the 1 600 km from Cape Town through the night. The welcoming committee got to see us at our worst: two travel-worn parents with four noisy boys aged 10, 8, 5 and 4 released at last from captivity, shouting excitedly as they explored their new home. The two-storey manse at 120 De Korte Street stood in the heart of Braamfontein with the old Clifton Methodist Church and its crooked spire next door. Both were marked for demolition because my predecessor, Reverend Jack Cook, had done a deal with developers in which they got our land in exchange for a brand new church complex in Rissik Street just below the new Civic Centre. A tall cylindrical apartment block was already rising in our back yard and we were told that the boys would need hard hats to play out there.[110] The move to Clifton Church was part of a deal too; my Cape Town Bishop wanted Jack Cook for the Metropolitan Church in Greenmarket Square and his Johannesburg counterpart agreed, provided he could have me. I had no objection to the swop because it rescued me from being sent to the Methodist Publishing House and because anyone excited about urban ministry would welcome the chance to engage with Southern Africa's largest, most dynamic city. Elizabeth struggled at first with the idea of living in Joburg with its thin air, red soil and dusty mine-dumps, but we ended up spending 25 fruitful years there, during which she built a significant career and made three happy homes.

After the excitement of the day we got the boys down and collapsed into bed ourselves, only to be startled awake next morning by what sounded like a giant gong booming in our heads. Leaping out of bed, I discovered that the Dutch Reformed Church over the road was tolling its mighty bell, announcing Sunday worship. When it finally fell silent I went searching for a shower and located it oddly positioned on the back stoep. I was luxuriating under the stream of warm water when the door opened and an elderly lady in black stood before me, wide-eyed. I grabbed for a towel and missed, but the second attempt covered what I thought was important. I should have remembered the Oxford don in a similar predicament who covered his face instead, explaining later that he prided himself in being better known for his face than his genitals. Then I said the only thing that came to mind: "Good morning!" Without a word my visitor retreated and closed the door. I was not to know that the addition on the back stoep of our home also provided the only toilet for people coming to the old church next door. Nor was it the end of the story. A few days later when being introduced to the church women's group, I found myself face to … well … face once more. I shook her hand and decided to brazen it out: "I believe we've met before," I said cheerfully. To her credit she looked me straight in the eye: "Nice to meet you too, Reverend," she replied. Three years later she died and, sitting next to the undertaker on our way to Westpark Cemetery, I recounted how we had first met. I'm not sure what other motorists thought seeing a hearse with two gents laughing hysterically up front of the coffin.

Clifton was the oldest church building still in use in Johannesburg but its congregation was probably the youngest. Jack Cook had done a sterling job as Chaplain to Wits University and JCE – the Johannesburg College of Education – as well as the nearby Nurses' College and Johannesburg Hospital. I inherited these chaplaincies and the vital young students who went with them. Their youthfulness was a tonic, although I struggled with inevitable comparisons between these privileged white youngsters and those whom I had left in District Six.

I was still working out how to respond to the very different challenges of inner-city Johannesburg when another 'Jane Abrahams' came into our lives, appearing on our doorstep with some welcome cookies. It was a serendipitous encounter. Like Jane, 23-year-old Helen Muller had just qualified as a teacher but was now leaning toward psychology. She was a highly motivated young Methodist with a grasp of student issues and a passion for developmental work with young children. I soon discovered that she was one of those many-gifted people able to turn their hand to almost any task. She was also something of an organising genius and to cap it all was excited about the role *Dimension* could play in church and nation. I was enormously pleased when she agreed to put her psychology studies on one side for a while to work on *Dimension* and help prepare the congregation for the new mission we were shaping.

Two further events helped move us in a new direction: the first was a training weekend in the Magaliesberg and the second a cry of need right on our doorstep. Most members felt that their church was 'doing fine, thank you,' and wondered why new training was needed. In a way it was, but a simple experiment made them think again. I sent someone armed with a tape-recorder out into the busy streets around us, stopping passers-by with two simple questions: "What do you know about Clifton Methodist Church and what do you think of it?" Members were surprised to discover that hardly anyone interviewed was aware that they existed – such was the impact they were making on our immediate surrounds. At the training I shared the priorities that should drive our approach to city ministry. Essentially, we would focus on four: to *tell* the story of God's love affair with the world, *teach* its implications for every aspect of our lives – personal and public, *demonstrate the meaning of true community* in our life together, and *serve* Jesus in the suffering, pain, oppression and need of "the least of his sisters and brothers"[111] in the city. If we could be faithful to these priorities, we would be doing all God required. These were not my ideas, of course, they come straight out of the New Testament; but many congregations had lost sight of them.[112] We also looked at how a congregation could learn to discern 'calls' from God. If a conviction began to speak inside any of us, we should be free to bring it to the community for rigorous testing. If we discerned together that it was a ministry God was calling us to take on – and provided a small group was prepared to 'own' it – then we would recognise it and ensure that it was resourced.[113]

Following hard on the training weekend a JCE graduate named Les Lageson came to see me. At our weekly School for Christian Living, she had raised her concern about the number of 'latchkey children' in the local primary school where she was teaching. These small kids came to school with keys hung around their necks so that they could make their way home through the teeming streets of Hillbrow each afternoon, to wait alone in some high-rise flat until a parent returned from work. "I can't get these children off my heart," said Les. "I wonder if we are being called to care for them?" This was exactly the kind of call I had been talking about so I put Les together with Helen and started the discernment process with a series of tough practical questions which they would need to work through. A second test would be whether, on hearing Les speak of her call, others would feel themselves called – not pressured – into it. Sure enough, as Les 'sounded her call' in church a small group responded and the vision of Careways Children's Centre was born.

Under Helen's direction, with a small staff and 30 volunteers, Careways opened on 1 May 1973. Every weekday 26 children between six and ten years began to make our premises their after-school home until parents fetched them around 5.30 pm. Incredibly, Careways was the first specialised after-school care centre we knew of anywhere in South Africa. More than that, we were pioneering a new kind of children's community. "Not a homework centre, nor a Sunday School, nor a recreation centre," Helen told journalist Christine Thuillier. "Careways is a programme designed to provide opportunities and experiences which will enable these children to grow into 'whole' happy people." I used to be astounded when dropping in to 'Council', for instance, to see the elected 'Mayor' – all of nine years old – mediating a conflict between two younger kids with helpful suggestions from the rest of them, and adult staff gently steering things with minimal intervention. Listening in on 'Thinking Day', I was again often touched by the sheer wisdom and inner strength of these children, many of whom were living in challenging circumstances. I marvelled at the infectious sense of love and life that Helen and her team evoked each day. At first children were walked from the local Roseneath Primary School but the principal was so impressed by the change in their lives that he soon lent us the school's minibus to ferry more of them. The numbers doubled and Careways touched about 100 parents, who attended monthly Family Evenings with growing enthusiasm, supporting the centre and – more importantly – each other. Careways became officially registered for training Wits social work and JCE students, many of whom spoke about it as a life-changing placement. Soon other churches were inviting our team to share the Careways story and after-school centres began to spread. As I contemplated the widening impact of obedience to just one 'call', I began to understand Jesus' reference to a single mustard seed growing into a broad tree offering shelter to many birds.[114]

The university work at Wits drew me into an ecumenical group of Catholic, Anglican, Presbyterian and Methodist chaplains who shared an office on the campus. The Methodist Society (METHSOC) at Wits was strong, as were some of the other church-based groups. The political climate required some unusual activities for student chaplains. In February 1973 we led services of protest on the Wits campus following the banning of black and white student leaders. I spoke of a South Africa "riddled with the idolatry of race, power and nation", and of the need to be confident that truth, right and justice would prevail. When open warfare broke out between protesting students and the police I found myself with others trying to act as a buffer between them and to lower the temperature of the confrontation. We reckoned ourselves successful if students got home without bruised heads. Our church, being fairly close by, became a sanctuary for some of those who needed to go into hiding.

Word spread through students and Careways volunteers that the church up the road had something different to offer and was eager to engage with their concerns. When we moved into the brand new sanctuary in Rissik Street in June 1973, it was virtually full house from the start. The newly named Civic Centre Methodist Church (CCMC)[115] included a coffee bar and lounge and offered hospitable spaces for building community. In the afternoons Careways kids thronged most of the building, while the evenings saw students and others dropping in for coffee and a chat, plus the weekly School for Christian Living programme. An annual Academic Service sealed our close relationship with the surrounding campuses. The work was fulfilling and joyful.

Three months into 1972, a stranger in his 60s had come into my office with a surprise request: he had been married in the old church and as a sign of gratitude for a "specially blessed life" he wanted to donate a stained-glass window for the new sanctuary rising in Rissik Street. My response was careful. First, he needed to see the sanctuary: because it was designed for one ten-foot high window running its entire length, the cost would be enormous. Second, whoever the artist, we would need veto power over the design. Third – and I wasn't sure how he would take this – whatever the cost, I felt he would need to double it so we could use the balance for serving the poor. I quoted the ancient saying: "If you have two loaves of bread, sell one and buy a hyacinth for your soul,"[116] suggesting that the reverse was equally true: for every gift of beauty to God and for our souls, we needed to gift those who had nothing and whose stomachs were empty. To my joy he saw the point immediately and agreed, then added a condition of his own: the stained-glass artist would need to be his son. Oh Lord!

I thought. That could be a deal-breaker! But I needn't have worried. When I met with his remarkable 24-year-old son – today the widely known artist Paul Blomkamp – we warmed to each other immediately. We spoke about God's commitment to the concrete world in which we live, about how the story of humankind may have begun in a garden but Jesus' battle with evil was fought in a city, and how the Bible ends with God reclaiming the city as a place of justice and peace. I left Paul to meditate over a hymn by Frank Mason North, *Where cross the crowded ways of life, where sound the cries of race and clan, above the noise of selfish strife, we hear thy voice, O Son of Man ...*[117]

Soon he was back with a design for *Christ in the City* – it still hangs in my study. Dominated by a rich but sombre blue it spans the story of humanity's pretentious Babylons, trapped in the serpentine coils of evil and lost in conflict and gloom. Then, in a flood of red and gold that can only be described as 'glorious' it has God's grace breaking into our world, not in triumph, but in love and service. The central focus is Christ crucified at the crossroads of the city, releasing new life into the world and leading to the beginnings of a new community. It was a breathtaking vision. In the months that followed I watched the window take shape, praying that its theme would always remind us that God's concern was more about bringing heaven's *shalom* to this world than getting souls to heaven. And yes, Paul's dad honoured his promise to fund the needs we struggled with on the city streets; all I had to do was lift the phone and his generosity did the rest. The first wedding in the new sanctuary was appropriately Paul Blomkamp's. It was a diamond morning when I married him to his sweetheart, with brilliant sunlight scattered into myriad colours by Paul's magnificent window and softly filtering down on the joyful couple. We needed nothing else to adorn the occasion.

Soon after our opening, the Group Areas Act struck again, this time taking aim at black congregations in the city. The Braamfontein Methodist Church not far from the university and led by Reverend

Mahlabegoane, was told it had to shut down. Sad as this was, it offered an opportunity to address the historic separation of white and black Methodist congregations. We invited his members to make CCMC their home, fully sharing the new facilities. The venerable Reverend Ezekiel Mahabane, sometime ANC luminary and President of the SA Institute of Race Relations joined Mahlabegoane in leading the whole congregation in a march up De Korte Street and into our new Sanctuary.[118]

Our usual services were beginning to integrate too. A handful of black worshippers were joining us, especially in the mornings. An incident reminded me just how deeply rooted racism was in some whites. I was called to a Braamfontein flat where an older Afrikaans couple lived. He was in the last stages of emphysema and I was able to journey with him through the days of his dying and conduct his funeral. Their past links had been with the Dutch Reformed Church, but his widow began to worship at CCMC and seemed to find sustenance from our community. Then one Sunday, she was sitting alone in a pew when a group of black latecomers moved in beside her. As more arrived she finally found herself shunted up against the side wall, for the first time in such close proximity to people of colour. I could see that she was distressed and at the close of the service, instead of shaking my hand she rushed past me in tears. When I visited her she upbraided me for permitting what had happened; black people were not supposed to sit with whites. "Find your Bible," I said. "I think it's time for some Bible study." And for the next hour or so we went on a journey through the Scriptures, beginning with the Genesis story where God creates all living creatures "according to their kind" – all except for humans, who are all made instead in one image: "the image of God". Then all the way through Peter's discovery that "God has no favourites", to Paul's great statement that in Christ there is "no such thing as Jew and Greek, slave and freeman, male and female".[119] For a long time my listener was silent, then in Afrikaans she said angrily,

"I went to church most of my life and this is the first time I hear these things. Why did my dominee not tell me?" Another long pause before she said quietly, "*Dis a hoë hek, maar as dit in die Bybel is, sal ek moet leer om daar oor te spring.*" (It's a tall gate but if it's in the Bible, I'll have to learn to jump over it.) The encounter inspired me to resurrect the My Brother and Me courses that had been so effective in District Six. One of them was to play a significant role in events leading up to the 1976 youth uprising in Soweto, but that lay in the future.

Further ministries were launched out of CCMC: HR officer Michelle Muller opened a typing college for black women in spite of being told that "no one would employ blacks", and banks refusing to do so on the grounds that their customers "wouldn't accept them". She nevertheless was able to place each of her graduates into employment, breaking yet another taboo. By 1975 we were also deeply involved with setting up Hillbrow House, an ecumenical ministry to lonely elderly people living in the teeming flatland.

At the end of 1974 the unexpected happened. I had been looking forward to a lengthy stay at CCMC when a group of lay leaders from the Central Methodist Church downtown requested a meeting. When they asked if I would consider moving to Central at the beginning of 1976 I swallowed hard. At one level the question was a no-brainer: CMC was the most influential Methodist pulpit in the land, known far beyond Methodist circles for famous preachers like William Meara and Dr JB Webb, as well as its popular radio broadcasts and magnificent choir. It also had a special emotional significance for me because in the 1920s my dad, as a young engineering apprentice, had been converted in that very congregation while listening to the preaching of William Meara, and had become Central's first candidate for the ministry. For someone only 36 years old it would be an astounding appointment.

On the other hand, I knew the current CMC well because our CCMC was in the same Circuit. Reverend Stanley Pitts, the minister there at the time, was also my Superintendent as well as Bishop of what was then called the South-Western Transvaal District. Conservative in many ways, he was a person of great integrity and I enjoyed working under him, but his congregation carried an even more conservative reputation. All white, it boasted having given the city a number of mayors over the decades and had a distinctly 'United Party'[120] flavour, with many World War II veterans and British immigrants among its members. Unlike the days of the old Methodist Central Hall, which had focused strongly on inner-city needs and the poor, the congregation had changed its name to the more dignified Central Methodist Church and now occupied a new cathedral-like sanctuary. My concern was its 'suburban' character. I had preached there on occasion and sensed that its key people were not from the inner city; nor were its programmes much different than those one would find in any white suburban church, focusing more on the needs of its commuting suburban worshippers than on the city itself.

So I thanked my visitors sincerely, but in fairness to them I needed to be up front with my thoughts. If I came, I would want to turn the church in at least three new directions, none of which would be easy for the congregation. "My first priority would be to work toward integrating Central," I said. The nation needed working models of God's future for our land, of blacks and whites finding one another. I had come to the conclusion that one couldn't preach the Gospel with integrity in South Africa to a segregated congregation. If they were unhappy with that, they should not invite me. Then there was the need to turn the congregation away from itself and toward the needs of the city. This would mean profound changes – a whole new set of priorities – in the life of the church. I paused to check their reaction, but Ken Roberts, the senior amongst them and a doughty WWII veteran, indicated I should continue. "I believe passionately in the power of preaching," I said, "and I respect the CMC pulpit enormously, but I must preach the whole Gospel, both personal and public. You will find me to be a faithful evangelist but I can never be silent about apartheid and what's going on in our country. I would use the Central pulpit to engage injustice, and you must know that will not always be comfortable."

There was a long silence as the four grey-haired men glanced at each other. Then Ken spoke up: "Thank you for being so straight with us. Can we let you know in a week?" And we parted.

A week later the formal invitation arrived.

16

Spreading Wings

Looking back at those first four years in Johannesburg, they were a time when I began to spread my wings. Far from a quiet life to edit *Dimension*, they exposed me to wider worlds of ministry and opportunity and things were soon every bit as pressured as they had been in District Six.

As chaplain to the hospitals I met some remarkable luminaries of the healing professions, including the famous Dr Chris Barnard, human geneticist Professor Trefor Jenkins, and palaeoanthropologist Professor Philip Tobias. Tobias was small in stature but a moral giant. I admired his steadfast public opposition to apartheid but saw another side of him when he asked me to preside over the annual dedication of cadavers at the medical school. He wanted his anatomy students to begin their first dissections with dignity and reverence. It was an eerie scene: the large dissecting room and the rows of covered corpses on tables with white-coated students – some clearly nervous of what lay ahead – standing by them; then the simple service in which I reminded them that each of the bodies they would carve into was once a living, breathing father or mother, daughter or son, with hopes and loves and fears – a human being of infinite worth to God. Hopefully it helped them approach their coming task with humility.

Trefor Jenkins was a congregation member and good friend. He was concerned that apart from one hour-long lecture, medical students were receiving no training in ethics. I found myself drafted into the medical school to assist and am still rather chuffed that a paper of mine, Ethical Implications of Genetic Practice, made it into the *South African Medical Journal*.[121] I also appeared with Professor

Chris Barnard and the senior Matron of Nursing on a panel about 'Communicating with the Dying Patient' and watched her put the great surgeon firmly in his place. My contribution had been about relationship. "The word 'patient' should be replaced by 'person'," I said. "Your 'dying patient' is first and foremost a *person* to love." I called for interdisciplinary teams, including a suitable trained chaplain, to ensure fully rounded care. To the 200 doctors present I suggested that they might have problems of avoidance because death bruised medical pride: "After all, it's rather humbling that in spite of all your efforts the mortality rate of the human race is still exactly 100%." Barnard took issue with me in a haughty response punctuated by long medical words. I wanted to remind the heart transplant pioneer that it was "all about heart", but before I could reply the matron did my work for me: "That is all very impressive, Prof Barnard," she said, "but you know as well as I do that when the end comes, you doctors tend to walk away and we nurses are left to hold the dying person's hand."[122]

In the mid-70s I had my first experience of the body that was to play a pivotal role in my life. The MCSA asked me to attend the National Conference of the South African Council of Churches. It was my first exposure to national-level ecumenical relations. Here were the leaders of the major Christian denominations of Southern Africa worshipping and consulting together and reminding me very importantly that God was not a Methodist. Great church denominations were free to rise above parish-pump concerns and address the larger issues shaping people's lives in the nation. I recall very little else from that first time, except that the young General Secretary, John Rees, who I knew through the MCSA's Renewal Commission, was determined to inject an entirely new activism into what had been something of an ecclesiastical talk-shop. The SACC churches were beginning to strengthen their opposition to the apartheid regime. John was to become my close friend and spiritual companion and our destinies would be entwined – for better and for worse – until his death.[123]

March 1973 saw a brave attempt by Rees on one hand, and Michael Cassidy of African Enterprise[124] on the other, to bridge the gulf between the more liberal SACC churches and the conservative-evangelicals and Pentecostals, who tended to eschew any engagement with political issues. They convened a Congress on Mission and Evangelism in the Athlone Park Hotel in Durban. Getting the 700 delegates of all races under one roof was a miracle in itself, requiring agonising negotiations with multiple government departments, every one of which initially refused permission.[125] For many blacks and whites it was a 'first' to share rooms and other facilities. It was certainly the first time any South African hotel had accommodated black and white South Africans together. At a personal level many bridges were built, and the experience of togetherness was initially both euphoric and surreal, but, as I wrote later in *Dimension*, "every single session ... was reminded ... of the great divide which wounds the body politic and the body of Christ in our land,"[126] and too many whites seemed tone-deaf to black concerns. Ultimately, frustrated black delegates shocked the rest by demanding a separate session to caucus. When they rejoined us they offered a number of critiques of the congress and then "spoke in love" to the white Christians: "For us to leave here with just words of repentance will be futility ... you must do something to lift the foot on our necks."[127]

My contribution was a paper on *The Strategic Importance of the City*, hammering home my conviction that the battle lines for the Christian faith ran through the great cities, not the sleepy suburbs of the world. "The city is the focus of population, political power and economic strength ... it is in the cities that the prototypes of our future culture are designed and tested," I said. After much more about serving the city, I declared that the one great, overriding challenge from God in our time and place was that of racial reconciliation. "Any evangelism which ignores the gaping, bleeding wound of racism is preaching in a cuckoo-land of unreality. Any message or any agent offering no healing for this wound is simply not speaking to the South

African situation."[128] This last sentence was not an accident: I was speaking just a day or so before Billy Graham was to make his first appearance in South Africa. With many others I had questioned the wisdom of inviting him to the congress – we feared that the hullabaloo around his coming would distract from the real issues that needed thrashing out between Christians of different stripes. John Rees confided to me that agreeing to a Billy Graham rally was the price paid to get conservative-evangelicals on board for the congress. Now that he was coming and would preach to a massive rally in King's Park Stadium on the Sunday, a small group of us determined to engage him about our main concern.

When the great man arrived, there was hullabaloo indeed, but we managed to get him alone late on the Friday or Saturday evening. I have to admit that we were fairly blunt: "Dr Graham, we are here to tell you that unless you denounce apartheid on Sunday you will be harming the Gospel and it would be better if you went home now." We knew that Graham had preached in countries with unpleasant human rights records and always refused to comment on these issues. "Maybe the Christians there asked you to be silent," we said, "but we are asking you to speak out, otherwise your silence will shatter the hopes of black South Africans and give encouragement to an evil system." Billy was clearly taken aback but he listened courteously and then spent some time explaining why he felt called to preach only the "simple Gospel of salvation". He assured us that among the people who had been converted at his rallies there were those who later did see the need to work for human rights and justice. "Then why not tell people up front?" we countered. "On Sunday you will be inviting people to confess their sin. Why not declare that in this land the most widespread sin to confess is prejudice – that you can't follow Jesus and hate your neighbour?" Our discussion went on for a while and Billy was gracious to the end. He said he would think and pray about our words.

On the Sunday, facing a multi-racial crowd of 45 000 people, Billy preached one of his standard "simple Gospel" sermons to great effect, but with one difference. For the first time ever, he crossed his self-imposed line and made a cautious and oblique reference to our nation's original sin: "If we don't become brothers – and become brothers fast – we will destroy ourselves in a worldwide racial conflagration." He went on hastily to diffuse what might be seen as an attack on South Africans alone: "This is not just a South African problem, this is a world-wide problem ... the problem is deeper than the law. The problem is in the human heart. We all need a new heart."[129] As hundreds of people streamed forward to make their commitments, I breathed a not very happy prayer to God. This man who back in North Carolina still opposed interracial marriages had at least said something, but I couldn't help comparing his timidity with the forthright challenge to apartheid Alan Walker had brought us a full ten years before. People in power, no matter how evil, had little to fear from Billy Graham.

I still had strong links with the Central Methodist Mission in Sydney and late in 1973 spent some weeks as guest preacher during Alan Walker's sabbatical. It was a privilege to step into my mentor's shoes and I had joyful reunions with friends Elizabeth and I had made in 64 and 65. The big surprise, however, was when CMM's two lay leaders asked me to think about succeeding Walker "if and when he might move on". Being thus considered was immensely affirming but disconcerting. I said that if the "when" happened and they still felt this way, they should tell me. Meanwhile I tried to put it out of my mind.

I had helped initiate the first five Life Line centres in South Africa. After that the network began to widen on its own by a kind of osmosis. The world movement also grew and I addressed international conferences in Chicago, Berlin, Los Angeles and Taipei, never wearying of speaking about the unique way Life Line brought together the ready accessibility of the telephone, the trained lay counsellor, and the intimacy of an anonymous telephone conversation.[130] Thousands of calls across the world were proving that this combination was "an idea whose time had come".

Overseeing the growth of the Southern African umbrella body was not all plain sailing. There were pressures from the state around our ignoring of apartheid's racial strictures and inner tensions about the movement's Christian roots. On the day we opened our first centre in Cape Town the government Social Welfare Department threatened to close us down unless we agreed to use only "professionals" and serve "persons of the white race group only", absurdities we flatly refused to go along with. Conflict with them continued for years. The 'Christian basis' got us into trouble from both secularists and religious extremists. Life Line was never about pushing faith or proselytising on the telephones – our counsellors were trained along Rogerian lines[131] to be strictly non-directive – but we were unapologetic about our roots and argued that when it came to human healing, the insights of Jesus were as relevant as those of Freud or Skinner, Rogers or Frankl. In Australia Alan Walker leaned toward a more rigid interpretation of our basis than I did, but because of their immense respect for the social work of the Central Methodist Missions, Aussies of all stripes saw no problem with Life Line's church links. In South Africa things were different. From the get-go our Johannesburg centre wanted nothing of the movement's Christian roots.[132] Interestingly, the most strident opposition came, not from Jews or Muslims, but secularists eschewing any kind of spiritual emphasis. As Life Line International's sole Africa representative I needed to honour its declared Christian ethos but unlike Walker I believed we could do so while at the same time freely welcoming volunteers of any or no faith as long as they understood and respected where we came from. He was finally grudgingly persuaded of this position but it made no difference to secularists determined to work with one eye kept tightly closed. A Jewish counsellor in our Johannesburg centre, who I will call 'Sam', lost patience with them: "Life Line has never asked me to compromise my Jewish faith," he said. "Neither has Life Line ever implied that I have less to contribute than anyone else here. All it has asked of me is to take seriously the insights of this man Jesus, about life, people and relationships – things that can make me a better counsellor. I've learned from Carl Rogers and I've learned even more from Jesus." Then he went on: "My Scriptures talk about 'how the Gentiles rage'. I think some of you Gentiles are transferring your own doubt onto those of other faiths. I think I respect your Jesus more than you do."

I could not have said it better.

Years later 'Sam' came to see me. He was suffering from terminal cancer and would die soon. "I've never forgotten what I learned in Life Line," he told me. "I'd like you to pray with me." Then he smiled. "I'm still a Jew, of course, but anyone who could care as much as Jesus could be of help right now."

Looking back at the controversy, I wonder now why it was such a big deal. The largest and most admired aid organisation South Africa these days is called Gift of the Givers. It cares for anybody and welcomes support from everybody, yet it is unapologetically Muslim and inspired by the Q'uran. Nobody questions its effectiveness because of this.

At the other end of the spectrum the *Sunday Times* announced one day that an Afrikaans religious group in Bloemfontein was launching a Life Line centre open to "white evangelical Christians" only. With friends like that we didn't need enemies. I gave them short shrift, denying them the use of our name and we never heard of them again.

We ultimately achieved the birth of Life Line Southern Africa, affiliated to the movement's world-wide network of 24-hour telephone-counselling centres. After ten years of intensive commitment I felt my work was done. I was grateful to have played a part in bringing Alan Walker's vision of a 'mantle of safety' to the cities of my own country, but was increasingly uncomfortable about the – albeit unintentional – 'whiteness' of the movement. In the 60s and 70s the black community

Top left: The family in Brakpan: Valmai, age three, and myself, age one.

Top right: The Mission House at Kilnerton with the College Chapel on the hill.

Right: In the garden of the Pretoria manse in 1947: Valmai is eleven and I am nine.

Above: Mom and Dad outside Rosebank Church in Cape Town in 1957.

Top: Dad (*left*) protesting the "Church Clause" of the Native Laws Amendment Bill in Adderley Street in Cape Town in 1957.

Above left: Elizabeth and I on our wedding day in 1960.

Above right: Midshipman in the South Africa Navy in 1957.

Top: Young sweethearts at Betty's Bay in 1957.

Above left: With Jane Abrahams in District Six in 1966.

Above right: From left to right: James Leatt, Audrey Pieterse, Alec Gordon, Joan van Heerden, Jackie Hartze, Kathleen Edwards and myself in a staff meeting in the Carpenter's House.

Above: A protest meeting in 1970 against the District Six removals in the Buitenkant Street Methodist Church, which is now the District Six Museum.

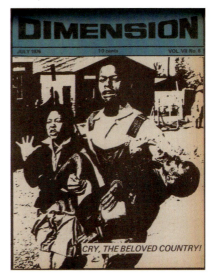

Above left: Handing the first issue of *Dimension* to the President of the Methodist Church, Rev Derrick Timm in 1970.

Above right: The banned July 1976 issue of *Dimension*: "Cry, the Beloved Country!".

Top: The "Plaque of Conscience": the first memorial anywhere in South Africa to the shame of apartheid, 21 November 1971.

Above: In the garden of the Civic Centre manse in Johannesburg with our boys: John, David, Christopher and Alan in 1973.

Left: The new Civic Centre Methodist Church in Rissik Street, Braamfontein, in 1974.

Above: A 1976 painting of the Central Methodist Church (CMC), later to become the Central Methodist Mission (CMM), in downtown Joburg.

Top: With Lindi Myeza, CMC's social worker and the *Star* newspaper's "Woman of the Year" for her work after the June 16 uprising.

Above: Visiting drought-stricken Atamelang in the Western Transvaal in 1985.

Top left: A 1982 cartoon in *Beeld* lampooning Bishop Desmond Tutu and myself after our exposé visit to Namibia.

Top right: John Rees in conversation.

Right: Preaching in the burnt-out Shaw Memorial Church in Grahamstown, which was destroyed by fire two days after hosting the funeral of a riot victim in 1985. In the foreground is the Grahamstown District Bishop, George Irvine.

Below: The president with his people – outside CMM in 1985 with members of the *Amadodana* or Young Men's Guild and Women's Manyano. Alongside me is Rev Sizwe Mbabane.

Left: Riot police invade CMM in 1988: with Rev Frank Chikane and Dr Allan Boesak in the pulpit while an armed police captain attempts to halt my prayer.

Above: CMM's congregation in 1990: the new South Africa already happening.

Top: The CMM interior in 1997: a special service honouring Bishop Stanley Mogoba with the World Methodist Council Peace Prize.

Above: Elizabeth and I meet Winnie Mandela for the first time in the Brandfort house where she was exiled by the apartheid government. Kimberley and Bloemfontein District Bishop Jack Scholtz is on the right.

Top: Welcoming Bishop Desmond Tutu to the Methodist Church of Southern Africa conference in 1984 after his Nobel Peace Prize.

Above: "O God, you and your people have done a great thing today!" Leading the crowd in prayer from a roof opposite security headquarters at John Vorster Square. PICTURE: ANA PICTURES/*THE STAR*

Top: March of the 25 000 on 15 September 1989: approaching the security police headquarters in Johannesburg. The marshal in the foreground with the yellow bandana is our student activist son David.
PICTURE: ANA PICTURES/*THE STAR*

Above: Alfred Woodington hands in his AK-47 in the CMM chapel witnessed by interfaith leaders on Reconciliation Day, 1994.

Top: Conferring with Peace Accord monitors in Soweto during the first democratic election in 1994.

Above: Preaching at a United Methodist Conference in Ohio, USA, in 1992.

Top: The first Freedom Day, 27 April 1995: presenting a sculpture made from melted guns to President Nelson Mandela.

Above: The Seth Mokitimi Methodist Seminary campus in Pietermaritzburg nearing completion in 2010. PICTURE: STEVE MCCURROCH/WWW.AIRSERV.CO.ZA

Top: Distinguished Professor: with Elizabeth at Duke University in North Carolina.

Above: With sons: David, Alan, Christopher and John in 2006.

Top left: Elizabeth at 50 on Blouberg Strand.

Top right: Sailing *Flash*, my beloved 25ft Flamenca, off Simon's Town in 2018.
PICTURE: CHRIS STOREY

had extremely limited access to telephones, private or public,[133] so it was understandable that interest was mainly among whites. Walk-in Life Line centres were set up in some black townships, but with limited success. Life Line Southern Africa was by then in the capable hands of wise colleagues like Ray Light, George Irvine and Colin Andrews.[134] Elizabeth's brother Allan Hardie and his friend Noel Wood were other stalwarts. From around 1977 onward I found myself attending national conferences more as a guest than a participant. Like 'Sam' I was deeply grateful for what Life Line had given me but I had also felt every one of its labour pains and carried some bad bruises from its controversies. I hadn't done the job perfectly but Life Line was now alive and well in South Africa and it was time to stand back. At the 1989 conference of Life Line Southern Africa the movement honoured my founding role by naming me Honorary Life President. By 1996 there were 24 centres[135] in our region.

In 1996 another honour came that completed a precious circle for me. I was invited to deliver the Sir Alan Walker Lecture at the 30th Anniversary Conference of Life Line International. Appropriately, the venue was in Sydney, where it had all begun for me. I took the chance on an international stage to thank my mentor Alan Walker: "... I have never worked for a more stubborn and difficult boss," I said. "He needs to know that he has given me more grey hairs than any other, but he must also know today that I have learned more from him than any other."[136]

Ironically the subject was 'Counselling and Christian Faith', and after all the heavy weather around the issue back home I offered what I hoped was a sensitive yet unapologetic case for the role of *sensible* faith in the healing of human beings. "The fact is that we are spiritual beings and we will never escape our hunger for spiritual meaning," I said. Criticising the movement for conducting this debate "within a therapeutic comfort zone ...", I reminded them that there was a real world out there of "people and their pathologies ... also needing to be considered when wrestling with the relevance of faith". Recalling the arduous process of selecting the South African Truth and Reconciliation Commission, I said it was no accident at all that in the final choice prominent people of faith easily outnumbered all the others, with an archbishop as chairperson. "The nation placed the task of healing its wounds in the hands of those most familiar with the way God has sought to heal people through the ages." Life Line too, I said, lives by the spirit of God. "It does not ask of you some credal orthodoxy, but it asks that you come increasingly to love this powerful resource of God's Spirit upon which you sail into the future … it is there to bring life to your voyage."[137]

As I write, Life Line in Southern Africa is 50 years old. Since we answered the first call in Cape Town with the words, "This is Life Line. Can I help you?" thousands of lives have been saved and millions of South Africans helped and healed. More recently, however, the internet, smartphones and social media platforms have eclipsed the simple technology that we used so effectively 50 years ago. Everyone can talk to anyone now – simply by reaching into their pockets. Yet the longing for real human contact is arguably even more desperate and the cries of the lonely, depressed, alienated and soul-damaged as urgent as ever. The question is how and whether the movement can find new ways of penetrating and humanising this different world with the same innovation, courage and faith Alan Walker showed in the mid twentieth century.

The year 1975 saw the World Council of Churches hold its first Assembly on the African continent, in Nairobi. I was to be among the South African delegates but decided to go early to meet with Alan Walker about launching Life Line in Kenya. The WCC had negotiated with the Kenyan government to temporarily relax their ban on South Africans and my early arrival made me the first to test their hospitality. Arriving at Nairobi airport it appeared that the good news had not reached the immigration gate and I was held there until dark while the higher-ups decided my fate. A group of curious immigration officers gathered round me, pumping this white South African with questions about his homeland. It was all very friendly and I was finally released and made it to the motel where Walker was staying. This was but the beginning of my Kenyan saga, however. A couple of days later, we received a call from John Rees in Johannesburg. The Kenyans had reneged on their agreement: no South Africans would be allowed into the country after all and I needed to know that Kenyan police were looking for me.

Checking in at my WCC-allocated hotel would have meant immediate deportation so I decided to throw myself on the mercy of some trusted WCC friends and bunk down with them. My hope was to keep a low profile and stay at the Assembly as long as I could before being kicked out of the country. I found myself in a four-bed hotel room sleeping on the floor with borrowed bedding and a thin mattress they had managed to purloin from somewhere. There were only three companions when I went to bed but they said the other bed would be filled by a late arrival from the UK. I woke at about 4 am and in the half-light was mildly alarmed to see a ghostly white apparition on the other side of the room. Then I discerned that it was a person covering himself with a sheet while he knelt at prayer. Later, when I introduced myself and mentioned the fright he had given me, he let out a delighted chuckle and apologised without any sincerity at all: "I'm Desmond Tutu," he said, and we shook hands, beginning a friendship that remains sacred to this day. To its credit, the WCC, regularly vilified in South Africa as 'communist' and 'anti-South African', leaned very hard on the Kenyans. They threatened to abandon Nairobi and take their Assembly to London unless all delegates – including South Africans – were allowed into the country. After another couple of days I found I was 'legal' again and could joyfully welcome John Rees and the other South Africans when they arrived.

Two memories from Nairobi stand out for me. The first was meeting with a group of South African refugees who had been marooned in the Kenyan capital for some years, living in a limbo of poverty and rejection. They had left South Africa to become cadres in the ANC's armed wing but had fallen out with the organisation. Now unwanted in Nairobi, they couldn't return home for fear of prison. It was heartbreaking to hear their homesick questions about the Joburg skyline and receive into my hands pathetic letters to families. The second memory was the furore over Canon Burgess Carr's provocative and frankly absurd statement that Christ, by dying on the Cross, had "sanctified violence".[138] It would not be the last argument I would hear justifying "armed struggle" but it was certainly the most bizarre.

For some time, both in Cape Town and at CCMC, I had been broadcasting the occasional morning and evening devotional slots on radio. The SABC had already been co-opted by the state and we called the public broadcaster 'His Master's Voice', but I determined that I would continue until and unless they interfered with anything I said. Television went operational in South Africa on 5 January 1976 and two days later, by accident rather than design, the beautiful sanctuary at CCMC was the venue for the very first televised church service in South Africa. I was asked by a man named Cliff Saunders if the SABC could use our church to telecast the special 'prayers for the nation' called for by Prime Minister Vorster. The circumstances were very unclear, but there had been serious military encounters and loss of life involving South African and Angolan armies in the border area.[139] I didn't believe that prime ministers should be telling the church when to pray but I saw an opportunity and acceded on condition that the service went out in its entirety – no cuts at all. To my surprise Saunders, who went on become the SABC's most notorious apartheid propagandist, agreed. As TV cameras and endless cabling cluttered our sanctuary for the first time, I began by telling viewers that I would not allow the telecast to "serve any interests in conflict with the Christian Gospel" – that we could pray for those in danger but there was no evidence in the New Testament that God sanctioned armed might, nor that God had favourites: "God grant that we be saved from false patriotism this day."

I went on to pray for all in danger and for their families, whether friend or foe, and for the bereaved, and that "the horrors of war may drive us to seek more ardently for peace". Also that we may be saved from hate ... that we were commanded to love our enemies ... respecting people "of whatever race, nationality or ideology". We needed to acknowledge that "the use of arms would never bring permanent solutions to human crises – and that those who lived by the sword would die by the sword".

Then I prayed for South Africa: "Let us pray for that higher patriotism which, rather than being blind to all that is wrong in our land, will root it out ... to love South Africa in such a way that ... she may not only be defended, but changed – that all that is evil may perish from our nation and all that is true and just and right and loving and merciful may flourish."

There followed a time of penitence and the service was over. I have no idea how many viewers there were, but messages that flowed in affirmed my decision to go ahead. Most were appreciative and some came from parents whose sons had been mysteriously called up in October, and from whom they had heard nothing. A few were predictably hostile and racist, accusing me of putting the black enemy on the same level as "our boys on the border". For many years to come, until one Sunday when the SABC cut me off in mid-sermon, I trod the tightrope of trying to use this tainted medium to good purpose.

17

No Soft Landing

Whatever hopes I had of a soft landing at Central Methodist Church were to be dashed by June, but in the months before the storm broke I felt as if I was back in the 1950s. Every Sunday worship in the magnificent sanctuary began with Rupert Stoutt's choir singing, "*Drop Thy still dews of quietness, let all our striving cease …*"[140] which was all very well; I loved the hymn but it seemed out of touch with the energy of the city outside and the travails of a land edging toward upheaval. Most of the worshippers – decent people mainly in late middle age and above – commuted in from the white suburbs. Weekday organisations catered for their various fellowship needs but none were addressing the central question of our time: "What does it mean to follow Jesus in apartheid South Africa?" In fact, very few CMC members would have felt that *was* the central question. Nor were programmes engaging the city's needs. The old Methodist Central Hall had launched Johannesburg's first welfare organisation – a team of deaconesses[141] who visited the poor and needy – but that ministry had long been hollowed out and the Deaconess Society I inherited was just a fund. My staff – an associate minister, an office secretary approaching 80 years of age and four cleaners – was smaller than the team I had left in Braamfontein. CMC was like a giant ocean liner with no crew sailing serenely to nowhere in particular. Turning it around would require enormous effort, over the objections of most of the passengers.

One evening during my first week I slipped into the huge sanctuary[142] illuminated only by the light of the street lamps outside. The beautiful space with its 900 seats lent itself to awe. It was also deeply intimidating for one who was now expected to bring "a word from God" from its pulpit each week. I knelt at the altar and asked for insight and courage. Insight so that what I preached would always have the ring of truth, and courage that I would never be afraid to declare it. A preacher's greatest foe is fear and I sensed that a stern test was coming. Without a big dose of guts I would fail. But I also asked for love – something I wasn't very good at – because as I sought to move the people of this congregation in a direction they would not like, I would need to love them without expecting to be loved back. I knew it would be hard, but then I had what some would call a vision: in the gloom I looked up at the gallery and imagined my dad sitting there as an eager 24-year-old half a century before – not in this very building, of course, but its predecessor – listening to the great William Meara's preaching and being moved to offer his life to the ministry. I felt connection and a strong sense of continuity. The truth was that I was just part of a story God was writing. It had begun long before me and would continue long after I was gone. All God was asking from me was enough faithfulness to help write one chapter.

Another early insight also helped. Rather than mess unduly with the weekly rhythms that were dear to the congregation, I would go around them. The old could live on while the new was built and the test of relevance would ultimately decide what lasted and what would fade away. Thus liberated, I began to plan ahead. I wanted to involve the four Circuit congregations[143] in a common strategy, pooling our meagre staff resources and working as one. A number of training events to this end were held that year. Helen Muller became our first Circuit-wide appointment, and when immense state pressure forced Beyers Naudé's Christian Institute to shed personnel, this brought us our first black staffers. I was glad to offer positions to Lindi Myeza and Motlalepula Chabaku, two powerful women of great talent. Chabaku was not with us long before leaving for the United States[144] but Lindi stayed for six years and became what the deaconesses of old had once been. In those days most destitute people approaching CMC for help were white, and I enjoyed watching their faces when I referred them to "our social worker, Ms Myeza". It was Hobson's choice – either submit to being interviewed by a black person or go with your prejudices and get nothing. Lindi started Zulu and Black Culture classes and began to endear herself to the congregation. It was tough to be the only black person at worship, but she brought real pizazz to the task and opened the way for others. Tentatively, a handful of black worshippers began to appear.

Not all the clergy colleagues I started with were as persuaded as I was of the way ahead; my successor at CCMC was unhappy about my plans and he felt my leadership style to be high-handed compared to more laid-back superintendents in MCSA. I'm sure he was right, but I was in a hurry: if we were to have any impact on a rapidly changing Johannesburg we needed to move fast and move together. I understood when he chose to move on. Ultimately, the Johannesburg Central Methodist Mission (CMM), as the Circuit came to be named in 1986, would have an inclusive team of five ministers and 24 lay pastors and staff, excluding janitorial staff. I guess that all of them would at one or other time feel the sharp edge of my leadership style, but most seemed to handle it and remain excited to be part of the CMM enterprise. One associate minister – David Newby – recalled that I phoned him at 6 one morning to invite him to join the staff at CMM: "My acceptance ... ensured that the 6 am phone call would become a regular feature of my life for the next four years." Speaking of times of disagreement, he said that while I would argue [my] case persuasively, I would also "listen to the views of others and respond accordingly without it affecting my relationship with them in any way".[145] I know that many also learned that there was another, very different side to me in times of trouble. At my farewell they gave me a light-hearted A+ for 'Leadership of Staff', which was definitely over the top, but I happily took it.

All the while, clouds were gathering over Soweto. The apartheid regime's intransigence in forcing black school children to not only learn Afrikaans, but also accept the language of the oppressor as a medium of instruction, made confrontation inevitable. We also had our own intelligence: Helen and Lindi were preparing to launch two Thlokomelong ('place of caring') pre-school centres in Soweto, one in Zola and the other in Jabavu. In the early months of 1976 future staff were coming to CCMC for training and each time the news they brought was more disturbing.

With Helen and Lindi I had re-started the Brother and Me courses pioneered in District Six and around March 1976 Lindi invited some 40 youths from Soweto to join a similar number of whites for a six-week course. It followed a pattern similar to the earlier ones but this time the atmosphere was especially tense. The Soweto youths were uneasy, bringing an edge to their encounters with the generally older whites. We sometimes had to wait for them because of 'difficulties' leaving the township. Around the fourth week – when in the normal course of events we expected things to be at their most tense – one of them approached me with tears of angry frustration on his cheeks. "I'm going home," he said, "I won't tolerate that white guy's arrogance anymore." It took a while to settle him. I knew who he was talking about – a particularly loud and insensitive white minister had objected to what we taught about white privilege and prejudice. In small group discussion this youngster had stood up to him and been steamrollered into silence. I tried to counsel him, affirming his courage: "You've got under his skin," I said, "he's hearing stuff about himself he knows is true and he's never been stood up to by a black person before. His real bullying self is coming out." I told him that most of the whites were profoundly impacted; he and his friends were doing an amazing job. He finally stayed and at the end of the course his evaluation included the words, "When I came I wondered if I was a person. Now I know I am a person." His name was Tsietsi

Mashinini. A few weeks later he was to lead the uprising that changed the political landscape of South Africa.

On Sunday, 13 June, things were going to change drastically at CMC too. I had received a plea from John Rees at SACC whose staff were convinced that something horrible was about to unfold. "Would you hold a prayer service for them?" he asked. I readily agreed and that Sunday evening my congregation was shaken by the presence of serried ranks of black and white SACC staffers filling the front rows of the sanctuary. To add to their anxiety Mrs Winnie Mandela had arrived too.

I welcomed the SACC as "Christ's peacemakers", who had been drawn by God into the struggle for South Africa's soul. In my sermon that night I spoke about their need to stay centred: that in times of confusion and conflict, "it is only when we are touched by the eternal that we know what to do in the here and now …" For real peace South Africans needed first to face the ugly truth and then to live the alternative. Racism was rooted in the "fear that casts out love" and people needed to see in us examples of the difference – people who genuinely sought to live and work together. Then SACC workers could be sure of the promise God gave to Jeremiah, to fortify them, "*to stand fast against the whole land*".[146] It didn't matter if they never saw the results of their witness … it was enough that peacemakers were called God's sons and daughters[147] – and were therefore the brothers and sisters of Jesus.

Later, John Rees wrote on behalf of the SACC staff saying they were strengthened: "All have mentioned in one way or another that it was as though we were being prepared for the week ahead."[148] If Rees was appreciative, others were not: letters and calls from white members reminded me that CMC was a "traditionally white congregation", and that a "convicted terrorist's" wife should not have been welcomed. My warning during the sermon of a possible violent uprising because of "the violence that is breaking [people] now", was condemned as "stirring up violence".

NO SOFT LANDING

The morning of Wednesday, 16 June broke like any other. I had a full schedule of appointments and a funeral at 2.30 pm. During the morning rumours began to spread of a massive school strike in Soweto. Looking down on Pritchard Street from my third-floor office I saw people gathering in small, earnest, very segregated groups. The funeral was barely over when John Rees called. Could I come to Diakonia House[149] right away – children were being shot in Soweto. When I got there SACC President Reverend John Thorne and a couple of other executive members were huddling with field worker Tom Manthatha. He had just come from Orlando and described the stand-off between hundreds of scholars and a large police detachment, of flying stones and a volley of shots. Now, he said, schoolkids were scattering and police chasing them down. Orlando West had become a war-zone.

Two things happened in Rees's office while I was there: the first was a speaker-phone call to Prime Minister John Vorster. John Thorne asked him if he knew what was happening and he said he did. Thorne begged him to intervene by ordering a stop to police shooting. Vorster refused. "This was organised to sabotage my meeting with Dr Kissinger,"[150] he growled, and we looked at each other helplessly, wondering at the overweening hubris of politicians. What would kids in Soweto care about that? "This is on your heads," he said. "You people started this, so you can stop it." He was callous and the call pointless.

Then we heard that railway authorities had cancelled commuter trains between Joburg and Soweto, presumably fearing that restive youths might bring their uprising into the city. Rees, who had superintended sections of Soweto for many years before the SACC job, saw it very differently. He began calling every authority he could, warning that if worried parents working in the city were stopped from getting back to Soweto to see if their kids were safe, then indeed, the city *would* go up in flames. His wisdom prevailed and the trains began to run again. Nobody knows how many lives John saved that afternoon.

Later, Desmond Tutu, recently appointed the first black Dean of

St Mary's Cathedral, arrived at Diakonia. He had driven out to Soweto but seen nothing. "I hear that police are driving up and down the streets just shooting at youths," he said, and broke down in tears. "How can they do this? How can they just shoot kids?"

The days following were a blur of crisis meetings, emergency parents' committees and the setting up of the Asingeni Relief Fund for victims. It was not a week conducive to quiet reflection over what was happening. When Sunday came I mounted the CMC pulpit to look out on a half-empty church. Angered by last Sunday's service and frightened by the events of Wednesday and following, many members boycotted the service. I read Jeremiah's words, "*Would that my head were all water, my eyes a fountain of tears that I might weep day and night for my people's dead!*"[151] and began: "Last week I said that we had a choice between creating a real peace based on facing the truth – or having people rise up against the violence that is breaking them. Some of you protested that those words were too dramatic but now we see, God help us, that they were not strong enough. In the horrors that came just three days later, the choice was made ..." I spoke of our guests from the SACC, who now were "haggard, drawn and broken-hearted ... risking their lives to ... stand between their people and the police, pleading for an end to the violence of both ... Nobody cared enough until blood was shed and death came to visit." Whites believed apartheid propaganda that the line of racial separation helped "avoid friction" but instead it had become a battle line: "In war opposing armies wear different uniforms; apartheid has made our uniform the colour of our skin," I said. Yet there was still time to be "courageous with love". I told the story of the black Soweto minister's wife who had ignored skin colour, giving sanctuary to a terrified Afrikaans social worker who had run to the church for protection. "She incarnated our conviction that in Christ the dividing wall cannot stand ... while the ruins still smoulder we must reach out our hands and ask and receive forgiveness.

The blood has already been shed; we need not, we should not, we dare not shed each other's blood."

Things could never be the same at CMC after that. A war of attrition began between a section of the congregation and their new minister. It took various forms, none of them pleasant: there were the appointments with good, decent people who informed me regretfully that they could no longer remain at CMC because of "politics from the pulpit". Anonymous letters were less polite and other members simply slipped away to join suburban congregations. However, the only open rebellion was redeemed by farce: a rather tubby choir member (I can't resist mentioning that his day job was rat-catching) organised his male colleagues to stage a walkout the next time I mentioned apartheid. They didn't have to wait long. The large choir sat in steeply tiered seats immediately behind the pulpit and as I moved into my sermon I must have mentioned the forbidden word because the congregation seemed suddenly to be interested in what was happening behind me. Determined to ignore it, I ploughed on, but then some of the people in front of me burst out laughing and I had to look round. The walkout had apparently begun well: the rat-catcher and his fellow black-gowned choristers had trooped down the steep stairs on one side of the choir gallery. At the bottom there was a sharp turn to exit into the choir vestry and this is where rat-catcher came unstuck – or actually the opposite. As he swung round in appropriate high dudgeon toward the exit, his gown caught on the balustrade. He was pulled up short, cannoning backwards into the person following, who did the same. By the time I looked round we had a Keystone Cops tangle of arms and legs and a highly amused congregation. The protesters finally sorted themselves out and left and I made a lame comment about demonstrations needing as much rehearsal as choir singing, but the event had made another wound that would need attention.

CMC's response to the Soweto crisis was multi-faceted. The church building became a refuge for kids wanting to study and we offered extra classes there. Elizabeth and I opened our home to some traumatised Soweto youths, offering them a respite from the townships. On one occasion we had Tsietsi's many siblings enjoying the pool in the manse garden until Alan had to dive in to rescue one kid whose excitement exceeded his swimming abilities. By far the most critical work, however, was done by a youth group Lindi Myeza assembled to assist families who had lost young victims to police shooting or detention. The Phanani group, among them Becky, Oupa, Cyril and Linda – I remember their names because I thought them so brave – visited some 300 affected families and searched mortuaries looking for the bodies of missing schoolkids. One terse report of their work at the time lists 32 homes visited and makes grim reading: "White City, Jabavu: Young girl shot by police at Sekano-Ntoane High School, Mashabane Family: Jackie Mashabane died in detention, Makletha family, Klipspruit: 15-year-old school boy killed by police, Mlhele family: young man killed at the Zondi koppie on day of Mashabane funeral; Rasmeni family, Mofolo North: 21-year-old boy killed by police at graveyard, and so on. Two of the Phanani group were ultimately detained without trial for more than three months. Lindi tells how the group would come to her home after a heavy day for supper, debriefing and prayers. The 'Cyril' in the group was Cyril Ramaphosa,[152] whom she said was the theological conservative among them, not too keen on political discussion!

Late in 1976 Lindi herself was arrested and detained without trial. I was outraged and demanded to see Security Police General Johan Coetzee. I told him about Lindi's work and berated him for detaining an innocent person. Unmoved, Coetzee lectured me for some time on the "wiles of the communists", then, using his index finger, began to draw concentric circles on his desk. "We are going to stop this thing," he declared. "We arrested everyone in this circle, and it didn't stop. Then the next circle, then the next, and we'll go on until it stops." Then he looked at me with dead eyes. "And let me warn you, Reverend, that you're in one of my circles." I at least got to locate Lindi in the cells at Protea police station and got to see her briefly. In short order three SACC staff – Elizabeth's close friend Bernadette Mosala, Tom Manthatha and Barney Ngakane – were detained without trial. Barney was a beautiful person, a long-time activist now in his seventies. In the 60s he had spent five months in solitary confinement and then been banned. The SB knew him so well that they sent him a note 'inviting' him into detention and John Rees and I accompanied him to the tenth floor of Security Police headquarters where he handed himself over. He kept a little suitcase ready for such eventualities so he had no need to pack anything.

Elizabeth was working overtime with Soweto victims too. She had become John Rees's personal assistant in 1975 but took over as administrative officer when Bernadette was detained, interviewing bereaved families to aid them with burial money. Day after day she heard ghastly descriptions of desperate searches through various police mortuaries and the heart-wrenching moment of discovering a loved child's bullet-riddled corpse, often lying under a pile of others. It was traumatic work.

Security police were meanwhile combing the townships for the leaders of the uprising, especially Tsietsi. He sought help from the Methodist Youth Centre in Jabavu, where a courageous Reverend Dan Katane hid him. An informer told the police and they came looking for him, only to be met at the door of Dan's manse by a demure teenage girl dressed in a white shirt and black gym tunic – the standard school uniform of the day. She opened up for them and watched while they searched every inch of the centre and Dan's manse. Thus disguised, Tsietsi lived there for some time before going into exile in August 1976.

Unbelievably, Helen, Lindi and others were able to open the first Thlokomelong in Zola in August. How they did it in the midst of the mayhem throughout Soweto remains a God-mystery to me. Both centres were staffed by Careways-trained pre-school teachers. In a time and place where police killed more than 660 schoolchildren before the end of the year there was something crazily defiant about successfully birthing a pre-school centre whose aim was "To help children feel a sense of worth, become excited about life and the world around them, and come to know God as a loving Father."[153] The second centre was opened at the Methodist Youth Centre in September 1977. Early evidence showed kids who had passed through Thlokomelong doing "exceptionally well" in their first year at school.[154]

The reshaping of our work at Central had been interrupted but the reaction to my June preaching made it even more imperative to go ahead. My next step was to plan a weekly Academy for Christian Living which would be central to transformation. To act differently people need first to think differently. Churches without a strong formational tool soon have a 'balance of payments' deficit, becoming importers of how society thinks, instead of exporting transformative thought and action outward. People need a forum where they can drill down into the bedrock of Christian faith and practice and be helped to think and act like Jesus. The Academy took education seriously. People registered and paid per course. A mandatory plenary at 6 pm was followed by supper, then four electives: one focused on Biblical Studies, a second taught Theology, another addressed Public Issues and the fourth offered skills. The Academy drew on all ministers in the Circuit as well as guest lecturers. Desmond Tutu, who is by discipline an Old Testament scholar, was one of our early lecturers, as were Dr Beyers Naudé and radical Bible scholar Dr Wolfram Kistner from the SACC.

In the years following, between 60 and 120 people came each week to learn and grow. Some had been at CMC for decades and welcomed this new opportunity to deepen their lives. Others had been turned off traditional church but relished getting their teeth into a serious teaching programme. They may have represented a modest percentage of the total membership but it was the Academy graduates – old and new – who became the leaders to help transform CMC.

It was while on a Life Line trip to Taiwan and Australia in 1977 that the temptation came. I had joyful reunions with Life Line friends from my days in Sydney and preached in Alan Walker's pulpit on the Sunday. Next day I found myself at lunch with the executive of Sydney's CMM and the penny dropped. CMM treasurers Peter Tebbutt and Jim Pendlebury were keeping their word, and on the day I was to fly home, popped the question: would I follow Alan Walker when he moved on? The flight from Sydney to Johannesburg is a very long one and little else occupied my mind. It should have been a no-brainer, of course: Sydney's CMM was the most effective and exciting city church I knew of anywhere in the world. The offer represented the kind of challenge I had often dreamed of. When I shared the news with Elizabeth she too was excited. Our days in Australia had been deeply happy and she longed for our boys to be free of the shadow of military service in the apartheid military. Yet ... we decided not to rush it but to let the matter filter through our prayers for a while. Alan Walker's retirement was imminent but no date had been set yet. In the end we decided that it came down to a simple conviction: unless we sensed a clear and positive call, we would be going for reasons of security rather than vocation. If we did that, then the pastor who touched down in Sydney would not be the same person they had invited. On the flight I would have lost something irreplaceable and they would be welcoming a minister who had compromised his integrity. I wrote to Peter and Jim in those terms, declining the honour. Almost simultaneously I learned that on their parish council were people who felt strongly that Alan's successor should be an Australian and in the end an Australian preacher, Gordon Moyes, was appointed.

Other international invitations were to come, from the United States and New Zealand, but while there was regret, there was no more temptation. We had worked it through together and were at peace.

18

Broken Open Church

In the years following 1976 CMM was drawn ever more deeply into the maelstrom of South Africa's struggle. For me, that was inevitable for any church congregation seeking to follow Jesus, but at the time many accused us of being political activists rather than Christians trying to be faithful. The distinction is important. My dad used to say that all discipleship "begins in theology and ends in politics"; in other words Christian activism needs to rise primarily out of what we believe about God, and then be acted out where people live and love and hurt and suffer. In any case the notion that political activism was all we were about would be a distortion. We were first and foremost a community where people came to discover their identity as children of God and to find purpose for their lives. The trouble was, of course, that we lived in a land where not everyone was respected as a child of God.

For me, the moment of preaching lay at the heart of what ministry was about and far from thundering Sunday by Sunday about political issues, my passion was to offer people what Jesus called "life in all its fullness". I wanted everyone to know what a difference this Galilean carpenter could make to their lives, leaving them with a fresh vision of what he called the "Kingdom of God" – healed people in a healed world of right relationships – a world of joy and justice and peace.

Nothing was more fulfilling than journeying with my people through the 40 days of Lent each year and into Holy Week. The drama of the Passion never failed to transfix and transform us. On

Holy Thursday the Service of the Tenebrae[155] would unfold publicly under a great wooden cross in our foyer, doors wide open to the busy pedestrian mall. Afterward in the darkness some of us would carry that cross upstairs into the sanctuary, where it towered over the crowded worshippers on Good Friday morning. Then the fallible preacher would dare the impossible: attempt to capture the mystery of God's great act of redemption in limited human speech. And each year, as if independent of my poor efforts, the impossible happened: the message burst through its confines and touched individual hearers. Many of the most effective new members of our church family traced their conversion to a Good Friday Service of the Cross.

Yet to preach a message aimed only at personal transformation would have offered a truncated 'half-gospel'. Good Friday could not have happened without Palm Sunday, when Jesus rode unarmed and alone against a great city to denounce the dead hand of legalistic religion and confront the crushing power of Rome. Equally, Easter could not have happened without Good Friday, when the cost of taking on the 'powers' was there for all to see – in a corpse on a cross. The crucifixion was engineered by powerful vested interests just as much as by deformed human character; therefore holistic preaching had to engage both. The surprise of Easter morning is about God gloriously endorsing the 'wrong' person: instead of mighty rulers and pious priests having the last word, it was the broken, bloodied carpenter and his radical selflessness who heard God's "YES!" and continues to have earth-shaking implications for the high and mighty everywhere.

So, when accused of stepping into 'political territory' I would argue the very opposite – that I was defending *God's* territory against trespassing politicians. It was South Africa's racist regime and right-wing clergy, not this preacher, who were the interlopers. Two thousand years after Jesus they were playing the same deathly games as Pilate and the priests of Jerusalem, trampling on the dignity of God's "little people". It was important to tell them: "When you mess with people made in God's image, you mess with God," and to warn them that no matter what suffering might lie between, they would lose in the end. Thus these words preached in 1986:

"Let me say to Mr Botha,[156] 'Apartheid is doomed!' It has been condemned in the Councils of God, rejected by every nation on the planet and is no longer believed in by the people who gave it birth. Apartheid is the god that has failed ... let not one more sacred life be offered on its blood-stained altar ... Open the prison doors! Call the exiles home! Burn the population register with its pornographic classifications of God's children by the colour of their skin! Do it now, for as sure as God lives and Jesus is Lord, you will have to do it in the end."[157]

Again, this was not a case of looking for something 'political' to say; it was stating a *theological* truth. Botha was tramping on God's turf and needed to get off. Of course not everybody saw it that way, and some exploited the resentment many white members felt. In the late 70s the now-famous Rhema Bible Church was launched and set up shop for some time in a nearby cinema. Its charismatic pastor Ray McCauley[158] was studiously silent on apartheid but didn't hesitate to disseminate adverts inviting those "tired of politics in the pulpit" and of the World Council of Churches to join his church. It was unprincipled huckstering but it worked. Ray loved to boast of miracles in his church but I told him the most amazing miracle to me was how his Pentecostals could wave their hands in the air and hide their heads in the sand at one and the same time. His congregation grew and mine shrank but I took strength from the number of our members who were bearing the heat and burden of those days and working for change. Prof Trefor Jenkins was one. He and a couple of colleagues were waging an unpopular battle to expose the doctors who had permitted the torture that ultimately murdered Steve Biko. Trefor wrote, "At a time when so many South Africans were being intimidated by the oppressive apartheid system and were being ground into a submissive state of passivity, worshippers at Central were offered the Christian hope and were sustained by it."[159]

However, the best sermons are more often preached without words. We searched for a way to ensure that whatever the theme of a worship service, we would always remember people in detention and those suffering torture or other forms of apartheid oppression. So the Candle of Peace, Hope and Justice came to the CMC altar. It was a simple white candle surrounded by coils of barbed wire.[160] At every service we paused to recall some or other victims or situation, reminding ourselves that no matter how cruel the barbs, the light "shines on in the darkness and the darkness has never overcome it".[161] Then we would light the candle and sing the prayer for Africa:

God bless Africa
Guard her children,
Guide her leaders,
And give her peace.[162]

The idea soon spread until similar candles stood on hundreds of altars across South Africa. I was amazed at the power of this simple symbol. Telling its story at the World Methodist Conference in Nairobi in 1986, a beautiful thing happened: British Methodist Ann Bird said that when they got home she and her spouse Derek planned to light their own candle every week, to remember Elizabeth and me and the CMC community. Such acts of encouragement cannot be measured. They not only kept that promise for seven years, but every week we received a card sending solidarity and prayers, signed by everyone at their Sunday dinner table. One carried four simple lines by Indian liberation theologian Samuel Rayan – words that have lived as a mantra in my head ever since and inspired the title of this book:

> A candle-light is a protest at midnight,
> It is a non-conformist.
> It says to the darkness,
> 'I beg to differ.'

Central's radio broadcasts had always held a special place in South African life, and an early dilemma for me was whether to continue using the unashamedly propagandist SABC. A message from Nelson Mandela via a prison chaplain clinched it: he thanked me for the encouragement my broadcasts brought them on Robben Island[163] and I resolved to continue unless there was direct interference. It came in 1988 and was ostensibly about the candle. We had already clashed over a June 16 sermon called *God's Future for South Africa* in which I had claimed that we were "... infected with the diseases of racism and ethnic pride, worshipping a primitive tribalism that will destroy us all". It was time "to tell the people who propagate this kind of thing that they are a disgrace to humanity ..." The little red light in the pulpit suddenly went out and I was off the air. The SABC claimed it was a fault in their studio link but I didn't believe them. Now we had an open row. They took exception to our naming detainees and referring to "Apartheid oppression" during our candle-lighting. In a tense meeting they demanded that we exclude the candle from future broadcast services. With a straight face I informed them that it was part of the Methodist liturgy and could not be excised. Loyally, Methodist colleague Austen Massey nodded in support. Then one of the SABC moguls gave us a glimpse of absurdity. "Well then, Reverend," he said, "can you simply light it without saying anything?" I couldn't suppress a chuckle. The notion of 60 or more seconds of total silence in a radio broadcast brought to mind listeners all over the land scrambling to adjust their sets. These were *broadcast* experts?

Our fate was sealed, however. The SABC overlords admitted that the order to suppress me had come from 'above' – their 'above', not mine – and I was off the air for good it seemed. In January 1990 they changed their mind and CMC was invited back to the airwaves. We agreed provided that "any further attempts to interfere with Methodist worship, including that very important moment when we light our candle and pray for the situation in our country, would not be tolerated".[164] When we returned, the national situation didn't seem to me that much different, so in my comeback broadcast I preached the same sermon, beginning with: "As I was saying when I was so rudely interrupted …"

But that was far into the future.

Integrating the congregation was not simply a matter of inviting black people to worship. In theory all Methodist services had always been open, but fixed attitudes and long custom were powerful deterrents. It took enormous courage for the few early black worshippers to walk into our imposing sanctuary with its all-white choir and pews awash with white faces. We needed a strategy to earn black trust. Part of it lay, of course, in educating the whites, 200 of whom ultimately decided to leave rather than change. I only learned much later that when Reverend Philip Mvunyiswa – the first full-time black minister to join me – presided at his first CMC Communion Service, one white communicant deliberately threw the consecrated bread to the floor rather than eat what he had received from Philip's hands. Such were the early indignities some black persons endured.

The crucial step to integration began, quite appropriately, 'underground'. Deep in the basement next to our 500-seat assembly hall was a large empty lobby space flanked by a well-equipped kitchen. This seldom-used area had direct access to the foyer and street via a broad staircase and elevators. From early on I was impressed by its potential. Some people can visualise new concepts but most need concrete examples before they catch on. All my talk about a different kind of church – hospitable, diverse and engaged with the needs of the city – could not match one working model, and the People Centre was to be that model. To a sceptical staff I sketched out my dream of a bright, welcoming space with comfy armchairs and a modern restaurant where the humblest street cleaner would be served with the same dignity as any advocate from the Supreme Court next door. It would be staffed by people with warm smiles, serving light snacks as well as tasty 'home-cooked' lunches. There was little initial support but I knew that unless this idea went ahead, nothing else would change. CMC needed to be irreversibly "broken open" so the real world could come in, and this was the way to do it. I didn't try to fund such a radical idea from CMC sources; a friendly foundation put up the capital needed and this went a long way to oiling the wheels. Lindi Myeza helped by demonstrating that nowhere in our environs could black people sit down to a meal. She challenged local well-known eateries to seat her, always to be rejected, and came back to tell her story. Now that finance was no problem, the project was grudgingly approved and that was all I needed. With a small team we set about transforming the basement. Much of the work was hands on, involving the indefatigable Ken Roberts as clerk of works. I was thrilled when a gifted and beautiful soul named Joan Rudolph left a high positon in the Central News Agency to become People Centre director. Joan was loved and trusted in the congregation and known to have superb catering skills. Soon she had assembled an excellent kitchen team and persuaded a group of white-haired CMC women to become volunteer table waiters. In April 1978 the People Centre opened. The night before, while fixing a large artwork to the wall high above the entrance, I fell off the ladder and landed on the concrete stairs fifteen feet below, so the Dedication Service was conducted on crutches.

From the outset the People Centre was a success, with 10 000 people of all races passing through its doors in the first six months. For fifteen years after that, it served an average of 200 meals each day. It was exciting to see black and white people eating together for the first time, but even more astounding was the notion of elderly white women serving black customers. Joan Rudolph was able to evoke a beautiful feel in the place. Clearing a table one evening, she found a paper napkin with these words scribbled by a customer: "Then there's all this – a stillness – a quietness – a people's place – an oasis in a steel city."[165] The People Centre was about lonely people finding fellowship and hungry people finding food. It was also about black and white people finding each other. Johannesburg *Star* journalist Denis Beckett described it as "not quite charity, not quite commercial ... at one table a millionaire Silk recharging from the pressure of prowess, and at the next someone who you suspect would never see a square meal were he not seeing it here."[166] I made sure I ate there on Wednesdays, when Joan's magnificent lemon meringue pie was on sale.

Of course it was illegal – apartheid's Separate Amenities legislation forbade mixed restaurants – and we soon attracted police attention. But we skated round registering as a restaurant by obtaining a certificate from the city health department permitting us to prepare food. That never ended the harassment but when the cops came we assured them that all we were doing was providing for our congregation – some of whom were black. It wasn't a lie: John Wesley had called the whole world his parish, so why could we not claim Johannesburg – and everyone in it – as ours?

The People Centre opened a new future for CMC: the building at last had a 'heart', a warm, human-scale place of hospitality. Black people began to feel at ease in the building, paving the way for deeper involvement in CMC and although it took time, most white members began to embrace the fact that this was what the future was going to look like. CMC was also gaining a unique reputation as the 'Church of the People' – the place in the city where black and white South Africans could break bread together.[167] Beckett recalled that, "The criterion for admission was simple ... you pitched up. This place was for anyone – not nominally for anyone, as is common – but really for anyone."[168]

Now that we were more confident of the hospitality we could offer, we moved outward. A talented new staffer named David Ching trained and led a multi-racial team to visit in the flatland around us. Each year they knocked on more than 1 000 doors, welcoming new arrivals, helping them settle into the city and inviting them to the People Centre and CMC – and many came. We developed a Charter describing who we were and the disciplines we were committed to. Unsurprisingly it contained those four priorities that I had articulated ten years before when we left Sydney. Following John Wesley's example of "Making it easy to come, but hard to stay",[169] we welcomed all unconditionally, but those desiring to deepen their relationship with us had to journey together for eight weeks in a New Life Group, learning to embrace our Charter disciplines while also exploring their own gifting. New members committed to be faithful at worship, attend the Academy for Christian Living, or the GIFT[170] groups that met in people's homes, give sacrificially and involve themselves in one or other of our ministries to the city. The growing of newcomers into disciples was the work of a succession of dedicated associate ministers – Revs Trevour de Bruyn, Trevor Hudson, Ric Matthews, David Newby and Janet Hudson. It was also where Elizabeth and a number of remarkable lay persons played an important mentoring role.

Other ministries followed with different degrees of success. When numbers of homeless men began to occupy and sleep around Hillbrow House, disrupting work among the elderly, our ecumenical partnership was challenged to set up a new ministry for them nearby and Genesis was born in 1980, offering a day centre, and counselling and accommodation to some 60 alcoholics and homeless men each day. That same year Reverend Sizwe Mbabane became the first black minister on our staff – albeit part-time – when I asked him to pastor the hundreds of cleaning and janitorial staff who lived in the 'locations in the sky' – accommodations on the roofs of office blocks and flats in the city. Sizwe did an outstanding job but some of his black clergy colleagues seemed to think that they had a lien on the black dwellers in the city and pressured him to desist. They never replaced his ministry. At CCMC Reverend Errol Gray launched Release, providing a welcome to prisoners being processed out of the Fort[171] at the end of their jail sentences. Two supervised flats were made available to help ease them back into their new lives of freedom. CCMC also offered a deep healing ministry linked with its work in the hospitals nearby. When Lindi Myeza left CMC in 1982[172] we entered a shared ministry with St Mary's Cathedral called City Care, supporting social worker Charity Tsotsetsi together. A team of eighteen people visited hospitals and nursing homes. At CMC we launched an Afrikaans-language service which failed to win a following but Workers' Worship every Wednesday lunch hour did take hold, offering prayer and a brief message to about 60 people from surrounding workplaces. A dramatic moment in its life was when a man walking past heard the singing in our chapel and came in, standing uncomfortably at the back until everyone had left. He told me that he had been on his way to the Tollman Towers Hotel next door, intending to throw himself from its roof, but the hymn had been a boyhood favourite and he felt impelled to come in. That moment began a way back from his despair.

At the beginning of the 1980s rent control in the city ended with the passing of the Sectional Title Act.[173] I attacked it in the media as a "Landlords' Act" gouging poorer tenants and forcing thousands of them to either purchase their flats at unaffordable prices, or have them sold under them. After one radio interview, an irate landlord called me, saying I was naive and ignorant of the problems he had to deal with. When I disagreed, he suddenly said: "I'll tell you what, Reverend, you can have my block of flats! I'll sign it over to you right now. Let's see if you can make ends meet trying to run it." And he did. I was gobsmacked but was not going to duck the challenge, so we soon found ourselves legal owners of Villiers Court, a slightly shabby block of 56 apartments a couple of streets away from CMC. With it came its tenants, most of whom were elderly disability pensioners, and Mrs Roestoff, its tough Afrikaans-speaking caretaker. The vision we set for ourselves was to prove we could bring a block like this up to acceptable standards and create a sense of security, community and mutual care among its residents – all for the low rental of R60 per month. I knew this was a job for miracle-makers and asked John Rees to manage the property while I gave Joan Rudolph the job of "creating community". We had to raise R100 000 for renovations – an enormous sum in those days – and we did. Every flat was repainted, rewired, re-carpeted and fitted with a new stove, and Presiding Bishop Khoza Mgojo officially named the building Cornerstone House in October 1981.

Not all was plain sailing with our tenants. One had been a famous boxing promoter and journalist with an easily aroused temper. He was known to walk the passageways brandishing a revolver. For a time I was probably the only Methodist minister in the world keeping a brothel because one resident was definitely earning a living that way. A lesbian couple occupied another flat, which was no problem for me, but Mrs Roestoff, of conservative views and limited English, sometimes got confused between the two flats and grumbled about the "lesbitutes" in the building.

Our tenants were initially suspicious of us. On Christmas Eve just three months after taking over the building, a group of us gathered in the open well of Villiers Court and began to sing carols. Looking up at the encircling six floors we could see one or two heads leaning over the balcony but nothing else. We were clearly not welcome and when a couple of unsavoury missiles came dropping down we decamped. But the residents had reckoned without Joan Rudolph's stubborn love: later that night, she and her team crept along every floor, pinning a bright Christmas stocking to each door. Inside were some useful gifts and a card from the "new owners" wishing the occupants a merry Christmas. Things began to thaw after that and when one tenant moved out we turned that flat into a Community Room, furnishing it with comfy chairs, tea-making facilities and a TV. Slowly, community began to happen. Cornerstone House operated for eight years until bad damage from the Khotso House bomb blast opposite and other factors forced its closure. When it did, I felt that a lot had been achieved. We had been the first to operate an ordinary block of flats on a non-profit basis, providing pastoral care for residents. "This ..." I said, "showed the way for other, better-funded organisations ... [and] at least we know that we began something with Cornerstone that lives elsewhere in a number of similar projects."[174]

We also had our heartbreaks, having to first amalgamate the two limping congregations of Bertrams and Victoria and finally close Victoria in 1984 as a worshipping congregation, although production of food parcels under Methodist Care, another one of John Rees's projects, continued there. Over the ten years since I had left CCMC that congregation had changed too, with a diminishing handful of students, while the black community who had joined us there grew. A reorganisation failed to resurrect the student congregation and we finally absorbed it into Central in 1987.

Financing the rapidly expanding work was a never-ending burden but in 1985 we clinched a unique property deal promising us a more stable future. The Tollman Towers Hotel next door was demolished and construction of the prestigious Johannesburg Sun begun. The developers came to me with an intriguing proposition: would we be willing to sell them our three floors of surplus bulk? 'Bulk' was apparently the amount of volume a building with our footprint was permitted to occupy and it seemed that because the CMC had built only four floors out of a possible seven, we had not used our full allowance. Selling our unused 'bulk' to the Sun people would enable them to add another couple of floors to their hotel. This kind of negotiation had never happened in South Africa but we were assured that it was common in New York, and we got down to business. In the end they got their 'bulk' in exchange for R320 000, plus eight permanent staff parking bays under the new hotel and 50 free bays on Sundays for our congregation. In addition, we would remodel our Smal Street Mall façade, replacing our small parking garage with three shops, two of which would be rent producing and the third given free to Operation Hunger. All of this for some fresh air! I dined out for a long time on that deal.

The 100th Anniversary of both CMC and the city of Johannesburg were celebrated in 1986. This was also the year that the MCSA Conference recognised us as the first Central Methodist Mission in the land.[175] The name change was significant because it acknowledged that we were unique both in our city location and our multi-racial character. Unlike suburban or township churches, a CMM was given freedom to seek financial and other forms of support from the nation-wide church. For me the new name was also a badge of courage, a salute to those people of colour who had risked so much to integrate CMM.

In 1988 another remarkable person came amongst us. With a name like Judy Bassingthwaite she might have been expected to be Anglo-Saxon but she hailed from the 'Baster' community in Namibia and was struggling to learn English. Judy was just about the bubbliest, most outgoing and warm person any of us had met. Her love for children brought her to South Africa for training as a Montessori pre-school teacher, sponsored by Harry and Bridget Oppenheimer of De Beers Diamonds fame. Billeted in their opulent home her descriptions in broken English of sitting at table with the richest couple in South Africa, trying to choose the correct cutlery with waiters hovering over her shoulder were hilarious. When Judy moved to the YWCA in Rissik Street she began worshipping at CCMC right opposite. An exhibition demonstrating the varied ministries in the Mission drew her to Central: "It was the candle with the barbed wire that blew me away," she says. "I always believed the church should be involved in the struggle for the oppressed and marginalised and here was one making it a central point every time they worshipped." Associate minister Janet Hudson encouraged her to think of full-time ministry and soon she was in my office to talk about it. She was turning away from a future R3 000 per month and all I could offer her was R250, plus accommodation and medical aid. Untroubled, Judy took up residence in one of the flats in our building and began her ministry on the unforgiving streets. Soon she had identified many colonies of homeless people, living in wretched conditions in alleys, broken buildings, vacant lots and refuse dumps – or simply under sheets of cardboard on the sidewalk. 'Sis Judy' as she came to be called, moved with extravagant compassion amongst these most vulnerable of human cast-offs, bringing simple acts of caring, a healing touch and her incandescent smile. With a child-like trust in prayer she walked the streets at night without fear, answering emergency calls at any hour. In 1989 our son Alan returned from Australia and joined Judy on the streets while preparing either for prison or for the ordained ministry.[176] She soon took charge of the joint Anglican/Methodist street team and the ministry called Paballo ya Batho ('caring for the people'). Every week their van, loaded down with soup and foodstuffs plus a medical team, roamed the streets and offered succour to the people who knew no other home. One of the more moving experiences for me was the annual memorial service attended entirely by homeless people, where we remembered those among them who had died on the streets. I found it hard not to choke up reminding them that no longer would their friends be classified as "of no fixed abode" – and that at last they had found a home nobody could evict them from.

Helen Muller had left us at the end of 1982 after eleven magnificent years of service in a multitude of positions,[177] but the work went on under new leadership. Careways birthed a second centre in Belgravia and in 1989 we opened a full-day pre-school called For Love of Children (FLOC). We now had some 160 children in our care. Given that Joburg's altitude was 6 000 feet and FLOC occupied the seventh floor and roof of Wynrop House down the street from CMC, we were confident that we were running the "highest pre-school in Africa". A second FLOC followed in 1991 and robbed Wynrop of the altitude prize by locating in the YMCA premises up the hill in Braamfontein, with 60 more children. FLOC was inspired and birthed by Wendy Young, another of the human gifts who seemed to arrive just when needed. A qualified pre-school teacher, she used to travel the 22 miles from Benoni to worship with us each Sunday, sitting unobtrusively in the gallery until one day out of the blue she expressed a sense of call to serve full-time with us. There were no funds but that didn't deter her. Off she went for two years to isolated Orapa in Botswana, teaching the Anglo-American mine's employees' children for a salary so generous that she could support herself for her first two years with CMM. Wendy first took over the People Centre in its eighth year of operation and also used her considerable artistic talents in the publicity and communication cluster, editing our news-sheet called *What a Family*, setting up exhibitions, designing bulletins and the like. Her transformation of the chapel for Holy Week always had a powerful visual impact.

The recession of the early 80s had seen a gradual breakdown in residential segregation in the flatland around us, with landlords surreptitiously renting to black tenants who, because they were 'illegal', could be exploited without recourse. CMM hosted the tenants' rights group Actstop and associate ministers Philip Mvunyiswa and David Newby were often found struggling to help evicted tenants. David Ching's team ran Bible Studies for flat-dwellers, helped by Alan and others. Many were undocumented immigrants and Alan recalls an evening when they were settling down to Bible Study when the cry "Home Affairs police!" went up. Alan insisted on praying the Benediction, at the end of which he was the only one in the room. Everyone had fled, leaving him to smile at the Home Affairs officials as they came knocking on doors.

In 1988 my Annual Superintendent's Report noted that "the non-racial character of CMM has reached 'critical mass,' no longer a white congregation with black participants but a community of firmly non-racial character not only in our worship but in every part of our life". It recorded that we were now the most integrated congregation in MCSA and "the prophetic decision made more than ten years ago by what was then an all-white congregation – and the price that had to be paid – have been justified".[178] It had seemed too high a price at the time: there were days in the mid-60s when I truly feared I would be remembered for shutting down MCSA's flagship church. Yes, we had lost some 200 members, but looking at the smaller but much more diverse community we had become, I knew that in spite of the pain it had been cheap at the price.

Central Methodist Church had been broken wide open.

19

Ministry With a Whiff of Teargas

Years later when the post-apartheid Truth and Reconciliation Commission (TRC) began its work, one of the commissioners, Dr Fazel Randera, visited me. He was responsible for setting up the TRC hearings in Johannesburg and came with a request.

"Bishop," he said, "we're hoping very much that you will permit us to hold the Joburg hearings at CMM."

I was taken aback. "We would be deeply honoured," I replied, "but the hall only holds 500 people and it's below ground. If the air-con gives trouble you'll have problems. I really don't think it would work …"

"No," he interrupted, "I'm not sure you understand me. It's the *church* we want, not the hall."

"But, Fazel," I said, "Have you thought this through? You're a Muslim and some of the victims telling their stories will be of other faiths. Surely that's painful enough without being in a place with 'alien' religious symbols like our sanctuary …"

Once again Fazel hardly waited for me to finish. "Peter," he smiled, "there's nothing alien about your sanctuary. It belongs to the people. It's the place that gave us shelter, where we could speak out, protest and mourn our dead. In the dark days we came there time and again. We can't think of a better place for truth and reconciliation to happen."

For someone who believed as fiercely as I did that the church exists, not for itself, but for the world, here was an amazing affirmation that CMM had become that kind of church. I readily gave my blessing subject to the approval of Reverend Mvume Dandala, who had succeeded me at Central, and kept my composure until Dr Randera had left. Then I sat down and thought about the import of his words and of all the times when CMM had been in the eye of the storm, and how many, many people had been sheltered and embraced, encouraged and affirmed there – and I was overcome with gratitude.

Much of our witness for justice rose out of simply trying to be faithful pastors and was interwoven with the daily joys and frustrations of ministry, but that was not enough: God and the circumstances required more. As Fazel's words explained, in the struggle years CMC was impelled – not for the first or last time – to demonstrate the ages-long Judeo-Christian practice of sanctuary.[179] Believers in a God who is our "refuge and our strength", and a "safe retreat"[180] and who follow a Christ who began life as a refugee[181] are called to always offer sanctuary, which is why one of my earliest decisions at CMC was to replace the tall, forbidding wooden entrance doors with plate glass ones; people needed to know that this place welcomed them. We began to house vulnerable civil rights groups like the brave people of the Conscription Advice Bureau[182] and Actstop.[183] Our evening services provided a meeting point for Conscientious Objectors unwelcome in their home churches. The Detainees' Parents Support Committee (DPSC), who cared for the families of people detained without trial, met in our premises too and were teargassed there more than once.

Embattled trade unions gathered in the underground hall, and sometimes overflowed into the People Centre, much to our customers' discomfort. Joan Rudolph and her successors as People Centre directors – Beth Logan and Wendy Young – showed enormous grace when this happened, but the subtext was easy to read: "Peter, how can we run a restaurant with war-like chants thumping through the walls?" I did my best to say sorry, but how could we refuse? Where else could these people vent their frustrations without having their heads beaten in?

The largest such gathering took place during the violence-wracked transport strike of 1987.[184] Denied a place to meet, 2 500 railwaymen – most of them migrant workers brandishing *knobkieries*[185] – descended on us. I had two problems: the first that they were armed, and the second, where to put them? All I could do was stand at our doors refusing entry unless they stacked their 'traditional weapons' in the foyer, and to my relief they complied. We packed about 1 500 into every inch of the 900-seat sanctuary, then into the 500-seat hall, with the rest filling stairways and lobbies. The songs began in the sanctuary, rumbled down the stairs and ended a few beats behind, in the hall. They were remarkably well-behaved, but I didn't want to be around when they got back to the foyer and tried to sort out whose *knobkierie* belonged to whom.

CMC was also the venue for packed memorial services, the first being for Steve Biko when he died a tortured death in prison in September 1977. The sanctuary was packed with deeply shocked people as Dr Simon Gqubule delivered the eulogy. I do not recall another death in the bad days that so stunned South Africa's black population – until Chris Hani was gunned down in his driveway in 1993 – yet most whites had no idea who Steve was. His charismatic leadership had produced the Black Community Programmes that turned around many a hopeless rural settlement and gave them self-respect. Who is to know what our country may have looked like had he lived?

Another of the dead slaughtered on apartheid's altar was 31-year-old Jeanette Schoon, this time assassinated together with her six-year-old daughter Katryn in June 1984 by a letter bomb sent to her in exile in Angola. Her parents, Jack and Joyce, were amazingly brave. They buried their daughter and granddaughter in Angola but asked me to host a service for her at CMC. I'm not sure I've ever been more affected: the sheer calculated ruthlessness of this act of state terror touched an anger deep within me. As I prepared to preach, a picture kept coming to mind of a police explosives technician coldly assembling the fatal piece of mail that would take the lives of a mother and child in another country. Jeanette was a courageous student leader who had suffered 68 days of detention without trial, and then slipped across the border with her spouse Marius Schoon on the day of their wedding. When she became a mother, she withdrew from political work for the sake of her children. She had written to her parents assuring them that they would be safe – and then this. Marius was away and two-year-old son Fritz was playing outside the range of the detonation. They could not attend the service, of course. As I preached I was filled with a cold fury: "The Bible speaks of the fallen-ness of humanity," I said. "It speaks about people who 'love darkness because their deeds are evil'. Today we are reminded again of the depths of evil to which human beings can sink. We can only speculate on her murderer or murderers; but whoever they are, *I want them to know right now that they have damned their own souls*."[186]

Yet another 1989 victim of government assassination was Anton Lubowski, a lawyer committed to the struggle of Namibians fighting to throw off the South African yoke. After being prominent in the End Conscription Campaign as a student in South Africa, he practised law in what was then South-West Africa, defending political prisoners. He ultimately joined SWAPO and became its Secretary General. In the run-up to the first democratic elections there Anton was murdered while entering his home. A judge later found *prima facie* that CCB[187] operative Donald Acheson had killed him, assisted by a group of CCB colleagues. But the service in CMC left no doubt that the ultimate villain was the system that oppressed people in South-West Africa.

These occasions were not without enormous stress. Inside I was not always popular with the crowds. No matter how passionate or painful the event, party banners or flags were banned from the sanctuary.[188] Sometimes over-exuberant activists would sneak a big banner in and try to hang it behind the pulpit just before proceedings began, but I would have none of it. We may have been the 'People's Church', but in the sanctuary they were in God's space, not to be hijacked by any political movement. Outside, always the police surrounded our premises, and often they pursued some of those attending afterward. Sometimes the unmistakable sting of teargas wafted about. Describing one such scene, Denis Beckett used a sentence that gave me joy: "What struck this bystander," he wrote, "was that here, come to life, was that thing so often wished for, a 'relevant' urban church ..."[189]

A favourite police ruse was to call in a bomb threat, hoping to cause disruption or cancellation. CMC was a large, complicated building with a hundred possible hiding places and guiding the squad and their sniffer-dog through it all was tedious and time consuming. The dogs apparently thought so too, with one deciding to stop and poo inside an almost inaccessible air-conditioning space. We had mixed feelings about these searches, suspecting that if there were a device, it could quite possibly have been placed by the police themselves. In the end we ignored the threats.

The CMM building also became a venue for exhibitions, some of them very uncomfortable. I walked through our front doors one morning to be met by a gruesome sight: hanging with nooses round their necks from a long crossbeam spanning the foyer were six what appeared to be corpses, all in orange prison uniforms, with hands tied behind their backs and hoods over their heads. I had forgotten that lawyer-activist Fink Haysom had asked whether an anti-capital punishment group could mount a five-day exhibit. I had happily consented but had no idea how realistic it would be. Using dummies Fink's group had replicated the horrifying group executions that happened every Friday morning at Pretoria Central Prison. Once over the shock I was glad we could play our part in highlighting this barbaric practice, but People Centre business did suffer that week.

In 1980 our entire clergy staff got arrested. We had joined some 50 others in a protest march to Security Police headquarters to demand the release of Congregationalist leader Reverend John Thorne, who had been taken a couple of days earlier. The Security Police, headed up by notorious torturer Colonel 'Rooi Rus' Swanepoel,[190] swooped on us – somewhat unwisely – right outside the Star newspaper building and shoved us into waiting vans, getting us to our destination earlier than planned. Then we were dumped into some very unhygienic prison cells. There were eight of us in our cell dressed not very practically in our clerical collars and cassocks. The whole purpose of prison is to intimidate: the noise, shouting, rattling keys and clanging iron doors, the guards in their boots and leather belts and guns and the rest, are all about power. So with a slam and a rattle an officious young guard shoved his enormous key into the door of our cell and … oops … the key wouldn't turn. We watched for a while as he wrestled the key this way and that, but the door just wouldn't lock. I thought this a good moment to remind him in Afrikaans of the Bible story of Paul and Silas in prison – and the way an Angel of the Lord had freed them.[191] The young white Dutch Reformed lad in his big uniform began to look less sure of himself. Finally, in words that could have been written for a comedy script, he gave up and said, "*Ag, julle is priesters, belowe my asseblief dat julle sal nie uitkom nie!*"[192] In that comic moment, the power equation was inverted, testifying to God's sense of humour. The open door allowed us to go round and check on other prisoners during the night, but the next morning we were all back in place and able to offer our guard our own version of, "don't do yourself any harm, we're all here!"[193] Facing the magistrate the next morning was a noisy business. Clergy from all over had come to support us and were singing and chanting in the corridor and outside the windows. Some of us – including Beyers Naudé and Desmond Tutu – had decided to refuse bail, only to find that an 'anonymous person' had already posted bail for us. Clearly the authorities didn't want further publicity and wished us gone. It was the first of five arrests for me and I determined to always carry a toothbrush in future.

Each annual remembrance of the 1976 student uprisings brought nation-wide clashes with security forces – always followed by more deaths. As the tenth anniversary approached we searched for a creative way to commemorate June 16 that would demonstrate to the people of Soweto that their pain was felt by ordinary South Africans – the 'silent majority' who were perhaps too cautious for street marches and such. Then Elizabeth's brother Graeme and his friend Geoff Sifrin came up with the astounding idea of 'A Garland of Flowers for Soweto'. Why not invite people everywhere to send posies of flowers with messages to their compatriots in Soweto? The moment the idea was floated it caught on. We raised consciousness by placing newspaper ads with a daisy to cut out, colour yellow and display on the rear windows of cars. Then, on 15 June 1986, real flowers with their notes attached were to be sent or delivered to a couple of depots, from which they would be taken the next day into Soweto. To round off the day a service at CMC would follow the deliveries.

On the morning of 16 June, arriving at Berea Methodist Church in Yeoville, I found a squad of riot police outside the church, obviously hoping to intimidate donors, but not quite sure how to bully families, including small children, delivering little posies. Once inside I found myself wading into a foot-deep sea of flowers filling the church. There were flowers from every corner of the land and further afield: deliveries from celebrities like Sting, Sidney Poitier and Harry Belafonte were lying alongside tiny posies with touching messages …

> We come to Soweto to wish you 'shalom' and pray these flowers will keep the hope of freedom alive in your hearts;
> In anguished memory of the thousands who have died violently and tragically in Soweto and other tormented townships since 16th June, 1976. We mourn with you and pray for a just peace in our beloved land. May God be with you;
> My family is praying very hard that our country may have peace and justice. We grieve with you for the deaths of your children and the

suffering and fear with which you are not so familiar.
These flowers are a token of our sympathy and our longing to reach across apartheid barriers to our fellow citizens.

The police squad watched while we loaded cars and pick-up trucks and set off for the various entrances to Soweto, but armoured vehicles had preceded us, blocking all entrances. The police there dumped and trashed some loads and turned others away. The van I was in slipped through by following close behind an ambulance racing to Soweto's Baragwanath Hospital, but we got no further. Surrounded by police we laid out our flowers against the hospital wall, while across the road residents of the black township applauded. The police ordered us to leave but we insisted that one of our number, Rabbi Adi Asabi from Joburg's northern suburbs, should pray. In the magnificent tradition of the Hebrew psalmists Asabi offered a lengthy lament, calling down Jehovah's judgement on a long list of apartheid's sins. Later we heard that as soon as we had left the police trashed everything.

However, unknown to us, Graeme Hardie had a Plan B. He had hired a light aircraft, loaded it with posies and messages and flown over Soweto, throwing them out of the plane's door. No police could stop him up there, but as luck would have it, one posy got stuck in an air intake and it took all the pilot's skill to get Graeme down in one piece.

That day motorists with yellow daisies in their rear windows were being stopped by traffic cops and some were arrested. Flowers that had not been destroyed were delivered to the 'non-white' hospital in Joburg itself and the day ended with a packed service at CMM, dominated by a yellow flower wreath in memory of the 1976 victims. We could take comfort in the fact that their memory had been honoured – and while thousands of posies failed to reach their target, there was a warm response from Soweto residents and, more importantly, to our knowledge no more youths had died in confrontation with police.

Wednesday night, 15 June 1988 was the eve of another remembrance of the Soweto uprising and for the occasion our Sunday School children had decorated CMM's foyer with moving prayers for peace. That night CMM's exterior walls received a different decoration: in a crude attempt at disinformation, leftist political graffiti was splashed all over them, implying that some of the very human rights organisations whom we sheltered had desecrated our church. But one of our janitorial staff had seen the perpetrators at work in the small hours and the next day he identified one of the culprits among the Security Police when they arrived to monitor our June 16 remembrances. When I preached later I reminded the congregation that Jesus had anticipated people acting against the Church "because they do not know either the Father or me ..."[194] The people who did this were "heathens who had defiled God's temple",[195] and as such, worshipped another god: "Oh, they may have some god," I said, "most people do. My guess is that theirs is the tribal god of the white race ... they bow to the idols that so many worship in this land, but they do not know the God and Father of our Lord Jesus Christ." "That's why, if we identify them," I said, "we will prosecute them, and when they are found guilty, I shall ask the magistrate to sentence them to worship here every Sunday for six months, to sing with us, to pray with us, to pass the peace of Christ with us, to hear the liberating Good News of God's grace with us, to break bread with us ... so they may find God!"[196] When I went to lay a charge it became clear that it would make our only witness – a young black cleaner – far too vulnerable, so I left it.

At about 1 am on 31 August, the apartheid state committed its most violent act of terrorism against the Christian Church. Using between 60 and 80 kg of explosive, a hit-squad led by their most feared assassin, Eugene de Kock – nicknamed 'Prime Evil' – blew up Khotso House, headquarters of the SACC and a number of other organisations. The blast was enormous; the explosives had been placed near or in the elevator shaft in the basement parking garage – blowing the elevator out the roof and devastating each floor of the six-floor building. I was woken soon after by a call from John Rees; I dressed quickly and raced into the city to be met by a scene out of Dante's *Inferno*. Fires were still burning in De Villiers Street, now littered with rubble, glass and twisted metal. The windows of Khotso House gaped emptily, with ripped curtains and blinds hanging out of them. Part of the face of the building had been blown off, exposing the foyer, which now had no floor. In the unpredictable way of explosions it had been sucked down onto the demolished cars in the basement, taking the security guard named Welcome Ntumba with it. He sustained back injuries and I saw him sitting in pain on the kerbside. He later testified in court that I had taken him to Johannesburg Hospital – something I don't remember. Cornerstone House, CMM's apartment block for disability pensioners, was directly opposite and shrapnel from the explosion had ripped into its frontage and destroyed all its windows. Fortunately most of the residents had their beds under the window-sills of the sturdy building. Shrapnel had blasted through above their beds, embedding itself in the interior walls of their bedrooms. I found some of them wandering around in their nightclothes covered in dust and blood from lacerations on their faces and forearms. The total number of injured was 23.

As the dawn began to break SACC General Secretary Frank Chikane arrived and *The Citizen* newspaper later published a photo of police explosives expert Lieutenant Charles Zeelie escorting us away from the entrance after refusing us entry.[197] Some years later he was to ask the Truth and Reconciliation Commission for amnesty for having been one of the squad who planted the bomb. SACC staffers began to arrive with the morning crowds and it was gut-wrenching to see the shock and horror on their faces as they came around the corner to find their workplace destroyed. Frank and I moved among them, telling them quietly to remain calm and make their way to CMM, just two blocks away. There, at the usual time for SACC morning prayers, we gathered in CMM's chapel and began worship. It was a deeply shocked group who tried to sing Psalm 23 together, but they were also a sign that the Christian witness of SACC against the powers would not be deterred. Soon, every nook and cranny of the CMM building was cleared and turned into office space for the SACC. Other city churches followed suit but of course the destruction of computers, files and other records set the work back enormously. It would take some years before we knew that this devastating act of violence was done on the express instructions of President PW Botha, perhaps as his revenge for the failure of the Eloff Commission to act strongly enough against SACC.[198]

Early in November 1988 a man with a heavy Afrikaans accent phoned in a chilling threat to my secretary: "Tell your boss Peter Storey 'I'm watching you, your time has come. Some of your black servants are already suffering.'" He claimed to belong to the Wit Wolwe.[199] A matter of days later, 21-year-old right-wing Afrikaner Barend Strydom went on a shooting spree in Strijdom Square, Pretoria. He cold-bloodedly murdered eight black persons, wounding sixteen more. When taken into custody he claimed to be the leader of a right-wing group called the Wit Wolwe, something the police decided was a figment of his imagination – that he was the only wolf. If they were right, then the call to my office came from Strydom himself and it is still an uncomfortable thought that I was on his list.

The phrase 'Prayer and Protest' came to describe gatherings where CMC's pulpit was a platform for prophetic resistance. The biblical prophets – including Jesus – disturbed the sleep of the powerful with God's voice for justice and CMC made space for the prophets in our broken land to be heard. For a while we could offer better protection than more exposed venues, but as confrontation escalated the powers showed scant respect for church spaces. In 1977, for instance, the Security Police raided Khotso House and held the staff – including Elizabeth – hostage for many hours as they searched different offices. Riot police teargassed political funerals and trashed the Methodist

Youth Centre in Jabavu, leaving its premises in a shambles. Churches of other denominations, especially in the Eastern Cape, suffered a similar fate.

Our turn to be violated came later. On 6 December 1988 a meeting at Wits University protesting the Delmas Treason Trial[200] was banned at the last minute. Word went round to disperse and re-assemble at CMC and soon the church was packed. The protest was resumed, this time as a 'Prayer' gathering. SACC General Secretary Frank Chikane and I were sitting behind the pulpit, with Dr Allan Boesak addressing the crowd, when I got word that a "whole lot" of riot police were outside. I went to investigate and sure enough, a platoon of men in full riot gear and carrying sub-machine guns was formed up in front of our doors. Seeking out the officer in charge, I asked him why they were here – we were holding a perfectly orderly meeting. He replied that the meeting was banned and his men were there to clear the people out.

"You must be mistaken," I said. "The banned meeting was at Wits University. This is Central Methodist Church."

"Don't be funny with me, Reverend," he said, "we know who's in there and we're coming in."

"Listen, Captain," I remonstrated, "this meeting isn't in the hall. It's in the church sanctuary. You guys have never invaded a church. If you do that, you cross a line. There will be hell to pay if you dare to invade a Christian church."

In doubt for a moment, he turned and spoke into his radio: "*Ons het 'n probleem,*" he said. "*Die priester sê hulle's in die kerk self...*"[201]

Then came the reply and on hearing the word "*Beweeg!*"[202] crackling through his radio I turned and ran up the stairs and down the aisle into the pulpit, stopping Boesak in full cry. I told the congregation that we were about to be occupied by riot police and to stay absolutely still in their places. There were only two major staircases down to the ground floor and I was desperately concerned about what would happen if a crowd approaching 1 000 people stampeded. Before I got the sentence out the police were streaming into the church. The sight of some 60 men in full riot gear, positioned around our communion rail pointing their weapons at the congregation was frightening, but to their credit everyone stayed calm and seated.

The officer, pistol on hip, joined us in the pulpit and barked an order at me: "Tell them they've got four minutes to disperse."

Again I remonstrated: "That's impossible! It takes much longer to empty this church … I know this. Let me calm them and dismiss them."

While we were arguing in the pulpit, Ken Roberts, who I liked to call my 'resident conservative', now in his late 60s, did his own amazing thing. With dignified anger at the riot squad's lack of decorum he got up and approached them. "Take off those helmets," he instructed. "Don't you know you're in a church? Show some respect!" It seems that some of the young Afrikaners in the squad were from God-fearing homes, because a few of them sheepishly removed their visored riot helmets, trying to tuck them under their armpits. In spite of the anxiety of the moment I couldn't suppress a small smile. The police captain realised I was right about the dismissal and grudgingly agreed to my request, whereupon I announced that the service had been declared illegal and that we would have to leave … after a closing prayer. With that I lifted my hands and began to pray. It was a long prayer. I wanted to at least challenge the power equation: why should a bunch of policemen have all the authority? So, while the officer repeatedly growled, "*Maak klaar, priester, maak klaar!*"[203] I managed what I hope was a dignified ending and pronounced the Benediction: "The grace of the Lord Jesus Christ, the Love of God, and the Friendship and Protection of the Holy Spirit, be with us all." With that the people left quietly and there were no arrests.

Ministry in such a massively stressful context was never easy, and could not have happened without remarkable people – not only on the CMM staff, but among my lay leaders. At some time I asked the six senior leaders if they would meet with me and my associate ministers weekly at 6.30 am. It meant that we could deal with urgent issues, yes, but more importantly, that we could pray together and hold each other accountable. Some of them lived in distant suburbs, others nearby, but with deep faithfulness they came into the heart of the city before daylight each Wednesday for years. I see their faces now and give thanks for them. They kept me strong.

By 1991 I had been 20 years in the Circuit – sixteen of them at Central Church. Much of what I had hoped to achieve had come about. Central had been broken wide open in a number of important ways. We had turned to face the gritty needs of the city and committed to numerous ministries of healing and service. While a significant group of white congregants had rejected transformation and left us, our church family of around 600 had found a "painful togetherness" and begun to look more like God's future for South Africa. People of colour now topped 50% and one of my proudest possessions remains a 1990 photo of the congregation, showing a beautiful rainbow community. Our voice had been heard nationally and could not be ignored and CMM had become known world-wide for its effectiveness as a city church.

We had also waded right into the thick of the political struggle – not as a tool of any political formation – but retaining our integrity as *Church*. I never forgot that the Dutch Reformed Churches' early identification with suffering Afrikaners had later turned into theological capture by the Broederbond's[204] apartheid ideology. I also knew that in the present struggle even the 'good guys' would not be above using us and was determined not to get sucked in that way because no matter how noble the cause, there would come moments when those same 'good guys' would need to be held accountable too.

Quite early during these years I had also been thrust into national leadership positions, first as President of the SACC and then as Presiding Bishop of MCSA, followed by the ongoing task of Bishop of the District.[205] Crazy as it sounds, these additional responsibilities had been carried out while still leading CMM, but by 1991 my Synod judged that the burden had become too great and voted to separate me from Circuit ministry at the end of that year. I would now be like Anglican and Catholic bishops, without a congregation. I understood the need, but looking back I know that I lost something life-giving and precious. For a minister there is nothing more fulfilling than to walk with your people through their various life challenges, offering them each Sunday the "bread of life" and seeing them grow in faith and character. More than we admit, we ministers live by our congregation's faith as much as our own and my heart broke at the thought of leaving CMM's people and pulpit. For me, the sixteen years there – with four before that up the road at CCMC – would always be the apex of my life as a preacher, pastor and sometimes maybe a prophet.

20

Encounters in the Public Square

The work of a minister is much more varied than many people are aware of and the special circumstances of South Africa's years of travail made it even more so. During the CMM years and beyond, as I became involved in wider leadership, there were many fascinating, robust and sometimes life-threatening encounters with people on all sides of the conflict as well as the international arena.

In 1980 I returned from speaking at the World Methodist Youth Conference in Cornwall just in time for the meeting of church leaders with Prime Minister PW Botha on 7 August. It was our first and PW was somewhat taken aback when Bishop Tutu asked to pray before we started. He clearly wasn't happy with the prayer because he warned that the next time we met he would make sure that his Principal Military Chaplain was there to pray instead. We waded in with the calls that would become a mantra in the years ahead: commitment to common citizenship for all, abolition of the pass laws and forced removals, a uniform education system and a "national convention" which would include the jailed and exiled leaders of the people. My contribution was to remind him that the churches had "branches" in hundreds of places where his party had never been and that our take on the situation was far closer to the grassroots than his. Botha responded to the different inputs in a more conciliatory tone than expected and mooted a second, all-day meeting. We left with mixed feelings. On the one hand, I told the media afterward, that there was a "very wide gulf" between us, but that more genuine conversation had taken place that day than "in any other talks in 30 years". I said

I believed it was possible "to speak to people without surrendering principles".²⁰⁶ However, the promised all-day follow-up never happened. Desmond Tutu, Sally Motlana and I tried to negotiate terms for it with cabinet minister Piet Koornhof, but without success. The project died after we discovered that at the very time we were meeting the Prime Minister, his government was secretly funding the right-wing Christian League of Southern Africa, which was dedicated to smearing the WCC and SACC. Desmond had also made a long trip to Europe and America, infuriating PW by lobbying church and political leaders for tougher action against the regime. PW immediately removed the General Secretary's passport for a second time. Our next meeting with him would be a long time coming.

When the Security Branch became part of our lives, some were more secret than others. One of our sons – waiting for letters from his girlfriend – couldn't understand why mail seemed to arrive only once a week. When he asked the friendly mailman, he was told, "Sorry, man, but we have to wait for the Special Branch to come on Wednesdays to read it before we can deliver." On another occasion I was having a long telephone conversation with my Presiding Bishop Khoza Mgojo when a voice suddenly broke in, saying "*Ag, julle twee praat kak!*"²⁰⁷ Apparently we had tried our phone-tapper's patience once too often. More serious were the anonymous calls and occasional death threats. Our sons developed different ways of responding, Alan's being a pithy "F.... off!"²⁰⁸ Mysterious objects were left at our front door, one a parcel emitting an ominous ticking sound, which I gingerly carried to the back garden and dumped into the swimming pool. It turned out to be harmless.

In 1981 I had the exhilarating experience of leading the Focus '81 Australian Youth Conference with more than 1 000 young people attending from all over the continent. It was good for a while to be free of South African concerns and help these youngsters make choices for their lives. In my last service some 300 of them made serious commitments to be Christ-followers and just over 40 of them offered for the Christian ministry.

I had also been deeply involved with John Rees and others in a process at home called 'Obedience '81', the most remarkable assembly in the history of MCSA. For seven days 800 Methodists met to stake out our convictions about what obedience to Jesus meant in the 1980s. Apartheid's alienating power was driving deeper fissures into the already tenuous unity of the MCSA and black Methodists were despairing of whether their 'multi-racial church' could be trusted to stand by them in their struggle. Most white Methodists, persuaded by government propaganda, were shockingly ignorant of their fellow Methodists' suffering.

The gathering was unique in a number of ways. Clergy and laity, young and old, women and men, black and white, were selected on a proportional basis, ensuring that Obedience was completely representative. Delegates signed a covenant promising full participation and committing to stay through to the end, regardless of how angry or frustrated they became. The 'bottom-up' decision-making process was also unique: every delegate was required to journal each evening, recording all insights during the day. Early in the morning, each met for prayer with one other person – a "faithful friend" chosen for them from a different background – to share their journalling. These pairs fed their insights into a larger group of about 20 which met immediately afterward. There were 40 such groups deciding what concerns and convictions they would convey to a 'Listening Committee' which was also uniquely inclusive. Nominations for it were held open until all 800 participants were satisfied that their concerns were represented on it. I was tasked with chairing this committee and when we first met I wondered how this disparate crowd of some 40 people could ever reach a common mind. We met each day and brought drafts of the emerging message to no less than three plenary assemblies for discussion, revision and more work.

It became clear that two great concerns were paramount. The first was the need to rediscover and contextualise the missional and evangelistic passion of our heritage. There were powerful calls for a new commitment to spreading the Gospel in the Wesleyan spirit in Southern Africa. Moved by these calls, more than 50 participants offered themselves for full-time ministry. The second was whether black and white Methodists would stand in solidarity with one another in confronting the powers as the apartheid state entered its most oppressive decade. Midway through the gathering Reverend Wesley Mabuza from Natal brought things to a head with a brutally honest challenge to white Methodists: either they were with the struggle for justice or against it. They had to choose. For many whites this was the first time they had been upbraided by a black person, certainly in such terms, and Mabuza's address became the tipping point. Some broke down and others threatened to go home, but many more knew that it was time to change. Remarkably the covenant held and of the 800 participants only one – a farmer from the Free State – broke ranks and left the gathering. The moment when Obedience '81 came closest to exploding gave opportunity for God's truth to break in.

Seasoned political journalist JHP Serfontein wrote that he knew of "no other meeting of this size and lasting so long, where blacks and whites were in a situation of continuous and intensive confrontation and debate, telling each other with brutal frankness and honesty how they see and experience their fellow Christians on the other side of the apartheid fence".[209] The next days were marked by a quiet determination to move the MCSA into a more radical obedience. Resistance to change began to melt away, clear convictions emerged and the work of the many-opinioned Listening Committee became easier. After consulting the plenary for a third time they asked a small multi-racial team to work on a final text. I took four colleagues, Stanley Mogoba, Mvume Dandala, Donald Cragg and insightful layman Allan Hardie to my office and we laboured through the night. One by one sleep overtook our partners until only Allan and I were left. We put the finishing touches to 'The Message of Obedience '81' at 4 am and it was adopted later by a standing vote of all 800 delegates. Only the farmer was missing.

In the years that followed – the bloodiest years of the struggle for freedom – the Message was used to hold Methodists accountable. Its power lay not only in its words, but in the way it had come about. Methodists may have failed it in many ways, but none could deny the commitment they had made in a week of painful togetherness. In the Message of Obedience Charter MCSA pledged itself to "henceforth live and work to bring into reality the concept of an undivided Church and a free and just Southern Africa".[210] Serfontein called Obedience '81 "probably the most important assembly yet held by any church in South Africa".[211] Its impact lives on: a school headmaster who was a Grade 11 schoolboy when he attended Obedience contacted me recently. He had been part of the Brother and Me course some of us ran during that week and wanted me to know how that course was still informing the way he was dealing with issues of diversity and transformation in his school 37 years later.

Another powerful experience for me in 1981 was when I entered East Germany as part of the first ever WCC Central Committee to meet behind the Iron Curtain. My West German companion confessed to some dread as he drove us to the DDR end of Checkpoint Charlie. As we were searched by the East German *Volkspolizei* – Vopos – the suspicion and animosity was palpable. The autobahn to Dresden, some 200 kilometres into East Germany, was rutted and worn. As we drove we caught glimpses through the forests of tanks and artillery pieces, of observation posts and the other paraphernalia of war, and stopping in the 'forbidden zone' was not permitted on pain of death. The only exception was a petrol station halfway with a small picnic enclosure, where we paused to eat our sandwiches and where a lovely serendipity occurred. One other family shared the space and we sat silent and apart until the old man with them heard my accent. He immediately limped across to us and asked if I was a *Züd-Afrikaner*. When I nodded he grabbed my hand, telling me through my interpreter that he had been badly wounded fighting with Rommel's Afrika Korps in North Africa. A South African unit had picked him up and he had been nursed back to health in one of our field hospitals. His gratitude nearly 40 years later for the care of his 'enemy' was very moving.

At first sight Dresden seemed to have no heart. Its centre had been obliterated in 1945 when Allied bombers ignited a firestorm that killed 30 000 people. The centre was still mostly a wasteland of gutted ruins with just a few buildings, like the famous Opera House only now beginning to be rebuilt. Thirty-six years after the war, Dresden was a city with only one shopping street. Again the thought came to me that we had to stop reckless people doing this to South Africa. We moved into our accommodation wondering how we would relate to the people in this grey police state. I had no idea how their faith would move and humble me.

Later in the dusk our convoy of buses moved down to the square. We could see people in the gloom but they were being held back by the *Volkspolizei*. We disembarked into an eerie silence, thick with suspicion and fear. Then we moved into the great Kreuzkirche – the Church of the Cross – which had been rebuilt only that year. It was elliptical in shape, with three balconies, one above the other, all empty. As we took our seats on the ground floor, feeling uneasy and insecure, we heard a shuffling sound. The people of Dresden had been permitted to come and watch this service and were moving into the galleries. The shuffling of their feet was the only sound there was.

Then the service began. The organ thundered out with Luther's *A Mighty Fortress is our God*, and as we stood to sing, something happened: we felt what seemed to be like raindrops falling on us. We looked up and there were hundreds of faces looking down on us, hands reaching over the balconies, each waving a white handkerchief. The people were smiling and weeping at the same time, and their tears were falling on us. That is how our 'enemies' welcomed us, and continued to do so in the days that followed in spite of all their Communist rulers' attempts to stop them. The Christians of East Germany had endured 35 years of persecution, intimidation and harassment and had simply proved that when life gets most intense, God becomes most real. The atheist state had announced that it would take only fifteen years to rid East Germany of the Church, because once the Revolution was established, poverty abolished and everybody had a job – as indeed was the case by 1981 – people would abandon their religious superstitions and myths. Who would need an invisible God? Yet here we were in a city where every day people would come up to us in the street, smiling and saying, "I too am a Christian."

The young woman who cleaned the room I was sharing with Stanley Mogoba was named Barbara Blumel. She was a computer scientist who had taken special leave in order to meet fellow Christians from the West. She told us that when the most exciting job for her particular field was open, "they said I could have it because I had all the qualifications and beat all the others in the entrance exams, but then one of them said: 'You know, it will be easier if you join the Party.'" When she told them that she couldn't do that, she lost the job. "I was out of work, even under Socialism, for six months and that very seldom happens," she said quietly. Her witness was not uncommon. Bishop Albrecht Schonherr, the Lutheran Bishop of the DDR, told us that if you are going to be a Christian in East Germany "your outward lifestyle must correspond to your inward confession for there is only one thing that we have to offer a secular atheist state and that is the kind of people we are – and they are watching us".

It was at Dresden that a remarkable peace movement was born. Youth from East and West spent many hours together and the young East German Christians began to believe that peace with the West was possible. They began to live out that conviction in the candle-light marches that began in Leipzig[212] and other places, finally helping to bring down the Wall eight years later. Barbara Blumel was among them.

On that same journey – this time in West Berlin – I met Bishop Kurt Scharf. He had opposed Hitler and suffered, then opposed the occupying Russians and suffered, then when refused entry back into East Germany, he had become a thorn in the side of West Germans by protesting the treatment of the Baader-Meinhof Group[213] in prison and the circumstances of some of their deaths. When I asked him for advice to a minister trying to be faithful in South Africa, I was surprised when all he suggested was that I should always pray by name for the victims of the regime. I said this was something I tried to do. "Then," he said, "go to those for whom you pray." Again I said I would endeavour to do so. "And after that?" I asked. "Oh," he replied, "suffer."

In January 1982, Desmond Tutu and I discovered how true that could be. We had decided that rather than just speaking out and praying for victims of the 'system' we should try to visit them wherever and whenever we could. News came of two Lutheran priests being detained and tortured in Venda, one of the nastiest of apartheid's 'Bantustans' governed by a puppet president, Mphephu, known for his cruelty. We set off on the 300-mile journey northward to visit them. After overnighting with friends in Pietersburg[214] we went on to the Venda border post where we gave the reason for our visit as "wanting to visit some prisoners in the 'capital', Thohoyandou". The guard grudgingly let us through and when we got to the main police station the commander was expecting us. "So you want to visit prisoners?" We said that we believed he had Lutheran priests in detention and we wanted to pray with them. What we didn't know at the time was that a priest named Reverend Tshifiwa Moufhe had been tortured to death some days before and that the others were in no condition to be seen by us. "We have no prisoners here," he said. Then he told us to wait while he "sorted things out". After an hour in a grim little room, during which time we heard snippets of conversation, sometimes in Afrikaans and apparently with Pretoria, he came out and said, "You have been declared *persona non grata* in the Republic of Venda and you are to be deported immediately." With that a couple of nasty looking men entered the room. They wore berets and reflective dark glasses, and had low-slung trousers and guns on their hips, and all I could think of was the dreaded Tonton Macoute[215] of 'Papa Doc' Duvalier's Haiti. They surrounded us and took us outside where Desmond's white Toyota Cressida was now sandwiched between two military vehicles with more soldiers with sub-machine guns sprawling over them. It was all very menacing.

We drove in convoy for a while but instead of leading us to the 'border', our escorts turned off onto a track leading into thick bush. They stopped in a clearing where they pulled us out of the car. Some began to push us around while others took items out of the car boot and threw them on the ground. They were particularly angered when we couldn't produce passports – after all, they were an independent republic and we were foreigners – so the threats and the waving and pointing of sub-machine guns went on. "We are going to shoot you. You know we can kill you. Nobody will find your bodies. This isn't Joburg. Nobody knows Tutu or Storey here …" This went on for a while and then, as if in obedience to some signal, it ended. We were ordered to pick up our stuff and get back into the car. We drove back to the tarred road and were soon at the border, where our escorts peeled off and we continued south, deeply shaken.

If anyone doubts that for Desmond Tutu prayer and life are inseparable, I have scary proof. He was at the wheel as we drove in silence for a while waiting for our heartbeats to slow. Then he spoke: "Peter, we nearly died back there; they would have shot us as easily as swatting a fly." I answered in a not very steady voice, "Yes, it was close." Desmond said, "We need to thank God for preserving our lives." And immediately he launched into an impassioned prayer of thanksgiving. I looked at him and saw that not only was he lost in prayer but his eyes were closed. I grabbed the wheel and let him thank God while I ensured that death didn't get a second shot at us.

More than 20 years later at a conference I was approached by a tall Afrikaner with a military bearing. He asked me if I remembered Venda. It was the first time this deeply repressed memory surfaced and I felt anger course through my body. "Yes, I do remember Venda," I said. "That was when my wife was nearly widowed and my children orphaned." He said that he had been a Military Intelligence colonel seconded to the Venda government at the time, and he had passed on the order that we should be killed. He still didn't know why it had not been carried out, but was glad. Would I forgive him? I had been struggling to breathe as he spoke and muttered, "Of course, yes, I forgive you … I have to …" but as he walked away, presumably with his burden lifted, the anger remained with me. I realised that I had much to process still.

Soon after the Venda incident I went back to Namibia to do some teaching in Windhoek and drove to Walvis Bay to visit Chris, who was stationed there. Two encounters stand out. The first was when I stopped my car amid the high dunes of the Namib desert and climbed one of them until the road was out of sight. I was surrounded by nothing but the serried dunes and emptiness as far as I could see. I sat there a while, listening to the silence and pondering the likelihood that no human feet had ever trod where mine had just been. After a while it came to me that I was not alone, that the silence was not empty but populated. There was a sense of immanence, of awesome Presence all about me and I knew then why the three great 'revealed' religions – Judaism, Christianity and Islam – had all been born in the desert. God was there in an almost tangible way. It took great effort to leave that place, retracing my steps unwillingly until I saw the road and my car below me, small and insignificant.

At Walvis, Chris was serving out his term in national service, but had found an old broken Extra sailing dinghy. He could repair anything and soon had it sailing again. In spite of a strong wind we simply had to sail together on the waters off the port. They are shallow and the wind whips them up in a trice, which is exactly what happened. The little Extra was flying, somehow managing the outward leg, but turning was going to be very tricky and coming home even more so. We were both shouting with a mixture of fear and exhilaration and finally made it back on a half-sunken boat to the beach. If my desert encounter was one way of being close to God, this was another, more exultant one.

My position on disinvestment and sanctions was initially a cautious one, supporting "targeted sanctions" of white activities and strategic goods rather than a total blockade of the South African economy, but I tried to be nuanced about it because Desmond and other colleagues I respected stood for a stronger position. Not only do I know now that I was badly wrong, but I embarrassed SACC by being caught out in a debate with Professor Wiehahn at the University of South Africa in 1985. There I did express my doubts about disinvestment but said that my opinion was irrelevant: "People who are desperate enough will use such a weapon and will have the right to say that it is better than violent revolution," I declared. The government-financed *Citizen* newspaper pounced and next day had front-page headlines screaming, 'METHODIST NO TO DISINVESTMENT'.[216] The truth is that the sanctions and disinvestment campaign became a crucial pillar of the struggle and without it the chances of total war would have been much, much greater. The economic squeeze reduced the regime's military options and forced it to look in new directions. I was far too slow to see this.

In 1986 I had my first encounter with heart problems, while on my way to speak at a conference on disinvestment in White Plains, NY. Because of the embargo on direct flights, I usually travelled via

London, overnighting with friends Paul and Linda Keister before flying on to New York. The days before had been very stressful and while shopping with Linda I collapsed, regaining consciousness in the high care ward of a Wimbledon hospital. An NHS doctor was leaning over me telling me I'd had a heart attack. A battery of tests the next day established that I had not, and I was released after 36 hours in time to get to America and deliver my conference paper a couple of days late.

Meanwhile, on 20 June I was phoned in the early hours of the morning by the wife of Reverend Ike Moloabi to tell me that he had just been picked up by the Security Police and taken away in his pyjamas. Ike was a fine minister stationed in Ikageng, the black township outside of Potchefstroom. I set off right away on the 124 km journey to meet Errol Hind, our other minister in Potchefstroom. By 8 am we were making the rounds of the police stations looking for Ike. As was usual in these detentions, there were denials of any knowledge of him, but when we got to the town prison someone let slip that he was indeed there. As his Bishop I demanded to see him and it worked. We were put in a room with some rough benches and an Afrikaans prison officer brought Ike in. He was still in his pyjamas, shivering in the cold and obviously frightened.

We were not allowed to say much to each other, but I had brought in my pockets some bread, a small chalice and communion wine, so I asked the guard if we could give Ike Holy Communion and he agreed. Spreading a handkerchief on the bench between us with the bread and cup upon it, I told the guard that Methodist Communion was open to all, and invited him to join us. After some hesitation, he accepted. Having broken the bread and shared it between the four of us, I passed the chalice first to Ike and he drank. Then, because we had a 'stranger in our midst' it seemed right to pass the cup to the officer. Now this white Afrikaner had a dilemma: if he wanted to receive the means of God's grace, he would have to place his lips for the first time in his life on a cup from which a black man had just drunk. For what seemed an eternity he held the small chalice in his beefy hands, just looking at it. Then he lifted it and drank – and at last I saw the hint of a smile on Ike's face. Finally, I confess to introducing a variation in the liturgy. "We Methodists always hold hands when we say the Grace," I said, and asked the Lord to help me keep a straight face as prison officer and prisoner held hands while I recited the ancient words of benediction. There was no miraculous release after this. Ike was kept some time longer but for the time he remained there he and this guard were strangely bound to each other and the power equation between them was never the same.

In September of that year Desmond Tutu was enthroned as the first black Archbishop of Cape Town, leader of the roughly 2 million Anglicans in the Church of the Province of Southern Africa. After the pomp of the service in the cathedral Elizabeth and I went to join the 10 000 people who greeted the new Archbishop in Goodwood Stadium. There we separated because I had to be on the podium to welcome Desmond on behalf of the wider ecumenical church family. Bareheaded and in my black cassock, I looked a little out of place among all the be-mitred bishops of the province resplendent in their white and gold. I guess this is what it means to be a non-conformist, I thought. When it was my turn to speak I reminded Desmond that we had shared the same small town as children,[217] "I in privilege, you in poverty." South Africa had separated us, I said, but the Church of Jesus brought us together. We had prayed together, gone to prison together and been deported together, "and today we can thank God together that this vast gathering is a sign of a new South Africa," and there was thunderous applause. "Today we salute your service to the ecumenical movement but even more we salute you as a symbol of hope for the hopeless, as a voice for the voiceless and as a servant of the cross," I said. "Today is a word to those in power that apartheid is doomed."

Probably because of wide exposure through Life Line and also SACC, personal invitations to me to preach or teach internationally were coming thick and fast. One such was to offer the Hickman Lectures on preaching at Duke University, in North Carolina. It was my first visit to what was later to become our second home. I loved the gracious gothic campus and enjoyed preaching in the cathedral-like chapel that towers over it. In the coming years I would preach or teach in 140 American cities, giving me unique access to the heartbeat of that remarkable country and leading later to even being invited to be 'Secretary of State' for a day.

One Sunday evening in 1988 a distinguished-looking man in his early 60s slipped into the back pew of our chapel at CMM. He came to a couple more services before introducing himself as Ian McCrae, the CEO of Eskom, South Africa's giant parastatal energy company. He slipped his card into my hand and asked if I would lunch with him. Some days later we met in his office in Eskom's massive headquarters and as we ate he drew my attention to a large oil painting. It depicted one of Eskom's mighty generating stations with powerlines running off toward a distant city. But the painting held a surprise: under the powerlines was a tree and a small rude dwelling, with a black family living there. "I keep that in my office to remind me why I'm really here," he said. "We have more power than we need in this country yet families like that live by kerosene lamps." He went on to speak of his dilemma. Because he kept the lights on in South Africa PW Botha's Security Council and the military knew that he could also switch them off. He was being drawn into their web with a view to weaponising electric power as part of the 'Total Strategy',[218] but he wanted to use the massive utility to free people, not hold them to ransom. Could I put him in touch with the "real black leaders" so he could hear from them how best to do this? I was impressed with him and undertook to make the contacts secretly. He could not be seen publicly to be consulting any but the regime's 'tame' black surrogates. I met McCrae late one night in the underground parking garage of the Sun Hotel where we swopped cars and I drove him into Soweto to meet with Frank Chikane and a small group assembled to meet him. He listened intently as they described life in Soweto and the vagaries of the electricity supply, problems of payment for the poor and so on. As if by arrangement there was a power outage while they spoke and the meeting continued by candle-light. McCrae undertook to go away and process what he had heard, and report back. I know that he wanted to supply Soweto direct instead of through the corrupt local councillors and took seriously a 'block-by-block' billing scheme suggested by the group, so that block committees could assess households with a view to discounts for the poorest residents. My role ended by hosting the feedback meeting at CMM on 21 December, attended by Frank, and heavyweights Albertina Sisulu, Cyril Ramaphosa, Ellen Kuzwayo and Sister Bernard Ncube. I do not know what flowed from any further meetings, but got the feeling that he had run into a wall at the Security Council end.

Also in 1988 a number of church leaders went on the shortest protest march ever. Five days after the banning by the government of seventeen anti-apartheid organisations and a number of their leaders, a protest service was held in St Mary's Cathedral in Cape Town on 29 February. I spoke the 'sending forth' prayer: "Go now in the spirit of Christ into a land of hatred, take his spirit of love into this city of division, take his spirit of unity into these streets of violence, take his spirit of peace and go now with God." Well. We didn't really go anywhere. We set out to march on Parliament only to be confronted by a large group of police right outside the cathedral. They ordered us to disperse and we knelt on the sidewalk instead. Our pavement prayer was short: those of us in the lead of the procession were physically lifted off our knees and my feet never touched the ground until I was pushed into the back seat of a police car alongside Frank Chikane and we were driven off to Caledon Square police station. Why the police took all this trouble I don't know, because we were not even booked into the cells before being warned and released. The rank and file of the protest were not so fortunate. They were attacked with a high-powered water-cannon and 150 clergy were arrested – something of a world record, I would think. While they were being processed we returned to the cathedral and called a press conference.

A more scary encounter in the public space was with militant youths in 1990. Father Emmanuel Lafont was a courageous priest stationed in Moletsane in Soweto. He embarked on a hunger strike protesting the escalating violence. I wanted to go and pray with him and our son Alan joined me. Parts of Soweto were in flames and a heavy pall of smoke hung over the area. Emmanuel was lying on his bed with a group of people around him and we shared together and prayed. He was one of the most humble, yet radical followers of Jesus I knew.[219] Returning through Jabavu we found that trees had been felled across some streets, making driving very difficult. As we were picking our way slowly through these barriers, sometimes driving on the sidewalk, something rapped on my side window. It was a 9mm automatic in the hands of a youth of about sixteen. He was very agitated and shouted at me to roll down my window. As I obeyed the gun barrel was pushed into my right ear and I was told to get out. A group of youths, all very menacing, surrounded our car, opening Alan's door too and pulling him out. I didn't know whether they were an ANC self-defence unit (SDU), or drugged kids taking advantage of the general anarchy to hijack us. The youth with the gun seemed to be the only one armed and his weapon was now pointed at my chest while he continued shouting. It was a very tense stand-off and there was not much I could think of to say but I pointed to the dog-collar I was wearing and said "priest". It made no difference. Then, gambling that the law of averages would favour me, I said, "Some of you are Methodists. Do you want to shoot your Bishop?" There was a pause in the shouting and the group went into a huddle and I tried to keep calm while they consulted, presumably about our lives. At that moment somebody approached from across the road. Alan remembers that he seemed to be telling them who I was.

The huddle suddenly broke and the leader came back to me, stuffing the pistol into his trouser waistband. "Sorry," he said, and we shook hands and they let us go.

In November 1990 the SACC linked up once more with African Enterprise to bring churches together at a venue in Rustenburg, 96 km from Johannesburg. It was the first time in many years that SACC member church leaders were meeting their Nederduitse Gereformeerde (Dutch Reformed) counterparts as well as engaging the Pentecostal family of churches. The rationale behind the conference was simple: if South Africa's divisions were to be healed, it was time for the churches to heal theirs. I confess to having had little appetite to engage with church leaders who – either by support or silence – had nourished and extended the life of apartheid. But after a tense beginning where we eyed each other suspiciously, a Dutch Reformed theologian from the 'cradle of apartheid', Stellenbosch University, came to the podium. His name was Professor Willie Jonker and his words would transform the spirit of the gathering:

"I confess before you and the Lord not only my own sin and guilt and my own personal responsibility for the political, social, economic and structural wrongs that have been done to you, the results of which you and our own country are still suffering from, but vicariously I dare to do that in the name of the Dutch Reformed Church of which I am a member."

For a while there was a stunned silence; you could have heard a pin drop. And then Archbishop Desmond Tutu bounded up to the platform and looked at us all and said, "Well, my theology tells me when someone confesses I have no choice. I must forgive." That was a moment of breakthrough and from then on a spirit of confession moved amongst us all. Ray McCauley stood up on behalf of the Pentecostals and said, "We sinned. We preached individual salvation without social transformation. We were neutral and therefore we collaborated with apartheid." Once they had confessed, it left us – the people who had led the struggle, or so we thought – the good guys. And in the final declaration we also had to make a confession: "Some of us were bold in denouncing apartheid but timid in resisting it. We failed to give support to courageous individuals at the forefront of protest. We spoke for justice but our own church structures continued to oppress."[220]

The Rustenburg conference was costly for the Dutch Reformed Church, especially when Moderator Dr Pieter Potgieter stated "unambiguously" that his denomination fully identified with Prof Jonker's statement. As a result of that confession some 30 000 members of the denomination walked out in anger and started a new whites-only church.[221] Dutch Reformed leader Professor Johan Heyns, with whom I worked late into the night on the committee that fashioned the Rustenburg Declaration, was later assassinated by an unknown gunman. It is thought that his turning against apartheid was seen as an act of treason against his *volk*.

Rustenburg had many positive results, however, one being that it made possible a more united capacity for peace-making that was going to become very necessary between 1990 and 1994. If the churches had not found that moment of healing, if we had not bowed our heads and confessed our own failures, we could not have played the crucial role required of us in two important bodies that saved South Africa: the National Peace Accord and the Truth and Reconciliation Commission. Both of these uniquely South African initiatives required a new spirit of working with former enemies and I doubt that either would have been possible unless estranged churches had found each other first.

21

Shadows of War

The shrieking was almost unbearable. Every rivet in the big Super Frelon seemed to be crying out as we winged across the bush. The ground was so close that I felt I could lean out of the open door and touch our shadow as it leapfrogged the trees. I'd been told that we had to fly this way to avoid ground fire from the SWAPO 'terrs' or 'terrorists', and I could see it made sense. My escorts, an army colonel and two South African Defence Force (SADF) chaplains, were hooked up to the intercom system. I'd been given earmuffs to dampen the noise and couldn't hear their conversation. However, the colonel hadn't bothered to hide his dislike; I knew I was an unwelcome guest and my presence strongly resented. It was easier to stare out the door at the blurring scrub below than to try and engage them. Looking about me, I wondered again what I was doing in an SADF chopper in the middle of a war, on my way to visit fire bases in the Caprivi bush.

It was 1985 and I was then the head of the Methodist Church of Southern Africa, but ever since my naval ambitions of 28 years before, my path had continued to intersect with the world of the military in different ways. This was just one of the more bizarre manifestations of a complicated relationship.

As early as 1970, church and state in South Africa had engaged in an increasingly tense exchange over issues of military chaplaincy, conscription and the 'Border War'. And behind these loomed, of course, the overarching debate about violence itself. Under the influence of Gandhi and King, and mentor Alan Walker, I had come to a personal position of Christian pacifism, hoping that I would find the courage to live it out. As a cocky undergraduate at Rhodes I had argued confidently for the 'Just War' position, but no longer. Try as I might there was no way that I could imagine Jesus in military uniform. I had become convinced that non-violence was his way and that the church's compromise with war since the time of Constantine was its longest and most tragic act of disobedience. With war there were no winners, only blood and more blood.

However, I never lost empathy for the people in uniform. Not only had I been one of them for a while, but the sacrifices of WWII had been stamped too deeply into my early consciousness to join the peace movement's sometimes glib condemnations of the military. I still appreciated the Just War position even though I could no longer defend it and felt for those who made the dreadful death and life decisions of command – who had to just "… do these things and say our prayers at the end …"[222] I shared Gandhi's view that practitioners of non-violence should not scorn military bravery but exceed it by being willing to die but not to kill. For me, the real problem lay not with the soldiers but with the politicians who sent immature eighteen-year-olds to fight their wars and die for their ambitions. As a father of four sons I cared particularly about young conscripts sucked into the SADF, and as a minister I cared about colleagues tasked with giving them spiritual care as chaplains. This may appear to have been a conflicted position, and of course it was, yet perhaps no more conflicted than that of Jesus the non-violent liberator giving time and compassion to an officer of the occupying Roman army.

Defence Minister PW Botha's view was that "The honour and duty to defend one's country should not be made subservient to one's religious convictions." A statement like that asked for confrontation and that is what he got at the 1974 SACC National Conference, held at Hammanskraal. Reverend Douglas Bax proposed that because the SADF was defending an unjust and discriminatory society, young conscripts should be encouraged to refuse service and the churches should reconsider seconding ministers as military chaplains. I supported the main thrust of the resolution but decided to engage Bax about the withdrawal of chaplaincy. The vast majority of SADF personnel were young conscripts who would be abandoned to the care of Dutch Reformed chaplains, most of whom were part of the apartheid brainwashing machine. I was determined that they should not be left without some spiritual succour. After a tough debate, my amendment was carried, leaving our chaplains in place but calling for "reconsideration of the basis on which they were appointed". It also sought to investigate ministry to the pastoral needs of those "under arms beyond our borders".

The 'Conscientious Objection' resolution broke on the nation like a thunderclap. Botha immediately tabled the Defence Further Amendment Bill with a R10 000 fine or ten-year prison sentence for anyone who encouraged another person to refuse military service.[223] This was later watered down to six years, but still made counselling potential objectors a high-risk business. Meanwhile, choosing to be a CO carried an automatic six-year prison sentence. When I became minister of CMM in 1976 we offered an office to the Conscientious Objectors' Advice Bureau and I was in awe of elderly ladies like Nan Cross who trod a legal tightrope, risking their own freedom as they helped troubled conscripts make decisions that could involve six years behind bars. Theirs was a role truly subversive of the 'powers', played with sweetly innocent smiles and cups of tea in their office one floor above mine.

On Sundays CMM used to hold a small evening service in our ground-floor chapel and because we were known to be sympathetic to COs, numbers of them attended. Their own congregations had coldly rejected them; here there was warmth and welcome. The presence of these young men always challenged me. Some of them were already on trial, others had yet to face arrest. No cheap religiosity would do for them; they came for the real thing. The Gospel that had inspired them to sacrifice needed now to strengthen them for suffering.

Then, in one of God's amazing ironies, the dynamics of our evening worship became even more unique. Following the Soweto uprising, the townships had been occupied by the military. Young white conscripts who had been told they would be facing an enemy on the northern borders of the Republic were now patrolling the streets of Soweto and Alexandra. One Sunday evening, just as worship began, there was a screech of brakes outside the chapel, some barked orders and the clumping of boots in the foyer. I continued with the service but it was hard to concentrate and the COs inside the chapel were white faced and anxious. WWII veteran Ken Roberts went out to investigate and found an entire platoon of uniformed SADF medics in the foyer. They came from the Diepkloof barracks on the edge of Soweto and were in the charge of a young corporal – also a conscript – who was a Methodist and had decided they should go to church. We were the only Methodist Church he knew of in Joburg and he asked if they could come in. There was one problem, however. Ken pointed to the pistol on his belt and said, "You can't bring that into our chapel." The corporal was apologetic. They were not allowed to drive anywhere without one of them being armed, he explained. I know nothing of the negotiation that followed, save that the weapon was handed to Ken, who spirited it away to a safe place for the duration of the service, and the soldiers joined our conscientious objectors for worship. This arrangement went on for some months and it was fascinating to see the engagement between them over coffee after each service. Here were a group of young white South African males similar in all respects save one decision: to either accept conscription or resist it. After some stiffness and suspicion it seemed to me that an unexpected sympathy grew between them. Our COs knew how difficult their own choice had been and cast no blame on those who had found it easier to 'go with the flow' when the call-up came, while at least some of those in uniform expressed a sneaking respect for contemporaries who were facing six years in prison for their principles. Standing in the foyer after worship and watching a soldier and a CO talking animatedly about rugby caused me to wonder again at the never-ending weirdness of our strange country.

Army occupation of the townships was initially seen as an improvement on the trigger-happy police patrols they replaced, but as soldiers got involved in house-to-house searches, reports of some atrocities emerged. A 'Troops out the Townships' campaign gained traction and, particularly in Alex, resistance grew. Youths were digging trenches to trap the ugly armoured 'Hippos' used by the police, and stringing wire across streets to try and decapitate soldiers riding in the high, open 'Buffels'. In February 1986 a concerted attempt was made by the churches to get the government to withdraw the troops from Alex. After a fruitless trip to Cape Town to plead for withdrawal, Desmond Tutu, Bishop Manas Buthelezi and I went to the stadium in Alexandra to report back. The arena was packed with 45 000 angry residents. We squeezed our way through those tightly jammed on the field itself and climbed on the back of a flat-bed truck. As Desmond began to use the PA system on the truck, his voice broke. "I have nothing to bring you," he said. "We have failed." The anger in the crowd was tangible and he spoke again, in Xhosa and Sotho, but any attempt to offer hope was drowned out. There was nothing for it but to leave. We jumped down from the truck and some older men formed a wedge to get us to our car. Once there a group of youths surrounded us. "Why should we let you go?" they shouted. "You come here with nothing and leave us to these soldiers who are killing us!" It was a very scary moment but they finally let us leave. As we drove away Desmond wept. "They are right," he said. "We brought them nothing."

As a Bishop, one of the portfolios assigned to me was that of military chaplaincy, responsible for implementing our church's policy and caring for the welfare of our chaplains. I found very quickly that they divided between those who were clergy wearing uniform in order to do their job, and those who did the job *for* the uniform. There were ministers of integrity and courage who were willing to embrace this deeply ambivalent role for the sake of getting alongside the young and often frightened conscripts who were the cannon fodder of the apartheid wars. Other chaplains should not have been permitted near the job: they enjoyed the military too much and had absorbed not only its culture but big doses of the 'Total Strategy' ideology. These were the people we needed to weed out. Among the truly dedicated chaplains, some paid a heavy price for their loyalty to MCSA and its position on the South African struggle. The Chaplain-General to whom they answered was an NGK dominee. During the notorious 'ComOps' political indoctrination classes run by Military Intelligence he had warned against "Tutu and Storey and other dangerous subversives", implying that we were both communists. One of our chaplains[224] immediately protested, demanding that the general meet with the chair of the MCSA Chaplaincy Committee – myself. An embarrassed Chaplain-General ended up apologising to me, asking me to convey his regrets to Bishop Tutu as well. These moments of small triumph were of course meaningless in the larger scheme of things, but I admired the courage and loyalty of a young chaplain willing to call out his general in that way.

I had experienced something similar myself when Bishop Tutu and I travelled to Namibia in 1982 to investigate allegations of SADF atrocities in Ovamboland. We listened to horror stories of how the feared Koevoet police counter-insurgency battalion, co-founded by multiple murderer Colonel Eugene de Kock, used to rampage through villages in their Hippos, dragging the bodies of killed 'terrorists' behind them in the dust and often leaving flattened dwellings behind them too. More than one Ovambo chief had been killed for alleged sympathy with SWAPO and captured land-mines had been planted by SADF operatives near their villages, with deaths of innocent villagers blamed on the 'terrorists'. It was a dirty war.

On our return to Windhoek, we called a press conference to expose some of what we had seen, and demanded an immediate withdrawal by both sides to end the suffering. "South Africa is in an unwinnable war," I said. "Every military victory of the South Africans is a political victory for SWAPO."[225] Unknown to us the hotel we used was partially occupied by the SADF and the press were highly amused at attending an anti-SADF 'presser' a couple of floors below military headquarters. Less amusing for me, however, was the knowledge that my two eldest sons, John and Christopher, were naval conscripts serving right then in nearby Walvis Bay. There was no way they would escape some of the fallout of their dad now being a whistle-blower, and I felt for them. The press conference struck a nerve. Government-supporting media and the military were quick to counter-attack: the Afrikaans newspaper *Beeld* carried a cartoon showing Desmond and me welcoming a thuggish, heavily armed 'terrorist' with Tutu saying, "I greet you – not as Communists or Marxists, but as beloved Anglicans and Lutherans."[226] The SADF said it was "obvious that the Rev Peter Storey and the SWA churchmen with whom he had discussions, have either been misled by the stream of twisted propaganda emanating from that sinister tool of Russian expansionism SWAPO, or are in cahoots with that organization."[227] The day after the press conference we sat in the Windhoek airport lounge waiting for our flight home, surrounded by fellow passengers, all of them white and many in uniform. They subjected us to the most poisonous glares I can remember and I expected someone to get up at any moment and assault us. It was around the time of Evensong, however, and Desmond Tutu opened his Missal[228] and began to quietly say his evening prayers. Nothing would divert him from his spiritual disciplines.

Meanwhile, I had succeeded Anglican Archbishop Philip Russell as Chairperson of the recently formed Inter-Church Committee on Military Chaplaincy (ICCM). It was our job to try and implement parts of the Hammanskraal Resolution by finding ways on one hand to distance our military chaplains from the SADF structures, and on the other, to investigate chaplaincy to the liberation movements. We were on a hiding to nothing. We tried to take chaplains out of uniform, but the Geneva Conventions require that chaplains must be attached to military units and wear a recognised uniform. So we set about designing a 'non-military uniform'. It was all something of a waste of time, made worse by the fact that one of our number was an informer, ensuring that the Defence Ministry was one step ahead of us most of the time. It was even more difficult to organise pastoral care to the liberation movements. Those who called most loudly for this in our church were nowhere to be seen when we asked for volunteers. We did, however, establish contact with an Anglican priest who was offering ministry to exiles in Umkhonto we Sizwe, the ANC armed wing.

The real heroes of our conflict with the SADF were the COs. They were not many, but one after another they made their compelling witness, and suffered for it. As the years passed, their numbers grew. The state grudgingly introduced a 'Religious Objector' category but government remained unmoved by any 'selective objection' based on the immorality of the Border War.

In 1985, the year of my Presidency of MCSA, an invitation arrived for me to accompany other church leaders on an SADF-sponsored trip to the 'Operational Area' in northern Namibia and the Caprivi Strip. I knew of these tours, when VIPs were wined and dined and given the propaganda line from morning to night, and I refused the invitation. At the same time I felt a pastoral responsibility toward Methodist youngsters caught in the SADF web. So I waited for a decent interval and then made an official request to visit Methodist conscripts in the Operational Area. The SADF people were enraged but I knew that in terms of a longstanding church-state concordat, they were obliged to give someone in my position the access I asked for. The military just had to grin and bear it. On 21 May I met up with the unhappy colonel and the two SADF chaplains in Rundu on the Angolan border. We boarded the Super Frelon chopper and headed off into the bush. I had specifically asked to meet with conscripts in more exposed situations, and the low-altitude rush across the bush brought us to them.

We would come upon a fire-base in the middle of nowhere, where the bush had been cleared for a couple of hundred metres in all directions and high berms bulldozed out of the sand formed perimeter walls. A watchtower or two overlooked the bush and behind the safety of the berms was a small canvas village surrounding a headquarters tent and a mess-tent. To one side were makeshift showers and latrines and the helipad, on which we descended with an enormous racket, whipping up a stinging cloud of sand. This was as close as any civilian would get to the sharp end of the Border War. We never stayed longer than an hour before flying on to the next fire-base and at each one I was met by anyone not on patrol who wanted to join me. The largest group consisted of about 25 young conscripts. I was honest with them, saying that while the Methodist Church could not support this war I knew that they hadn't asked to be here, that they were maybe scared and that we cared about them very much. They were remarkably open with me: like soldiers everywhere, they hated the boredom and yes, when on patrol they were often afraid. One of them was bold enough to talk about the corrosive effect of hate. "We're taught to hate here," he said, "and I fear what that is doing to me." Others nodded as he spoke. I had already seen the evidence while drinking some coffee in a HQ tent: ghastly photos of mangled corpses looking down on us – trophies denoting the fire-base's 'kills' – and I had wondered what long-term damage these crude 'motivators' wrought and what price would one day have to be paid for such violations of human decency. It was not easy to respond to him. We talked about the God who I believed never left us, even when we walked into places [he] didn't want us to go. I asked them for telephone numbers of parents and girlfriends promising that I would call them all when I got home. Before parting we said prayers together and then I shook their hands and got back into the chopper.

The next day I finally flew back to Waterkloof Air Force Base in a military C-140 transport. At home, I began to place telephone calls: late into the night I called parents and girlfriends, to tell them that I had seen their soldier son or lover a dozen or so hours previously and that he was "okay". When I first identified myself the reaction was usually one of suspicion or outright hostility. Why would someone with my political reputation be wanting them – and at that time of night? Then, when the purpose of the call was shared and messages passed on, the chill slowly melted, to be replaced by thanks and appreciation. "We stand against this war," I said, "but we care about those caught up in it." It was a good night's work and I went to sleep alongside Elizabeth in the small hours thinking about young men on two sides of a dirty war, sleeping fitfully that night in exposed places, each seeking courage for this needless conflict.

At the 1987 Methodist Conference, some of us called for MCSA to make a radical break with its past and become the first 'mainline' denomination to declare itself a "Peace Church". In so doing we would join the small group of Christian bodies like the Mennonites and Quakers who renounced violence, refusing to let their members take part in war. After a vigorous debate, it was surprisingly agreed to refer the issue to all Circuits across the country, for discussion. My episcopal area as Bishop covered Johannesburg, Soweto and the mining towns to the south west, passing through arch-conservative places like Krugersdorp, Ventersdorp – headquarters of the Afrikaner Weerstandsbeweging (AWB)[229] – and Vryburg. In the middle of a war, Methodists got down to arguing whether their denomination should commit itself to pacifism, but many local Superintendent ministers ducked the issue rather than face uproar. I was invited to some angry Circuit meetings and was fascinated to see how this issue united whites and blacks in opposition. Whites were outraged that their church was asking them to "stand by and let the Communists take over the country" while blacks could not believe we wanted their liberation movements to lie down while the army and police "just mowed them down". I tried to interpret to each the dilemma of the "other", with little success and came away more convinced than ever of how different things might have been if MCSA had been more integrated at grassroots. Instead Methodists were shouting past each other – and in some places, no doubt shooting at each other. It was while driving out to one of these meetings – and having chosen a back road through Lichtenburg – that I came across the sobering sight of a long convoy of SADF tank carriers bearing heavily damaged tanks and other armoured vehicles. It was clear that there had been a major battle in which SADF armour had been badly mauled, and that they were choosing the back roads on their way back from Angola to Pretoria. None of us had yet heard of Cuito Cuanavale[230] and the horrendous battle fought there but the picture of those twisted wrecks stayed to haunt me. Men had died inside them.

The next Methodist Conference received reports from the Circuits and Districts and came somewhat regretfully to the conclusion that the Methodist people were not ready to embrace the Peace Church notion. Pacifists would remain a minority and the church would have no new prophetic word for a nation torn in two.

Throughout these years the shadow of the inevitable call-up of our four sons, John, Christopher, David and Alan, had hung over us. We were concerned for their physical safety of course, but there was the deeper matter of integrity. The concept of 'moral injury' is relatively new: it refers to the character damage soldiers experience, not so much from what they have suffered, but because of what they may have *perpetrated*. We hated to imagine any of our boys actually killing another person, never mind a fellow South African. Because of this, I had hoped very much that my naval background would count in getting them into the navy, where chances of this happening were far less. In spite of their putting up a good case, when John and Christopher's papers arrived, they were both headed for the army. We were still trying to come to terms with this when sheer coincidence gave me an opportunity. Passing the SA Navy recruiting office in Pretoria one day, I heard someone shouting my name. Looking in, I was surprised to see the very person who had once sat beside me in 1956 on the bus to Saldanha Bay. Now he was a naval captain and apparently in charge of recruiting. He surprised me with the warmth of his welcome, as if unaware of the wide gulf that these days alienated me from the SADF and its actions. After chatting for a while he asked me about my family and I took my chance: "Can you believe," I said, "that my two eldest boys have both been called up for the army? Two sons of a naval officer made to wear khaki!" My captain friend's reply made my heart leap: "Ag, we can't have that, Peter," he said. "Give me their details and I'll look into it." It was as simple as that. New papers soon arrived and instead of the army, John and Christopher both left for naval training at my old establishment, SAS *Saldanha*, and were later posted to Walvis Bay. I know that I compromised some principles that day in Pretoria, for interests that were very personal, but I think I can live with that guilt – and I remain ever grateful for that chance meeting and the generosity of Captain X.

Our third son, David, was reading law at the University of the Witwatersrand, and was a student activist deeply involved in NUSAS and SRC activities. He and his colleagues had been harassed by the Security Police but he had managed to get his military service deferred legally each year. In late 1989, 771 young white men from all over South Africa announced that none of them would fight in the 'Apartheid Army'. Over 100 of those based in Gauteng appeared dramatically at the home of SACC Vice-President Sheena Duncan in Johannesburg. As they sat together on Sheena's lawn I congratulated them on having denied "a whole company of infantry" to the apartheid army. I was grateful that three of our sons were there: David was declaring that with deferments ended, he would now refuse; John, who was about to become a chartered accountant, had completed two years and an extra camp in the navy, was refusing to report again, and Alan was there too. The only one missing was Christopher, who had graduated from the Johannesburg College of Education and married his lovely fiancée Kim. They were now teaching together in Mmabatho and he had made the same decision as John.

Needing space to think through his call-up, Alan had followed matric by spending 1988 working as a labourer in Australia and returned with his mind made up: he would be a CO. He had a profound commitment to non-violence and although his objection was solidly faith based, he decided to reject 'religious objector' status because it discriminated against secular moral and political objectors. So he began to prepare himself for six years in jail. He felt called to seek ordination as a minister and while in Australia he had preached his first sermon in a Sydney church. It was titled *The Only Thing God Cannot Do*, the theme being that God was incapable of ceasing to love us. It happened to be on my 50th birthday and news of it was a special gift.

In April 1989 a small group of Methodists, ordained and lay, met in retreat on a farm outside Johannesburg. Our purpose was to launch the Methodist Order of Peacemakers (MOP). A conference to plan this had been held five months before in strife-torn Pietermaritzburg. After much agonising and praying, those who felt ready to do so gathered in a circle to make our commitments. On the table in the centre of the circle, handwritten and fresh from our struggles, lay the Pledge of the new Order. It read simply:

> I desire to model my life on the non-violent way of Jesus;
> I therefore renounce violence and pledge myself to engage actively in the work of peacemaking.
> I will seek to live by the rule of life of the Methodist Order of Peacemakers.
> I accept that this commitment may be costly to me, but make it trusting in Christ who strengthens me.

Alan went first to the table, signing his name, followed by Elizabeth and myself in support of him and seventeen others. It was a holy moment, made solemn by the tremendous price that Alan and some of the others were ready to pay for that simple promise. South Africa now had the harshest laws in the world penalising conscientious objectors.

While waiting for the axe to fall Alan worked on his minister's candidature process, serving on the CMM staff, mainly among homeless street people. At age 22 MCSA accepted him as a Probationer Minister and in January 1991 Conference appointed him to a congregation in Rustenburg. It was a miserable situation: his supervising minister was a gung-ho part-time SADF chaplain with no sympathy for Alan's stand and the conservative congregation chose to simply ignore the agony he was going through. The day he was required to report for military training, he went to Doornkop base near Soweto as required, declared his refusal, was arrested and ordered to appear in court on 15 April 1991. The End Conscription Campaign (ECC) came to his support: "We need men of peace like Alan Storey working among South Africans and building the spirit of the new nation, not wasting time in prison," they declared.

Through all of this my bizarre relationship with the SADF continued. I was travelling to Heidelberg Military Base to meet with conscripted Methodist ministers who were making a stand against having to carry arms during their training and then attending MOP meetings the same evening. On 6 April, Elizabeth, a number of MOP members and myself were taken into custody by an army warrant officer for demonstrating outside the Armscor Defence Exposition at the Rand Show. Having confiscated our anti-SADF placards, he marched ahead of us, ramrod stiff, not knowing that he was displaying the top poster to good effect to the watching crowd. We followed happily.

Eight days later, on the evening before Alan's court appearance, we held a prayer service in our 'COs' Chapel'. It was crowded with friends and members from CMM and the Conscientious Objectors'

Support Group (COSG) and ECC, who had plastered the city with posters of Alan with the words: 'Rev Alan Storey – On Trial for Non-violence'. I struggled through a short homily, rather choked up with the thought that by the end of the next day, our fourth son might vanish for six years into the maw of South Africa's prison system. I wanted people to grasp why he was doing this: "Many say that the stand he is taking is unrealistic," I said, that because we live in a fallen world "... realism requires us to use imperfect methods like violence." Alan, however, had a different sense of what was real: his starting point was the Cross of Jesus – God's way of confronting evil with radical love. "That is the reality that Alan lives by," I said, "and that is why he cannot support the unrealistic and outworn way of violence." Our son was going further than simply refusing to use violence to defend apartheid. "He is saying that he could not use violence even to destroy it." This service, though painful, was also a deep celebration. I said that Al had made the biggest discovery of all: *being real was to be loved, to love and to refuse not to love* – even though, as the Skin Horse once told the Velveteen Rabbit, "it might hurt sometimes".[231]

And so we went to court. Alan was represented by Advocate Edwin Cameron, later to become a distinguished judge of the Constitutional Court. Our son was calm but his heart must have been racing. The courtroom slowly filled and we waited for argument to begin. In the end it was a strange anti-climax: the magistrate informed the crowded room that, at the request of the Attorney-General of the Transvaal, he was adjourning the trial. Something was afoot. We didn't know it at the time, but we were witnessing the death throes of the conscription system. Alan appeared again on 13 May with a similar outcome. Then on 17 June, at his third appearance, the SADF withdrew all charges against him. He was a free person – which of course he had always been – a truly free person. The entire conscription edifice had begun to unravel. His first public words afterward honoured the COs who had gone before him over the years, especially those who had been imprisoned. He hinted at his own experience of the cost: "I think back on the many days I broke down and wept, agonising over my decision ..." But, he declared joyfully, "I give testimony to the truth that God's power is made perfect in weakness ... when I am weak then I am strong."

My last duty toward SADF personnel was with Adele Kirsten, who was the genius behind so many of the ECC's imaginative protests. In May 1997 she and I spoke at an ECC press conference in a last-minute plea to ex-conscripts to come to the Truth and Reconciliation Commission while there was still opportunity. I felt deeply about this. "For those who carry guilt, it's time to be healed," I said, "and for those who deny guilt, it's time for the truth ... and for white South Africans it's time to pay a debt." I attacked the military for "sitting tight, arrogantly hiding behind a dubious code of unit loyalty and oaths of secrecy," and called for ex-conscripts to come forward and expose the human rights violations of the war. The apartheid military ideology had conscripted not only their bodies but their consciences: "By coming to the TRC you can reclaim your consciences ... and expose the truth." A last word was for those who had refused conscription: "Those ... who paid the full price, not only of imprisonment, but the sneers of a misguided white public ... I salute those young men today. They were the conscience of South Africa's white youth and the most obvious victims of conscription."

Over the quarter century that conscription was in place, some 600 000 white youth were called up, to become in the words of Theresa Edlmann, "both victims of a system and perpetrators in its name".[232] The SADF was never defeated in the field but too many of its members were internally damaged because of what South Africa's dirty wars demanded of them. Moral injury manifests itself still in men in their 50s, 60s and 70s today. Our culpability has yet to be exorcised.

22

A Blow Falls

I served on the executive of the SACC first during its rapid expansion under John Rees's leadership and finally as its President during Bishop Desmond Tutu's early years as General Secretary. The organisation had become the flag-bearer of church resistance against the apartheid state. Prior to the birth of the UDF[233] in 1983, we were virtually standing in for a black leadership that had been thrust into prison or exile. With the Catholic Bishops' Conference (CBC) and Beyers Naudé's small but influential Christian Institute, our actions attracted the glare of media attention as well as uncomfortable government and Security Police scrutiny. My time in leadership also brought a personal crisis that was to test my friendships and my sense of integrity to breaking point.

It was late on Friday, 10 April 1981 when the blow came. Desmond Tutu, Sally Motlana and I had spent the day engaging with church leaders from all over the country about the fallout from Desmond's latest overseas trip. He had enraged the regime once again with his calls for economic pressure on South Africa and they needed to hear first-hand what he had said, and why. Now they were gone and we were joined by Matt Stevenson, our administrator, and SACC legal adviser Oliver Barrett. Matt was a dour Scot and without any change in his customary expressionless manner, he brought the news that would shake SACC to its foundations over the next three years: it seemed that while the police were investigating misappropriation of SACC funds by another staffer, they had stumbled on *prima facie* evidence that John Rees had stolen money from the council. At that moment they were waiting outside wanting us to sign an affidavit laying a complaint against him.

Matt's statement sucked the oxygen out of the room. For a while we sat in stunned silence. It was too much to take in. My first thought, and I know Sally's too, was that this was the work of the Security Police and that if there was evidence, it must have been planted. Knowing John as I did, there could be no other possibility ...

I had first met John Rees in 1967 when we both served on the MCSA's Commission for the Renewal of the Church. I took an immediate liking to this dynamic young layman's quick wit, his sharp mind and seemingly boundless energy. At the time he was in the very senior echelons of the Johannesburg City Council's Non-European Affairs Department, having started as a humble clerk. He had been converted through the Methodist Youth Camp movement and ran the youth work in his local church in the Jeppe area. The turning point in John's life was his selection to attend the 4th Assembly of the World Council of Churches in Uppsala, Sweden. To this 30-year-old who until then had experienced little beyond Johannesburg Methodism, the discovery of the church's world-wide ecumenical family was mind blowing – and its agenda even more so. Uppsala was the first of the more radically engaged assemblies of the WCC. Its message spoke of listening to "... the cry of those who long for peace; of the hungry and exploited who demand bread and justice; of the victims of discrimination who claim human dignity; and of the increasing millions who seek for the meaning of life". God had heard these cries and ... acknowledging that human beings had not yet learned how to live together, the assembly vowed that "especially we shall seek to overcome racism wherever it appears".[234] John heard a personal call at Uppsala to live a more ecumenically inclusive, socially engaged Christianity. When the position of General Secretary of the SACC was advertised he decided to apply. The position in this modest, underfunded organisation had always been held by a senior clergyman, and John was not the only one surprised when he was appointed to succeed Bishop Bill Burnett.

His first year was marked by the firestorm over the WCC's Programme to Combat Racism (PCR). The world body's action in granting funds to South African liberation movements among others enraged Prime Minister John Vorster and millions of whites in the country. Not only did the young GS navigate the crisis with deft skill, but from the day of his arrival at SACC he infused a new energy and began to build it into a much more formidable organisation.

By the time our family moved to Johannesburg in 1972, the SACC was already hardly recognisable. New divisions had been established, staff hired and much wider contacts established with churches in Europe, the United States and the rest of Africa. My relationship with John grew at three levels: a personal friendship that would last until the night he died, a stimulating and businesslike engagement in the SACC, and an exciting and virtually indispensable collaboration in the development of the Central Methodist Mission. He and Dulcie were the first to befriend Elizabeth and me as we sought to settle in Braamfontein with our four boys. I recall our first dinner with them in the revolving restaurant at the top of the Hillbrow Tower and my wonder at their generosity: the R25 bill for the four of us was an amount I could not have afforded. John and I developed a strong friendship. We both came from relatively humble beginnings and had no interest in wealth. We were both deeply private people, ill at ease with heart-on-sleeve emotionalism. We also shared what some would call 'old-fashioned' values, prizing honesty, hard work, loyalty and discipline, and both of us regarded service to the church as a call we needed to obey.

Elizabeth became engaged in the SACC before me. Soon after we arrived in Johannesburg John's lone secretary used to bring Elizabeth her overflows of work and this developed ultimately into a position as PA to him. Elizabeth was to serve three General Secretaries in that position: John Rees, John Thorne and Desmond Tutu. For my part I began attending the executive in 1975 and was elected a vice-president in July 1977. John was punctilious in avoiding SACC shop-talk away from those meetings and never attempted to use our friendship to influence any position I might take as an officer of the Council. In any case we thought we would overlap for only a brief period because John had decided to move on.

It was his involvement with CMM that had us working most closely together. I have never met anybody more disciplined and indefatigable. John rose very early and after spending time in prayer and gathering his thoughts for the day, donated at least two hours to his church commitments before arriving punctually at his office at SACC, and later the SA Institute of Race Relations. His role at CMM expanded over the years: teaching a teenager class each Sunday morning, organising Big Walk fundraisers and flower shows with Dulcie, and being a Circuit steward[235] of the Mission. His biggest commitment was to manage Cornerstone House, our block of flats for disability pensioners. In the multitude of tasks involved, fundraising, preparation of leases, dealing with difficult tenants, the total renovation of the building inside and out, John was key and he accounted for any finances to the last cent. To be in a meeting with John – he was one of the faithful stewards who met with me each week at 6.30 am – was always exciting. Time and again he provided the creative edge to a conversation with new ideas about how to make CMM more effective. We also worked together more widely. He ran the African Old Age Pensioners Scheme and built the first home for the aged in Soweto. He established Meals on Wheels in three black townships and managed Methodist Relief, a massive feeding scheme. Together we worked at a national level on the MCSA Renewal Commission, and Obedience '81. While never quite acknowledging it to each other, we both told others that we were best friends.[236]

This then, was the man who I was now asked to believe was a thief.

Because I would not, my fate was to be inextricably bound to John's over some of the most painful years of my life.

After seven years heading the SACC, John had resigned. He had grown the Council exponentially from a handful of staffers to a complement of over 40 persons overseeing thirteen different areas of mission – home and family life, justice and reconciliation, theological education, bursary funds, inter-church aid, mission and evangelism ... and more.[237] He had also seen to it that the ratio of black divisional directors to white had changed significantly: seven of the twelve were now black persons.[238] We replaced him with Reverend John Thorne, a distinguished previous president whose tenure was very brief. Thorne had none of Rees's administrative flair and became quite immobilised in the face of the complex SACC task. When faced with documents he didn't grasp, his tendency was to simply stuff them – including donation drafts – into his desk drawers and hope they would go away. He was gone within a few months of being appointed and John Rees called back to hold the fort while we searched for another GS, this time the Anglican Bishop of Lesotho, Desmond Tutu. I was privileged to nominate Desmond for the job and he was appointed from 1 March 1978.

SACC President Sam Buti was often absent and as senior vice-president I found myself taking the chair by default at executive meetings and even national conferences, often at short notice. Thus I chaired Desmond's very first meeting where it was agreed that John Rees would stay on for a couple of months as the new GS settled in. During an extended overseas trip by Desmond in May/June 1979 and more frustrating absences by Buti, I found myself navigating two problematic issues involving staff suspected of dishonesty. The first was at the college that SACC and CI had established for the African Independent Churches at St Ansgar's Mission; the second was in the SACC Accounting Service (SACCAS). The St Ansgar's case was uncovered by SACC's ombudsman, Eugene Roelofse, who not only hounded me daily about it but began to set himself up as snoop-in-chief around the Council offices, upsetting staff.[239] It led to Independent Church Bishop, Isaac Mokoena, the Director of Church Development, confessing to forging cheques and being dismissed.[240] SACCAS had been set up to handle the Council's bookkeeping and provide employment and training for aspirant black accountants. In December 1978 questions had surfaced about all not being well there and outside accountants had been called in to investigate. The following year a secretary was found also to have neglected piles of paperwork simply because it was beyond her. Some things fell badly behind and when Desmond returned I wrote to him protesting Buti's absences and pleading among other things that the position of Director of Administration, which had been decided upon much earlier, be urgently filled.[241] A new search was initiated and, much too late, in October 1979 Mr Matt Stevenson arrived to take up this position.

Investigations at SACCAS showed some R29 500 missing and evidence pointed to the chief accountant there, Mr Elphas Mbatha. Desmond Tutu laid charges against him and he later stood trial for fraud. He was discharged for lack of evidence but it was during the police investigation into the Mbatha case that they claimed to have uncovered the evidence against John Rees.

That fateful meeting in Desmond's office would be the first of many agonising debates as people wrestled with their loyalties toward John on the one hand and the apparently damning evidence on the other. That first night, a pattern emerged that would typify most of what followed: I was adamant that on the basis of my knowledge of John's character, he was innocent of a crime; whatever the evidence, there would be an explanation. Sally was equally clear about John's innocence; the Security Police had to be behind this. Desmond took a more measured view: whilst we might have full confidence in John's integrity, we could not rule out the theoretical possibility that a felony had been committed. Moreover he was concerned about the racial sensitivities involved. We had signed the necessary affidavit to charge a senior black staffer and now we were being reluctant to do so in the case of Rees, a white man. Stevenson kept his own counsel.

The police then joined us in the person of Warrant Officer Allan Mills of the Commercial Branch. Mills was an unprepossessing, mousey man whose complexion matched his grey suit but he was on a mission. He produced evidence that sums of money had been placed by John into at least 21 different personal bank accounts and immediately applied pressure. Rees, now Director of the prestigious SA Institute of Race Relations, was about to go overseas on a fundraising trip. "We believe that he is a flight risk," Mills said, "because this case will ruin him." Meanwhile Matt Stevenson had been scrutinising the evidence and said he needed more to persuade him that the funds in those accounts were SACC monies. Mills became agitated and used the race card. "Mr Rees is a thief. You acted quickly in Mr Mbatha's case and now you are reluctant." We responded that this was completely different: in John's case he had absolute discretion over massive funds to disburse as he saw fit and could not be thought to have behaved improperly "at the first whiff of suspicion". While assuring the police that our records were open and we would not stand in the way of any bona fide investigation, we declined to sign the affidavit.

When Mills had left, we instructed Oliver Barrett to contact John and seek explanations around the disputed funds. I had listened with care and watched the interchange. Mills' smugness galled me. I had a strong feeling that something beyond the normal was happening here – something malevolent – but I couldn't put my finger on it. So I expressed the only certainty I had at that moment: "I continue to have full confidence in John's integrity and would be unable to sign that affidavit. If the Council comes to a point of doing so I will almost certainly have to resign." So, from the beginning of what became known as the 'Rees Affair' lines began to be drawn.[242]

Three days later Oliver Barrett reported on his discussions with John. He had ascertained that apart from the Asingeni discretionary fund John had also operated another unrelated secret fund involving some R250 000 over the last four years. He was bound to total confidentiality about its operations and the terms agreed with its principal, who he refused to identify. He said that this fund had made advances to the SACC's Asingeni[243] Relief Fund on occasions when Asingeni was in deficit and the cheques the police had produced of apparently SACC funds going into John's personal accounts were "repayments from Asingeni". Barrett confirmed to us that such a fund existed and was satisfied from John's disclosures and the "somewhat scanty documentary evidence" that John had not committed a felony, even though placing the monies into his private accounts "may not have been wise".[244]

Feeling the need for wider counsel we decided to invite all Johannesburg-based SACC executive members to meet at CMM the next day. At that meeting of thirteen highly trusted people I outlined the "very grave situation" and asked for their help. Some wanted me to recuse myself because of my pastoral relationship with John, and others felt I should remain in the chair, but ultimately I felt it best to leave the meeting, which decided – bearing in mind that Oliver Barrett was also John's attorney – that another senior attorney should look into the same matters as he had, and report back. Also, if the outcome was not to sign a complaint it would be unfair to place that burden on the Presidium alone; the whole executive needed to take responsibility. In my absence they obviously considered my position and apparently satisfied themselves that I should continue chairing these sensitive meetings because when I was invited back they asked me not to consider my recusal "as binding on any future meetings".[245]

I had meanwhile turned to Philip Russell – at that time Anglican Bishop of Natal and an honorary vice-president of SACC – for counsel. Philip was one of the wisest people I knew and his carefully reasoned reply confirmed me in my stand. Both the donors and the

SACC executive had entrusted John with a very large fund and placed it completely in his discretion. Given the circumstances of the times we were living in, it was no surprise that both donors and recipients might well demand absolute confidentiality. John had to make subjective decisions alone about large disbursements and having put him in that position, it was up to us to either remove him if we were not prepared for the risks involved, or to trust him. "When one moves in the area of trust, one is guided not simply by 'hunches' but by experience ..." Philip wrote, and went on to state "categorically" that nothing John had ever done during his time at SACC had given him any reason not to trust him completely. He did raise one flag, putting into words something all of us who knew John were aware of: "I refer to his love of the dramatic ... I do not regard this in any sense whatsoever as a character blemish, but it could have resulted in his over-reacting to a situation, overmoving in the direction of super-confidentiality." However, Philip continued, "if he believed the situation was of the critical nature he thought it was, then he would have to respond by placing of funds in such a way as to enable the wishes of the donor to be achieved as well as observing the secrecy of the recipient when that was required." The Bishop's firm view was that if any action was taken against John the initiative should not come from the Council. Further, if the majority of the executive did decide to sign the police affidavit, opportunity would need to be given to "those who feel strongly to the contrary" to demonstrate this ... "by resignation or other means".[246]

Then John broke his silence. In a letter to the Presidium he told us that he was "deeply hurt and affronted" and found it horrific that we had not come out immediately in "total and complete affirmation" of himself. Clearly we didn't trust him in a situation he believed to be masterminded by the SA Police. It was the SACC and its Executive and Finance committees that had put him at risk and he had accepted that risk. Now, "to support and be of help to the organisation that I love," he had revealed the totality of the operations to Oliver Barrett, including "the complete state of his personal finances." In his letter John reminded us that he had built SACC from a "six-person organisation with a budget of R30 000 to one of 70 employees and a budget of more than R2 million. Then he listed the five discretionary funds he had operated while GS, described their purpose and the amounts that had passed through his hands. In one case, that of Dependents' Conference – a fund to assist the dependents of detainees – in 1971 the police had tried to get John to charge the Dean of Johannesburg, the Very Reverend Gonville ffrench-Beytagh,[247] for the "misuse of many thousands of rands over a long period", including DC funds. "I totally rejected the suggestion on the grounds that we trusted him and he had total discretion," he wrote, and the point was not lost on us. Of the other funds the two that really mattered were the Asingeni Relief Fund and the one that had been unknown to anyone. John said that this super-confidential fund, which we later came to know as ACTIPAX, was within his total discretion and he had disbursed from it some R240 000 between 1974 and 1978. It had nothing to do with the SACC, he said. As far as Asingeni was concerned, he had made discretionary payments of some R205 000. Forty per cent of them, not being confidential, were recorded; the other 60% were confidential and made over in cash or in kind "to persons who fell within the definition of the parameters agreed upon for the Asingeni Relief Fund".

He said that it was no secret that he had opened up building society accounts to handle transactions for both of these funds and some had passed through his own personal banking account. The payments were of an extremely sensitive nature and for the safety of the recipients "I would not reveal ever to whom monies were given". He went on to enumerate other positions of trust in the City Council, Methodist Church and voluntary organisations where he had been or was presently custodian of hundreds of thousands of rands. "When I think of the confidences which I held in respect of that agonising period 1976 to early 1978, I am amazed that it is even contemplated by yourselves that this should be discussed … I am left cold." He pointed out that his lifestyle and place of abode had not changed substantially in 20 years – something I could attest to, having celebrated with the family when the last payment had been made on their R16 000 home in Kensington. "I am an active practising Methodist," he said, "and declare to you that I have not touched a penny of the monies which you entrusted to me." He vowed to fight "with every resource at my disposal to protect my name, my position in society and my present employment".

John then listed some of the ugly ways in which the Security Branch had sought to discredit him in the past and said, "Can it be – God forbid – that you are being used to get at me after so many years … what more do I have to say to you, and can I say to you?"[248]

It was a powerful letter but as the days passed it was clear that not everyone was convinced. I had been shocked when the meeting at CMM had appeared to doubt Oliver Barrett, who had served us with total integrity for years. What then did they think of me? Yet, by a strange irony on the very day that John wrote his letter, Desmond Tutu wrote to me asking that I permit my name to go forward to the National Conference for election as President of the SACC. Back in December 1980 Desmond, together with the Archbishop Emeritus of Cape Town, the Most Reverend Selby Taylor, had met with our absentee President, Ds Sam Buti, and prevailed upon him to resign. Now he wrote, "If you believe that the Holy Spirit has a hand in things such as elections then you should not want to frustrate him so early." Amidst the high drama, life had to go on.

The evening before the vote at the May National Conference, I recall sitting at supper with Desmond and Matt and thanking Desmond for the painful but rich privilege of working with him. "It's been quite a ride," I said, "but tomorrow it ends." I was quite sure I wouldn't be elected; not only was I one of only two white candidates out of six nominees in an overwhelmingly black Conference, but the shadow of the Rees issue hung over us all. Elizabeth was already picking up rumblings in the corridors of Khotso House about my protecting John "because he was white". I was proved wrong, however: to my utter surprise I was elected with three times the votes of the runner-up, my friend Dr Simon Gqubule. Desmond wrote again, thanking me and Sally Motlana for our "wonderful, costly and prayerful support". It had been all of those things. I was utterly committed to ensuring that Desmond should never be without my support both in prayer and action. I believed in him, believed that God had called him to this task and regarded my role as being his loyal shield. We had developed a friendship based on mutual respect and appreciation of one another's gifts. I admired his Christ-centred spirituality, natural warmth, prophetic insight and sheer guts; he liked my preaching, my "way with words", as he put it, my clarity of thought and the way I guided difficult meetings. He would come back to his office and tell Elizabeth how much he had felt supported by his President. Yet neither of us was afraid to challenge the other. That was the way it should be. We made a good team but we were about to be tested to breaking point.

23

Perfect Storm

As the weeks rolled on, Warrant Officer Mills seemed to relish dropping regular tidbits of added information by way of Matt Stevenson, who said he was now satisfied that "SACC funds were being held in accounts beyond the Council's control". While stalwarts like Reverend Joe Wing and Canon Michael Carmichael believed that nothing had changed in principle, Stevenson didn't. I had the growing impression that Desmond was moving that way as well.

At a full Executive in April I tried to sum up the situation. We had invited the police's attention by charging Elphas Mbatha. They had a *prima facie* case against John, i.e. evidence which, in the absence of a reasonable explanation, indicated that a crime had been committed. If there was political pressure behind Mills, they would probably go ahead whether or not we laid a complaint; therefore our decision came down to what we believed about John. He had vowed to go to jail rather than reveal details, so we had to rely primarily on our experience of him and the testimony of Oliver Barrett. It was all about John's character and the fact that we had trusted him with SACC for seven years, as well as giving him total discretion over very large sums of money. We also had Oliver Barrett's assurances regarding the existence of ACTIPAX. "If all these together amount to a 'reasonable explanation'," I said, "then we should refuse to lay a complaint."[249] If not ... I didn't want to contemplate that.

The Executive decided not to lay a complaint.

In August, accountant Tim Potter, who had earlier given SACC a clean bill of health, wrote to ask whether, in the light of the Rees revelations leaking out, he should withdraw his report. The Presidium responded that the information he referred to "does not in principle alter the position as we understood it after the last Executive meeting … and therefore there is at present no necessity for the withdrawal of your report." We were, however, taking steps to get a satisfactory certificate from John Rees in relation to the movement of funds after the appointment of the new General Secretary.[250]

On 10 and 11 August both Elizabeth and I had been summoned to John Vorster Square for questioning about John. Elizabeth was anxious beforehand but need not have feared. She found herself thinking more about others: "I felt God very close – he calmed me and cleared my mind, but what a horrible place to go as vulnerable young black person," she wrote afterward. My own interview was tense. "I will try to answer whatever you ask," I said, "but you need to know that I believe John to be innocent and will defend him in every way possible." The prosecutor then threatened to declare me a 'hostile witness' and I said, "Fine, that's what you'll get." In the end the state decided that neither of us would help their case.

In October, Elphas Mbatha was found not guilty for lack of evidence. The case was widely reported for two other reasons: First Warrant Officer Mills used his time in the witness box to reveal that John Rees had placed SACC funds in 51 different bank accounts and that the SACC had refused to lay a complaint; and then the magistrate had lambasted Desmond Tutu, accusing him of making Mbatha a scapegoat for SACC's "chaotic" finances. It was time to go public.

Desmond Tutu and I held a press conference on 13 October and I covered every step we had taken since April when Mills first approached us, saying that the National Executive had consistently concluded that Mr Rees had acted with complete integrity. Desmond followed up with a fiery response to the magistrate: "I will not be deterred by all the vilifications and denigrations and personal attacks ranging from Prime Ministers to magistrates," he vowed, and then outlined the steps taken to correct the SACC's financial problems. When Mr Potter had found nothing untoward "we insisted that he continue," he said. "Surely that would be odd behaviour on the part of someone who wanted to cover up."[251] I also issued a statement defending Desmond and criticising the magistrate for "emotive rather than judicial expressions of opinion".[252]

The hue and cry escalated, however, with newspapers like the *Rand Daily Mail* joining less friendly media in calling for full disclosure. The *Cape Times* recommended a "full and public inquiry with all due speed".[253] The *Sunday Times* front page yelled: CHURCHES IN NEW CASH ROW.

Facts unknown to me were also emerging. Sally Motlana had received R7 000 to start a shop in Soweto, and Desmond himself R14 000 toward his house in Orlando West. It didn't matter that Sally had suffered in solitary confinement for 56 days and certainly qualified under the Asingeni rubrics, and that John had identified a completely separate anonymous donor as being behind Desmond's R14 000. Events were outpacing us. By 27 October when the full Executive met I reported on the confluence of different problems, each of which was bad enough, but together had led us to a point of crisis. The matter was now one of public interest and we needed to satisfy the public about our bona fides. Then Matt Stevenson dropped his bombshell: while he accepted the existence of Rees's "other discretionary fund", he believed John had acted dishonourably in passing them through the Council's finances without our knowledge or permission. Further, he could not say that monies in Rees's personal accounts "are not the Council's property".[254] The upshot was that the Executive decided it had no option but to set up an "urgent commission of inquiry" headed by a senior advocate, to look into our financial affairs from 1975 onward.

But it was all too late. We had exposed ourselves and the regime moved swiftly to outflank us. Early in November Prime Minister PW

Botha announced a judicial commission of inquiry into the SACC headed by Justice CF Eloff. It had wide terms of reference and we soon received a letter demanding that we hand over – well, everything.[255] The list of documents was endless. Every nook and cranny in the SACC and of our lives would be under scrutiny for years ahead. Our intention to set up a church-driven commission stumbled on for months but became irrelevant. All attention would now be on the tribunal under Justice Eloff and on the almost inevitable trial of John Rees.

In spite of growing tensions, I still felt able to straddle the demands of my loyalties to Desmond and SACC and to my friend John. In November I chaired a particularly intricate meeting with church leaders to decide how to respond to the Eloff Commission and Desmond Tutu wrote me a gracious letter: "Thank for who you are," he said, "and for chairing a tricky session so competently." He felt that we had emerged from that encounter much closer to one another than before the meeting.[256]

That December, the Rees family and ours drove down in two cars to Cape Town. On Tweede Nuwe Jaar[257] they joined us at Betty's Bay for a picnic together with Gilbert and Jane Lawrence. John and Dulcie and their daughters Joy and Lynn took to the little Lawrence girls and John romped with them with un-Rees-like abandon. It was a blessed break for us all, almost as if God was giving us some clean, wholesome air before plunging us back into the smog of charge and counter-charge that lay waiting in Johannesburg.

Another precious moment was in January when our John managed to get leave from the navy to come home for his 21st birthday. Before returning he came and sat on our bed until 3.30 am sharing about the truths he had learned in our home – and now in faraway Walvis Bay. His time there had been enriched by new friendships and he intended being true to them. He had done incredibly well in his UNISA studies too. I recall thinking how good it would have been to live a normal life as a normal family, but what was 'normal' in our times?

There was family pain too. Later in the year our fourteen-year-old David was walking his own *via dolorosa*. His best friend Maurice had been in and out of hospital for months with leukemia. Dave's faithfulness in sitting for long hours with him had been one of the deepest lessons in love I had ever seen. Maurice, out of hospital, spent the Republic Day weekend with us but died at home two days later. Dave was utterly bereft and I was grateful we could be together at Maurice's funeral where Dave bravely helped carry his best friend's coffin. Because the family were Jehovah's Witnesses I was not allowed to say anything 'religious', but I didn't have to. All that was needed was to speak about Maurice and David's love for each other: what was closer to God's heart? Our son carries the love of that friend and the pain of his loss still.

Fast forward to June and the SACC National Conference – not the first I had chaired, but my first as their elected President. In my Presidential Address I didn't dodge our crisis. "The years of crying God's words of warning and calling for God's compassion and justice could be coming to a climax for us. The long shadow of State action stretches across this Council and therefore over the Church." There would be those hoping that this would be an excuse to strike at the heart of Christian opposition to injustice and to silence our voice. But we would not be silenced. Apartheid was "the most radical dismemberment of any nation since the partition of India". The sons of black and white South Africans were being poured into the bottomless pit of war, and churchmen were being beaten in churchyards, their arms broken by police sjamboks.

Yet, in all of this there was good news: "Jesus had said that *'when all this begins to happen, stand upright and hold your heads high, because your liberation is near!'*"[258] The stones of South Africa's temples were already tottering and the false god of apartheid was failing. Yes, the Council was not perfect and the powers were trying to discredit us, but that did not matter in any ultimate sense. I reminded them that just as the media were trumpeting our troubles and our "crisis", 123 ministers of the Dutch Reformed Church had just come out saying they couldn't worship at the temple of apartheid any longer. "When you see these things happening, know that the heart of the battle is already won." Whatever happened to us we needed to be confident of that. Our task was to live in "God's future" now: in that future compassion and caring would rule – so we should live that way now, while the world lived by the love of power – we should live by the power of love now, and by truth, and by justice and by non-violence. This was the Christian hope, not some sentimental optimism but "the insight which enables us even in the darkest hour to know that Christ is Lord".[259]

I would need a strong dose of my own medicine in the days following.

In a week of what the media called "high drama" Desmond Tutu announced that he was returning the R14 000 he had received from John Rees. Then on 24 June, while I was deep into chairing the conference, someone came in and whispered to me that the police had arrested John Rees. They timed it as dramatically as possible to coincide with our conference, marching into the boardroom of a company where John was accepting a donation for SAIRR, and taking him away. I delegated the chair to Sally, grabbed former Methodist leader Dr Donald Veysie and raced into Johannesburg. We reached the magistrates' court just in time to join a deathly pale Dulcie in one of the grimy courtrooms as John was brought in to be charged with fraud, alternatively theft. He was released on R30 000 bail. We spoke briefly and I returned to the conference, where I convened an emergency Executive during a recess. I was sick in my stomach as I reported the morning's events. Then I offered my resignation. A couple of faces in the group lit up as I did so, but the rest would not hear of it and I was instructed to continue in leadership. The conference later passed a resolution assuring John of their "love, concern and prayers".

That same day I was told that as a potential prosecution witness I was forbidden any contact with John. That was deeply painful: he was not only my friend but I was his pastor. The ban remained in place until the end of his trial. I was touched, however, when Dulcie came to see me soon after. She had been angry with me, unsure of my role in all of this, but when she saw my face as we sat together in that courtroom, she knew that my love for John would not be shaken. We prayed together and I was grateful that she trusted me because at times I was unsure of my own footing. Every day I asked for wisdom just for that day. There was also my congregation at CMM. They were stunned and confused, but after being apprised of the story in its entirety, the CMM Leaders' Meeting took a brave vote: John was told that they continued to believe in him and whatever other positions he might lose through all this, his role at CMM would continue as before.

Tensions rose in the months leading up to his trial. An example was a meeting where we struggled for hours over the complex question of privilege and of whether the SACC had an obligation to help John finance his defence.[260] There were clashes over whether Matt Stevenson should have handed a particular document to WO Mills and whether Oliver Barrett could handle being both the SACC's and John Rees's attorney. Barrett was threatening to withdraw unless Stevenson stopped frustrating his efforts and Matt admitted a longstanding unhappiness that Barrett was acting for us at all. On the matter of financing John's defence, neither Stevenson nor Desmond felt SACC had an obligation – Desmond reminding the meeting that no such help had been given Mokoena or Mbatha. But others, like Lutheran Bishop Manas Buthelezi, and Methodist GS Stanley Mogoba, differed. SACC had always helped accused people get a fair trial. Anglican Winston Ndungane[261] supported the principle, "but only if John doesn't have the necessary funding". When it looked as if the meeting was moving their way, Desmond drew a line: if we decided to finance John's defence, he said, he "would need to reconsider his position". Trying to prevent a complete fracture, I informed the meeting that the Methodist people were rallying around John and raising the necessary funds; he would not need SACC help. At the same meeting, we were warned that the Eloff Commission had been hard at work turning over every stone in our affairs and was ready for hearings.

It was a perfect storm.

24

Bearing Witness

We could either let the Eloff hearings intimidate us or we could use them as a platform to tell the world what the Church of God was really about. We believed that at the heart of the encounter lay the question of our theological identity: these turbulent priests who dared to speak truth to power and to defy the state, who were they really representing?

It was decided that Desmond and I would offer the SACC's evidence-in-chief. He would lead off by establishing the SACC's mandate from Scripture, the Church, and indeed from God. Then other witnesses would deal with nitty-gritty questions of detail and I would 'book-end' the SACC's case with a closing statement, also picking up on anything we felt might have been overlooked.

Desmond's evidence was a *tour de force*. Naming it *The Divine Intention*, he began ...

> "My purpose is to demonstrate from the Scriptures and from hallowed Christian tradition and teaching that what we are as the South African Council of Churches, what we say and do, that all of these are determined not by politics or any other ideology. We are what we are in obedience to God ... we owe ultimate loyalty not to any human authority however prestigious or powerful, but to God and to his Son our Lord Jesus Christ alone, from whom we obtain our mandate. We must obey the divine imperative ... whatever the cost.
>
> "I want to underline that it is not the finances or any other activity of the SACC that are being investigated. It is our Christian faith, it is the Christian churches who are members of the SACC on trial ... We are

on trial for being Christian ... It may be that we are being told that it is an offence to be a Christian in South Africa. That is what you are asked to determine. And that is a theological task through and through."

Then, much to the obvious bemusement of Judge Eloff and his tribunal and to the enthralment of the public gallery, Desmond waded into a sweeping journey through the Scriptures from Genesis to Revelation, spanning the doctrines of creation and the fall, of incarnation and salvation:

> "I will show that the central work of Jesus was to effect reconciliation between God and us and also between men and men (sic). Consequently ... I will demonstrate that apartheid ... is evil, totally evil and without remainder, that it is un-Christian and un-Biblical ...
> "I will show that the SACC and its member churches are not some tuppeny-halfpenny fly-by-night organisation. We belong to the church of God ... universally spread through the whole inhabited universe ... It is the body of Jesus Christ ... and it is a supernatural, a divine fellowship brought into being by God himself through his Holy Spirit ..."

Then an early ultimatum ...

> "With due respect I want to submit that no secular authority nor its appointed Commissions has any competence whatsoever to determine how a church is church nor what is the nature of the Gospel of Jesus Christ. With respect we do not recognise the right of this Commission to enquire into our theological existence and therefore into any aspect of our life as a Council. Only our member churches can call us to task. If we have contravened the laws of the country then you don't need a Commission to determine that. There is an array of draconian laws at the disposal of the government ..."

This Bishop of the Church was not going to be intimidated ...

> "I want the government to know I do not fear them. They are trying to defend the utterly indefensible. Apartheid is as evil as Nazism and Communism and the government will fail completely for it is ranging itself on the side of evil, injustice and oppression. The government are not God. They are just ordinary human beings who very soon like other tyrants before them will bite the dust. When they are taking on the SACC they must know that they are taking on the church of God. ... Christ has assured us that his church is founded upon a rock and not even the gates of Hell can prevail against it."

Some five hours later he completed his statement. It stands as one of the great documents of Christian witness.[262]

Then the examination began, led by Advocate Klaus von Lieres und Wilkau, whose Prussian name suited his demeanour. He set out to show that the SACC, far from being a primarily religious organisation, was a tool of the ANC and its communist allies, busy fomenting revolution. He grilled Desmond for some 20 hours, but there was something pathetic and clumsy about the bullying Von Lieres trying every which way to shake a theologian of Tutu's stature. The Bishop remained firm.

In the next weeks others came forward either to vilify or defend us. My old nemesis, secret police General Johan Coetzee was one of them, alleging that we were giving money to the terrorists and demanding that the SACC's overseas funding be cut off. The right-wing Christian League of South Africa (CLSA), a body secretly paid by government to smear the SACC and WCC,[263] also weighed in against us. On the other side, we smiled as the head of our Justice and Reconciliation Division, Dr Wolfram Kistner, when attacked for being the "brains" behind our alleged left-wing machinations, insisted on giving long, dry, theological and biblical responses to Von Lieres, clearly frustrating our prosecutor.

Then it was my turn. Early on 9 March 1983 I drove to Pretoria along the busy Ben Schoeman highway, praying that the knots in my stomach would ease. It was a Wednesday and I had spent the weekend in Oliver Barrett's office dictating my 84-page statement. There was no time for revision on the Monday or Tuesday because, ironically, Stanley Mogoba and I were leading a retreat for Methodist military chaplains wrestling with how to represent the Gospel in the deeply compromised context of the SADF.

The commission met in a modest hall in the optimistically named Veritas building just off Church Square. Supreme Court Justice Eloff and the other four commissioners – all white males – were seated at the far end. There was a small press and public gallery and to the left were the tables for counsel, ours on this day being Advocate Jack Unterhalter SC. Von Lieres sat nearest to the commissioners with his assistant and their pile of files. In the middle of the room was a single chair with a small table. This was where I was to spend a total of 26 hours and it suddenly felt a very lonely place. I muttered to myself Jesus' words about not worrying what to say when brought before "rulers and authorities",[264] and settled in for the ordeal.

The judge welcomed me courteously and asked if I had an opening statement. I answered "Yes, quite a lengthy one," and he bade me begin. I identified myself first and foremost as a minister of the Gospel of Jesus Christ. Whatever my status, nothing was more binding on me than my vows of ordination. All other loyalties, whether to nation, family, people or party, were subservient to this. None could live up to the high calling of Christ, but the "the supreme improbability" of the Good News was that when we failed, God met us with his grace and forgiveness. As SACC, we were not perfect but without disrespecting the commission, we were answerable to an authority way beyond them and would not accept having our motives and intentions decided by them. Any anger in my responses to the "hard and cruel things said about us", would not be because of personal grievance but because "truth had been violated, the church misrepresented and our Lord grieved".[265]

I said that it had been strange listening to the evidence thus far. Witnesses had painted a picture of SACC as serving dark intentions and designed to bring chaos in our land. "The SACC I know is a different one: it is an attempt against the heavy odds of prejudice, the captivity of the past and the oppression of the present, to be a light on a hill and a transforming leaven in a land of division, hopelessness and fear." Our detractors seemed to have read history with one eye closed. We were accused of being allies or willing dupes of international communism and its surrogates ... but I had waited in vain "to hear one word about the other makers of history in our time: the inventors of apartheid. To examine our role without taking cognisance of that context was like trying to understand Abraham Lincoln without mentioning slavery or Dietrich Bonhoeffer without mentioning Nazism." Our role in SA arose out of two great realities: the first being our understanding of Scripture, a point made powerfully by Bishop Tutu, and the second being the great corporate sin of apartheid. Quoting my dad 24 years earlier, I said, "Apartheid is a sin against the Father who wills that all should be his sons and daughters; and against the Son who died to reconcile all people to God and to each other; and against the Holy Spirit who makes all of us one in the bonds of peace." Further, if you once accepted that apartheid could be right anywhere, then you were saying that Christ's act of reconciliation on the cross had failed everywhere.

My task was to show that our concern with socio-political, economic, educational and human issues was as much part of the evangelical Gospel as winning disciples and I used John Wesley and the Wesleyan movement as my model. I reminded the commission that the eighteenth century evangelical revival was the most widespread since biblical days, yet Wesley insisted that it was never only about individual conversion. I listed the practical programmes he set in place to educate and uplift the poor and ridiculed the charge that SACC's support for the new black trade union movement was subversive. "It was in fact the Evangelical Revival that gave birth to Trade Unionism." The breeding ground for the SACC's concern for human rights, justice and reconciliation was not Marxist. "These very same concerns were the hallmarks of powerfully spiritual men who lived 100 years before Marx was heard of." I said that I resented "hearing my Christian heritage being cheapened by naive inferences reminiscent of McCarthyism".

Referring to the SACC and its member churches, I said it had two roles: the first was to reflect their position on issues and undertake the tasks they gave it; the second was to speak prophetically to them out of the insights that came from ecumenical engagement. When it came to who we chose to aid, our decision to help political prisoners and support their families was because they were the most despised ones of South Africa – the equivalent of the "least of Jesus' brothers and sisters"[266] in the Gospels. We were under Jesus' instruction to go to them.

To the accusation that we were in cahoots with political movements like the ANC I countered that an alliance with any political organisation would cause us to surrender our "prophetic distance", a vital element of our integrity. Further, the strength of SACC's witness was the very fact that it neither held nor sought temporal power. "The only man to be trusted is the one who seeks nothing for himself – so also in organisations." I quoted my own words to the Prime Minister: "We have no dreams of power, we pose no political threat. In secular terms this Council is quite powerless. You can close us down tomorrow. Can you not believe then that the cry we raise comes not from some strategy but from the heart … that [we] … are in touch with more grassroots people than your racially exclusive party can ever be? Why would we bother if it were not for the fact that people are suffering?"

To the accusation of being fellow-travellers with the communists I said: "If I walked out into the road yesterday and found that it was snowing, and if the person walking next to me was a communist and said, 'Oh, it's snowing,' I don't believe I would have a moral obligation to say it was *not* snowing." Some political formations might well take stances similar to those of the SACC but there was a radical divergence around the issue of violence. While we could understand those whose frustration led them to abandon peaceful methods of achieving their ends, we could not walk that way. "I could not belong to a body advocating violence as a means of change and I am confident that neither would any of our member churches," I said. Nor could we countenance acts of terrorism, whether by liberation movements or the SADF. There was a difference between guerrilla warfare and terrorism.

Speaking of Desmond Tutu's role as both servant of the churches and prophet in their midst, I defended his right to go out ahead of us. I quoted our member churches' declaration after his controversial 'Denmark coal' speech: "We will not allow any single member of the Body of Christ to be isolated for attack where we are sure that his primary commitment reflects – as does Bishop Tutu's – those values for which each of our member churches firmly stand ..." Other less major areas were covered too, tying up some of the loose ends left by other testimony before mine. Then I closed by reminding the commission that something similar to this hearing had happened a very long time ago:

"In the Book of Acts there is the record of the early Apostles on trial before the Sanhedrin. The reason why the work of the Church didn't come to an end that day was because of two actions: the first was the fearless witness of Peter the Apostle, standing for the truth even when threatened, and obeying God rather than men.

"The second actor was one of his hearers who was open to the truth, the Pharisee Gamaliel, who though he didn't have any reason to like the Christians, discerned the ring of truth in their words. He said 'Keep clear of these men … for if this idea of theirs is of human origin it will collapse, but if it is from God, you will never be able to put them down, and you risk finding yourselves at war with God.'

"The result of that encounter long ago, was there for all to see."

The presentation took four hours and I was questioned for two days after that. The details in the 250-odd pages of question and answer don't matter anymore.[267] I remember the judge showing a special interest in the social impact of the Wesleyan revival. He wanted a book about Wesley to read over the weekend. By one of those inexplicable coincidences I was broadcasting from CMM that weekend and on the Monday he told me he had listened. He grilled me himself on my definitions of apartheid and of what I meant by corporate sin – and about violence. He struggled to accept my argument that a young black man living under the humiliating constraints of apartheid might come to believe that "unless he did something, he would die with his dompas still in his hand … still condemned and branded by the accident of a black skin". I had said that any reasonable person would understand such a young man saying, "Let me rather die with a gun in my hand than come to old age that way," but Eloff couldn't get his head around that idea and engaged me at length about it.

Elizabeth was able to attend some of my testimony and felt that, "It was like an exam taken on all your learning, and studying and reading and living, your whole life." At some point she found herself descending in the elevator alone with a security policeman who had attended most of the hearings. Out of the blue he made some complimentary remarks to her about my "integrity". Taken aback, she tried to engage him further but he said nothing more and stepped out very quickly when they reached the ground floor.

For Prime Minister Botha the Eloff affair brought forth a mouse. I had come to sense that the judge was at heart a decent, fairly non-ideological person and his 450-page report reinforced that impression.

Of course there was predictable criticism of SACC's engagement in social, political and economic matters and especially the Council's financial affairs, but otherwise the commission gave Botha very little. It suggested framing legislation that could ensure tighter controls on the finances of bodies like SACC, but significantly failed to recommend declaring the SACC an "affected organisation",[268] saying that such an action would have "been seen as restricting religious freedom." It said that even though the money spent on helping the needy and deserving "can only be described as meagre compared to that used for political purposes, innocent people would suffer if the organisation were to be rendered largely ineffective."

There is no doubt that the government was both angry and disappointed but Desmond Tutu was not going to let the commission off without a scolding. He could find only one point of agreement with them – that they had little understanding of theology, so how could a fair judgement be expected? "It really was like asking (speaking respectfully) a group of blind men to judge the Chelsea Flower Show."[269]

For me the most significant moment of the Eloff Commission hearings was in mid-March when there was a stir and a shuffling in the public gallery and a group of churchmen from all over the world entered the hall and demanded to speak on behalf of the Council. They came from Germany, Britain, Scandinavia, the United States ... representing great bodies like the World Lutheran Federation and the EKD (Evangelical Churches of Germany), the Anglican communion and the World Alliance of Reformed Churches. They spoke with force and conviction, leaving no one in doubt that an attack on the SACC was an attack on the world Church. I remember my eyes filling in wonder at being part of this amazing entity – body – movement – and thinking at that moment of those in power in South Africa: "You guys can't win; you're up against the Church of God."

I also breathed a prayer of thanksgiving that we had been able to get through the Eloff hearings united and together.

25

Trial by Friendship

Meanwhile 30 miles away in Johannesburg another drama was moving inexorably toward its climax in the Rand Supreme Court, right opposite the CMM. There John Rees cut a lonely figure in the dock as the state piled up the evidence against him. The judge was Richard Goldstone, who would go on to stellar heights as one of post-apartheid South Africa's first Constitutional Court justices – and then the International Court of Justice in The Hague. He was one of those jurists who had managed to remain relatively untainted in a system badly distorted by its discriminatory context and I had no doubts about his fairness. Bishop Tutu's evidence in the trial became controversial: first he declined to comment on the state of the administration when taking over from John but when pushed indicated that he was "very unhappy" from the start. There were sharp differences with John's advocate, Johann Kriegler, over whether he had known and consented to the withdrawals John had made following Desmond's arrival. This was, as I recall, a major dissonance between the two narratives.

When it was John's turn Kriegler led him through what was almost a lone defence. Elizabeth was one of the few called to testify to his lifestyle. "He was so punctilious that if he sent a personal letter from the SACC office he wanted to know right away what the postage cost so as to reimburse it." She spoke of Dulcie Rees's "ancient Mini with flowers painted on it" and the modest home in Kensington, always in mint condition but offering no signs of extravagance. It also emerged that some of the "51 bank accounts" that Mills had made so much of had never contained more than a few rands.[270] But in the face of John's silence there could only be one outcome. His main defence was no different than what Oliver Barrett had come back with almost exactly two years previously. Now, as then, his only hope of proving it was to offer up names of people who could verify his story, something he had vowed never to do, even at the price of going to prison.

Like so many others the judge seemed to be looking for a hidden key to the puzzle. Joseph Lelyveld wrote that Goldstone "leaned over backwards to avoid any suggestion that he was joining the Government's vendetta against the Council", and that even John's convinced supporters agreed that he "helped to convict himself with evasive and contradictory testimony ..."[271] On the face of things Goldstone appeared to have no option but to convict him. Much had revolved around the existence or otherwise of the mysterious "second fund" named ACTIPAX, which Goldstone labelled as "highly improbable". He found John guilty of 29 of the 43 counts of fraud and alternately theft involving R296 500 of SACC money. All that remained was for pleas in mitigation of sentence and John's likely imprisonment.

Late that night I ignored my ban and visited a very broken man. What passed between us remains in the sacred space of pastoral confidentiality, but it was a conversation of searing honesty and I came away affirmed in the one certainty that had held me throughout the long saga: John may have made stupid mistakes but he had not enriched himself by one penny. When it came time for the pleadings, I didn't hesitate to join others, like Professor John Dugard and Reverend Stanley Mogoba, in witnessing to John's virtues and long list of accomplishments on behalf of the poor and marginalised. Elizabeth had created a scrapbook with a similar record and messages from around the world which we handed in too. The judge was clearly struggling to match the man we described with the acts he had found him guilty of. He quizzed me at length about what he called the "riddle" of John's character. I spoke about John's love for the dramatic but more of the psychological danger that lurked for people placed where they could daily dispense large sums to others – that with the obvious good they were doing sometimes came a sense of omnipotence, and with it licence. But I also underlined the reality of the risks involved in helping political fugitives and the effect that had on him.

In the end, John was sentenced to an effective ten years imprisonment, suspended conditionally for five years, and fined R30 000. I rejoiced that he would at least go free, but being familiar with his deep pride in his name and integrity I knew he had suffered a blow from which he would never recover.

It remained for me now to consider my position with SACC. Unlike some others of John's friends I had no difficulty in understanding Desmond Tutu's anger at John, and therefore to some degree at me. Here he was – the first black SACC General Secretary – just three years into his tenure and under sustained attack from the regime, plunged into a crisis threatening the very life of the Council all because of the actions of one man. Whether John acted rightly or not, his case doubtless emboldened Botha to trigger the Eloff Commission, which in turn dominated our time and energy and virtually immobilised the Council for two years. Desmond's own affairs had been subjected to unwanted public attention too. If I were in his shoes, I would have found it impossible to hide my frustration but he held it in through the multitude of meetings around this issue and, whatever he felt, went along with the decisions not to lay a complaint. After the trial, however, his anger exploded in ways that were unhelpful. His charges that John Rees had "racially divided the SACC"[272] perpetuated the simplistic view that we on the Executive had charged Mbatha because he was black and defended Rees because he was white – yet it was Desmond himself who had charged Mbatha and a thoroughly multi-racial Presidium and Executive who repeatedly expressed their trust in Rees. Of course race would rear its head – it always does in South Africa – but I recall absolutely no one on the Executive who spoke of race at any time except for Desmond's warning that people would see our actions in those terms. Now he was stoking the fire. He was even angrier at the Methodists, attributing their continued support for John to "latent racism".[273]

Though desperately torn at times, until Goldstone's verdict I felt that I had managed to honourably balance my loyalties to both Desmond and John. I had duties to my General Secretary and to a key member of my congregation, and to each as friends. The Friday night after John was sentenced, the SACC Executive met to discuss the implications of the trial. On the Sunday I woke to a story in the *Sunday Express* reporting on the meeting, quoting Desmond saying that I "had accepted the guilt and betrayal of trust" by John, and speculating about my probable resignation.[274] The story was by Wilmar Utting, who I had found to be a particularly unpleasant reporter. Desmond and I had a pact that we would always offer the media a united front and Utting had managed to fracture it. I was furious. I called him, berating him for speaking about me to her. Desmond didn't hold back either, letting fly with some of his frustrations too. It was short, sharp and painful – and the only time we ever had words. Within hours I sat down and wrote to him apologising for "losing it", acknowledging that it was foolish because however this disastrous situation ate into us, we should not be divided. We had prayed together, marched together, gone to jail together and looked death in the face together. Surely – whatever happened – our friendship should not be allowed to founder under the weight of this crisis. He replied with a gracious apology himself.

However, the National Conference was fast approaching and the next Executive would be discussing whether or not to sue John for the money he was supposed to have stolen. I couldn't be part of that. The time had come to end the agony. My last duty as President of the SACC was to receive John Rees's resignation as an Honorary Life Vice-President of the Council. Then, on 27 May I opened the Executive meeting as usual and asked permission to read my letter of resignation. It was well known, I said, that from the very first meeting with the police two years before, I had declared my complete trust in John Rees and had held steadfastly to that position. I did not in any way regret that stand, "which was taken in total sincerity and based on both principle and personal trust". I would continue to place the best construction on John's actions … and remained convinced that he did not seek to enrich himself. I did accept, however, "that in the process of those actions, there was a deception of the Council".

"The Presidency of the Council is a symbol of unity in the SACC, which is itself committed to the unity of the Church," I said. "By God's grace we have been enabled to demonstrate that unity throughout the Eloff Commission and the Rees trial." Both had now come to an end and, "I have been given to understand that the position I have taken … could prejudice that unity and thus be a disservice to the Council. To imperil that unity would be out of character with the love and respect I have for the SACC."

I reminded my colleagues that circumstances had dictated that I had chaired the Executive for five of the nine years I had served with them and we had become a non-racial ecumenical team "tested by fire and made stronger by difficulty". I fully understood the hurts which had come recently to each member of the team and the anger which some felt. I added that I continued to hold Bishop Tutu in the highest esteem together with all those with whom I had walked.

"I pray for you today," I said, "in the hope that now that the Law has been the Law, the Church will be the Church."

It was a deeply sad moment for me, made even sadder by Elizabeth's resignation as Desmond's PA later that day. She loved Desmond deeply but had been asked to type one too many personally painful documents and felt she had to end their five-year working relationship. From one of the most significant secretarial jobs in the country, she became a 'Kelly Girl' looking for piece-work.

John had to resign as Director of SAIRR, and his sentence prevented him from being in any kind of business. He took a position as head of the Avril Elizabeth Home for mentally challenged children and poured his prodigious energy into ensuring their well-being. To visit him there was a beautiful thing. Children with these needs have few boundaries and I loved seeing them mob and lovingly maul John every time he emerged from his office. This warm, yet private friend who had left the courtroom not long ago with his reputation in tatters seemed to be finding healing in their embrace.

One day John went into hospital for some tests and called me on one of the newfangled cell phones. When I got there he told me he had just been diagnosed with the most virulent strain of leukemia and we talked about what might lie ahead. He was not afraid but deeply concerned for Dulcie and the girls. Typically, he said he was determined to "fight this thing with all my might". That night, Elizabeth and I were at CMM fairly late and found the lights on in the chapel. There was Dulcie, arranging flowers for Sunday, and John carrying vases and water buckets. He had not yet told her – this little job had to be done first.

My strains with Desmond took very little time to heal. As a pastor I think he understood how standing by one of my parishioners could be a priority. However, according to Shirley du Boulay, what he *did* question was my refusal to admit John's guilt. She wrote that, "His final wistful comment on the matter was 'I only wish I had a friend like that.'"[275] He sent me a letter following the June National Conference telling me of the standing ovation they gave me *in absentia* and of their invitation to become a Life Vice-President. I asked for time, but later accepted the honour.

John lived just long enough to see the birth of a new democratic South Africa. There were many warm and happy times at his home or around his hospital bed as he moved in and out of remission. A unique mark of respect came from the judge who had sentenced him: he asked John to chair the Goldstone Commission's Committee on

Children and Violence – a monumental report which he just managed to complete. There were deeper talks between us about hurt and forgiveness, life, love and death. John and Dulcie came to our home for the last time on 7 October. He was in a lot of discomfort that evening and eight days later, in the small hours of the morning, he died in hospital. The paroxysms of pain that lifted his body were too much and my last service to him was to convince the nurse to increase his morphine dose to bring quiet.

More than 1 000 people of all races packed the CMM Sanctuary for John's memorial service. Offering the eulogy I said:

"Many opponents of apartheid suffered, but John's crucifixion was of a uniquely excruciating kind. It was not his vision, nor his convictions that were put on trial, but that place within himself that he prized most dearly, his integrity. ... Given the evidence before him, the Judge had little option, but the real truth, which will one day be revealed, lay in what wasn't before that court.

"I pray that one day, those who John saved and hid and fed and enabled to escape the Security Police with the money he is supposed to have stolen, will find the courage to stand up and testify. But even if they never do, from the times we talked together, prayed and wept together, I testify today that John's conscience was clear. His family knows that and so do many others.

"But who was this man?

"I was reading the Beatitudes of Jesus this morning. They tell of the kind of people who Jesus needs to build the Kingdom of God. Those Beatitudes are appropriate for John: he knew his need for God, he knew sorrow, he was of a gentle spirit, he hungered and thirsted to see right prevail in this land, he showed mercy and he was pure in heart. He was a peacemaker and he suffered every kind of calumny for the Lord's sake.

"And he was my friend ..."

26

National Leadership

Being elected Presiding Bishop is the highest honour the MCSA can bestow on any of its ministers – and the toughest job. In my day the expectations were almost absurd. Known then by its more humble Wesleyan title, the 'President of the Conference' carried all the responsibilities of leading the largest multi-racial denomination in South Africa while still serving a local church and running the District it was located in. The saving grace was that the term of office in those days was just one year before handing over to a successor.[276]

Time-honoured usage required that voting for the top position be without nomination. This was designed to discourage individuals from promoting themselves as 'candidates' and to make politicking distasteful. As a young minister back in 1969 I had enthusiastically lobbied for another to be elected to this position but the experience – if not the goal – had left me uncomfortable and I decided 'never again'. So when delegations came to me in 1982 and 1983 asking me 'stand' for the office I shooed them out: "Nobody 'stands' when an election is without nomination," I said, and I truly meant it. Nevertheless, I found myself runner-up in the voting in 1982 and was voted President-Elect a year later at the Durban Conference. I would take office in October 1984, presiding over the ten-day Pretoria Conference before leading the denomination until October 1985.

The Conference made a big moment out of such elections. Elizabeth was flown down from Johannesburg to join me as I tried later to respond to the vote, bringing to mind the people and influences that had shaped my life. I was somewhat overwhelmed, recalling that my dad had been similarly honoured 28 years before, something unique in MCSA history. What I didn't say was that the vote offered some healing after my anguished decision to resign the SACC presidency six months earlier. I knew I had done right to stand by John Rees, but it had left me in a very empty place, feeling bereft and alienated from the ecumenical community that Desmond Tutu and I had led. Now, here was my 'mother' – the Methodist Church – seemingly affirming the path I had walked and inviting me back into national leadership. Elizabeth had also gone through real struggle after resigning as Desmond's PA, having to resort to temporary secretarial jobs while looking for new employment. Her solidarity with me had cost her enormously and it was with deep awareness of her hurt that I paid tribute to her as the "rock of strength and love of my life". Later, Reverend Bob Stead and Milly opened their home to us and a few close friends for an impromptu party and we were put up in a lovely suite in Durban's Royal Hotel. I doubt our Conference hosts knew that because we didn't have that kind of money it was the first time we had been in a hotel since our honeymoon. We made the most of it.

The election, while presaged by the close vote in 1982, was still a punch to the solar plexus. Was I ready for this? I was 44; only Alex Boraine had been younger than me when elected. Given that, like him, I was not wildly popular among white colleagues and was elected on the first ballot,[277] it had obviously happened with overwhelming black support. While I was grateful for that, South Africa was hurtling toward the abyss and my year of office – 1985 – would be the most fraught and violent yet. Only a brash fool would not have quaked at the prospect. The President-Elect year was meant to be used for spiritual and mental preparation and to shape the five major addresses required at the coming Conference. Fortunately, long leave was due in mid-1984 and I was taking over the pulpit of the main Presbyterian Church in Sydney, Australia, for a couple of months. The time away promised a quiet space to prepare and for us together to gird our loins for what lay ahead.

Then came an unexpected challenge. I was asked to co-lead an ecumenical delegation to the United States and Europe in March/April 1984. Our task was to alert the outside world to the way the forced removals juggernaut was re-engineering South Africa and ripping up the fabric of black community life, and to seek additional pressure on the regime. My co-leader was Roman Catholic Archbishop George Daniel and our delegation was a mix of seven clergy with on-the-ground experience in the barren resettlement areas where victims of the policy were dumped. We were armed with a powerful exposé of the government's 'Relocation' policy[278] and the group appointed me as spokesperson. The first engagement was at the United Nations in New York addressing the ambassadors of the Africa Bloc. We then went on to meet with UN Secretary-General, Dr Pérez de Cuéllar. He listened intently to the case as I put it. Already 3.5 million black people had been robbed of their citizenship, uprooted – some more than once – and sent to so-called tribal 'Homelands' or Bantustans. The regime was planning the same fate for at least 2 million more black people and the only thing that could stop them was massive international pressure led by the UN. Pérez de Cuéllar needed no convincing; he assured us of maximum support and we went from his office to a press conference.

There I faced the US media for the first time. I wasn't sure why there was such a buzz in the room until the first questions came: "What do you think of your Prime Minister signing a peace treaty with Communist Mozambique yesterday?" On 16 March 1984 – while we had been travelling – PW Botha and President Samora Machel had signed the Nkomati Accord. It was a public relations masterstroke for PW. One of the 'frontline states' had buckled under South African pressure and agreed not to harbour the ANC any longer. South Africa for its part promised no longer to support and arm Machel's guerrilla foes,

RENAMO.²⁷⁹ The details don't matter here; nor does the fact that neither side meant a word of it. What mattered to us at that moment was that Nkomati threatened to pull the rug from under our mission. If the regime was so bad, how come Machel and Botha were cosying up to each other? I had to think on my feet. "This is troubling news which our delegation will have to process when we have more detail," I said, "but it changes nothing for the millions of victims of forced removals. Machel may have been bullied into submission, but we have told Prime Minister Botha repeatedly that the frontline of South Africa's struggle is not on our borders. It is inside our country in every place of pain and oppression and injustice where human beings are treated as commodities to be picked up and dumped down at the will of the white government. If Botha turned away today from apartheid and its forced removals, problems on our borders would soon cease."

In New York we also met with President Reagan's Under-Secretary of State for Africa, Dr Chester Crocker. He was pleasant enough but clearly committed to Reagan's policy of 'constructive engagement', which he felt would win through. We could not agree. He had the cold detachment of a distant analyst, but was unconvincing to those among us who had recently come from the suffering of South Africa's dumping grounds. As we left, we found the South African Ambassador to the US, Mr Brand Fourie, waiting in the ante-room. He doubtless felt the need to follow up on our visit with Crocker in case we had been too persuasive. As we passed him he spat out the word, "*Skande!*"²⁸⁰

In Washington DC, we covered the same ground with both Democrat and Republican members of Congress. The courtesy with which we were met from both sides of the aisle was very different from the coarseness of present-day US political discourse, and the anti-apartheid cause gained endorsement from significant Republicans like Mark Hatfield and Richard Lugar as well as the more predictably supportive Democrats.

We then left for Europe, visiting the United Kingdom first and then the foreign ministers of a number of European countries. There was a not-so-funny-for-me comic moment in London, where we arrived on a Saturday afternoon. Our delegation was to supply the preacher next day at Westminster Abbey and we had delegated the task to Archbishop Daniel. While we booked into our hotel George went off to his accommodations at a Catholic convent. At supper a waiter came round reminding us that British Summer Time began at 1.00 am Sunday morning and clocks needed to be advanced by one hour. Next morning we reached the Abbey in good time and robed for the service but as the minutes ticked away there was no sign of the Archbishop. We were finally formed up to process into the Abbey and everybody looked at me. "Looks like you're the preacher," said Jimmy Palos, and my stomach heaved. There was no way I could pluck a decent sermon out of the sky. At that moment, by the grace of God, Archbishop George appeared with his usual beatific smile, thinking he was just over an hour early. Nobody at the convent had told him of the time change and his smile vanished when he saw us lined up and beginning to move. "Did they change the time of the service?" he asked as he hastily donned his many-buttoned cassock. "No, George," someone said. "God changed the time all over Britain. Now get in line!"

Our itinerary had been designed to pre-empt a trip PW Botha was planning for June. He had secured his first meetings with some European heads of state, including Prime Minister Margaret Thatcher and Chancellor Helmut Kohl of West Germany. We wanted to make sure that wherever he went he would be dogged by questions about forced removals. Soon, however, it was I who found myself at the centre of controversy and, sadly, on the wrong side of a spat with one of my heroes, Alan Paton. Calling the forced removals policy "apartheid's own version of a 'final solution'", I listed some of the similarities between the ways in which unwanted people were treated by Nazi Germany and the way they were being treated by the SA government – the stripping of citizenship rights making people aliens in the land of their birth, shipping them off into a limbo where their continued existence was totally ordered by the whim of their rulers – all because of their race and the determination to be rid of unwanted people. I added: "If the six million people treated this way by the Nazis had been dumped in those places without being killed, there would have been very little difference between the two policies." The statement was not strictly untrue but it received an outraged response. We had been followed everywhere by South African newspaper reporters and they pounced with headlines like: *'Storey – SA policies like those in Nazi Germany – Only Gas Chambers and Mass Murders Missing'*.[281] Then lion-hearted author and liberal prophet Paton ripped into me in the *Sunday Times*.[282] He scolded me for violating truth and the English language. "How the two situations are 'fully comparable' when the two most terrible happenings in all history are missing, I just cannot comprehend," he wrote, warning me that I would never win over "backward White Christians" with such "unhelpful hyperbole". I defended the accuracy of my comparison as I had originally stated it but tried to learn something from this most trenchant of apartheid's critics: if comparisons are too emotive they become the focus instead of the evil they are intended to highlight.

When PW Botha arrived in June, the media did tackle him wherever he went about his forced removals policy and when he met leaders like Thatcher and Kohl, the *New York Times* wrote of a "staged frostiness". In fact, Helmut Kohl who typically sat on a large upholstered sofa for photo opportunities with his foreign guests actually had the sofa moved out of his office for Botha's visit.[283] Hopefully the work of our delegation contributed some of the frost. Botha seems to have got the message anyway because forced removals tailed off and the additional two million people marked for 'resettlement' stayed put.

In June 1984 I received a letter from Nelson Mandela, now prisoner number 220/82 in Pollsmoor Maximum Prison. He wanted to congratulate me on my election to lead MCSA and mentioned my broadcasts from CMM. Knowing that his letter-writing privileges were still limited, I was deeply touched by this kindness. He recounted some funny stories about Reverend Seth Mokitimi's preaching at Healdtown, and also his memories of attending the old Methodist Central Hall (now CMM) when he first came to Johannesburg. "This letter also gives me the opportunity of thanking the Church, through you, for all they have done for my family. Without that help Winnie's burdens would have been much more difficult to endure," he said, ending with, "I look forward to the day when I will meet you and your wife in the flesh and shake your hands very warmly."[284]

Approaching the 1984 Conference in Pretoria I decided that the theme would be 'Hope'. We were entering a make-or-break period in the South African struggle and I wanted to point the nation toward the high road of peace-making and justice rather than the violent abyss yawning before us. I began my addresses by offering a theological foundation: for Christians the *wellspring of all hope* lay in the Jesus event. That was the centre of all history for us: "When Jesus mounted his cross, that day proved evil to be only the second strongest force in the universe." Christian commitment to justice was less ideological than relational – it rose not out of some cold political theory, but "because we have gazed into the face of Christ and seen there his suffering love for humanity". Because it was the night of my Induction, it seemed right to speak very personally about my own faith:

> "My testimony is simple: Jesus told a story once that leaped across 2 000 years and flashed into my life, of a son and a father, a far country and a family home. That story explored the geography of my soul ... it told me I was a long way from home. But it also told me something else: that there was someone back there scanning the road each day ... Since then I have come to discover something about myself: there is the self I know and despair of – the self-truth if you like. But this is not all: there is another truth about me in the heart of God. The self-truth

says, 'make me a servant, I have sinned.' The God truth says, *'This my son was lost and is found again, was dead and is alive.'* Tonight I celebrate Jesus for showing me the God-truth about myself. That is the truth I must trust for him to make me the person he sees in me."[285]

I invited all our ministers to be Messengers of Hope challenging two forms of theological despair, "obscurantist spirituality that led to pietist escapism – and ideological captivity that led to ultimate disillusionment." Each was a heretical "half-Gospel" and only the whole Gospel of Christ would suffice. Turning to Methodism's founder as an example of wholistic faith, I reminded them that "John Wesley's theology was beaten out on the anvil of his daily battle with personal and social evil in a brutalised society very much like our own." Real hope was born in the inward life of the soul because "hope's final fortress is the heart", but needed to be realised in concrete action. Rather than being part of the nation's disease, the Church had to be the place where "the love of God leaps across the parallel lines drawn by history". I pleaded for a much more rapid implementation of racial integration within the denomination. Undeterred by claims that many blacks were also uneasy about full integration, I said, "All that proves is that the Bible is right – none of us has a monopoly on sin. There are times when God's Spirit requires of us something none of us wants, but which all of us need."[286]

The beginnings of the nation-wide unrest and security crackdowns that were to bring 1984–85 to boiling point were already upon us and the Conference was anything but placid. Early on, news came of 6 000 police and soldiers invading Sebokeng. I despatched a task team to the Vaal townships to investigate and after hearing their report-back, brought the Conference out in a two-hour vigil of protest, calling on national service conscripts to "refuse to be part of such actions". The Conference went on to encourage opposition MPs to resign their seats to demonstrate that Parliament had lost any legitimacy. Among other actions I was glad to offer a platform for Ds Beyers Naudé to speak publicly after being recently unbanned and welcomed Bishop Desmond Tutu to receive our congratulations following the announcement of his Nobel Peace Prize which, I said, was the world's emphatic rebuke to the findings of the Eloff Commission. "Now you belong to the world," I said to him, "but we are so proud that you first belonged to us." A decision that brought animated discussion was asking Reverend Ernest Baartman to educate the Conference about the meaning and significance of Black Consciousness, a subject the church had tiptoed around for too long.

My main address began with its own comical mini-drama. Earlier I had dubbed the SABC "the prostitute of the airwaves" for selling itself to a slavish propagandist role and the public broadcaster had withdrawn their TV crew in a huff; but now, because of a leak that I would be calling for an end to the armed struggle, they wanted to come back. They made the mistake of arriving noisily to set up their cameras in the church aisle after my address had begun. I ordered them out.

The address dealt with *Finding Hope for South Africa*. I had recently come into possession of intelligence showing that both the SADF and the ANC had arrived independently at similar estimates of what the deepening conflict across South Africa was going to cost in human life: they believed that a full-blown civil war on our streets would take around 3 million lives – most of them black – before it was exhausted. Listening to some of the self-proclaimed 'radicals' around me I was convinced that few of them had any idea what a real war looked like. The current clashes in the townships were horrible but they were minimal compared with the Beirut-like devastation and bloodletting that could lie ahead. I began by saying that the intensifying violence across the nation had exposed a widespread despair. The regime may have been at the peak of its military power, but had actually run out of road: "… the granite wall of apartheid is riddled with cracks,"

I declared. "It is ready to fall on its builders, and they don't know how to dismantle it. They are haunted by the knowledge that no government can defend itself indefinitely against its own people." On the other hand, the dispossessed in our land were lashing out with "the rage of a despairing people", and the liberation movements were equally bound by narrowing options. There were now thousands of exiles who saw their choices in starkly simple terms: "they have only two ways of returning to this country – on their knees or with a gun in their hands, thus their commitment to the armed struggle." South Africa was like Gulliver, a great giant bound and made helpless by a web of consequences, and the desperate danger was that we would adjust to them so that they became inevitabilities.

There was need for a "strategy of hope". The Church had to live a *prophetic evangelism* that offered the Cross "not as a formula whereby to escape our dilemma, but that place where we nail ourselves to God's passion – and where God nails us to our neighbour". Turning to the convictions that had for so long sustained my own faith, I said that the first need was for *fearless witness to the truth*. Then we needed to *bind up the broken* because compassionate caring was not a diversion from the main struggle for freedom; it was a sign of hope: "It is by the costly caring for the broken that we earn the right to speak at all." A third priority was for the Church to *live the alternative* in what I called the "pain of togetherness" ... "I say to black and white today, South Africa waits to see a working model – a visual aid – of things we believe to be the will of God." Calling for ways to bring change that were "consistent with the mind of Christ", I wanted to confront the war-drums now beating so loudly on both sides of the struggle:

> "In war violence is glamourised, people are dehumanised, truth becomes propaganda, morality is destroyed and reconciliation is impossible ... war is always the *ultimate despair* ... To those who believe that military might can repress the aspirations of a subject

people, I say: 'in the long-term your hope is vain and your war unwinnable.' To those who believe only war will bring the change they want, I say: 'the instrument you are using will bring more suffering on this land than it has ever known and you will inherit ashes.'"

Therefore a failure urgently to explore every avenue for negotiation now was "criminal". There were certain steps that *could* lead to a just peace. Namibia needed to be dealt with decisively. Free elections should be held there immediately and South Africa should abide by the result. "Statesmanship," I said, was when "leaders are willing to risk greatly for the sake of averting even greater catastrophe" and, for South Africa itself, two great acts of statesmanship could break the impasse:

- The liberation movements should renounce the armed struggle.
- President Botha should withdraw troops from the townships, unban the liberation movements and invite them home to "talk instead of fight".

"Then," I said, "let there commence the long process of seeking together with other authentic leaders … a truly new dispensation for South Africa to which each party can say 'yes'." [287]

My proposals sound tame with hindsight but at the time they were almost unthinkable and sparked widespread debate in the media. The *Sunday Star* saw my "dramatic call" as "an attempt to break the impasse between the Government and … movements like the ANC",[288] while the *Rand Daily Mail* asked, "Who can deny the relevance and force of that message …? The deadlock has to be broken, and as Storey notes, it requires a two-fold commitment: the exiled movements must abandon their armed struggle, and at the same time the Government must unban the movements and invite them home to talk."[289] Desmond Tutu, who was present at my address, supported my call, but wanted an assurance that it included authentic leaders in prison and exile, which in my mind, of course it did. Dr Allan Boesak rejected it, indicating that only the government could end the cycle of violence because "it started the violence in the first place".[290] I wondered whether the dead in the coming holocaust would care much who started it; the question was how to end the cycle of death in a way that opened new possibilities of life. I knew that my call needed much refining, but I also had no doubt that the path of negotiation was the only alternative to bloodshed on a massive scale unimagined by some of the more shrill voices on the stage.

My final address at the Conference Communion Service was a simple evangelical sermon accompanied by an altar call and I was surprised – as always – by the numbers of people who came forward to kneel in commitment. Now, having successfully navigated the Conference, the real work of leadership would begin.

27

Among God's People

The President traditionally spent much of the year visiting the eleven Districts and I had asked to hold 'teaching retreats' for clergy and laity on my travels. These went well and I enjoyed the teaching role, but the real work of leadership was dictated by the escalating crisis in the land. In January 1985 I found myself in a light plane rushing to preach in the burnt-out ruins of Grahamstown's historic Shaw Memorial church, destroyed by fire two days after hosting the funeral of a riot victim. "God's tears flow with yours," I said. "This place of peace is now one of the symbols of South Africa's pain and division. Violence will lead us all to hell but we cannot preach against violence unless we can show people a better way. We have to plant the tree of justice in our land, then we'll see that one of its fruits will be peace."

A visit to Atamelang in the Western Transvaal took me into the heart of a murderous drought, with animals perishing and people scratching for water in the mud at the bottom of dried-up wells. Later the 160 children of farm labourers who we housed in the Vryburg Children's Centre greeted me with great enthusiasm. The centre was deeply unpopular among the white farmers round about because without it providing them access to education almost all these kids would have been sentenced to virtual servitude on the farms their parents worked. Then on to the Orange Free State District and the long drive to Kuruman, with Jack and Joan Scholtz, where in a dusty, wind-swept settlement Elizabeth and I met a 100-year-old Women's Manyano member, dressed in her perfectly pressed uniform with its snow white hat, red blouse and black skirt. Her mind was sharp and she could remember

President Paul Kruger and many more Methodist Presidents than I could. We came away touched by the faithfulness and sheer strength to survive among the poorest of our people. It was during this visit to the Orange Free State that Jack and Joan took us to the farming town of Brandfort for our first meeting with Winnie Mandela in the township of Majwemasweu, where she lived under banishment.[291]

Just six days later, on 21 March, police shot dead 24 funeral mourners right in front of the Methodist church in Langa township near Uitenhage. With the townships ablaze and increasingly under siege I felt it crucial to expose white Methodists to what was happening to their black counterparts. "It is wrong that many of our members continue to worship serenely while innocent people are being killed on the doorsteps of our township churches," I declared[292] and directed that all Districts should convene one-day 'Crisis Synods'[293] and locate them right in the conflict-ridden townships, where they could see the devastation and listen first-hand to the experiences of the suffering people. The more than 1 500 clergy and laity who had the courage to leave their privileged 'bubbles' to attend these Synods in the burning townships were deeply shocked by what they saw and heard. In a message to be read in all pulpits in the land, they said: "We are living in a time of tragically fulfilled prophecy. Our pleas and warnings all went unheeded and we must now minister in the chaos and suffering which has resulted." There followed a list of actions taken or planned in regard to confronting government, calls for withdrawal of soldiers from the townships and that conscripts be allowed to refuse such duty, reaffirmation of our unequivocal opposition to violence as a means to both prevent and achieve change, and a repeat of our call for a National Convention involving all authentic leaders. It was time to "end this agony".[294]

I have written elsewhere of my foray into the Border War zone in May of 1985[295] but prior to my starting the SADF trip Elizabeth was with me to visit Angolan refugees in Rundu on the edge of the Kunene River. Whole families had risked the crocodiles of the river to escape war-torn Angola and MCSA had an effective ministry among them, with school and chapel and clinic. Pastor Ludwig Hausiko ministered to them and wanted to show us a new clinic in the bush. Together with Namibian bishop Demetri Palos we got into his jeep-like vehicle and set off on the rutted road parallel with the river. The pastor had only one speed – flat out – and it seemed soon that our wheels were more off the ground than not. When I suggested he slow down before he killed us, he looked round, white teeth bared in a wild smile, and shouted one word above the noise: "Land-mines!" I never said another word.

The clinic was a tiny prefab on the banks of the river, and was sadly lacking in supplies. I wondered what good it could be. Then Ludwig took us on a hike along a narrow defile cut through the tall thick grass until we came to a small clearing. There, on the carefully swept sand, logs had been laid out like pews and a forked stake with a flattened paraffin tin nailed on it had been driven into the ground, forming a lectern. Under the scant shade of a thorn tree, in the silence and the heat, we waited. Then we heard singing. Into the clearing came a number of women, all very thin. Their clothes consisted mostly of sacks – either of rough hessian or the lighter muslin used for flour bags – with holes for head and arms. These women were victims of the war, their menfolk dead or fled, who were trying to survive in the bush. Yet here they were, carrying millet-fronds and waving them as they sang. Ludwig turned to me: "They are saying that they are glad to meet their President and they want to say thank you for the clinic." Their faith and devotion was mind blowing. We had church together for an hour and then, as we left that little clearing in the middle of the bush, Elizabeth whispered, "We've just been in a cathedral."

Returning to Johannesburg I ran straight into the 'Prayers for the Downfall of the Government' controversy, dealt with in the next chapter. For some hectic days it threatened to open up a breach among SACC church leaders and other prominent church activists. I was to discover – not for the last time – that while I always seemed to find reserves of courage and energy to take on the regime even in the depths of weariness, tension within our own ranks was another matter: it drained the life out of me. But, days after this my Annual Synod met. Election as President of MCSA had also made me *ex officio* Bishop of what was then called the Southern Transvaal District and the clergy and lay leaders now had to decide whether they wanted me to continue as their District Bishop when I vacated the national position. In a vote that was therefore something of a 'mid-term' judgement on my work as President I was gratified to be elected by a 144-9 plurality.

In July it was the turn of war-torn Mozambique. The Nkomati Accord was already a dead letter and Samora Machel's Marxist government was once more locked in a grim war with South Africa-backed RENAMO forces. Elizabeth had decided 'for the boys' sake' that it would be too dangerous to have both their parents in the war-zone and I agreed, but on the evening of 14 July she changed her mind. "I just had a strong feeling that I must go," she said. "I felt God saying, 'You can walk with the people in their pain … just be obedient.'" We were met by our local Bishop, Reverend Isaac Mahlalela, who packed us into his pick-up truck. The capital, Maputo, was derelict. Electricity supply was sporadic at best, with people in high-rise buildings cooking their food on open fires at ground level then climbing maybe eight storeys to their apartments. There being no spare parts, cars that broke down stood abandoned in the streets, their wheels removed. An air of fear and decay pervaded the tree-lined streets as we drove to the only major hospital. There we visited Reverend Chikona Matussi, one of our clergy who had lost a leg in a RENAMO ambush. It was a battle to get to him because of the other beds crowded into the ward. There were no serious medicines and he was in anguish, surviving his amputation without painkillers.[296] Later I met with the government director of Justice, a Mr Cicarni, and the Secretary for 'Protestant Affairs' to talk about Methodist Relief[297] and how best to deliver aid to the impoverished country. Cicarni was frank about the need. "Mozambique is like a baby," he said, "born in pain and naked, needing food, clothes, shelter and education." Then he made a rueful confession: "I'm a Marxist, Reverend," he said, "but I'll tell you now that the only people I can trust to get food to those who need it most are the churches." He thanked MCSA for what it was doing in this regard.

The country was effectively cut in two by RENAMO and we couldn't reach Methodists in the north but we took the ferry across the harbour estuary and deep into the bush on the southern side to visit Reverend Matussi's former congregation at Ncekane. There we were welcomed with a heartbreaking song:

Only a true friend comes when there is trouble,
You have come when it is not safe to come.

These people could live relatively normal lives between sunrise and sunset, but when darkness came they took their children and faded into hiding places in the bush while RENAMO roamed. The little corrugated-iron church was full of people, many of them youngsters. It had bullet-holes in its walls, letting in pencils of light while I preached. Elizabeth spoke with great power about the woman whose backbone was straightened by Jesus:[298] "With his healing touch this stooping woman was freed to stand up straight and look into eyes filled with grace and love, and could now look other people in the face too, with dignity and full personhood." My wife spoke of her fears about coming to Mozambique. "Violence makes us fearful," she said, "but God straightened me and said 'Go and do not be fearful.'" Wherever we went, her message touched the women, who were clearly suffering most in this war. Nobody ate before noon but, amazingly, people in abject need shared out of their poverty. A bowl of water was brought for us to wash our hands, then another bowl containing rice and cabbage leaves soaked in hot water. That was it, washed down with tea.

On our second-last day in Mozambique I preached in a four-hour service at the main Methodist church in Maputo. I spoke about God being most real when life was most intense – something we had found to be deeply true in this war-torn land. Then we went to a settlement on the fringes of the city to visit Americo Tivane, another preacher who had been badly wounded; he had been shot through the stomach in an attack on the area. We listened to his story, held hands and prayed. I had little doubt that the faith we found in this pain-filled land would outlast the promises of Marxist utopianism. Whatever inspiration and encouragement we might have brought, it was the courage, resilience and inextinguishable faith of the people that strengthened us. And well it might, because in our absence PW Botha had declared a State of Emergency in South Africa and already some of my colleagues, including Reverends Mvume Dandala and Andile Mbete in Port Elizabeth and Reverend Victor Madikiza of Brakpan, had been picked up in early-morning swoops.

Stanley Mogoba,[299] now Executive Secretary of the MCSA, warned by phone that I might be on PW Botha's detention list and shouldn't leave the airport when I arrived back in South Africa – I should travel straight on to London. A quick conference at the airport with my deputy, Sizwe Mbabane, John Rees and *Dimension* editor Theo Coggin confirmed the decision. Theo had brought me a packed bag and I took the night plane. I had already planned to be at the World Methodist Peace Conference there and simply arrived a little early. I was now in a position to speak out against what was happening at home untrammelled by emergency regulations. On arrival I made a comprehensive statement about the state of emergency, spoke on BBC and gave a number of media interviews. I said that South Africa's rulers were "prisoners of their own immoral policies, and reduced to the desperate measure of martial law". I described the ongoing exclusion of blacks as "the final foolishness, closing the door on hope" and urged the recall of Parliament, an end to the state of emergency and the announcement of a National Convention involving all recognised leaders to decide a new constitutional formula. "I say to Mr Botha, 'You cannot defend a country indefinitely against its own citizens.'"

The Peace Conference was a first – a joint enterprise between the World Methodist Council's divisions of World Evangelism and Social & International Affairs, two wings of the Council with very different emphases. The one tended to focus on individual faith-sharing and discipling, while the other was more issue-oriented. Not surprisingly, the conference reflected this dichotomy. I had been invited to preach at the closing service in Wesley's Chapel[300] in City Road. For a full week we had struggled with the issues of world peace, with some arguing that the only way was through changing people one by one, and others convinced that only the transformation of social structures would bring peace. The thought of ascending John Wesley's pulpit was intimidating. What, I wondered, would he say on this occasion? Wesley would eschew each extreme because the genius of his theology was the way he married personal piety and social transformation. Those who clung to one or the other alone were betraying that crucial balance. I also believed that no matter how elite and highly educated the congregation might be, the grand old man would have made a call to commitment, so I decided to do the same. When I got to the end of my sermon, I said: "Some of you here have been so busy with your personal spirituality that you have drowned out the cries of the poor and oppressed with your hallelujahs. You need to repent and ask God for a new commitment to social justice. Others have been so busy changing the world that you have neglected your own personal piety. You've been so busy protesting and picketing that you've forgotten how to pray. You need to repent and commit yourself to a new personal walk with Jesus. So, come together, kneel here and ask God to help you get your Gospel together again." And they came! Some 40 clergy, professors, experts and analysts, believers and sceptics came and knelt in a sign of contrition and a yearning for newness. I thought, Well, Father John, that one worked. Thank you!

My return to South Africa at the end of July was without incident except for the usual harassment at the airport.[301] I had let it be known that wherever I visited I expected Methodists of all races to meet me together, but when we visited Cradock in the conservative Eastern Cape, a mixture of local intransigence and fear created a small crisis. Cradock was where popular anti-government activists Matthew Goniwe, Fort Calata, Sparrow Mkhonto and Sicelo Mhlauli came from. On 27 June they suddenly disappeared. It would later emerge that while driving to Port Elizabeth they had been kidnapped by the Security Police, assassinated and their bodies burnt. Here we were, a month later, and Lingelihle township was boiling; it was described by Alan Cowell of the *New York Times* as "a crucible of violence … in the manner of Northern Ireland or Beirut …"[302] and had been under massive military lock-down for some time. I felt that we should hold our official gathering right there as a sign of solidarity with the people; I also wanted to visit the widows of those now known as the 'Cradock Four'. On the Sunday morning, with Bishop's deputy Dr Donald Cragg guiding us, we passed numerous armoured vehicles perched on the hill above the township and drove down into its mean streets, where we saw a body partly covered by a piece of cardboard, still lying by the side of the road, a pathetic reminder of some encounter the night before. We were met at the Methodist church by Reverend Gladwell Tunyiswa and his brave wife Margaret who took us into a church packed with black worshippers. The white Methodists of Cradock were conspicuous by their absence – except for one white couple sitting in the front row with their two small children. I was told that this family farmed in the nearby countryside, and was known and unpopular in the white town for their stand against racism. I was awed by their courage: to make a stand in a one-horse white *dorp* where everyone knew everyone else seemed to me to take so much more guts than I would be able to muster, and then to make their way into Lingelihle under the guns of the SADF to come to worship.

We had church and I tried to offer some hope and encouragement. "This evil will end," I said. "Through the bravery of people like you, mothers, fathers and specially you young men and women who refuse to co-operate any longer in your own oppression, you will be free. And when you are free, those white police and soldiers on the hill will learn that they can be free too – free from prejudice and hate. Until then you must know that God is with you in your pain."

But there was also work to do with the white Methodists. After a visit to a very brave Mrs Goniwe in her little house, we drove back into Cradock to see why the whites had snubbed us. I had asked Reverend Tunyiswa and a lay leader from Lingelihle to accompany us so they could see that there would be no inconsistencies in my message. The white Methodists had finished their service and – as if they were living on another planet – were holding a *braai*[303] in the manse garden, which was where I found, or shall I say caught, them. Our arrival elicited first shock and then hostility. Their minister, who had done nothing to get his people to the official service in the township, was tongue-tied. I requested him, as politely as I could, to re-assemble his people in the church. There was grumbling and there were some angry words, and some people stormed off, but most of them filed sheepishly back into the sanctuary, expecting a dressing-down from the head of their church. I did speak briefly, expressing my sadness at their absence earlier and telling them just how gracious and brave the people were whom they had refused to meet. Then I said, "And it seems you didn't want to meet me. Perhaps you'd like to tell me why, or ask me any questions?" There was a surprised silence before one or two people spoke up with questions about some of the stories they had seen in the media about me. As I responded to more of them there was a discernible thaw in the atmosphere, with nods in places replacing stony frowns. The ogre was more human than they thought. Then a middle-aged man stood up: "I am a policeman," he said. "A real policeman, or a security policeman?" I asked. He reddened, and admitted he was the latter. "Welcome," I said.

"I often have you guys in my services." He then proceeded to accuse me of being a stooge, aiding the "Communist Total Onslaught" on our country and peddling the Marxist line. I let him go on for a while before I stopped him. Then I asked whether he had read the Obedience Charter. His look of puzzlement was enough. "You seem to be an expert on the Communist Manifesto," I said, "but you haven't read the charter that guides the Methodist Church. I have it with me. It expresses the collective mind of the most representative gathering of Methodists in our history. It is rooted firmly in Scripture and our Wesleyan convictions and it defines what our church believes about the struggle in our land. So it's not me you have to decide about – but the Obedience Charter. If you call yourself a Methodist, you will stand with it. If you cannot stand with it, there are other churches to join." That silenced him and the meeting ended fairly soon after. We prayed and the people went their way. I never received an apology from the minister for refusing to bring his people into the pain of Lingelihle to hear their President, nor for failure to educate his congregation about the Obedience Charter. Experiences like this confirm my view that apartheid could have ended years sooner were it not for cowards in our pulpits.

On 19 August a group of church leaders led by Anglican Archbishop Philip Russell met again with State President PW Botha to confront him with a five-point call: repeal the pass laws, withdraw your troops from the townships, end the state of emergency, release Nelson Mandela and hold a National Convention to write a new constitution. It was the first such meeting with him since 1980 and Botha had assembled his senior cabinet around the long oval table, with the nine of us parked at the bottom end. On his left sat National Intelligence Service head Dr Niel Barnard with a pile of files in front of him. Each time one of us spoke Barnard would open a file and hand it to PW, who would then alternate between perusing it and fixing the speaker with a malevolent stare – all this to intimidate. When it was Catholic Archbishop Denis Hurley's turn to speak, Botha launched a vicious attack on him: "I don't want to hear from you, Bishop Hurley," he thundered. "You openly support the communists. I am not listening to you." Botha went on to quote something Hurley had said recently which had particularly angered him, and then he simply bullied him into silence. Turning immediately to one of the black churchmen there – representing a much tamer denomination – PW turned on the charm: "Now Reverend X here is a real Christian; he cares about the upliftment of his people, not supporting revolutionaries." It was an ugly encounter and we came out angry. Apart from agreeing to appoint a magistrate to investigate some of the security force atrocities we had reported, Botha had shifted not at all.

At the press conference afterward, Hurley said with good reason that "communication had been virtually impossible". I said it was clear from the meeting that "there are two clocks running in South Africa – one at five past midnight and one long before. We are trying to represent those for whom midnight has struck … where hopelessness and despair have welled over into rage." I didn't think there was any indication that Botha had heard us. "We can only hope that on reflection he will see," I said. That same day, presumably to neutralise any impact from our visit, Botha entertained two Dutch Reformed groups and right-wing Moral Majority founder Reverend Jerry Falwell from the USA. Falwell came out full of praise for the regime, to which I later responded that Falwell's view was a disservice to justice: "He hasn't the slightest notion what is going on in the hearts and minds of the majority of people in this land."[304]

In late August a local mob of 100 Inkatha supporters armed with *knobkieries*, axes, knives and other weapons, attacked the Federal Theological Seminary in Imbali township outside Pietermaritzburg in Natal, demanding that seminary president Khoza Mgojo and Dr Simon Gqubule come out "to be dealt with" and that all students leave the premises by 30 August. Because many students were critical of Buthelezi and refused to "dissociate the call for justice from the training for ministry",[305] his supporters blamed the seminary for anti-Buthelezi protests in the township. That night I phoned Chief Minister Buthelezi. I emphasised that our talk would be confidential and in a long conversation thought I had got a commitment from him to call his followers off. In public he continued to refuse to accept any responsibility for the incident but there was no more violence. The seminary closed for a brief period and court injunctions were obtained restricting further harassment by residents of Imbali.[306]

My dear friend Abel Hendricks, now Bishop of the Cape Town area, was in the thick of the tumult on the Cape Flats, trying to keep the police in check and protecting 'coloured' schoolkids as they rebelled. On 29 August, when I heard that he and Methodist ministers Charles Villa-Vicencio and Alan Brews had been arrested together with Reverend Allan Boesak on a 'Release Mandela' march near Pollsmoor Prison,[307] I flew to Cape Town. I got to the Wynberg magistrates' court with Abel's deputy, Reverend James Gribble, in time for their appearance. The magistrate remanded them in custody and I asked James to convene an emergency meeting of as many Methodist ministers and lay leaders as possible for that night while I visited the cells to try and make contact. I was refused permission to see them and was about to leave the cell block when somebody hailed me. It was Sergeant George Slade, father of my old friend Don, from Camps Bay days. He had run the small police station there for many years and was a beloved figure in that part of the world. "What are you doing in Wynberg, Sergeant?" I enquired. "I could ask the same of you Rev," he replied – then told me he was excited because this was his last day in the police force; he had only five more minutes before retiring. "Well then," I pleaded, "maybe your last action can be a favour to your church: can you get me in to see Reverend Abel Hendricks?" And he did. I couldn't see the others but I did spend some time with Abel. He was not afraid for himself but deeply shocked at police actions over the past few days.

That night a large crowd came to the meeting in my old church in District Six. Early on Charles Villa-Vicencio and Alan Brews arrived, having been released from custody. I asked them to speak, explaining what they had done and why and then tried to put the day's events into the wider context of the insurrection and cruel repression spreading round the country. There was much anger, not always for the same reason: most were outraged that the police had dared to arrest their Bishop, while some conservative white and 'coloured' Methodists were angry that he had "got himself involved like this". Looking back I know I failed somewhere that night. I came without a plan and gave too much weight to holding the Church together. While many thanked me for coming so quickly and "shedding light on the situation", I was also accused of having failed Abel and the rest by not immediately leading the crowd out on another march to demand their release. A night march would of course have been foolish, giving security forces' *carte blanche* in the darkness, but we should have done something more than vent.

Around this time the Kairos Document burst on the South African scene, raising all sorts of issues (which I address in the next chapter).

A last major involvement before handing over the reins of MCSA leadership was with the National Initiative for Reconciliation (NIR), another effort to try and shift the logjam in our country. NIR brought 400 church leaders from 48 denominations to the city of Pietermaritzburg to wrestle with the crisis in our land. I was deeply touched when ageing anti-apartheid icon Alan Paton stood to read the words of Psalm 130: "Out of the depths have I cried unto you, Lord hear my cry ..." There he was, this man who was crying for the beloved country while I was a schoolboy, yet still believing, still standing for the values we had come to seek together. African Enterprise's Michael Cassidy laid down a marker by pointing us to the Exodus story: for the Hebrew slaves to cross the Jordan and arrive safely in the promised land, "the priests who carried the ark of the covenant of the Lord" had to lead the way, holding back the waters until the last of their people had passed over.[308] "There is no hope for national reconciliation without the church first showing the way and paying the price," he said. Other speakers like Desmond Tutu and Professor David Bosch spelt out that price. Reconciliation was not about "making nice"; it was about facing the truth about ourselves and our culpability – and changing our ways. It was at the NIR gathering that Tutu made his famous statement, "It is very hard for me to reconcile with you when your foot is on my neck."

For me, there was another, unexpected pilgrimage required in those days: 46 dominees of the Dutch Reformed churches were attending rather tentatively and I found myself in a small group each day with a few of them. As they shared their stories I became conscious again of how deeply they resented English speakers like myself – to the extent that before addressing the black/white gulf they wanted first to talk about this. It came to me just how different South African history may have been if, after the Anglo-Boer War, my forebears had found the grace to ask forgiveness for the disastrous concentration camps where Boer women and children where crowded together in dangerously unhygienic conditions and where so many of them – as well as their black workers – died. I felt the need to make that apology to the group I was part of and I hope that, coming from the leader of the largest English-speaking denomination, it made some difference for them.

The most dramatic outcome of the NIR gathering was the decision to bring South Africa to a halt on Wednesday, 9 October. A 'Pray-Away' was called – a day of prayer, fasting and humiliation on which we invited the entire nation to stay home and go to their local churches to pray for transformation in our land. PW Botha was outraged at the prospect and some unions growled about churches mimicking their strike tactics and not consulting them, but in the end the Pray-Away broke all records. Soweto at times looked like a ghost town and it was estimated that 60% of its population participated. At CMM in Johannesburg a steady stream of people came to pray throughout the day, and the service we held at lunch hour was strongly attended as large corporations closed their doors for two hours. Cassidy wrote, "The most moving picture to me was the front-page headline and full-length picture of what they called 'the busiest road in South Africa', from Soweto to the city. It was totally deserted except for one lone cyclist. The huge headline, surely the strangest in South Africa's history, came from the heart of Soweto and simply said, 'HEAR US, O LORD'."[309]

I went to Bloemfontein to hand over to the new MCSA President, my friend Reverend Ernest Baartman, grateful that my final engagement had been one in which God's power to bridge the chasms of history and ideology had been affirmed in a small way for me. Having been battered throughout the year by an unbroken torrent of hostility from the racist right – as well as from time to time the slings and arrows of the hard left, it was good to lay this burden down. Reviewing my year of office I noted that the call I had made twelve months before had been greeted by shock but that now "it has become the conventional wisdom among all sorts of people in politics, business and industry – all except in the Union Buildings". I decried the breakdown in solidarity among those who opposed the regime: "We are in an era where the assassination of someone who thinks differently than yourself is almost as important as resisting the system and where the Church is seen as a rich prize to be co-opted by one or other wing of the struggle."[310] I was determined that the Church not be hijacked.

I had begun my year of office pledged to be a "messenger of hope", and Elizabeth and I had sought to bring the gift of hope in the places we visited. In some of those places I know that she and I had done so. In others I had failed, but we had both been the recipients of something very precious in return: the people we had met, especially among the "least of Jesus' brothers and sisters",[311] had left an indelible mark upon us. The Church may give us many reasons to be cynical but in touching these lives, time and again we had found the real thing – Christ-like courage, rock-like endurance, humble faith and love beyond understanding.

28

Stress Fractures

The years of struggle were extraordinarily stressful and some inner disharmonies were inevitable. Those of us leading the Church's witness were not always of one mind about how best to go forward. Labels like 'radical', 'liberal', 'moderate', 'conservative' – and the relatively new 'progressive' – were often too readily applied. I tried not to take them too seriously because they have little meaning independent of context. My label changed depending on who was talking about me. To most whites I was a dangerous radical, but to the most ideologically driven activists I was at best an irrelevant liberal. They saw their role as pushing leaders like me into more aggressive positions or writing us off. We needed their impatience but understandably, individuals and bodies unconstrained by large constituencies were freer to decide and act than the SACC member-denominations. An example of this was the ongoing polite but discernible tension between Beyers Naudé's Christian Institute and the SACC. We were allies working hand in glove, but overseas funding support was often attracted by presenting a more 'radical' image and the saintly Beyers was sometimes less than a saint when it came to stealing a march on the SACC in this regard. The CI didn't have to bring along thousands of local congregations as did churches like MCSA. Ironically, in the early years Beyers wooed me for a staff position and it was this factor that decided me to refuse: I felt that the real test of my effectiveness was not whether I could play the gadfly – which was the CI's role – but whether it was possible to transform ordinary local congregations into agents of change. After all, if we couldn't mobilise congregations on the ground against South

Africa's original sin, we should stop speaking of the Church as being engaged in the struggle.

Another reason for occasional differences amongst us was our theological, cultural and psychological dispositions. Calvinist churches, especially those breaking out of the Afrikaans Dutch Reformed family, were generally more pugnacious and militant than the English-speaking denominations. I decided that it was simply the nature of the beast. While travelling in Europe for SACC I had found the Netherlands churches to be the most self-righteous and shrill about apartheid; perhaps they needed to compensate for the guilt they felt about their descendants in South Africa. Similarly, those who had been part and parcel of the apartheid-justifying Dutch Reformed family seemed to be longer on militancy than grace. Calvinism has a big dose of exclusivism in its DNA and Afrikaans culture refers to something called *broedertwis*.[312] When both are in play the gloves are really off. I remember my first meeting with Ds Nico Smith, who earned fame for moving with his family into a black township after becoming convinced of the wrongs of apartheid. Nico scolded some 30 black and white veterans of decades in the struggle as if we were neophytes. My feelings were mixed. When these Afrikaners change they certainly go all the way, I thought admiringly, but also, it's a pity that the later they come to the struggle the more they think they're the only ones here. Maybe Nico's freshly opened eyes enabled him to see with the clarity of a convert the weaknesses of those of us who had trodden this path for many years, but I will not pretend that he didn't get up my nose.

One more factor needs to be added to the mix. The more 'radical' of my counterparts were often either members[313] or close allies of the ANC or PAC and that did raise a question as to who they were speaking for. I remember saying of one of them that "the politician in him always seemed to be a few steps ahead of the theologian", and sure enough, his political ambitions emerged openly later, only to be swatted aside by the party he thought owed him a position. With few exceptions "men of the cloth" have made dismal party politicians, with little to show for it except a dented credibility. By contrast, people like Desmond Tutu retained their moral authority precisely because they eschewed such ambitions. I remember saying to PW Botha once, "Prime Minister, you should listen to what we are saying because we're the only people who come into your office who don't want your job." We need to be sure that is always true, which is why I believe that the Church needs to keep some "prophetic distance" from political formations. This is not to be confused with avoidance of engagement: it is about being free to speak an uncompromised word into the situation – a word emanating from a theological, rather than ideological place. It is hard enough to discern God's word above the cacophony of our own cultural and ideological conditioning without being hitched to a party line as well. Mvume Dandala once summed me up this way: "Peter is not a party man: as a result of his struggle with the Gospel … his challenge to the church is not to sacrifice its independence … he has called passionately for the unbanning of the ANC and PAC while firmly objecting to the stance that puts people in the Nationalist camp beyond redemption."[314]

There is of course a theological position born largely out of Latin American liberation struggles, which invites the Church into unashamed identification with political movements fighting for justice. The problem with that is writ large in South African history: the Dutch Reformed churches were so closely identified with the Afrikaner liberation struggle that it resulted in their becoming co-inventors and defenders of the apartheid project. It is one thing to obey God's call to identify with the oppressed in our land and stand against the powers, but quite another to place the church at the disposal of those seeking political power, no matter how God-pleasing their agenda might seem.

These tensions broke surface most prominently twice during 1985, the first being over the 'Prayers for the Downfall of the Government' controversy. Returning to Johannesburg from the Namibian border

I landed in a flurry of SACC meetings around this issue. In 1984 Dr Allan Boesak had called for "a day on which to pray for the downfall of the government". He went on to say, "If the rulers will not hear the cries of the people, if they will not change, if they continue to prevent justice, let us pray them out of existence. God will hear our cry."[315] An SACC-appointed work group later produced a document called *A Theological Rationale and a Call to Prayer for the End to Unjust Rule*. Without officially adopting it, the SACC Executive sent it as a study document to all regions, including the Western Province Council of Churches (WPCC). They jumped the gun by releasing it at a Cape Town press conference on 24 May claiming it had the SACC imprimatur. Allan Boesak preferred to name it *Prayers for the Downfall of the Government.*

The row that raged for a while over the *Theological Rationale* and its *Call to Prayer* lay in a combination of factors. First, the premature release of the document was seen by some of us as a ploy to avoid a final vetting by the SACC and church leadership. Anglican Archbishop Philip Russell and I both protested that we were being asked to commend to thousands of churches a document which had not yet been adopted. WPCC insisted erroneously that it *had* been adopted but if their real intention was to impute a distinction between what they felt was their more 'radical' position and that of the SACC Executive and church leaders, they got what they wanted. Second, countless prayers had been raised asking God to rid South Africa of its oppression, but this was the first theological statement seeking to justify the actual removal of those in government, praying that God "*... may remove from his people the tyrannical structures of oppression and the present rulers in our country who persistently refuse to heed the cry for justice.*" The Archbishop questioned whether he could support a call that essentially revised some of the Prayers in the Anglican Prayer Book and said it was hardly honest for churches to make representations – even on behalf of the oppressed – to a government "when one is asking God to remove it from office".³¹⁶ I was as committed against PW Botha's regime as anyone else but my Wesleyan doctrine of grace would not permit me to put them beyond the pale of transformation by praying prayers that I said seemed to limit the operation of that grace to one option only. God might well decide upon that option, but "it is not our business to limit him to it".³¹⁷ Desmond Tutu also distanced himself but did so privately in a letter to Reverend Frank Chikane "because of my loyalty to the SACC". He wanted to know why the call never named the sins, for instance, of "young people again resorting to necklacing", or bodies like Inkatha and the ANC.³¹⁸ The media pounced eagerly on Boesak's provocative phrase and, as Charles Villa-Vicencio put it, the questions that intrigued them were: "Precisely what was the document calling for? Was it the violent overthrow of the regime? To what extent was Allan Boesak responsible for it, and to what extent is he isolated from the rest of the church? Was the document an SACC document? Was it the work of a few radicals?"³¹⁹ The controversy would not have lasted very long without the whiff of division in the air. Headlines trumpeted a 'split' in the SACC. There was anger on both sides, with church leaders believing they and the SACC Executive had been blindsided by Allan Boesak's penchant for publicity, and his WPCC supporters feeling betrayed by our distancing ourselves from him. But there was no split. By 3 June the SACC had met and cobbled together a statement that left most bruised egos – but much more importantly, the witness of the Church – reasonably intact. It confirmed that the *Rationale* had not ever been adopted by the SACC, but included an assurance that the Archbishop and I were in no way seeking to undermine SACC unity in our statements. On that June 16, we all went to prayer in our thousands, and while the semantics of our prayers might have differed, their intention and intensity was the same. Things are always clearer from a distance, and looking back I don't think any of us covered ourselves in glory. Both parties would have done better to talk to each other before addressing the nation. The misunderstandings of those days were unhelpful and we needed a much deeper conversation about what was really happening behind the furore.

This tendency was even more marked when later in the year a group of anonymous theologians published a document called *Kairos – Challenge to the Church*.[320] The way it was released had ambush written all over it: on that day, CMM's primitive fax machine began to overwork and soon rolls of paper were snaking all over the carpet. My secretary was still trying to cut, collate and staple them when Catholic theologian Father Albert Nolan walked in and told me that "a document is being released today that may be quite controversial. You should get ready for something of a media storm." With a little smile he then apologised for having "forgotten" to bring a copy with him and left. He was right about the storm. The most basic courtesy would have ensured that we could read and digest the content before its release but I hadn't read the first page before the press was clamouring for a response. The anonymity of the authors added more unnecessary drama. Since when did Christian theologians make their witness hiding behind anonymity? Could that be called 'witness'? Were they hoping to give the impression that all the authors were black Christians writing from the dust and struggle of Soweto when perhaps this was not the case?

Kairos named three theologies: "State Theology", justifying the status quo and represented mainly by the Dutch Reformed churches' close identification with the regime; "Church Theology", typified by the liberal multi-racial SACC churches such as my own, with their emphasis on calling for justice and reconciliation and nonviolence; and "Prophetic Theology", which they said, "analyses the conflict in society clearly, examines oppression and tyranny in the Christian tradition … states unequivocally that God sides with the oppressed and calls for participation in the struggle for liberation and a just society."[321] "Church Theology" and the multi-racial churches of SACC were the main target and came in for a hammering. We were rightly accused of a gap between public profession and actual practice and falsely accused of equating state aggression with insurgent response, which was nonsense. The churches had been fastidious in distinguishing between the primary violence of the state and the counter-violence of a violated people. We were told that our problem was that we elevated concepts like reconciliation and non-violence into "absolute principles" without emphasising justice – again untrue. Ignoring years of unequivocal opposition to the regime, *Kairos* scorned any belief in the value of talking to both sides of the struggle and accused us of being weak neutrals wanting to become a "third force" between oppressor and oppressed.

However, nothing was as neat and tidy, nor as black and white as the sweeping generalisations of *Kairos* made out. Attaching one theological typology to the "liberal multi-racial" churches was not very good analysis because no denomination was homogenous. The MCSA, for instance, was itself a site of ongoing struggle. There were Methodists of all the above types constantly engaging, disputing, learning and painfully growing. What else had Obedience '81 been about? And when Moses went time and again to Pharaoh on behalf of the Hebrew slaves, did that mean he had become a neutral "third force"? Yes, we had often failed to act on our convictions, but *Kairos* insisted that our convictions themselves were faulty. We were told that if only we analysed the context properly we would see the futility of our approach.

In spite of many pungent and uncomfortable truths I agreed with, *Kairos* seemed to me to be driven more by political calculation than theological principle. Rebel Afrikaans theologian David Bosch agreed, saying that it was "strategy posing as theology" and when that happened "it became ideology".[322] I was troubled by the ease with which the Jesus commitment to non-violence and the New Testament emphasis on reconciliation were dismissed and David concurred: "The dividing of reality into absolutely black and white categories is a pernicious theological position,"[323] he said. So what was *Kairos* after? If one looked at the 'Challenge to Action' at the end of the document there was no help there: it ended with a whimper. There was nothing new except a patronising and revealing instruction to the churches "not to duplicate what the people's organisations are already doing ..." but to consult, co-ordinate and co-operate with them.[324] For the rest, churches were already involved in doing to a greater or lesser degree all the things *Kairos* was "challenging" us to do. I concluded that the long-term aim of the document was to persuade readers that the regime was completely irredeemable, and that any hope of achieving change by protest, economic and other forms of pressure was long gone. If our churches could be persuaded of this, then the way would be opened for a more supportive stance toward the "armed struggle". That would be an enormous coup for the liberation movements, whose armed wing, MK, had failed in 24 years of existence to achieve anything more than small, sporadic acts of 'armed propaganda'.[325] Was that what *Kairos* was really about?

Both Desmond Tutu and I declined to sign the document. He felt it falsely caricatured the witness of earlier Church opponents of apartheid whom he admired and who had inspired his own witness. He also believed its theology of reconciliation was "less than Biblical and that the Church needed to continue to witness to reconciliation for all, at all costs, even death".[326] Being the son of one the earlier witnesses *Kairos* scorned, I concurred. Also, as with the *Prayer* document, I would be denying a central tenet of my theology by concluding that anybody – *anybody* – was beyond redemption. His stance and mine were not popular; for some, in a struggle as intense and painful as the one we were in, to demur was treason. One was supposed to go along with documents like these, whatever one thought of them, "for the sake of the cause". When a clergy colleague who was enduring a long, six-year punishment for refusing to go to war against his black compatriots wrote a careful and compassionate critique of *Kairos*, he was dismissed arrogantly as a "supporter of the *status quo*". I warned of a danger "that this document tends to replace the blasphemy of a tyrannical state with the absolute rectitude of a people's struggle ... *Kairos* lays the foundations for a theology of political resistance, legitimising the violent overthrow of a violent and tyrannical regime, but it may be that because of *Kairos*' poor understanding of the theology of non-violent resistance, others will take another way."[327]

Looking back, the irony of *Kairos* is that the incisive analysis it claimed was already behind the curve. While the churches were being urged to give up entirely on the apartheid regime, God was inspiring other options: by September 1984 Nelson Mandela had already written to Minister of Justice Kobie Coetzee inviting him to visit, thereby setting in motion the long, risky and complicated set of negotiations that led ultimately to his release, the unbanning of the liberation movements by President FW de Klerk on 2 February 1990 and ultimately the first democratic elections. Mandela knew that the armed struggle had achieved little more than "armed propaganda" and was going nowhere. "I started *Umkhonto we Sizwe* (MK)," he said later, "but I never had any illusions that we could win a military victory; its purpose was to focus attention on the resistance movement."[328] Allister Sparks adds: "So, getting to see the government had always been a primary objective."[329] This was going to happen, not because of armed action by MK; it was happening because increasing numbers of black South Africans were refusing to co-operate in their own oppression, and more and more countries around the world were squeezing the regime economically and in other ways.

29

Hostage Crisis

Like most South Africans I was glued to my television set for many hours as South Africa bade farewell to Winnie Madikizela-Mandela, freedom struggle hero in her own right. As I watched, I felt the sadness of having lost someone I had known and admired at her fearless best, but mixed in with that was anger because of my painful recollection of events when she was at her worst. I was intimately involved in those events, so it was hard to watch one speaker after another either ignore or aggressively deny the dark shadows that they still cast. By the time of her funeral her life story was already being rewritten with every ounce of heroism recalled and every notorious deed airbrushed out. None involved on the day found the moral courage to at least acknowledge her transgressions. Instead, her funeral was a state-sponsored canonisation with serious implications for the truth.

Winnie's saga was a tragedy of Shakespearean proportions, which also inflicted deep injury on the ANC. I believe that the movement's failure to hold her accountable for her offences in the late 80s and early 90s marked its first public slide from the moral high ground of the struggle. This woman who in her prime had stood for an unwavering, almost superhuman resistance to wrong, became a troubling liability. She often said, "I am the product of the masses of my people and also the product of my enemies," and it may well be that the wounds those enemies inflicted on her soul damaged her irreparably. My engagement with her certainly marked one of the most painful chapters in my life.

We first met in 1985 in Majwemasweu, a bleak reservation for blacks outside the white farming town of Brandfort, where Winnie had languished under official banishment since 1977. Located in the Orange Free State 350 km from Johannesburg, her new home might as well have been in a foreign land. The language spoken there was Sesotho, while Winnie was from the isiXhosa-speaking Eastern Cape. Winnie's roots, like those of Nelson, were in the Methodist Church and as leader of the denomination I wanted to bring her some encouragement. Elizabeth and I were driven from Bloemfontein by the local Bishop, Jack Scholtz, and his spouse Joan, both of whom had offered spiritual and practical care to Winnie since her banishment began. Jack and Joan had had their own problems defending Methodist social principles in conservative Bloemfontein, and right-wingers had once stoned their home.

Arriving in the township, we were joined by the local minister, Themba Mntambo, who had made it possible for her to launch a day-care centre for pre-school children in the church building. We drove up to House 802, just another dreary two-room matchbox house typical of black townships across the land. A Security Police vehicle was parked up the road but we ignored its occupants and walked up the short path. Some flowers planted around the front door were a brave attempt at home-making in the dust. Standing in the doorway with arms spread wide in welcome was a smiling Winnie Mandela. We exchanged greetings and went inside the small living room cum kitchen. Jack and Joan wanted to check that certain supplies had arrived safely, and that all was well with the small clinic that the MCSA and other donors had helped fit out for her. Having become the first qualified black social worker in South Africa, and in spite of the language barriers, Winnie had lost no time making herself useful to the desperately poor people around her. We compared notes about our different experiences visiting her husband on Robben Island and she spoke of her work among the people of Majwemasweu. Then she and I went into the small adjoining bedroom where I told her of the call I planned to make at the coming Methodist Conference for an immediate unbanning and return from exile of the liberation movements on the one hand, and a cessation of the ANC's armed struggle on the other. She was enthusiastic about the first and less so about the second. "This is an important call," she said. "It will encourage my husband and the movement, but it is too early to end the armed struggle." She nevertheless understood that my position was consistent with the Church's emphasis on non-violent forms of resistance. Before we left, we all prayed together and then each received one of the effusive embraces she was famous for.

Winnie was strikingly beautiful. In addition to her intelligence and warmth, in her presence I had no problem understanding why a young Nelson Mandela had become smitten by this fiery woman – and why other men later became entangled with her. During the Brandfort exile reports of alcohol, drugs and men had begun to surface and I sensed that the layers of pain behind the smiling welcome were manifesting in damaging ways. By this time in her life, Winnie had been horribly abused both in and out of jail. Her times of imprisonment were hellish, with long periods of solitary confinement – sometimes completely naked – plus physical and mental torture. Back in Soweto not a day had gone by without intrusive surveillance or worse: police dragging her out of bed in the small hours of the morning, demanding to search her bedroom. Her resistance was fierce but the harassment was unrelenting. Despite all her courage Winnie was becoming a damaged person. Throughout these years the Methodist Church offered what support it could and Mandela himself never failed to express his appreciation. He wrote to me from prison that same year: "This letter gives me an opportunity of thanking the Church, through you, for all that they have done for my family. Without that help Winnie's burdens would have been far more difficult to endure."[330] Sadly, however, no help was sufficient to prevent the emotional damage even then corroding her character.

A year after our visit and with typical defiance, Winnie broke her banning order and came home to Soweto. She took up residence again with her daughter Zinzi in the house in Vilakazi Street that she had shared with Nelson before his imprisonment. She literally dared the authorities to arrest her, but they were hesitant because her bold move coincided with the growing international momentum of the Release Mandela Campaign. All over the world people were demanding that Nelson be set free and in his absence Winnie, with her Evita-like magnetism, became the obvious pin-up for the campaign. Her home was seen as an essential stop for visiting dignitaries and diplomats and she was showered with gifts and honours. Somebody coined the title 'Mother of the Nation' and the African-American community in the United States in particular elevated her to celebrity status. In their eyes Winnie could do no wrong and I would argue that this unqualified adulation added more damage to her psyche on top of all the horrors of police brutality.

Then, fatally, she surrounded herself with a shady group of tough youths nicknamed the 'Mandela United Football Club', who may have worn sweatsuits and trainers, but played little soccer. Instead they became Winnie's enforcers, doing her bidding in Soweto with whatever brutality they thought necessary. Winnie carried no official position with the underground ANC cadres, but she set herself up as an alternative authority in the area, issuing orders and demanding obedience. Emma Gilbey describes how Mandela United began to "almost ape" the behaviour of the Security Police: "Winnie's boys would burst into a house with much clamour and show of force, before compelling an intended victim into a vehicle and driving him off to a place of interrogation – Winnie's house. Once there, a mutated form of police questioning would occur, with verbal abuse, kicking, punching, whipping, beating and slapping. Instead of mock executions at gunpoint, victims would be hung from the ceiling; instead of being hooded or blindfolded, they would have plastic bags placed over their heads, and have their faces shoved in buckets of water. Instead of electric shocks, their flesh would be carved and, as cited in one case, battery acid would be smeared into the wounds. And instead of being dangled out of the window by their ankles they would be thrown high up into the air and left to hit the floor – a practice known as 'breakdown.'"[331] Around these activities there was a curtain of silence. Proof of the fear inculcated by the Mandela United thugs was that although I moved in and out of Soweto regularly at the time, I remained unaware of the growing crisis. I saw Winnie from time to time to arrange for international guests to meet with her clandestinely in spite of her banning order. On these occasions she was full of charm and nothing appeared to be amiss. Visitors went away enthralled by her. It was only in July 1988, when news came that the house in Vilakazi Street had been burned down, that I heard another narrative. I went to the site hoping to offer her some sympathy, but found the charred ruin deserted. Over the road an elderly man leaned on his gate watching me. I said, "This is so evil. The system never stops persecuting her." His reply was unexpected: "Bishop, this was not the system." He pointed up the road. "The boys from that school did it. This was done to punish her Football Team for raping one of the schoolgirls there." I was aghast, wanting deeply not to believe him. I drove to Winnie's office in the valley below, trying to process what I had just heard. As if to confirm the old man's words, I found the gate closed and guarded by a couple of surly youths who demanded aggressively to know what I wanted. I was irritated by their attitude. "I've come to minister to Mrs Mandela," I said. "I am her Bishop and I don't have to answer to you." There were bullying undertones to the brief altercation that followed but I was finally admitted and found Winnie in a mood of deep depression, staring into nowhere. She and daughter Zinzi sat in silence while a wealthy African-American friend, Robert J Brown, hovered in the background, acting as if he was the authority in the household. I later learned that Brown was a North Carolina businessman with a dubious background who hoped to cash in on his ties with Winnie. She ultimately indicated without much conviction that "the system" had burned her house but the conversation left me concerned that the neighbour may have been right.

After that, reports of other bullying actions by the Football Team began to surface and I learned from SACC General Secretary Frank Chikane that a 'Crisis Committee' had been formed to try and rein in their activities. It consisted of Frank and anti-apartheid stalwarts Sister Bernard Ncube, Cyril Ramaphosa, Beyers Naudé, Sydney Mufamadi and Aubrey Mokoena. Nelson Mandela himself had requested them to act. Meanwhile, with the help of Brown, Winnie moved into a much more commodious house in Soweto's upmarket Diepkloof Extension. This was to become the site of the horrifying excesses that sucked me into the Mandela United violence.

Late in the night of 7 January 1989, Kenny Kgase, a 29-year-old man who had done some caretaking work at CMM, arrived at the church horribly bruised and terrified, saying that he had escaped from Winnie Mandela's house and pleading for protection. It transpired that twelve days previously, he and three others, Thabiso Mono (20), Pelo Mekgwe (20) and Stompie Seipei, who was only fourteen years of age, had been forcibly abducted from the church mission house of Reverend Paul Verryn in Orlando East. The kidnappers were members of Mrs Mandela's football team. Suddenly the most famous woman in the anti-apartheid struggle appeared to be involved in kidnapping and brutal assault.

I had appointed Verryn as the only white Methodist minister in Soweto because of his remarkable ability to relate across racial lines, his deep commitment to the black struggle and his longstanding therapeutic work with people damaged by the apartheid system. He had credibility in the community and I believed that he had the theological tools to interpret the Gospel effectively in that context. Paul was not married and would have had the small mission house to himself had he not thrown it open as a sanctuary for fugitives from the apartheid system. Young men fleeing harassment and others, coming out of detention, sought refuge with him and so there were often as many as a score of them around the house. They would sleep wherever they could and, as was the case in thousands of Soweto homes, the idea of anybody, including Paul, having an entire bed to himself, was unheard of. Members of the underground movement knew they could entrust to his care youths threatened or damaged by the 'system'. This was a risky ministry because, in the overheated political tensions of Soweto in the late 80s, the ruthless Security Police were not the only ones to fear; the merest whisper suggesting that one might harbour informers – *impimpi* – could lead to retribution. Youths coming out of detention were twice victimised, first by torture in the police cells and then by the understandable suspicion that they may have been 'turned'. Paul had practised his ministry of sanctuary consistently for some years, and seemed to be a master at treading the fine line required, but as is often the case with passionately committed people, he had little respect for anybody's authority except his own and was obstinate to a fault. Very quick to lay down the law with others, Paul jibbed at taking instructions himself.

In late October of 1989, he had reported to me that rumours were being spread in Soweto that he was sexually abusing youths under his care. He had also reported this to Frank Chikane. Paul's sexuality was not an issue for me. To me, whether he was gay or straight was irrelevant, and later, in Winnie's trial, when her advocate tried to make homosexuality an issue when cross-examining me, we clashed strongly. But Paul's stewardship as a minister toward vulnerable youths in his charge needed to be morally blameless. I asked for an assurance that the rumours were false and given my trust in his integrity, accepted his word on that score. Chikane had suggested the closure of the sanctuary ministry but I felt the work was too important and in any case was not prepared to take such drastic action on the basis of rumour. I did, however, instruct Paul to enforce a couple of simple rules to protect himself. First, a line had to be drawn at the bedroom door; no matter how crowded the house, he was no longer to permit anyone to sleep in his bedroom, let alone his bed. In addition, a supervising committee was to be formed in the Orlando East Methodist congregation to share the responsibility of care. Paul agreed, but unfortunately never implemented the first and most important instruction. What was seen by me to be a sensible safeguard for his reputation was probably dismissed by him as his Bishop's ignorance of the pressures under which he and his charges lived. He was to pay a dreadful price for this disobedience.

During November 1988 there was some good news: Paul reported to me that a woman named Xoliswa Falati, with her daughter, had sought shelter because her house had been burnt down. She was now providing a "maternal, stabilising presence", he said. I was pleased to hear that discipline had improved and with an adult woman in the house Verryn also felt better protected from rumour. Neither of us realised that Falati had been planted by Winnie Mandela. Two other newcomers into the manse at that time were Stompie Seipei and Katiza Cebekhulu. Katiza was a highly strung, very damaged youth on the run from Natal. Stompie was a thirteen-year-old legend hailing from Tumahole township outside of the rural town of Parys, where he had a reputation for leadership amongst the youth activists. Because of his commitment to the struggle he had become something of a mascot to the Mass Democratic Movement (MDM). I once found him in my office after a protest meeting at CMM. Looking at this child sitting on a chair with his feet not reaching the floor, I asked what he was doing there. I was told, "He's waiting for the Security Police to leave, so he can get out of the building." Laughingly I enquired what he had to fear. "He led the march," was the reply. In spite of his tender age, by the time Stompie entered Verryn's house he had already been detained for a year and tortured. Some suspected that he had been turned.

The scene was now set for the drama that followed.

At around 8 pm on 23 December 1988, while Paul Verryn was on leave, members of Mandela United suddenly burst into his house. Falati quickly pointed out Kenny Kgase, Thabiso Mono, Pelo Mekgwe and Stompie, and these four were grabbed and bundled into a waiting van. Katiza Cebekhulu was also taken but I am still unsure whether this was against his will. Led by a very nasty character named Jerry Richardson the abductees were taken to a room behind Winnie Mandela's house where, according to Thabiso and Pelo's later account to me, and Kenny Kgase's evidence, they were confronted by Winnie herself. She accused them all of having sex with "the white priest" and Stompie was also accused of being an informer. Winnie began hitting them with her fists, then a sjambok, and then others, including Katiza, joined in. The vicious assaults continued until, in Pelo's words, "our eyes could not see for a week". He said they were told to accuse Verryn or be killed. During the mêlée, perhaps because of the 'informer' charge, or because of his small size, Stompie was given the 'breakdown' treatment – thrown up into the air three times and allowed to drop with a sickening thud to the concrete floor. According to one version of events, when the others were finally told by Jerry Richardson to go and clean up, Stompie's torment continued. In Emma Gilbey's reconstruction, after further assaults, Stompie confessed to having sold out four comrades in Parys, which would have sealed his fate.[332]

The prisoners were kept under careful watch for some days after being forced to clean up their blood in Winnie's back yard and the room where they had been assaulted. There are claims that highly respected activist doctor, Abu-Baker Asvat, was called in to examine Stompie at some point and said his brain was seriously damaged. Sometime on Sunday, 1 January 1989, Stompie was told to gather his things and go with Richardson. He was told he was going home. According to Katiza, by then he was "soft on one side of his head and couldn't see out of his eyes. He was also vomiting." We now know that Stompie's throat was cut later that night by Richardson and another thug named Slash, and his body left in the veld.

Between the kidnapping and Kenny's escape, the three remaining prisoners were first held incommunicado in Winnie's premises and then on 3 January they were taken by Richardson for what turned out to be a gruesome induction into the Mandela United team – an execution. Some months before, a member of the football team named Lerotodi Ikaneng had fallen out with Winnie and Zinzi's current boyfriend, Sizwe Sithole. He had lain low for some time, but the football team had caught up with him. In the veld near Mzimhlope, Thabiso, Pelo and Kenny were forced to hold Ikaneng down while Richardson and Slash cut his throat and stabbed him with a pair of garden shears. He was left for dead. After having apparently proved their loyalty, the three abductees were welcomed back at Winnie's house, given sweatsuits, and addressed as 'Comrades'. Their faces and bodies were still horribly bruised, but they were now paired with other members of the club and given sentry duties. It was during sentry duty on the night of 7 January that Kenny Kgase found himself alone for long enough to escape over the fence and run away.

Paul Verryn learned of the abduction two days after it happened but at first kept me out of the loop, seeking help from community leaders. Early in the new year, first Aubrey Mokoena[333] and then Dr Nthato Motlana visited Winnie, enquiring about the abducted youths. Winnie first flatly denied that the youths were at her home, but when the much more senior Motlana arrived, she admitted they were there, but refused him access to them.

To anybody in a relatively normal society, it might seem absurd that the police were not brought into the matter, but the Soweto of 1989 was not a normal society. The police were the enemy, their ubiquitous, abrasive presence a daily reminder of oppression. Calling them in was out of the question. For all anyone knew, the Security Branch might themselves be involved in some way. If the matter was to be resolved it would have to be done without them.[334]

Two days after Kenny Kgase arrived at CMM, Verryn finally briefed me on the crisis, which was to occupy most of my waking hours for the next few months. I made immediate contact with the Crisis Committee and we agreed to work in close collaboration. We were now dealing with a hostage situation and before trying to untangle the roots of this saga, our first priorities were to ascertain Stompie's whereabouts and obtain the release of the two – or three, depending on Katiza's status – remaining youths before they were also 'vanished'. I was content to let the community leaders, who were better placed than I, do the direct negotiating. On 12 January, during a visit by them to Winnie's home, Zinzi made the first admission that the youths were being held against their will, when she let slip that one of them – Kenny – had "escaped". What then had happened to Stompie? That day, three committee members were at last given brief access to the kidnap victims, who first claimed to be there voluntarily, despite the fresh wounds on the bodies of Thabiso and Pelo. Katiza, finding himself alone with the committee, broke down and pleaded to be rescued. He said, "I'm going to die anyway, so I might as well tell the truth." He confessed that they had been told on pain of death to accuse Verryn of sexual abuse. Meanwhile, I informed Winnie's lawyer that the church was now monitoring the situation and would hold her accountable for the safety of the remaining youths and Stompie.

The days following involved more visits to Winnie's house and further torturous negotiations. I was concerned that we increase the pressure on her without her feeling completely cornered. I had a ghastly premonition that Stompie might already be dead and had to stifle my panic about the others. It seemed to me that there could be only two possible outcomes: either Winnie would release the youths or, if she panicked, they would vanish like Stompie. It would be easy for her to claim that they had crossed the border. Meanwhile I had briefed the national leadership of my denomination, who were anxious that if the news got out that we were confronting Winnie head on, people with no knowledge of the facts could either misinterpret our actions politically, or suspect a sex-abuse cover-up. The rest of the country would be astounded and enraged. I was left to handle the matter but, fortunately, by this time I had access to human rights lawyer Fink Haysom, whose advice at different moments in the crisis was invaluable. Geoff Budlender, another courageous attorney, took a watching brief in the interests of the hostages themselves.

Late on Friday 13 January, Nelson Mandela's lawyer, Ishmael Ayob, visited Winnie and threatened to take the matter to her husband in Cape Town's Pollsmoor Prison. At the same time, he conveyed a message from ANC President Oliver Tambo in Lusaka requesting her to release the youths. The ANC in exile was by now alarmed about the implications of the 'Mother of the Nation' kidnapping youths from a church sanctuary. When Winnie repeated her allegations of sexual harassment, Ayob proposed that he be allowed to take the youths to me so that they could repeat these charges. Winnie at first agreed and then changed her mind. Finally she demanded I come to her house. This message only reached me a couple of hours before her deadline of 11.30 the next day and after much wrestling and with Fink's concurrence, I demurred. The youths would not be free to tell the truth while still in her house, and I had been unable to locate any Crisis Committee member to accompany me, something I deemed imperative if Church and community were to work transparently with each other. In any case, when I tried to call Winnie to convey my decision, she was nowhere to be found.

Ayob did visit Nelson Mandela that same Saturday and returned with his instruction to Winnie that she was to release the youths immediately. She flatly refused. On Sunday Ayob made another unsuccessful attempt. Meanwhile I was making a new approach through Dr Motlana, who had just returned from seeing Tambo. I was also seeking guidance from Fink as to whether I could, in the name of the Church, bring a writ of *habeas corpus* or failing that, an interdict preventing Winnie from harming the youths. It turned out that neither option would be open to me, the first because we would have to locate each of the youths' parents – impossible in the timeframe – and the second because none of the Crisis Committee members who had actually seen the bruises and wounds was ready to give evidence against Winnie. They were willing to be go-betweens, but I was discovering how deeply they all feared crossing her. In the end it looked like it would be Winnie in one corner and the Church in the other.

On the same day – 15 January – that Motlana confirmed Oliver Tambo's instruction to Winnie, I had to take an action I had been strenuously avoiding: I pulled Paul Verryn out of Soweto and sent him into hiding. I hated doing it because it could convey a wrong message, but by now there was convincing evidence that the Football Team was planning to kill him. Then I got a cryptic message from Ishmael Ayob: "They're coming out" – and they almost did. The youths were taken that night to Ayob's office but escorts Richardson and Falati began to haggle. Ayob refused to take the youths unless their release was unconditional, and they were taken back to captivity. This may be the reason why Ayob fell out of favour with Winnie and was suddenly replaced by another lawyer named Krish Naidoo.

By this time it was decided to consult a much wider group of underground leaders about the impasse. A secret meeting of representatives of about 60 community organisations, some from as far as Tumahole township and Ikageng outside of Potchefstroom, was being convened for the next evening, Monday 16 January.

When the actual release came, it was something of an anti-climax. That Monday I received a call at around 3.30 pm telling me that Dr Motlana had taken the youths to Krish Naidoo's office and left them there. "There are four of them," I was told, "and one seems high on drugs." I quickly called community leaders Steward Ngwenya and Nat Ramagope to witness the handover and rushed to Naidoo's office. There we found Naidoo and Pelo, Thabiso and Katiza sitting round the boardroom table, with a scowling thuggish escort who gave his name as 'Manois Maseko'. It was my first meeting with any of them. 'Maseko' immediately took a bullying stance. A long and heated discussion ensued in which he, backed by Naidoo, insisted that the youths were there to lay charges against Paul Verryn. I said I had not come to negotiate, but to take them back into the care of the Church, and was not going to leave without them. I would listen carefully to any allegations they might make, but would also be asking hard questions about how they came to leave the mission house in the first place. Pelo and Thabiso looked totally traumatised, with heavy facial bruises still visible, while the one introduced as Katiza was wild-eyed and jumpy. I told them of the meeting planned for a few hours later and indicated that any charges against Paul could be laid there. In the end Pelo and Thabiso said they wanted to come with me, while Katiza refused and elected to stay with Naidoo. I had done all I could and decided to leave with Pelo and Thabiso while the going was good. The three of us left the office and then 'Maseko' stepped into the lift with us and I could almost smell the two youths' fear. Once on the street, he muttered some threats and went off. Only then did one of them speak: "He is Richardson, he is the killer," said Pelo.

Once back at my office I arranged food and ablutions for the two youths. I indicated that they should hold their stories for the evening meeting – especially anything related to Paul Verryn – and also forbade contact with him. I didn't want to be accused of priming them in any way. Nevertheless, on the drive to the meeting, they broke their silence. They told me how badly they had been beaten, until "our eyes could not see for a week", how they never ever wanted to go back to the Mandela house, and how worried they were about Stompie. They had been told to accuse Verryn or be killed. They had been assaulted by Mrs Mandela herself and Jerry Richardson was "the worst of them all". All I could say was, "You need to tell the truth tonight, do not be afraid – just tell the truth."

Getting to the meeting itself was a tortuous business. Fear of both the Security Police and the Football Team thugs made secrecy imperative and we were directed to two false addresses before being sent to the real venue, a small church hall in Dobsonville. The room was filled with about 150 people and the meeting was chaired by trusted community leaders Sister Bernard Ncube and Steward Ngwenya. Some key clergy were there too, including Paul. Also present were about ten of the remaining residents in Verryn's mission house. The atmosphere was tense but controlled. After prayers and an introduction, a statement by the residents of the mission house about the abduction was read, followed by Pelo and Thabiso telling their stories. They had been taken to Mrs Mandela's house against their will, beaten and sjambokked, first by her and then beaten by the Football Team. There was shock when they showed their livid scars. In the middle of their evidence a frisson of fear shot through the meeting when Krish Naidoo suddenly appeared, accompanied by Katiza and a Football Team member. There was a debate as to how security had been broken and whether it would be safe to continue but in the end it was decided to go ahead, not permitting the newcomers to leave until the meeting was over (we learned later that Krish had tried to persuade Winnie to come, but she had refused). Pelo and Thabiso then told of Stompie's vicious treatment and how he had been taken away early in their detention.

When Katiza spoke, he admitted participating in the beatings. Asked whether he thought Stompie was dead, he answered, "Yes." He also alleged that Verryn had once "lain on top of him". Verryn was then asked to reply to this allegation and strongly denied it. Thabiso had made a similar allegation when interviewed in the Mandela house earlier on. He was asked to confirm it but withdrew it unconditionally. "I was forced to say it," he said.

It was crucially important for the credibility of the Church that Paul's behaviour be properly interrogated, so I addressed the meeting, calling for anyone with any evidence of inappropriate behaviour on the part of our minister to come forward. I promised that if there was the slightest credible evidence the Church would institute proceedings against Paul. No allegations were made, and instead a youth named Thomas stood up and indicated that he had lived in the mission house since 1987, often sharing a bed with Verryn, and that no hint of any kind of misconduct had ever taken place. He asked the other nine residents present whether they supported his claim, and they all did. It was left for me to put the same question to the meeting at large. There was silence, followed by a unanimous motion of confidence in Verryn and a commitment to ensuring that he return safely to his workplace. Much relieved, I indicated that I was unwilling to proceed with any charges on the basis of just one allegation made by someone (Katiza) who had collaborated in the assaults. The meeting concluded that Winnie Mandela was using the allegations against Paul as a smokescreen to justify the kidnapping.

The most dramatic evidence of all came toward the end of the meeting, when Lerotodi Ikaneng, who had been left for dead by Richardson and Slash, entered the hall. He uncovered his throat, showing ghastly fresh stitches from ear to ear and told his own story of near death. He had managed to drag himself across the veld to get aid and had been in hospital since then. Pelo and Thabiso, together with Kenny, had of course been forced to assist in killing him and the two of them were deeply shocked, both relieved that he was alive and terrified that they would be held accountable for his attempted murder. The crowd in the hall expressed horror and anger. Some demanded that we march immediately on Winnie's home in order to "deal with her", but cooler heads prevailed and it was decided that a delegation would visit her the next day. However, the meeting did agree that she had lost the right to use the Mandela name and that the movement should distance itself from her.

HOSTAGE CRISIS

I got home well after midnight, deeply thankful that a minister who I trusted had been cleared of suspicion and that at least the hostage phase of this nightmare was over. I had also been impressed by the thorough and scrupulously fair process I had just witnessed. The mystery of Stompie, however, remained unsolved and a different ordeal, this time in the full glare of the public eye, had just begun.

30

Confronting Expediency

Unknown to us, Stompie had already been found. Just a few days after his murder and ten days before the hostages were released into my care a passer-by had stumbled upon his broken little body in a stretch of veld near Noordgesig on the edge of Soweto. He notified the police, who delivered the body to the government morgue in Diepkloof. There it was to lie unidentified, until 9 February.

Looking back it is amazing that the entire drama had thus far escaped media exposure, but on Thursday, 26 January I was contacted by the *Weekly Mail* to tell me they were running a story about the abduction the next day and warning me that it included an attack by Mrs Mandela on the Methodist Church. Reporters had been tiptoeing around the story for days but none of their papers was going to risk getting out front on it – none, that is, until the *Weekly Mail*[335] took the plunge. I had no option: I gave a guarded statement and waited for the deluge, which was not long in coming. After the story broke the next day I was mobbed by news organisations desperate for further details. With Crisis Committee members refusing to go on record I was fielding interviews with NBC, BBC, ABC, WTN, *The Guardian*, News of the World, Sky News – it felt like everybody but the Eskimo Times. The street in front of our home was jammed with TV vans and I was wondering how many versions of my short statement there could possibly be. I had said simply that an abduction of youths had taken place at the hands of "Winnie's Football Club", that the Methodist Church in consultation with community leaders had been involved in confirming the youths' whereabouts and securing their release, that we were still concerned about a fourteen-year-old boy, that the perpetrators' claimed they were protecting the youths from improper conduct by our minister, that community leaders had investigated and found the allegations to be groundless, but notwithstanding this, that the minister concerned had requested an investigation by the Methodist Church to clear his name (Paul had indeed made this request to me after the community meeting). I concluded hoping that the "deeply felt resentment toward this group's physical attacks on people in Soweto can be channelled constructively to bring them to an end". I had been careful not to name Winnie as being directly involved, but that did not stop her from unleashing the first of a number of escalating attacks on the Church, and when it became clear that the story was about to break, she had seen to it that Katiza was taken late that Thursday evening to a police station to lay charges of sexual misconduct against Verryn.

Much worse was to follow. That same Friday, Dr Abu-Baker Asvat, the doctor reportedly called in earlier by Winnie to examine Stompie's terrible injuries, was shot dead in his surgery. This gentle community healer, beloved by the people of Soweto, had been visited by Jerry Richardson the day before, complaining of an illness. The doctor found no problem, making the purpose of Richardson's visit suspicious. Then, on the day the media storm broke, two youths pretending to be patients entered his surgery and shot him. A paltry R130 was taken from his desk and they escaped using an electronic button behind his desk to open his consulting room door – something they could not have known about unless someone had told them about it. This horrible act set two new narratives in motion: Winnie immediately hinted that the Church was implicated, declaring that Asvat had been murdered because he was to be an expert witness in the sexual misconduct case. At a meeting I convened with community leaders the next day Dr Nthato Motlana rubbished Winnie's claims: "She's lying!" he said. Winnie had also asked him to confirm sexual interference and he had told her, "No such medical evidence is possible." A second, much more plausible scenario, however, was that the one expert witness to Stompie's life-threatening condition after his dreadful beating had been silenced.

It was becoming worryingly clear to me that the Crisis Committee and I were diverging: their mandate might have been to rein in Winnie's excesses but they would not speak against her and they lacked urgency in the matter of Stompie's fate. I was shocked to discover that nobody had troubled to inform Stompie's mother in Tumahole of what we knew about her son, and unlike some of their courageous younger UDF comrades, the committee members were acting with one ear cocked toward Lusaka, where the ANC in exile was extremely loath to see their fiery 'Mother of the Nation' struggle icon discredited. Ironically, another struggle hero was now involved: Asvat's nurse, who took the details of his killers, heard the fatal shot and found his body, was Albertina Sisulu, spouse of Nelson Mandela's closest comrade, Walter. Many believed that if anyone deserved the title 'Mother of the Nation', it was the strong, principled, modest Albertina, but she had none of Winnie's pin-up charisma.

On Wednesday, 1 February, Paul Verryn and I left early for Parys and by 8.30 am found ourselves squatting on a couple of packing-cases serving as chairs in the modest township shack where Mrs Joyce Seipei lived. Nobody had told her anything about her son's disappearance and it fell to me to break the news of his abduction and torture at the hands of Winnie and her gang. It would not be the first or last time during the struggle years that I had to bear such news to a mother, but there was something infinitely sad about the blank, unbelieving look that crept across her face as I spoke. I had to tell her that the outlook was grim and that she should expect the worst. When she finally spoke, it was to affirm her faith in God, "who had kept Stompie alive up till now". We prayed together and then left her in her pain.

I returned to another media clamour. Winnie had given a TV

interview blasting the Methodist Church and now also the SACC, for a "gigantic cover-up". Denying any abduction had taken place, she claimed that the Football Team had been dismantled long ago. Accusing Verryn of "sodomising black children", and continuing with these activities with "the full knowledge of some of the top leaders of the church", she said Verryn had a medical problem "which needs to be addressed by responsible leaders". She accused the SACC of covering the matter up to protect its overseas funding. Her allegations were becoming more bizarre each time she spoke. I made one more attempt to urge the Crisis Committee to rein her in. Beyers Naudé had rejoined the committee after an absence overseas and now seemed to be in charge. When we met late that night he told me that Winnie had reneged on three meetings that week and they had now given her an ultimatum to meet the committee and myself the next morning, or they would hand her fate back to the community. I questioned what they hoped to achieve. Naudé said that she would have to hand over the Football Team and its future to the Crisis Committee, and agree to "negotiate a solution" with me; then we would all face the press together on the Friday with "an agreed statement". I was shocked that somebody as wise as Beyers could believe – with murders piling up on each other – that there was anything left to "negotiate". He also showed me two statements, from Orlando West and Diepkloof Civic Associations, both strongly backing Paul Verryn and the Church and the decisions of the community meeting. *New Nation* and the *Weekly Mail* already had these statements but the Crisis Committee was attempting to stop their publication "for the sake of not hurting negotiations with Mrs Mandela". Listening to all of this, all I could see was the face of the stricken mother I had left earlier that day. I told Beyers that nothing would be achieved until I had answers to the questions about Stompie. He surprised me by saying that that was my problem. "We are not mandated to do the work of the church," he said. "That is up to you." My patience with the Crisis Committee was fraying. It seemed to me now that they were more concerned with damage control for the ANC than the brutal murder of a little boy.

The next morning Fink Haysom and my Methodist Church superiors urged me to hang in a little longer, but I was dubious. I later learned that Beyers Naudé and Sister Bernard had held an "off the record" meeting with Winnie and Zinzi. I don't know what transpired, but when I met again with Beyers, I was told that Winnie and Krish Naidoo had asked that I be excluded from the planned meeting with them, now set for noon. I was not surprised and indeed a little relieved, requesting that the committee come to brief me immediately after, which they did. Beyers Naudé opened with another plea that the Church and Crisis Committee "move forward in unity" for the sake of all concerned. He and Sydney Mufamadi[336] said that they had laid before Winnie all the evidence they had about the abduction, including the allegations made by the youths while still in custody. They briefed her fully on the community meeting that had cleared Verryn and censured her, and told her that the Church also had evidence that may or may not agree with theirs. Winnie in turn wanted me to know that she was willing now to "enter a wider discussion involving the Committee, the church, the Mandela family and possibly Ishmael Ayob". Instead of offering any explanation about Stompie, she said that "an ex-captain of the Football Club" had been arrested for his disappearance and other arrests were imminent so she couldn't comment because the matter was now with the police. She confirmed that Katiza had laid a charge against Paul Verryn. After Krish Naidoo made a further appeal for unity, Aubrey Mokoena made a poorly veiled threat. "The Church ought to be careful not to go its own way," he warned, "because the Church also has enemies." I felt my hackles rising. Earlier, Mokoena had been the most craven in refusing to help get a restraining order; now he had the cheek to issue warnings to God's Church! I replied as calmly as I could that while I had always been committed to working together, the Church would be guided by its conscience above any other consideration, and that we would not take kindly to threats. We left it that I would meet Winnie at 3 pm the following day to confront her with the evidence in the hands of the Church. Next day, once again I waited and she failed to arrive.

The weekend and the following few days passed by quietly, as if everyone was drawing breath. I was utterly drained but dragged myself to the Methodist Bishops' meetings in Durban, where the news came through on Thursday, 9 February that Stompie's body had been located after an anonymous call to the police, and finally identified. I rushed back to Johannesburg for a flurry of meetings. We were now definitely dealing with a murder, but before the implications could sink in a new emergency arose. On 13 February underground leader Dan Moshage called me with the terse message: "Football Team out on the hunt!" We knew what that meant. They had decided to go for broke and anybody and everybody seen as a threat by Winnie's thugs could be in danger. We immediately rounded up the remaining youths at Verryn's mission house and moved them to a hideout in the country. We could not protect everyone, however, and during the night the house of a Dudu Chili was firebombed by members of the Football Team. Her son Sibusiso had earned the wrath of the Football Team and while he and Dudu were absent and escaped death, her sister Barbara was set on fire and a thirteen-year-old child, Finkie, shot in the head and incinerated.

Things were now horribly out of hand. On Wednesday, 15 February, Winnie travelled to Cape Town to see Nelson in prison but got short shrift from him. He banned her from talking to the media. Meanwhile the Mass Democratic Movement had made a final decision to 'distance' themselves from her. A hall at CMM was packed with journalists from all over the world as Murphy Morobe, Archie Gumede, Elijah Barayi and Azhar Cachalia denounced the Football Team's "reign of terror", and bluntly accused Winnie of complicity in the abductions. They called for a "dignified distancing" from

Mrs Madikizela-Mandela, using her maiden name for the first time. I recall standing near them and thinking to myself, This is what moral courage looks like. I couldn't help comparing their sheer gutsiness with the shilly-shallying of the Crisis Committee. When a reporter shouted the question, "Why has it taken you so long?" the painful answer from Morobe said it all: "Because it was very, very difficult."

31

Soul Wounds

The identification of Stompie Seipei finally brought the police fully into the picture. They now had a body and Winnie's house had become a crime scene. Nevertheless, they were treading very warily. I couldn't help a wry smile at the politeness of a very senior officer – Major-General Jaap Joubert of the Soweto Murder and Robbery Squad – requesting to interview Pelo Mekgwe and Thabiso Mono in connection with their abduction. I knew they were too terrified to return to Soweto and I also knew all about police interrogations, so I agreed on condition "that it takes place outside of Soweto and that their lawyer and I can be with them". So it was that the day after the MDM press conference lawyer Geoff Budlender and I accompanied the youths to Bryanston police station, where they made their statements. Three days later two men appeared in court in connection with the Asvat murder and four days later Jerry Richardson and Football Team member John Sithole were charged with the abduction of four youths and the murder of Stompie Seipei. Winnie was left untouched.

The cracks between the ANC in exile and the MDM in South Africa were widening: Lusaka was urging that Winnie "not be shunned" while Morobe, Cachalia and other MDM leaders stood firmly by their call to "distance" her. As usual, she herself was way ahead of anyone in stirring new confusion. Speaking on 21 February to the *Daily Telegraph*, she claimed that Stompie was not dead. "The body is not his. I am a victim of an orchestrated hate campaign by white churchmen." She charged that the SACC was plotting her downfall and "someone wants to destabilise the country to make my husband's release more difficult". Denouncing the MDM leadership, she alleged that the "black democratic movement is now infiltrated at the highest level". Then she repeated her charge that Abu-Baker Asvat had been shot because he held evidence of Paul Verryn's sexual assault. Arriving at my office one day during that week, I found the walls of the Central Methodist Mission daubed with slogans: 'Kid Killer Winnie' read one, and another, 'Storey pray for Winnie'. It was becoming very difficult to keep things clear. I felt as if I was spinning in a vortex of competing political agendas and while I understood some of what was happening, I was determined not to be sucked in. The only thing that kept me sane was the remembrance of that little fellow sitting in my office not so long before, and the face of his mother. Winnie was not the victim – Stompie was.

Throughout this unfolding drama, one man endured a lonely anguish. Nelson Mandela could rely only on newspaper reports and fragmented messages. After I had gone public, I received a heartbreaking message from him, conveyed by Ayob: "Please ask Bishop Peter why he is doing this. Why can he not deal with Winnie pastorally as her Bishop?" I appreciated how pained and helpless Madiba must be feeling, but clearly he was not being given the full story. I had already given Ishmael Ayob a full memorandum to give him, but he showed no sign of having received it and I don't believe he did. It was desperately important to rectify this. By a perhaps providential coincidence, my Presiding Bishop Stanley Mogoba was due to visit Mandela in prison on 23 February, giving me my opportunity. I prepared a note consisting of fourteen brief points – the evidence against Winnie and how and why the church had acted thus far. Mogoba undertook to put it into Madiba's hands. Essentially he needed to understand that we had only broken silence after Winnie had spoken to the *Weekly Mail*, that we had made superhuman efforts to get the youths out safely, but that everything changed when Stompie was confirmed dead. Since then Winnie had cast the blame far and wide, but the bottom line was that she was implicated in high-level common law crime and the matter could no longer be contained.

This time Madiba got my message. After the meeting Stanley Mogoba phoned and gave me a verbatim report. The pain-filled grace of Madiba's reply brought tears to my eyes:

Mandela: "The fault is hers. My apology to the church, but why couldn't Bishop Peter have come closer to her instead of it being discussed in the press?"

Stanley Mogoba then offered my note and testified to the many attempts to meet her. He himself had been present on one of the days she failed to appear.

Mandela: "I owe Peter an apology for what I've been thinking. It is an ugly situation."

Mogoba: "She is the one who has broken press silence."

Mandela: "Yes, I see."

Mogoba: "We are under great pressure from community and church for answers on the whole issue."

Mandela: "How would it be if I advise her to call a press conference – public apology – 'I have done wrong, seek forgiveness and want to begin again'?"

Mogoba: "It has merits but may be too late."

Mandela: "I need to thank the church for all it has done over the years."[337]

It takes a great soul to bend to an apology under such circumstances, and I have always treasured that reply, but it worried me that even at this point Madiba himself could still harbour hopes of the matter being dealt with by a press conference and an apology. We were way beyond that.

On Friday 24th, my response to Winnie's bizarre allegations in the *Daily Telegraph* was front-page news, but I was getting ready for another sad journey to Tumahole, this time to bury Stompie Seipei. Although the body had been identified by its fingerprints, Winnie continued to insist that Stompie was alive and now safely over the border. *City Press* stoked the rumour with a huge "Was it Stompie?" headline. The funeral the next day was attended by about 2 000 people, far too many to fit into the sweltering church. The atmosphere was drenched in sweat and fear. There were rumours that Winnie and the Football Team would arrive to demand that the coffin be opened. I seemed to be the only one who knew that was the last thing she would want to happen. As I delivered the eulogy, I tried to keep my eyes on Stompie's mother, stoic to the last, but now with every spark of hope extinguished. I addressed her …

"I'm so sorry, Mama," I said, "that I had to come into your home and tell you that your child, blood of your blood, flesh of your flesh, bone of your bone, was in all likelihood dead …" I recalled watching her face and seeing in it the faces of too many mothers in South Africa. Today she might have the proud sorrow of a great funeral but tomorrow she would be alone and her son would still be dead. Looking at the small coffin, I spoke to Stompie: "Your terrible and violent death was an unspeakable crime and when I think of the way you died, I am deeply angry, but before your body was so brutally broken, your childhood was already dead. *South Africa killed your innocence long ago*. That is the greater infamy and deserves the deeper anger … in another land you might have been a choirboy but South Africa made you a boy general. God forgive us …"

Acutely aware of the anger in the crowd, I spoke against revenge. "If there are those who have come to stoke the fires of retaliation, you should go home because you do [Stompie] no honour." I said that the facts of his dying had probed beneath the surface of South Africa's pain and exposed the deeper wounds carved into an oppressed people's soul … "the erosion of conscience, the devaluing of human life, the reckless resort to violence and the evasion of truth." I said that the South Africa we were struggling for was one in which a mourning mother's pain and the life of a Tumahole child should be infinitely more important than the loss of political face. Finally I reminded the apartheid regime: "Long before his life was so brutally taken, Stompie Seipei was already willing to lay it down. And there are millions like him. If a fourteen-year-old child is willing to die for freedom, nothing will stop freedom coming. And when that day comes we will remember the Stompies and know they have had a part in fulfilling the Scriptures that declare, *a little child shall lead them.*"[338]

Two days later Katiza joined those charged with Stompie's murder. I returned to the seemingly never-ending meetings trying to contain the crisis. By this time we were running out of ideas. At my last meeting with Ishmael Ayob he had floated suggestions including a *mea culpa* speech by Winnie, admitting herself for psychiatric treatment, silencing her again and moving her to Cape Town. Murphy Morobe had gone to Lusaka to face the ANC in exile – an unenviable encounter because his integrity was resented. When the ANC came to power, he and his courageous colleagues never fully recovered their deserved place in the new South Africa.

Matters were now in the hands of the police and the Attorney General, and they were biding their time for reasons we only understood in early 1990 when State President de Klerk's bombshell announcement of Nelson Mandela's release swept everything else off the front pages. On 11 February, the world stood still as Madiba strode to freedom, with Winnie beside him, her clenched fist triumphantly raised. For me, with millions of others, it was a moment to savour, but it was shadowed by the sight of Stompie's nemesis, still defiant, still not held to account, still acting as if the child's death, and many others linked with her football team, had not happened.

In May 1990 I gave evidence in the trial of Jerry Richardson. He had been arraigned for the murder of Stompie and the attempted murder of Lerotodi Ikaneng with various counts of kidnapping and assault. Falati and others were charged with some of the counts too. Richardson was tried first and alone. Emma Gilbey called it a trial run: "If it was successful, then Winnie would be tried ..."[339] In the witness box I related the long struggle to free the youths, and under cross-examination was asked only a couple of questions. Paul Verryn testified and was able for the first time publicly to deny the sexual abuse allegations. Kenny Kgase, Pelo and Thabiso told their stories, implicating Winnie as well as the various accused, but Winnie herself declined to give evidence for Richardson and was not subpoenaed. Richardson was determined to protect her, denying that she had been in Soweto at the time of the kidnapping, and his defence team produced a Brandfort resident who testified that Winnie had been with her that weekend. Significantly, it was the first time in the eighteen months since the kidnapping that anyone – including Winnie – had suggested that she was absent from Diepkloof that night. In the end Justice O'Donovan found Richardson guilty and sentenced him to various periods of imprisonment for the kidnappings and assaults. For the murder of Stompie he was sentenced to death.[340]

By September, the state took the leap and added Winnie's name to the others charged with the kidnappings and the events that followed. The trial began amidst a media frenzy in February 1991. Again I had to give evidence, and covered similar ground as in the Richardson trial. This time, however, there were differences: Winnie's defence counsel was the famous human rights lawyer George Bizos, who had defended Nelson Mandela and his colleagues in the Rivonia Trial and had built a formidable reputation over the decades between. His strategy was to deflect attention from Winnie to Paul Verryn's sexuality. Journalists remarked that at times it appeared that Paul, not Winnie, was on trial. The other difference was that the drama was not limited to the courtroom. On the first day of full hearings, news came that one of the key witnesses, Pelo Mekgwe, had vanished after being fetched by "a senior ANC person" from the Orlando house. Whether he went willingly or not is not known – it was rumoured that the ANC had spirited him across the border – but his disappearance spooked Thabiso and Kenny, who the judge had to threaten with imprisonment before they agreed to testify. When they did, Kenny had a torrid time. He had written and spoken much to overseas journalists, embroidering his story somewhat, and Bizos was able to trap him in a number of inconsistencies, but when it came to the key events on the night of the kidnapping he stood firm. Thabiso was unflappable and unshakeable on the key facts.

Now it was my turn. I had spent the night wrestling with why, through this tortuous train of events, I now had to mount the witness box to expose someone who had been my hero, who had suffered immeasurably, and who millions idolised as a symbol of defiance and liberty. Yet she had become something else, denying not only liberty, but life itself to some of her own people. I had tried so hard to ensure that when she was confronted, it would be by her own comrades, rather than one with the skin colour of her oppressors. None of the Crisis Committee had been called, however, and when the crunch came, I a white person would stand in what was still a white-dominated court, to help seal her fate. The Methodist Church had stood faithfully by her and her husband for all the years of their suffering, yet now the Church, which had defended so many prisoners in the apartheid dock, would speak from the other side of the courtroom. It was a gut-wrenching positon to be in.

In the morning, my son Alan, who would himself go on trial just two months later for refusing to serve in the apartheid military, gave me a note to take with me. It read: *"Be strong in His love and don't lose sight of the vision God has given us that there is a butterfly in everyone – try to free the butterfly in Winnie, which only comes through love and the truth."* It was a poignant and important reminder of what my faith taught about every human being and I think it helped me speak truth without letting my emotions about the whole saga cloud things.

When we got there I saw Winnie standing with her legal team and found myself walking across the courtroom to greet her. I shook her hand and said how sorry I was that things had come to this. She seemed surprised but we had no time to say more. I was sworn in and according to Gilbey's record, was treated very differently than the earlier witnesses: "Storey was highly respected by all sides in court," she wrote, "the esteem in which he was held matched the deference with which he was treated."[341] But this did not mean that I had an easy ride. My evidence about the kidnap and events following was detailed and fairly straightforward, but when George Bizos rose to cross-examine me, he ignored most of that and seemed concerned only to explore Paul Verryn's sexual proclivities in as much detail as possible. I objected to this focus, suggesting he had a homophobic agenda. Bizos appeared taken aback and vehemently denied my accusation, but I felt I had struck a small blow when he proceeded more cautiously after that. In his memoir he recalls that the gay community and some editors accused his team of mounting a homophobic defence. He asks: "suppose Verryn had shared a bed with young women who had sought refuge in his house, what accusation would then have been made against us?"[342] That argument was specious and unworthy of a lawyer of his calibre. While the sharing of beds between siblings of the same sex in crowded homes was common in Soweto and therefore unremarkable in the mission house, no Soweto family, however crowded their home, would have countenanced bed-sharing between sexes. Therefore why would Verryn? When the judge later vindicated Paul and ruled that there had been "a deliberate and protracted campaign" against him I was gratified to have had some role in countering this part of it.

In the end, Winnie was found guilty of four counts of kidnapping and of being an accessory to the assaults. The judge slammed her "complete absence of compassion toward the victims of the assaults suffering in your own backyard, just outside your window". However, to the surprise of many, the judge accepted Winnie's Brandfort alibi in spite of the fact that it took eighteen months before she mentioned it.[343]

At one level I still feel deep sadness about the circumstances that placed me in that witness box, and the dreadful harm the whole saga was doing to the freedom struggle, but at a moral level I have no regrets. With their reign of terror Winnie and her thugs had become the very thing they claimed to abhor. The simple truth is that freedom won at the cost of destroying a fine person's character and killing a fourteen-year-old child is a stained freedom. Gilbey records: "... the transformation provoked by Storey's appearance went beyond the manner in which he was addressed. As he stood ramrod straight, swearing his oath with authority and conviction, Storey appeared as *deus-ex-machina*, a soldier of God, restoring sanity and order to the proceedings."[344] If by that she means that I helped get closer to the moral heart of the matter, then I am grateful.

Of course there were other voices. The government-funded *Citizen* accused Frank Chikane, Stanley Mogoba and me of "hiding a terrible evil" by keeping our "knowledge of the murder of Stompie" from the media and seeking to negotiate with Winnie for the release of the other youths. "... if they had spoken up more forcefully at the time, the reign of terror ... might have been brought to a speedier end."[345] The truth is that we did not know Stompie's fate, but even if we had, a hue and cry in the media might have done just the opposite – the other youths may have been executed too. Like most hostage dramas, we had to walk a fine line. I cannot claim that all the decisions I made in the midst of the whole messy business were right, but I am infinitely grateful that none cost anyone else their life. It turned out that Stompie was beyond help before I even knew of the abduction, but the rest of the kidnapped youths came out alive.

My final engagement with this saga happened at the Truth and Reconciliation Commission. The TRC held a special hearing on the abductions and other gross human rights violations by Winnie's Football Team. Some of the hearing was in camera – which I felt was a mistake – but Winnie herself demanded a public hearing as well, and

I was asked to testify. By that time (November 1997) I was teaching in the United States and had to return to Johannesburg. I arrived at the hearing jetlagged and tired, and more emotionally vulnerable than I realised. I had never thought to seek counselling following the trauma of those days and as I sat waiting for my turn to testify, suddenly it all became too much. I saw the lonely figure of Mrs Joyce Seipei sitting against the wall, marginalised as always. I listened while various people I knew and respected tiptoed around the truth. I was shocked when Dr Motlana denied point blank something he had said directly to me. I was saddened to see even the redoubtable Albertina Sisulu taking refuge in forgetfulness rather than identify her own handwriting on the card that proved Winnie had visited Dr Asvat's surgery when she claimed to be in Brandfort. Earlier Sisulu had confidently identified her writing in a BBC television interview. I saw the imperious, seemingly impervious Winnie Madikizela-Mandela seated like royalty at the centre of it all, dressed in full fashion. Then Paul Verryn had spoken movingly of his pain. He looked directly at Winnie:

> "I have been profoundly, profoundly affected by some of the things that you have said about me, that have hurt me and cut me to the quick. I have had to struggle to come to some place of learning to forgive, even if you do not want forgiveness or even think that I deserve to offer that to you. I struggle to … to find a way in which we can be reconciled – for the sake of this nation and for the people that I believe God loves so deeply. And so I … I sit before you and want to say that to you …"

His plea brought no response. Later I was to watch my friend Desmond Tutu humiliate himself, begging Winnie to acknowledge some – any – responsibility for the terrible deeds that had been done. And in the middle of the packed hall I wept. Our third son, David, who had accompanied me, took my hand and I think we managed my breakdown as quietly as possible.

I had kept a contemporaneous record during the hostage drama, which the police knew about but had never asked for.[346] For the first time I was able to go through it publicly. David Beresford of the *Mail & Guardian* described it as a "devastatingly detailed account" and said that I exposed Winnie "as a liar of terrifying ruthlessness ..."[347] It was not me, but the record which did that. When laid out as a day-to-day diary, it was devastating. But I also felt it important once more to try locate the horror of the abduction events in the wider tragedy of our land. Yes, Winnie was responsible and needed to be held accountable, but she was not the only one; the whole bloody saga of cruelty and pain that was apartheid, including the damage done with cold intent over many years to this woman was also present in the room. That is what the TRC was about. After lengthy questioning by lawyers representing Winnie and other interested parties I asked to make a statement, because, I said, throughout the saga, the truth had been trimmed to prevailing political whims by politicians, or suppressed because people feared for their lives. "I really believe that to dispel this suffocating fog of silence is very important for the future of our country."

I talked about four wounds these years had carved into people's souls – the erosion of conscience, the devaluing of human life, the evasion of truth and the reckless resort to violence. "The primary cancer may be, was, and will always be the apartheid oppression, but the secondary infection has touched many of apartheid's opponents and eroded their knowledge of good and evil."

"A tragedy of life is that it is possible to become like that which you hate most and to be remade in the image of your oppressor," I said. "I have a feeling that this drama is an example of that. Unless this fact is recognised, then all the truth will not have been told ... The torture and murder of Stompie Seipei are important beyond the normal horror we should feel because ... they may have been common-law crimes, but they are also about the ruthless abuse of power. Even given the latitude of a time of struggle, they resemble far too closely the abuses of apartheid itself." I concluded by underlining the moral significance of it all by quoting theologian Walter Wink, who said, "It is not enough to become politically liberated, we must also become human."[348] I said, "This case is about recognising the inhumanities which too many of us were capable of ... and becoming human again."

I kept silent about my disgust with some of the Crisis Committee's cowardly evidence, but commended the MDM leaders who had the moral courage to take the stand they did. Then I turned to the matter of Paul Verryn, accusing the media for consistently associating his name with the words "sodomy" or "rape" in spite of the fact that the allegations against him had been thrown out by the community leadership and two judges. Everybody who had publicly accused him had, to my knowledge withdrawn their allegations, except one. Looking at Winnie, I said, "It is my hope that before these hearings are ended, that last remaining accuser will withdraw her words and take back the accusations she has made against him."

She never did.

Her contribution to the hearings was a string of denials, but she did finally respond to Tutu's pleas with the grudging admission that "things went horribly wrong" and she was sorry. A reconciliation hug between Winnie and Mrs Joyce Seipei followed: it was poor theatre and unconvincing.

The next day I gratefully settled into my seat for the 24-hour flight back to the tranquillity of a university campus far, far away from South Africa's tormented story and the sad flotsam it kept washing up from the wreck we had made of our past.

When the commission's findings were announced it found Winnie "politically and morally accountable for the gross violations of human rights committed by the Mandela United Football Club"[349] and that the abductions from Verryn's house had taken place on her instructions".[350] She was present during the assaults on the youths and "initiated and participated in the assaults".[351] It also found that Winnie had "deliberately and maliciously slandered [Paul] Verryn in an attempt to divert attention away from herself and the associates of her household".[352] The finding about Stompie was less clear, although the commission accepted the corroborative testimony that placed her at the scene and implicated her in the assaults. It stated that "in all probability she was aware of his condition" and "compounded her complicity" by failing to get the necessary medical help for him".[353] Also, that he was last seen alive at her home and that she "was responsible for his abduction and was negligent in that she failed to act responsibly in taking the necessary action required to avert his death".[354] Despite the fact that it made these strong findings, I felt that the Madikizela hearings were a low point in the commission's life.

32

The Thin Orange Line

The National Peace Accord (NPA) was the best kept secret of South Africa's transition to democracy. The 'miracle' could never have happened without it but it has gone deliberately unacknowledged by politicians of all stripes, and historians have given it nothing like the weight it deserves. We owe more than we will ever know to the 'thin orange line'[355] of peacekeepers who demonstrated a degree of bravery and selfless patriotism that demands our esteem and gratitude. It is fashionable these days for people who were hardly out of nappies in the 1990s to rubbish the transition as a 'sell-out'. They have absolutely no idea how desperately near we were to conflagration and how close they came to growing up in a blitzed wasteland. The National Peace Accord was a major reason why they didn't.

I had often wondered how we would know when our adversaries had run out of road and what we would do with that moment. President De Klerk's famous speech on 2 February 1990 is usually regarded as the marker, but for me and thousands of others it happened four months earlier in Cape Town when Archbishop Desmond Tutu, Allan Boesak and the city's courageous new mayoral couple, Gordon Oliver and Joanna Stern, led 30 000 citizens in a peaceful march from St George's Cathedral to the City Hall. Only a week previously, there had been chaos in those same streets when police used a high-powered water cannon firing purple dye to disperse demonstrators – leading them to amend the Freedom Charter's "*The people shall govern*" to "*The Purple shall Govern!*" This time everything was different.

Two days later, on 15 September 1989, it was Johannesburg's turn. After a service in St Mary's Cathedral a number of faith leaders, led by SACC General Secretary Frank Chikane, Bishops Duncan Buchanan, Wilfred Napier and myself, and Presbyterian and Congregational leaders Alan Maker and Ron Steele, set out for Security Police headquarters at John Vorster Square two and a half miles away. Most of the 1 000 people who had worshipped with us followed. The march had been banned, so we waited for the inevitable clash with the riot police but they never appeared. We picked up pace, and as we marched, instead of the expected police attack, onlookers began to join us. They left the sidewalks and swelled our ranks. Now there were two thousand, and then five. Halfway along the route, still no police action and the crowd had grown to 20 000. Then, trotting breathlessly alongside us was a little grey man typical of the civil servants of the apartheid regime. He was waving a piece of paper, begging one of us to take it. We were not going to unlink our arms – so we asked him what it was. He told us it was permission from the Chief Magistrate to hold the march. We looked at each other in amazement and then glee, telling him to keep his piece of paper. We knew that we'd won. When we got to Security Police headquarters we walked right into the lion's den and delivered our protest.

Then Frank Chikane, Duncan Buchanan and I climbed onto a roof and looked down at this amazing crowd of around 25 000 people standing in silence, stunned at their achievement. They stretched a couple of city blocks and then out of sight around the corner. Frank handed me the bullhorn and I asked them to sit down in the street and then led them in prayer: "O God, you and your people have done a beautiful thing today!" ... and as the first words of the prayer reached them, without being asked, they began to repeat it aloud. Phrase by phrase, the words of thanks to God and the cry for a new South Africa were picked up and carried through the gathering – like a sacred Mexican wave – until all had joined in. It was a mystical and unforgettable moment. Then I spotted David below me. He was one of the marshals for the march and was mouthing something urgently. I finally got his message and called everyone to their feet to sing *Nkosi Sikelel' iAfrika*.

Later I wrote: "It was as if the people of Johannesburg were coming out of a long, dark shadow – as if this momentary throwing off of oppression was a foretaste of the future everybody longs for." But it was even more than that: together with the great march of the 30 000 in Cape Town it was the end, the last protest march under apartheid.

Nine days after De Klerk's speech, like millions of others, I watched Nelson Mandela's triumphant walk from prison with a sense of unreality and wonder. The new day we had prayed and worked for was beginning to dawn. But I remember warning my Synod that a majority of white South Africans knew in their hearts that the days of supremacy were over, though some would retreat into a "fanatical bravado typified by groups like the AWB"; nor should we underestimate the destructive power of "the shadowy security establishment". I warned that "the worst of the cruelties may still be ahead".[356] And they were. We were entering South Africa's most murderous years, not only because of the violent rearguard actions of white racists. Most of the killing that lay ahead was by black political formations, notably Buthelezi's Inkatha and Mandela's ANC. They had sniffed power and their contestation let loose a flood of violence. It had begun in Natal as far back as 1987, when UDF and Inkatha supporters began staking out territory. Having had some experience mediating between such groups, I was not surprised to see the "solidarity of the oppressed" begin to unravel but I doubt that many of us had any idea how vicious the ensuing war – aided and abetted by the "security establishment" – would be. More than 14 000 men, women and children would be killed between 1990 and Freedom Day in 1994. The causes of this violence were complex, but among them were attempts by Inkatha to sabotage the process altogether and by all the parties to destabilise their political opponents and achieve political hegemony in certain areas. Not least was a "third force" within the security apparatus of the state, carefully stoking the violence and ensuring that the mayhem continued. There was also opportunistic violence by criminal elements. As horrible acts of murder and destruction spread, government and political leaders seemed either helpless or unwilling to stem the violence.

That was when civil society stepped in and a remarkable alliance – one not often seen – was born. Religious and business leaders, trade unions and human rights lawyers and other deeply concerned citizens, came together to intervene. Many of the lawyers we worked with had paid a heavy price since student days for their commitment to democracy. The business leaders knew that war and chaos could only torpedo the economy. Church leaders were determined that all these years of costly witness and painful struggle by ordinary people would not be squandered by reckless and ambitious politicians. Together, after tense shuttle diplomacy this alliance dragged the politicians kicking and screaming into one room, and said, "Enough already! You're not going to leave here until you agree to compete in a way more appropriate for the birth of a democracy." The result was the National Peace Accord (NPA),[357] headed up by John Hall, former executive director of Barlow Rand, and Stanley Mogoba, Presiding Bishop of MCSA. The NPA laid down Codes of Conduct covering all of the signatories as well as the police and security forces.[358] It was a unique construct: because the police and military were so mistrusted, the government was outsourcing the task of keeping the peace, inserting between them and the population a parallel organisation run by church and business people and the best of civil society, with the other parties agreeing to abide by the NPA's rules. National, regional and local peace committees were to hold police and the political parties accountable. It was going to be a tough job. On 26 October I addressed a mixed bag of politicos about the hypocrisies that they would need to be rid of: "How can you say 'I believe in peace' while still using hit squads to assassinate black activists?" I asked. "How can you say 'I believe in peace' and demand to carry 'traditional' weapons? How can you say 'I believe in peace' and insist on arming defence committees? How can you say 'I believe in peace' and shout 'one settler one bullet'?"[359]

It took two years to put these committees in place because it often meant bringing to the table people who were literally shooting at each other by night. The task of NPA Local Peace Committees (LPCs) was described in the Accord as: "*creating trust and reconciliation between grassroots community leadership of organisations including the Police and Defence Force*" and "*settling disputes causing public violence by negotiating with the parties concerned*".[360] This was a massive ask. While the setting up of these committees in most places prevented violence from taking hold, where it was already endemic the story was very different. There, NPA mediators and monitors risked their lives daily in the crossfire of heavily armed antagonists. One of the key persons trying to set up LPCs in Soweto was Elizabeth's boss Charles Nupen, director of the Independent Mediation Service of South Africa (IMSSA). She was his PA and they would drive deep into Soweto to wait in some church hall or other – often in an atmosphere thick with fear – for representatives of the warring groups to turn up, often having to do so three or four times before succeeding. Given such levels of suspicion and the fact that nothing quite like this had been tried anywhere in the world before, it took months rather than weeks to put the Regional Peace Committees (RPCs) and LPCs in place. During this time the violence continued to escalate and the media were unfortunately far too quick to write the NPA off as a failure. In the end they would be proved wrong.

The only people with the credibility to chair these bodies were trusted human rights lawyers, business and church people, ironically most of them white. It was a new experience for those of us involved.

I found myself co-chairing the Wits/Vaal RPC with Rupert Lorimer, a retired Democratic Party MP and businessman, as my partner. Our RPC had responsibility for the most volatile areas outside of Natal.[361] Chairing a committee of all political parties, including those who were fighting each other, as well as the SADF and police was like herding wildcats. To get these people to begin to listen to each other took months. I had my own lesson in the pain of peace-making when we went away for a weekend of "team building" and found myself in a small group with a colonel of the Security Police whose task had been to harass me for years. He had seen to the death threats my children used to hear when they answered the telephone, the strange-looking objects left on our front doorstep at night, and other intimidating actions. Now I had to sit in the same group with him and actually *listen* to him. I found that very difficult, and it helped me understand a little of the depth of mistrust and memory that especially our black compatriots had to overcome.

The Wits/Vaal office was headed by Peter Harris, a tough lawyer and brilliant negotiator who chose our law graduate son David as his deputy director.[362] Staff appointments for the RPC team took an eternity, with every single one having to be "by consensus" – which meant getting every party to accept each name. The effort was worthwhile, however, and slowly an outstanding multi-racial, multi-party team emerged. Together they recruited and trained thousands of peace monitors – many of them unemployed black youngsters. These youths had known nothing but violence from the apartheid system and became increasingly excited to learn that there were non-violent ways of resolving conflict. Once trained, they went out unarmed into places of dreadful strife, intervening and often placing themselves between warring groups. They, not the politicians, were the real workers of South Africa's 'miracle'. COSATU member Alfred Woodington was an example. In a stand-off at Sebokeng between angry ANC demonstrators and a police detachment whose tense commander had already ordered them to aim their weapons, Alfred approached him across the dividing no man's land armed with nothing but the orange Peace Accord vest with its two doves across his chest. As he approached he repeated quietly, "Do not fire. It's okay. I know these people and I can calm them." And he did, preventing yet another massacre. Encounters like that were not uncommon.

The violence in our area was focused primarily in Witwatersrand townships where single-sex hostels housed migrant labourers from Natal and from the Eastern Cape. In some hostels, both groups had lived together for years but now were killing each other at the slightest provocation, each group trying to expel the other. Hostels housing mainly Zulu Inkatha Freedom Party (IFP) supporters were often located in ANC-supporting townships and they became armed fortresses from which these men would sally forth bringing death to nearby homes, or be attacked in turn by armed youths of the ANC 'Self Defence Units'. One such situation was in Alexandra township. The IFP had infiltrated battle-hardened fighters and weapons into the Alex hostels and people walking in streets nearby became targets of snipers. The local population had organised themselves too. It was during one crisis between the two groups that I was called to try and mediate. Our key NPA volunteer there was Reverend Liz Carmichael, a quiet Anglican priest of prodigious stubbornness and courage. I found myself back in Alex Stadium where thousands of people had gathered fearing that an IFP attack was imminent. Some were arguing for a pre-emptive strike. We pleaded with them to hold off while we tried to make contact with the Inkatha commanders, which meant braving the dreaded hostels.

Armed men grudgingly allowed us through the barbed wire perimeter and we asked to meet with their senior *indunas*. I wondered how these Zulu patriarchs would respond to a woman, but Liz was undeterred. This was her NPA area and she was going to see it through. We were taken down a maze of passages deep into the dark bowels of the massive building. More armed men. Filth was everywhere, and one wondered how human beings could live in these conditions. Finally we found the commanders and were able to speak with them. I remember telling them that there were thousands of people at the stadium, convinced that the IFP was about to unleash their fighters, and there was great danger that they would strike out of fear of being attacked. I had experienced Inkatha's aggressiveness on a number of occasions so had little trust in them, but Peace Accord business required strict impartiality and I thought I could detect not so much aggression as fear. These hard men seemed to be convinced that the crowd in the stadium was arming to attack and overwhelm *them* – and were asking why they should not strike first. We assured them that their fears were unfounded that day; their men could stand down. Then, hoping we had been convincing enough, we threaded our way out into the daylight and back to the stadium. There we conveyed the news that if people returned to their homes, no attack would happen. We knew that if we were wrong people would die undefended that day, but we were not wrong. I came away utterly drained and with two thoughts: the first was how life or death hung daily by such slender threads; the second was sheer awe for the courage of Liz the priest who had no need to be there at all, except for her allegiance to the one who said, "Blessed are the peacemakers ..."[363]

The brutality of the internecine violence seemed to have no limits. Our monitors saw things no human being should have to look upon: dismembered and gouged bodies, dazed people crawling on the ground searching for an amputated body part, disembowelled infants, a taxi-load of dead ... and they sometimes came back at the end of the day with glazed eyes, ashen and silent. Some asked me to write a prayer they could pray before setting out or refer to in stressful moments, and I did:

A PEACE MONITOR'S PRAYER
God of the nations and of all people,
I ask that today you will be with me
in the work that I must do.
Let my heart be open and my mind clear,
In my attitudes keep me fair,
In my decisions make me wise,
In my actions hold me impartial.
If I encounter danger, give me courage,
Under pressure keep me steady,
Help me to treat each person
as equally important to you.
Hear my prayer that today
not one of your children
will die or suffer injury
and that peace may prevail,
AMEN

The Swedish government had sent a team of specialised trauma counsellors to help monitors who were breaking under the strain. They were a great gift to us for many months and there were tears when they went home.

The 'thin orange line' was sometimes stretched to breaking point and I instructed churches in my episcopal area to release their clergy for at least one day a week for "peacemaking or peacekeeping" work. Not all complied because there will always be ministers and congregations who think that it's all about them – rather than the broken world Jesus died for. They were the losers, however. Many other colleagues and lay people did magnificent work all over the Reef, learned new skills in the doing and can look back on their part with quiet satisfaction, knowing that they helped to birth the new South Africa.

One of the most dramatic encounters I was involved in happened in Kagiso township on 16 September 1990 and was not so much an NPA exercise as something of a 'Methodist miracle'. It was my second visit in a few days. Earlier, I had come with Bishop Desmond Tutu and Reverend Frank Chikane to these same dusty streets, under a pall of smoke from still-burning houses. Wherever we went, crowds pressed us with stories of the horror they had endured. Earlier that week, Zulu hostel-dwellers had swarmed out of their hostels on a killing and burning spree, leaving scores of houses destroyed and many people dead. "Don't speak peace to us!" they shouted. "Give us guns or go away!" Now it was Sunday and I was back in Kagiso accompanied by a group of courageous clergy. We had come to express solidarity with the victims of the raid. Our Methodist church was packed and during the singing and crying we laid hands on grieving mothers who had lost loved ones, and prayed for them.

Then came the sermon from the Bishop – one of the many times when words threatened to fail me. But as I sought to console these people, my mind kept being invaded by a vision of the hostel where the violence had come from. I have seldom felt such a clear sense of being led. Did God not care also for those lonely migrant men? Was it not unscrupulous politicians who had preyed on their frustrations and fears and whipped them up into doing this? I began to speak about them: their lonely and desperate circumstances, far from their wives and children, often despised by the more educated and settled families around them. As I spoke, I sensed a response and, most remarkably, even some of the bereaved mothers were nodding as if their pain gave them an extra measure of empathy. Next, almost not believing my own words, I told the congregation that God needed someone to reach out to those hostel-dwellers to start building a bridge of healing between them and the people of Kagiso – and that I felt impelled to do that now. Announcing a hymn, I invited whoever felt similarly called to come with me. God would go with us, I said, then headed for the door.

Some 70 people joined me. We marched the mile or so singing the hymns of the faith, hoping they would signal our peaceful intentions. I was also grateful for the identifying cassocks and gowns of my fellow clergy and the bright red blouses of our Women's Manyano. As we approached the fortified hostel our hearts were in our mouths. Armed men patrolled the rooftops and gun muzzles were visible in darkened, broken windows. Once in those gates there would be no easy way out.

But we sang our way through the gates and into the compound – surrounded now on all sides by hostel buildings and sullen armed men. Their leaders listened incredulously as we explained our desire for peace and reconciliation, and asked their forgiveness for the years of marginalisation they had suffered at the hands of the local people. The need for peace, the importance of families, both here and far away, the danger of being dehumanised by political agendas – these were the things we spoke of. Everything I said had to be interpreted into isiZulu, a slowing-down process that may have helped in the danger-laden atmosphere: each phrase had two shots at being understood. And we spoke of God, the God of their ancestors and ours, who wished all of us to live in peace.

It didn't happen quickly or all at once, but after a time, the atmosphere began to subtly change: weapons began to fall to sides and hands began to reach out to each other. Slowly the tense stand-off gave way to something different. Voices began to lift in song, heads bowed in prayer. Fear and hate had given way to compassion and consequently a slender bridge had been built back into the hearts of these violent men, making a chance for future peace.

Driving home that day I couldn't believe what had just happened. I was overwhelmed by awe at what God was capable of drawing out of us poor, fragile and frightened creatures.

Such dramatic moments were few. In most cases we had to think beyond peace as a concept and embrace it instead as a tough *process* involving painstaking steps: opening lines of communication, building trust, developing a problem-solving culture, agreeing on codes of conduct and committing to be held accountable to those codes. Holding the peace committees together was a superhuman task. Initially tirades and walk-outs were common, but over a period of two years, the stubborn impartiality of NPA staff, mediators and monitors slowly began to win through. Antagonists began to recognise the humanity in one another, trust deepened and grudgingly relationships began to be established between enemies. We were experiencing at close hand the birth pangs of a new South Africa.

In April 1993 Chris Hani, the most charismatic young leader of the black liberation struggle, was assassinated by a white man. The country teetered on a knife's edge as two million angry people marched in cities all around South Africa. As many as 200 000 of them came to his funeral in Johannesburg's 100 000-seat Soccer City Stadium. The burial was to be in a 'white' suburb 22 km away. Clashes between angry mourners and both whites and Inkatha supporters seemed inevitable. At the last moment the ANC leadership recognised that they couldn't handle it and asked the Peace Accord to organise the logistics. The Wits/Vaal RPC swung into action, holding at least 21 meetings with different parties in a matter of hours, arranging food for the thousands gathering in and around the stadium the night before, and organising hundreds of buses to get them from there to the graveside afterward. Peter Harris and his team set up a Joint Operational Centre (JOC),[364] bringing leaders of all political, police and military formations into one room. The police agreed to keep 500 metres away from all activity unless called in by the RPC, leaving the job to them and their monitors. That day, when a racial bloodbath could have erupted, less than 20 people were killed in the whole of South Africa. Tragic as those deaths were, the NPA and its peace committees had proved their worth.

Ahead lay the sternest challenge of all – South Africa's first democratic election. In the Wits/Vaal region we would be monitoring as many as 40 political meetings each night. Would the thin orange line hold?

33

Taking on the Guns

Late in 1993 I was sitting in our lounge in Newlands in Johannesburg. Alan was on vacation from seminary and he walked in saying, "I saw something on CNN about a hand-in of guns in Chicago. Why can't we do something like that here?" He had already written some thoughts down by way of a proposal and I don't remember much discussion because the idea seemed to speak for itself. We were both involved in the National Peace Accord. The land was awash with guns and political violence was still at horrifying levels – in the Wits/Vaal region nearly 4 000 people were killed in 1993 alone. What if, in addition to all that the Peace Accord was doing, there was a campaign inviting people to hand in their guns before the first democratic elections in April 1994? So began the story of 'Gun Free South Africa', something many still think was my most quixotic, naive and foolish quest. Yet few memories bring me more satisfaction and gratitude.

One of my sadnesses had been the SACC's hesitancy to come on board with the Peace Accord. They were suspicious because the government provided its budget and simply wouldn't believe that the NPA had total autonomy over how it was spent. They also had other queries which I had been happy to take directly to national NPA chair, John Hall. I had tried desperately to persuade them but believe it was one moment when the SACC failed to read the signs of the times. Among their leadership were people stuck in 'resistance mode' and unable to make the leap required by that moment in our history. I was not prepared to see people dying in their thousands while others quibbled about the only plausible peace-making organ in the land, so

I persuaded the Wits/Waal RPC to let me set up a 'Religious Bodies Sub-Committee' to recruit and train peace-workers from churches, and later synagogues, mosques and temples, and to explore the unique role faith communities might play in making peace. Many fine faith leaders joined it and eight of them now sat on the RPC itself. We organised numbers of peace-building workshops, created guides for preachers to use in their pulpits and committed ourselves to recruit and train 1 000 of the 5 000 peace monitors our RPC needed for the coming election.

It was to this body, on 13 January 1994, that I spelled out the vision of a Gun Free Election Campaign, proposing a two-week amnesty a couple of weeks before polling day for people to hand in firearms. The idea was initially met with incredulity and scepticism. One member pointed out that my suggested starting date of 1 April was appropriate for such a foolhardy quest – and given the timeframe I soon found out that he was right about the date. But I persisted: "Guns are the symbol of all our fears; they now dominate life in South Africa," I said. Whether guns were used to wreak political violence on left or right, were stockpiled by fearful whites or were at the heart of the massive spike in crime, the campaign would be a statement by the unarmed majority in this country that they refused to be held to ransom and were determined to hold peaceful elections. Why could we not do it? Slowly the group began to come around and when I put it to the full RPC and promised them that the religious bodies would drive it, they gave it a somewhat bemused blessing.

At the request of the police the idea soon expanded beyond the Wits/Vaal to a national hand-in but when I lobbied Tokyo Sexwale, soon to be Premier of the new Gauteng province, he was adamant that he would never hand in "my Kalashnikov", nor would any ANC cadres, until after the elections. Power needed to be transferred first and once that happened, he would be willing "to lead the march to hand their AK-47s himself". Sexwale unknowingly did us a favour because much as a 'Gun Free Election' was to be desired, we soon found that we needed much longer to organise the hand-in. Consequently, 16 December 1994 was chosen instead. One of the most divisive public holidays in the past dispensation[365] and now named Reconciliation Day, it was appropriate for our purpose.

How I was going to manage all of this, I was not quite sure. The months leading to the April elections had thrown up a pile of responsibilities that were incredibly demanding. In addition to my normal duties as a Bishop responsible for 100 clergy and some 300 congregations I was involved in a number of key processes. One was preparing for the 500-strong World Council of Churches Central Committee coming to South Africa for the first time in January 1994. Another was piloting a massive two-year process called *Journey to a New Land*, designed to reshape and position MCSA for the advent of democracy. Then I was still chairing most RPC meetings, which were becoming more frequent and tense as the election approached, as well as the very first Police/Community Relations Committee in South Africa.[366] I was also chairing the inter-church committee designing the great thanksgiving service to be held in a Soweto stadium the day before Nelson Mandela was expected to be inaugurated as President. Ironically, the SABC now felt that I had an important word for the country because I found myself being called to broadcast special messages every time new crises arose in relation to the country-wide violence.

It was a full plate.

The team that gathered around what was now the Gun Free South Africa (GFSA) Campaign was rich in commitment and talent. Thomas Cochrane, an American law graduate from Albion College in Michigan, became my first full-time assistant and Methodist ministers Kevin Behrens and Lawrence Smith were seconded from their churches to give invaluable direction to the campaign. I turned to the peace activist, media, NGO and corporate worlds for wise and experienced leadership. Among the early committee personnel were Sharon and

George Trail, faithful friends who I had married years before.[367] Both worked voluntarily until George had raised enough funds for us to employ them, with Sharon becoming our indefatigable full-time co-ordinator and George our fundraiser. Veteran peace activist Adele Kirsten would go on to drive some of GFSA's most significant achievements long into the future. Reverend Mvume Dandala was making life-saving differences in his Hostel Peace Initiative, as was Reverend Brian Smith on the dangerous East Rand. Anglican Bishop David Beetge and Chief Rabbi Cyril Harris were staunch supporters, as was Bob Tucker, Banking Council chief and passionate community builder.

Alan, back at Rhodes, threw his weight into the Grahamstown area. In July 1994 Sheena Duncan, a human rights campaigner with giant moral clout, became our most valuable addition. She wrote offering the full support of the Black Sash[368] and went on: "It is quite clear to me that I must offer to do more than just write you messages about the gun-free campaign. I am VERY ENTHUSIASTIC so if you need me for anything please ask." Then in typical Sheena fashion she added: "The only thing I am not co-operative about is meetings which start late!" I was quick to accept and happy to welcome someone as obsessive about punctuality as I was. Sheena arrived when we were struggling with limited funding and growing opposition, and wondering if we could sustain a national hand-in after all. We were also being urged to soften our 'gun free' position: Rabbi Harris had received sharp opposition to the campaign from the Jewish community and wanted something more moderate. I was dog tired and somewhat discouraged and might have given in if it was not for Sheena. She steeled us all with her uncompromising commitment to a "Gun*free* South Africa" while offering wise strategic and practical ways forward.

Early media converts were *Saturday Star* editor Shaun Johnson who committed regular space to the campaign and gave us robust support. The slightly more cynical Harvey Tyson, editor of the *Star* itself, offered some humorous yet basically supportive columns and later ensured daily exposure in his paper. Later some others came on board as well. Ken Owen of the *Sunday Times* and the Afrikaans papers were either hostile or uninterested.

In a statement released near the hand-in date, I said that GFSA had three main goals. The first was to open a debate South Africa had never had: on the culture of guns. This certainly happened – an early surprise was the wakening of a gun lobby that we didn't know existed. After I addressed a meeting in Durban two white men identified themselves as from the South African Gun-owners' Association (SAGA) and soon afterward an article appeared in *Man Magnum* magazine panning my presentation and warning members that GFSA was determined to take their guns. From then on SAGA never stopped rubbishing the hand-in project. Its followers sent a steady stream of letters to newspapers.[369] Apart from the debate about whether civilian access to firearms made a society safer or more dangerous, gun owners were outraged that we were calling for licensed as well as unlicensed weapons to be handed in on 16 December. We decided this because as many as 15 500 licensed firearms were being lost through theft or carelessness every month, most often ending up in the hands of criminals. Also, until recently only white South Africans had been permitted to own firearms; a focus on unlicensed weapons only would look like GFSA was discriminating against blacks. While the level of the argument was sometimes fairly low, SAGA's regular attacks made sure that the issue of guns was seldom out of the media. They say there is no such thing as bad publicity.

Our second goal was to educate children to the dangers of guns. At GFSA's launch on 3 November eight-year-old John Wessels became the first child to hand in his precious toy gun and this element of the campaign ballooned beyond all our expectations. Many of us were kept busy attending hand-ins at schools and youth clubs. It was especially moving to stand in a dusty Soweto school campus and see children handing in even the wood or wire 'guns' they had fashioned for themselves. In some cases we were able to give books in exchange, but most brought their toys in a spirit of real sacrifice. Thousands were handed in and OK Bazaars climaxed the toy gun phase on 14 December by crushing their entire stock of 'realistic' guns under a steamroller outside Johannesburg's city hall. I have since met some of those kids – now men and women – who say that the hand-in formed their thinking about guns for life.

The third goal was to "reduce the number of guns in circulation through the voluntary hand-in on Reconciliation Day". This was obviously the biggest challenge. On 30 August a small multi-faith delegation went to our new President to seek his endorsement: would he let us issue a certificate of appreciation signed by him to each person handing in a gun? It was the first time I had visited Madiba in his new offices and was surprised to find the portraits of former prime ministers and presidents lining the ante-room where we waited. New Justice Minister Dullah Omar was present and I asked him, "What are these guys still doing here?" He looked at the pictures and said, "Well Peter, they are our history," and then added with a smile, "… and believe me, they *are* history!" When President Mandela came in he looked tired and was wearing a comfy old pair of slippers. Listening to our presentation, he examined the documentation we had given him and though our group covered the Christian, Jewish and Muslim faiths, typically he wanted to know whether the Dutch Reformed Church was among our supporters. I replied that we had not had much luck with them: "You know, sir, how difficult it is to part *die Boer van sy roer*."[370] In the end we got his backing. He said the campaign was both "timely and necessary", and told us not to give up on the Afrikaans churches. Right away we put in orders for the all-important certificates carrying his face and magic signature, with the words: "Your brave deed has helped free our country from violence and fear. I pray you will be an example to others."

We kept up a barrage of press releases, TV and radio contributions, all aimed at persuading people that their trust in firearms was misplaced. "There is a difference between feeling safe and being safe," we would say. "Many more people have been robbed of their guns and worse, killed with their own weapons, than have successfully defended themselves against an intruder." Eighty per cent of our population was not armed and did not want to live in an armed camp. There was still time to reverse our growing gun culture and help turn the tide toward a safe and secure nation.

Fundraising was tough. We received nothing from the NPA budget and some large corporations that showed enthusiasm in the beginning took fright when the campaign became controversial – which had not taken long. Time and again we found that if just one key person in a corporation was an avid gun owner, our chances were greatly reduced. We were promised free advertising by SABCTV and went ahead preparing a week of hard-hitting TV adverts to take us to hand-in day, but permission was suddenly withdrawn. We learned that the chairperson of the Public Interest Advertising Committee had waited until we had made the ad, and then torpedoed us. Ultimately 65 corporate donors and trusts produced just under R600 000, while others donated office space, equipment or attractive prizes. Apart from receiving the 'Mandela Certificate', persons handing in firearms would be entered in a draw with a R100 000 first prize and about 30 other smaller cash and 'in kind' prizes.

Getting the amnesty was a far more complicated matter than I had anticipated. Without amnesty the police would be obliged to arrest anyone bringing an unlicensed firearm to one of our reception points. Long hours spent with police lawyers, the relevant cabinet minister and our own legal advisers brought no satisfaction and all the time the hand-in date was drawing closer. Twenty-four hours was all we would be permitted and it turned out that to achieve it Parliament itself would need to suspend the relevant laws. The problem was that

Parliament was about to rise for its December break and in the end it took a late-night phone call to the formidable Speaker of the House Frene Ginwala to secure a commitment to get it done on the final day of business. Safety and Security Minister Sydney Mufamadi was at last able to announce a "24-hour indemnity" from midnight 15 December to midnight 16 December. We were cutting things very close.

Our staff and regional committees had worked like Trojans. Apart from 800 police stations across the land, Smith and Behrens had to organise around 170 places of worship as hand-in points. We believed that many people would feel more secure handing in their firearms at such places and this proved to be the case: 80 per cent of the arms and other items that did come in were brought there. A police officer would be present, however, to oversee the cancelling of licences, where relevant, and safety, while clergy were allocated to each police station as observers. Someone would also be on the spot to render weapons harmless, using a grinder or welding equipment. All weapons handed in would later be melted down.

At 8.30 am on 16 December we held a special inter-faith 'hand-in service' in the CMM chapel focusing on what we hoped would happen all around the nation. Leaders of different faith communities stood behind the altar to witness one of the peace monitor heroes of pre-election days – Alfred Woodington of COSATU – come forward with an AK-47 rifle and two grenades, weaponry he had kept hidden for many months in case he would have to resort to them. He had called me the night before confessing to a deep struggle because he realised that the act of handing them over would also mean parting with his trust in the use of force and he still found that very difficult. It was therefore very moving to see him approach and to take his assault weapon and lay it on the altar. During the day others around the country would have similar experiences. Some other people also came forward and then the service was over and the waiting began. I found the inactivity hard to bear. Apart from dealing with the odd question or administrative hiccup somewhere across the land, waiting for news in the GFSA headquarters was like being a political candidate while the votes were being counted – almost unbearable.

And the news was not good.

At the end of the day, by any ordinary measure the hand-in had failed. The enormous efforts we had made over the past months to move our nation in a new direction yielded a paltry 327 guns plus 6 800 rounds of ammunition and 200 other bits of lethal weaponry. As chairperson of the campaign I felt the heavy weight of having drawn so many people into such extraordinary labours for so many months – just for this. I couldn't believe that in the whole nation, so few people had got the message and for a while I was gutted. Around me others seemed less downcast, reminding me that "every gun taken out of circulation represents possible lives saved", and that this was "only the beginning", but it was a hard moment. The next day the *Star* carried an honest headline: "MILLIONS HANGING ON TO THEIR GUNS", but it rather kindly told readers that I was unperturbed, reminding them of my words early on the 16th: "Even if no guns come in today the campaign has already succeeded in its first objective – it has opened a debate on the growing gun culture in our land."[371]

I needed more reassurance than that and it came in an odd way. The day after the hand-in, I received an anonymous call from an Afrikaans-speaking man saying that he was "tired of killing people", and asking me to come alone to a certain place where I would find "something I wanted". I asked why he hadn't made use of the amnesty and he said he had been thinking about it but was only finally persuaded by the *Star*'s picture of "that guy giving you his AK". By then the deadline had passed. Given the venom my leadership of the campaign had stirred up, especially among white males, the whole idea was risky, but something in his voice convinced me. I confess I watched the pick-up area for quite a time before approaching it but it turned out that he had been true to his word. I found an SADF

R1 automatic rifle with a large supply of ammunition, plus a haversack full of hand-grenades. Very gingerly I brought the dangerous load home and started telephone negotiations with the police about handing it in without being arrested myself. Elizabeth hated having it in the house and wondered aloud how many people this R1 had killed or maimed, but seeing it up close and knowing it was about to be put out of action affirmed the campaign for her. However disappointing the results, this seemed to make all the agonising effort of GFSA worthwhile.

So without 'spinning' what had been a meagre result, my media statement thanked everybody who had made the hand-in possible, detailed what had come in, and stated that the results "confirmed the need for the campaign to continue". South Africa's love affair with guns was deeply rooted ... those weapons handed in were just the tiniest tip of the iceberg and "December 16 was just the beginning of the process of change".[372]

Writing some years later, Adele Kirsten said: "The sense of failure at the small number of guns taken in was strongly mediated by surprise at some of the unexpected results and the excitement of being part of an emerging movement."[373] My old CMM associate David Newby had chaired the GFSA effort in the Western Cape, aided by the hugely enthusiastic Father John Oliver and they were more successful than anywhere else in the country. Speaking to Adele, he was untroubled about the numbers of guns handed in. "... only on the day of the hand-in did he realise that this had the makings of a long-term campaign," involving "a succession of small victories ... one step at a time, heart by heart, square metre by square metre ..."[374]

That has been the story of Gun Free South Africa ever since. Before long, a campaign had become a movement. I continued to chair the emerging organisation until the end of 1997 but I was happy for the creative energy and vision to pass increasingly into the hands of Sheena Duncan and Adele Kirsten. Adele Kirsten was appointed national co-ordinator of GFSA in March 1995 and immediately her wide experience as an activist and organiser helped the movement to clarify its objectives over the coming years. They were: to influence public policy on firearms legislation, to engage people at grassroots through projects and campaigns, and to shift public attitudes by raising awareness about the danger of guns.[375]

In September 1996 some of us sat in the gallery of the Gauteng Provincial Legislature to watch the passing of a bill declaring its precincts a 'Gun Free Zone'. We had worked hard for the concept of gun-free zones to be accepted and dozens of businesses and schools and other entities were now making similar declarations. The right to say 'no guns in my space' was widening. To those who scorned GFSA's vision as an 'impossible dream' we pointed to the remarkable advances made by the anti-tobacco lobby, another 'impossible' campaign. Like them, GFSA was increasingly demonstrating that gun violence was a public health issue, causing massive drains on the nation's scarce health care resources. In the Constitutional Assembly hearings David Newby and I went up against the gun lobby, successfully arguing that there was no place in South Africa for the gun-rights cultism spawned in America by the Second Amendment to their Constitution. There should be no "right to bear arms" clause in the new South African Constitution. Private gun ownership could never be a right, but always a carefully circumscribed privilege, and the right to be safe from the threat of death by firearm far outweighed any "spurious right to own one".[376]

GFSA was the obvious body to play a crucial role in the framing of new firearm legislation that would finally be passed in the year 2000. There was a new mindset in government ministries and when we lobbied for more stringent controls we found we were pushing at an open door. But the task still took years of skilful and determined advocacy. Adele Kirsten's experience and know-how, together with consummate networking skills and the ability to gain the confidence of widely differing constituencies helped forge a Gun Control Alliance

(GCA) with other sympathetic and like-minded organisations. GCA in turn stayed the course over the years it took to see the final passage of the new Parliamentary Act[377] and we were gratified at how much of it reflected our concerns. Kirsten summarised: "The Act has made it more difficult to get a licensed firearm, and also makes it easier to remove guns from those who are abusing them. Fewer gun licences are being issued and fewer guns are available." She also pointed out that a direct result is the reduction of gun traders. "In 2000 when the Firearms Act was passed, 720 gun dealers were licensed to operate [in South Africa]. Six years later 640 of these dealers were out of business … almost 90% of the trade."[378] There was also compelling evidence of a reduction in gun deaths based on figures from South Africa's four largest cities over the period 2001–2004. In Cape Town, for instance, the firearm homicide rate almost halved: from 34.1 per 100 000 to 18.7 per 100 000.

Today GFSA remains extremely lean and agile. It has a minuscule staff but I doubt any non-profit of its size has punched so consistently and effectively above its weight. Paul Graham of the Institute for Democracy in South Africa had followed Sheena Duncan as chairperson in November 2004 but she remained an inspiring presence until her death in May 2010. Those she left behind in GFSA's leadership have stayed the course. Adele Kirsten left the staff for a period but returned as Director in 2013. I find deep joy in the fact that Alan, whose idea on a sunny afternoon in 1993 was the spark for all of this, himself became a nationally known advocate for the principles of GFSA and was elected chairperson in 2007. He served in that capacity until resigning in 2018.

Was the campaign quixotic? Maybe, but for some reason that has never been a worry to me – and here's the thing: there are more people than we realise out there who feel the same. They are the makers of God's tomorrow.

34

Days of Grace

"Welcome to South Africa's day of grace!"

The words of BBC anchor David Dimbleby as dawn breaks over the Union Buildings in Pretoria are wonderfully appropriate. It is Tuesday, 10 May 1994 and we are about to witness our first democratically elected President take the oath of office. Getting our scarred nation to this place has required more than the usual supply of grace – perhaps the "grace upon grace" that Scripture speaks of.[379] The road has been arduous and deadly. South Africans, especially black South Africans, have come through hell to celebrate this moment.

Watching the event unfold on my TV screen, I see the leaders of the nations, the great and the good – and the not so good – assembling to be part of history. It is the biggest assembly of heads of state since … whenever. But they are not uppermost in my mind today. Instead I am seeing flashbacks from the recent past, some horrifying and others awe-inspiring. They are mainly about ordinary people enduring excruciating horror or doing extraordinary things.

I think back to the atrocities I had seen at Boipatong two years before, where an Inkatha *impi* slaughtered 45 children, women and men in an orgy of killing. I recall travelling to meet with survivors in a community hall and not being able to finish what I wanted to say. I broke down because there were no words for pain as deep as theirs – only tears.

I think of how terrifyingly slender was the thread holding us back from disaster after Boipatong when Mandela's anger drove him out of negotiations, and how some church leaders shuttled back and forth across the land, sitting first with him, then De Klerk, then Buthelezi in Ulundi and then doing it all over again. I remember Madiba's thunderous visage as he accused De Klerk of betrayal, and De Klerk's fatuous response: "Cowboys don't cry." And Buthelezi's penchant for long typewritten lectures blaming everyone but himself. The future of 40 million people was literally in the hands of these three proud men. I marvel at how, in spite of the centrifugal forces tearing at them, each grudgingly came to accept that he was bound to the others by the mysterious alchemy of our nation's history – and perhaps, at this critical time, by a greater Providence.

I picture Chris Hani dead in his own blood and how the voice of a stricken Nelson Mandela came across the airwaves, slowly, harshly enunciating his people's shock and anger at the white man who had done this. Then, with the inspiration of a soul acutely tuned to the greater good, he spoke of the white Afrikaner woman whose vigilance ensured the perpetrator's arrest. A brief speech that saved the nation from disintegrating into chaos.

I think of 26 000 peace monitors, more than 90% of them black youth from volatile townships, going out day and night to form that thin orange line separating enemies, listening, calming, reasoning and most times bringing a measure of peace. Alongside them I saw the faces of our international friends, public policing experts from Scotland Yard, trauma counsellors from Sweden, United Nations monitors … I saw Barbara Nussbaum patiently teaching her umpteenth batch of new monitors how to behave under extreme stress, and Elizabeth, seconded from IMSSA, meticulously compiling the database of our 6 000 Wits/Vaal monitors so we could contact them at any time – and trying to memorise some of their names so as to pray for them.

I recall the TV documentary showing our David and Peter Harris, with Alf Woodington of COSATU and IFP leader Gertrude Mzizi literally putting their bodies between two massive opposing armies about to collide in Vosloorus. What other country anywhere, I ask myself, would virtually outsource its security to lawyers or the churches, or the business community and township kids at the most dangerous moment in its history?

I remember the bomb that detonated two streets away from CMM just before the election, killing nine people, one of whom was on her way to morning worship. Ninety-two people were maimed and injured. How other bombs exploded in and around Johannesburg that week, killing and dismembering people as the AWB's 'Iron Guard' made their final cowardly effort to stave off the democracy they feared. And the last massive explosion at Jan Smuts airport on election day itself.

But I also recall the many Afrikaners, most of them once staunch supporters of the regime, who in these last years wanted to be part of something different. One was the Security Branch colonel I have written about earlier. I was once his target, but he never let us down. Others were civil servants. We were far apart in so many ways yet were finding each other around the shared challenge of bringing South Africa through to this moment.

I see in my mind's eye Mr Jacob Dhlomo, the elderly Zulu hostel-dweller who in the midst of a season of gruesome killings openly approached the gates of an enemy – isiXhosa-speaking – hostel. Convinced by Reverend Mvume Dandala's Hostel Peace Initiative[380] this dignified migrant worker stood before his foes asking to see their leaders. He came with a request and a question: "My request is that if you kill me now, you will let my body go home to Zululand for burial." Then the question: "How many more of us have to die before the killing ends?" The guards at the gate were struck by his quiet courage. They took him in to their leaders and the beginning of a new reconciliation was born.

I remember the surging hope in the Carlton Hotel ballroom as we welcomed Henry Kissinger, Lord Carrington and others when they arrived just fourteen days before the election to try and end Buthelezi's boycott of the polls. Then the sinking feeling when they left 48 hours later, saying it was hopeless.

I have learned that one of their group, Kenyan Professor Washington Okumo, never left but stayed to do the impossible. The story of how he almost single-handedly hammered out the agreement that brought Buthelezi into the election reads like a fast-paced thriller. It is a story of miracles, an encounter with God's "grace upon grace" that even the most hardened unbeliever would be hard put to dismiss.[381]

And now we are here at South Africa's 'Day of Grace'.

Buthelezi's entry into the election just seven days before voting began probably saved us from civil war, but it created almost insuperable problems for the Independent Electoral Commission who now had to find a way of adding his name to the 80 million ballot papers already printed. Fortunately there was just room below the eighteen others on the ballot to affix a sticker with the IFP's name, Buthelezi's portrait and the all-important blank square where people could place their X. Every sticker had to be carefully affixed by hand. Problems multiplied. During the voting days just about everything needed for polling stations ran out: extra ink had to be manufactured at night in university laboratories, extra ultra-violet lamps fetched from Lesotho and millions of extra ballots printed. The entire election was a race against catastrophe, yet somehow every obstacle was faced and overcome.[382]

David had left the NPA office for Harvard in August 1993 on a Fulbright scholarship but Peter Harris, now in charge of the IEC Monitoring Directorate, called him back for the last two weeks before the election to help handle the challenge of setting up some 550 extra polling stations in Buthelezi's very dangerous rural back yard as well as in the Eastern Cape. Inkatha may have ended its boycott but many of its followers were still in aggressively undemocratic mode and four days before voting three ANC canvassers were shot in Ulundi itself. Meanwhile Alan, in his Honours year at Rhodes University, was responsible for all the peace monitors in the Grahamstown region. For Elizabeth and me the voting days were the culmination of months of unremitting work. Her database was the core of the peace monitor deployment operation enabling the RPC to sometimes monitor 40 political gatherings per night. My job during the voting would be to patrol between voting stations in Soweto ensuring that all was well.

Early on Wednesday, 27 April Elizabeth and I went to the nearest polling station to vote. We had hoped to take John Munyai who worked in our garden once a week, but he was long gone, already in the line. This was his day! The sight that greeted us was deeply moving. Our voter education programmes had stressed four crucial facts for our often illiterate audiences: "You *can* vote, your vote is *secret*, everyone has only *one* vote and your vote is *worth the same* as Mr de Klerk's or Mr Mandela's or Chief Buthelezi's." Now here in front of us it was happening: whites and blacks, some being white 'madams' with their domestic workers, were lining up together and knowing that when they went into the booth to make their X their votes would have equal weight. Nearly a quarter century later nobody bats an eyelid at the thought, *but you had to be there!*

Later in Soweto, armed with an unfamiliar cell phone provided by the NPA and with bright orange Peace Monitor stickers on my car, I drove from one station to another, marvelling at the kilometres-long queues of people waiting their turn to do something they had never done before in their lives. Soweto was quieter than I had ever known it. As I drove by people waved happily at my Peace Car and I remembered the not-so-distant past of burning buildings, teargas and rock-strewn streets, growling armoured vehicles and roving bands of armed youths. All was now quiet. At one voting station deep in Soweto the UN observer there grinned widely as I arrived and said, "I from Nepal," reminding me of just how many people around the world cared about our freedom. He could hardly speak English yet he was getting on wonderfully with the IEC staff, monitors and voters and enjoying himself immensely. Everywhere I got the impression that our international guests had a sense of the immensity of these days, not only for South Africa, but for the human project.

Only one ugly incident marred an otherwise miraculous first day. Driving with another monitor along a quiet portion of the Moroka-Nancefield road we came across one of our Peace Cars stopped alongside a minibus with a large Peace Accord sticker on it. The car doors were open and so was the sliding door of the minibus. There were a number of men inside it and one of our peace monitors was standing as if carved of stone, facing into the van. As we arrived I caught a glimpse of guns pointing at him, then the sliding door was slammed shut and the minibus roared off. When our monitor got his voice back he said that we had saved his life: "Those were Inkatha guys from Nancefield Hostel; they had a whole lot of guns on the floor and they were ordering me to get in." It was worrying that a vehicle with peace stickers was being used for running guns into the hostel but I thought better of giving chase and instead reported it in. We then drove in convoy to the nearest voting station for a much needed coffee.

The drama wasn't over, however. Having fallen into a deep sleep I received a call around midnight from Piet Coleyn, director-general of Home Affairs, whom I had never met. He was an old guard civil servant and would normally have been in charge of the whites-only elections of the past. Now his department had to render logistical assistance to the new IEC. He was extremely stressed and put a surprising question to me: "Bishop, can you assemble 500 church people at the Civic Centre by 4 pm tomorrow?" I asked why and he said that he had come out of a stormy meeting of the political parties at the IEC headquarters. There had been serious altercations between party representatives over real or perceived irregularities at counting stations and mistrust of IEC impartiality. The parties were demanding that there be another layer of 'outsider monitors'. The problem was that they couldn't agree on who they could trust to do the job. "Then I had an inspiration," he said. "I asked them if they would trust the churches and they all agreed. So can you help us? It could save the election." I immediately called other church leaders and we set in motion an all-night telephone chain to our clergy who in turn called their lay people. The plan was to get as many as possible to Johannesburg's Civic Centre the next day.

That Thursday morning in Soweto the voting remained peaceful. At some point I stopped at the memorial where Hector Pieterson had been shot on 16 June 1976 and two men recognised me. Full of smiles, one shouted, "Hello, Bishop! We have the vote now, Father, you can die now. Your work is done!" I think I know what he meant, but still …

The Civic Centre was a ridiculous choice of venue. It stands on an island at the top of Rissik Street and rush-hour traffic was tearing around it. Amazingly, not 500, but 900 people had risked life and limb to get to it. They were crowded around the entrance to our venue but a big padlock prevented entry. Fuming, I used my primitive cell phone to locate Piet Coleyn, who apologised and told me that the parties were still locked in negotiations. Could I bring the people back the next day – Friday – at 4 pm? I couldn't believe my ears. Here I was with 900 people, some of whom had travelled long distances. How would they react? Someone gave me a bullhorn and competing with the traffic noise, I tried to explain the situation: "I apologise for the inconvenience," I shouted, "but everyone at IEC is stretched to the limit. They still need us to save the election – just not today." The Rhema Bible Church in the suburbs would make a far less problematic venue and I asked the crowd if they could gather again there the next day. With remarkable goodwill, they agreed. I said a prayer and reminded them: "We can be the difference as to whether this election succeeds or fails."

That night, again near 12 pm, the phone rang. Piet Coleyn's voice was cracking with anxiety and fatigue. He was sorry about the disaster at the Civic Centre, but it was important now that we get our people to the Rhema Church by 9 am rather than 4 pm. Once more the telephone chain was set in motion and I tried to sleep, wondering how many would arrive. I needn't have worried: next morning a staggering 1 200 people waited expectantly in Rhema's commodious sanctuary to hear what was required of them. After a further agonising wait of two and a half hours, Coleyn and his team arrived. After a couple of hours' training the IEC expected our people to leave for 720 destinations immediately without having given much thought to the logistics involved, so a group of church leaders took over the entire operation. Calling in travel agents, they deployed 420 people to the Pretoria, Witwatersrand, Vereeniging area and sent another 706 to counting stations in every part of South Africa. Some went by car, others by air and most arrived at their destinations during Saturday, 30 April. Many slept in their cars for two or three nights, some in the clothes they had worn to the briefing. Reverend Jack Scholtz and Joan ended up in Nyamazame township outside Nelspruit,[383] where he said they were welcomed by exhausted controlling officers near the end of their tether. "There was a genuine desire to get things right but people couldn't keep their eyes open. Our group fanned out into Kangwane and got the system going again." He added that the presence of the church had added credibility to the process.[384]

Speaking later of the emergency mobilisation I said that "their intervention was crucial to getting the election back on track". I was also proud of the contribution religious bodies had made to a peaceful election by putting 1 000 monitors into the field, and of the Peace Accord as a whole: "We had 6 000 monitors in this region alone and ... I was deeply impressed by the mature way they handled lots of little crises. Their highly visible presence was a powerful assurance to people that voting would be safe."[385]

And so to the Union Buildings and our day of grace.

Nothing could have prepared me for the waves of emotion now

rolling over me. A kaleidoscope of sights, sounds and experiences coming too rapidly to process: our new multi-hued banner flying at every mast and my heart feeling pride for the first time, listening to the rich accents of the Chief Rabbi reading Isaiah's magnificent words:

> "For a small moment I have forsaken thee … in a little anger I turned my face from thee for a moment … in righteousness shalt thou be established; thou shalt be far from oppression … and from terror … violence shall no more be heard in the land, nor ruin and devastation within thy borders."

and:

> "Though the mountains shall depart and the hills be removed … never … shall the covenant of my peace be removed from thee."[386]

In the crowds on the lawns below, joy overflows and South Africans of all races are baptised into a new spirit of oneness. A centuries-long yearning has at last been unleashed. A white man on crutches, struggling as they sink into the soft lawn, is lifted up by the mainly black crowd and passed over their heads to the front. White policemen smile and join in the dancing …

… and the roar rising from the packed masses when they hear Mandela's words echo those of God's prophet:

> "Never, never and never again shall it be that this beautiful land will again experience the oppression of one by another and suffer the indignity of being the skunk of the world."[387]

I go to my kitchen window with tears streaming down my face and look out toward a church on the promontory south of our Newlands home. It stands on the edge of what was once the vibrant black ghetto called Sophiatown, renamed Triomf by the racists who ejected its people back in the 1950s. I remember that its white priest was ejected too. He wrote one of the early books damning apartheid called *Naught for Your Comfort*.[388] All must have seemed lost then, but it was not: unknowingly the priest of Christ the King church in Sophiatown had nurtured one of the champions of justice who was to help reshape South Africa. For eighteen months he had faithfully visited an altar boy named Desmond Mpilo Tutu confined in a tuberculosis sanatorium. Young Desmond never forgot that care and the Christian compassion that inspired it. Looking up at the church on the hill I am glad that the ageing Huddleston is back in South Africa for this season of grace and wonder if he has any real comprehension of how powerfully that youth brought comfort – in the real meaning of the word, *strengthening* – to the millions of oppressed people now set free. "Thank you God, thank you!" I say over and over again.

The days following Mandela's swearing in were magical. In July, having taken up residence in the imposing mansion in Pretoria now named Mahlamba Ndlopfu,[389] the President threw a banquet – not just any banquet, but one with a Biblical touch. He invited those he called "veterans of the struggle" who had made some stand against apartheid in the 50s and 60s. When we drove up the winding drive for the first time in our lives, Elizabeth and I couldn't suppress our laughter because parked on the pristine grass of ex-President De Klerk's golfing greens were now rows of dusty buses from rural South Africa. From now on those rutted greens would present a putting challenge second to none. True to his character, Mandela had invited unsung and unrecognised stalwarts from all over the land. So many were people who had stood up to apartheid where it was most dangerous, in rural towns and farmlands far away from the media attention that could sometimes ameliorate the harshness of the 'system'. We sat near a man who was a Methodist from Uitenhage, an ex-MK cadre. He had been interrogated and tortured for a year before spending

22 years on Robben Island. Now he was 65 years old and this was the first official recognition of his sacrifice. Rather too lightly I said, "So you're a 'graduate' of the Island?" He replied, "No. That would make it sound too easy." Then he thought for a while and said, "But yes, I am a graduate; on Robben Island I learned to forgive."

When President Mandela got up to speak, he took a moment to upbraid us: "When you sang the National Anthem you mumbled through the second part,"[390] he scolded. "We are one nation now. Make sure you learn *Die Stem* for next time." His next few sentences took my breath away. "You honour me because of your presence," he said. "Please know that I am here only because of you." Then he continued: "I have invited you so you can see for yourself the place where the evil deeds of the past were planned." A rumble of anger rolled through the audience. Then he said, "I have also invited you here so that by your noble spirits, you can cleanse this place." All around us there was a collective intake of breath. You could see the straightening of old shoulders as this remarkable man who had sacrificed so much humbly affirmed *their* dignity and *their* sacrifice. It was a golden moment.

In September that year, the MCSA Annual Conference met in Umtata, the one-time 'capital' of the Republic of Transkei. This was the apartheid 'Bantustan' that once declared the MCSA an "unlawful organisation", so there was a sweet irony about meeting in the very chamber that had been their 'Parliament' where the banning had been promulgated. President Mandela was to be our guest of honour and I was touched and not a little nervous when I got a call from his office asking me to write his speech. I sweated long and hard on the draft but knowing that he was at his best when he removed his spectacles and went off text, I left spaces for him to do so and I think he enjoyed that. It needed to be a warm speech made amongst friends, and began: "To visit you is a personal homecoming, because of the role this great Church has played in my own life …" He delivered the speech much as I had written it, but made one significant change: wherever I had spoken of the role of the churches he spoke of "faith communities" instead, showing once more his desire always to include. I admit that I had written one paragraph as a kind of litmus test of his position on church-state relations but he never hesitated, saying firmly, "All governments, no matter how democratic, need constructive criticism and advice from those who live close to the people and who listen for the voice of God. I ask you therefore to continue to play your prophetic role, always seeking to hold this nation and all its leaders to the highest standards of integrity and service."[391]

Sadly, before the year was out *realpolitik* intruded. On 25 October a small group representing the National Peace Accord went to Parliament to meet the new Government of National Unity. We were there to plead against the closing down of the NPA, lock, stock and barrel. We could not believe that an instrument with so much potential was going to be dumped on the trash heap. Pared down, yes, but closed altogether? Our database alone was a treasure-trove of young South Africans trained and motivated to be a healing force in the land. There was still so much to do to ease tensions and teach non-violent ways of resolving conflict as people tried to cross from past to future. What other country had the privilege of starting out with 26 000 peacemakers at their call?

We waited gloomily in a conference room for the politicians to arrive, hoping still that we might dissuade them. When they arrived they were led, not by Nelson Mandela, who I believed might be open to our case, but by the suave Thabo Mbeki. He was accompanied by all the other party leaders. Early into the meeting it was clear that their collective mind was made up. Some of their remarks were revealing: this was not about costs; the NPA nation-wide had never cost more than R80m each year – a pittance compared to what it had achieved. No, this was more about hubris. I believe the politicians were embarrassed that a motley band of priests, lawyers, businesspeople and kids had done what none of their parties could do. While their followers were shoving the nation recklessly toward civil war it was the NPA that had held the line and clawed South Africa back from the precipice. Sitting listening to the smooth words of Mbeki it came to me that our existence – which should have been celebrated as another unique South African solution to a desperate dilemma – was felt by them as a judgement on their failures. The axe fell. As we walked out I found myself alongside Mbeki's closest ally, Essop Pahad. Filled with anger, I said to him, "Essop, I've been so wrong about the Peace Accord, I always thought that our job was to save the people and bring peace to our land, but I see now that we really existed only for people like you to get your bums on those seats in Parliament without any bullet-holes in them. Now you're there the rest doesn't matter." He had the grace not to respond and we went home to dismantle the best kept secret of South Africa's 'miracle'.

Let the last word on the NPA be a more gracious one than I could summon up that day. Susan Collin Marks laid herself on the line often in the bad days and helped change them for the better. She says: "The Peace Accord provided an institutional home for peacemaking, wove it into the fabric of society, and imprinted it on the hearts of countless South Africans … for the first time in history the methodology of conflict resolution was used to transform a nation."[392]

That 1994 election year brought some wonderful family achievements: John completed his MBA at Wits and David his LLM at Harvard, while Alan added an Honours degree to his Rhodes BTheol. In February 1995 Chris and his wife Kim, teaching now in Knysna, gave us our first grandchild, Simone. She was to be followed over the next years by a sister, Frances, John and Desiree's Jessica and Sarah, and Dave and Alex's Adrienne and Scott.

Days of grace continued under the benevolent and deeply human influence of Nelson Mandela. On 27 April 1995, our first officially marked Freedom Day, Elizabeth and I were at the Union Buildings for the ceremony. Somewhere in the programme I was to present Madiba with a small sculpture made out of melted-down guns from the Gun Free hand-in. A couple of hundred 'VIPs' jostled for the front seats facing the podium. It was easier to take seats in the back row of the platform, with the crowded lawns behind us. When the President arrived he took one look at the set-up and said he would prefer that the podium be moved to the rear edge of the platform so that he could see the people on the lawns below. The result was that everyone had to turn their seats around, leaving the most pushy VIPs now in the back row and Elizabeth and I by sheer luck right next to him. Suddenly the last were first, the first last. As he sat down with a smile and polite handshake I wanted to laugh out loud. As if it were the most natural thing in the world, this amazing man had just got us all to act out one of the more uncomfortable parables of Jesus.[393] I wished I could preach that kind of sermon, but you needed to go to prison for 27 years to do so.

At the MCSA Conference later in the year the 'Journey to a New Land' process I had chaired came to some fulfilment with significant changes in the way the church would go about its ministry. It represented the culmination of two years of work, particularly by my friend Ross Olivier – the best equipped all-round minister I knew – who had driven the process on the ground and run workshops all around the country. I also took some satisfaction in having a Methodist resolution on abortion accepted after a tough five-hour debate.[394] It began where I believed Jesus would begin, at the very human place where people struggle painfully with dilemmas that have no easy or 'right' answers. No woman desires or plans for abortion. The issue only arises in pain-filled circumstances and because it is unlikely that there will ever be consensus on this matter, the law needs to respect the consciences of those who eschew any form of abortion, as well as the rights of choice and health of those who do not. Beyond placing limits on the period and conditions within which abortions may take place, the question of who is permitted to perform such operations and possibly the degree of consultation necessary, the law should be silent. The bottom line is that the decision to have the procedure needs to remain a matter of conscience for the woman concerned. The role of the church is not to judge, but to be supportively present to her whichever choice she makes.

During that same Conference I heard that President Mandela had appointed me to the panel that would select the Truth and Reconciliation Commission.

35

Search for Healing

The Truth and Reconciliation Selection Panel met for the first time on 21 October 1995. It was chaired by Fink Haysom, who was now President Mandela's legal adviser. Our task was to deliver a list of 25 names to the President from which he would appoint between 11 and 17 Truth Commissioners. Those chosen would shoulder the awesome responsibility of bearing the pain of apartheid's victims, deciding the fate of its villains and delivering the truth about the struggle years. Uniquely, the TRC would not stop with apartheid's wrongs: those in the liberation struggle who had committed gross human rights violations or atrocities would also need to seek amnesty and their victims be heard. In this regard South Africa's TRC was like no other. It took the huge moral step of acknowledging that, no matter how noble the cause, there were no clean hands. Even though there was no moral equivalence between the inhumanities of apartheid and the struggle for a more human South Africa, as Justice Minister Dullah Omar put it, "We would never want to see ourselves condoning human rights violations simply because they were committed by freedom fighters."[395]

The panel consisted of four political party representatives and four others from civil society and the churches.[396] The act required commissioners to: "Be of moral integrity with a commitment to human rights, reconciliation and the disclosure of truth; not a high-profile member of a political party; be able to make impartial judgements; and should not be an applicant for amnesty."[397] Any South African could nominate candidates and we were each given a pile of Lever Arch files containing details of the 299 nominations and sent away.

Wading through them I was appalled by some of the names: how could people so compromised have the cheek to let their names go forward? After a couple more meetings, in which the politicians sparred with each other inconclusively, I felt we needed to get honest so I sent round a memo[398] making it clear that I could not recommend anyone who by their action or inaction had implemented, or collaborated with, apartheid. To me that was a moral absurdity. Nor would I vote for anyone involved in the violent dimension of the anti-apartheid struggle. Also anyone – black or white – who in the bad years had been concerned simply with advancing an academic or professional career without engaging with the moral and political struggles of the day. "For people who ignored the pain of apartheid to think they can adjudicate on others' suffering is a terrible arrogance," I wrote. I wanted to ask them all: "Did you suffer?" or at least show me where you used the skills and position you gained on behalf of the oppressed. There was also the issue of *memory*: "Many nominees were babes in arms when some of the worst evils were perpetrated, but now put themselves forward as 'experts.' I can't see how they could possibly empathise with victims or understand the impersonal forces which drove some of the evil-doers." Finally I was uncomfortable with the degree of self-promotion among many nominees. "Those who promote themselves in order to get onto the Commission will use the hearings for the same purpose," I said. The TRC was not about them; it was about those who endured suffering and those who bore guilt. In my voting I would be looking for some humility and selflessness.

Having delivered my soul, I wondered how on earth we would achieve consensus. After we had each narrowed our preferences down to 40 names we could begin to decide who should be interviewed. The interviews were held in public in Johannesburg, Cape Town and Durban and were variously absorbing, boring and troubling. We were struck by just how many South Africans had amazing stories to tell and how rich were the people-resources of our land. Equally there were still some who seemed to think that long lists of academic achievements somehow qualified them for the task. One professor seemed surprised to be asked whether he had ever been a member of the Afrikaner Broederbond, wondering why that was relevant. We also needed to probe uncomfortably into the sensitivities of some who had endured long spells of detention and torture. When we invited one prominent candidate to speak about his experience it was clear that his wounds were still too fresh. Listening for months to multiple stories of similar suffering would undo him.

I began to appreciate how shrewdly the panel had been designed. The politicians had instructions from their principals to push certain names but more often than not they were checkmating each other. When they failed to get a candidate favouring their constituency they realised that the next best thing was someone who would at least be fair and impartial. That was when those of us who were non-party appointees could suggest names more widely acceptable to all. Another development that impressed me was how attitudes to certain high-profile candidates changed. Some panellists were meeting people like Bishop Desmond Tutu face to face for the first time in their lives, rather than the caricatures they had known in the media, and were frank about how the encounters affected their thinking. Toward the end, we all had a fairly good idea of who would have made the most quite outstanding 'first team', but considerations of race, gender, region, profession and language made compromises inevitable. I am bound not to report the choices of any of the panellists, but when we finally reached consensus and sat back in weary relief one member said, "Hey, guys, I hope you won't ever tell my party who I voted for. It wouldn't go well for me!"

When we handed our list of 25 nominees to President Mandela his first act was to count the number of women among them and he seemed satisfied. In the dying hours of our deliberations the women on our panel had caucused across party lines, demanding more female nominees and saying that they might withhold support from other names unless they were successful. I admired their *chutzpah* but not all their choices: one woman had lived in America for 20 years furthering her academic career during the worst of the bad times, and she raised more than one red flag for me. Presumably they came up with this name because ideological differences prevented agreement on anyone closer to home. In the end the President named seven women – including her – among the seventeen commissioners he appointed. She left the TRC before it had run its course.

The President, sensitive to the delicate situation in KwaZulu-Natal, asked why there was only one name from that region. I answered perhaps a little too frankly: "Because, Mr President, they were all crooks." Maybe it was because the region continued to be wracked by violence that people were still unwilling to be transparent, but apart from human rights lawyer Richard Lyster we had found the candidates interviewed in Durban to be uniformly unimpressive; some were evasive and others downright dishonest. KZN remained a minefield in all sorts of ways.

When the final slate was announced many were shocked at the omission of my Presiding Bishop, Stanley Mogoba, who had topped our list. It was a hurtful blow and many, including Mogoba himself, believed that he had been snubbed because of his PAC roots. I didn't believe Mandela to be so small-minded and knew that over the years he had developed a high regard for Stanley's wisdom and charity. I believe that the problem was the KZN dilemma. Mandela had to find a credible black commissioner from that troubled region and made the shock decision to import somebody whose name had not come before us at all: Methodist Bishop Khoza Mgojo,[399] whom he felt was trusted on all sides. Unfortunately, having resolved one problem he had created another: two Methodist bishops (plus that Dr Alex Boraine had once also been the leader of the Methodist Church) would draw charges that Mandela was favouring his own church. If he was to keep Mgojo, he would have to let Mogoba go. I believe it was as simple and painful as that.

I am an unabashed champion of the TRC process. I followed it, participated in it, defended it in my newspaper column[400] and have spoken about it in every corner of the world. It may not have been perfect but I believe it to have been the most magnanimous and healing process any nation has devised for dealing with a shameful past. The awe with which it is regarded internationally is unquestioned, yet the fashion in today's South Africa is for critics, most of whom never lived through those days, to rubbish it. Together with our Constitution it is derided as a 'soft option' that let off the main perpetrators – the whites – far too cheaply. I hope its critics will think again or at least tell us what they would have offered in its place. At the time those who belonged to the 'prosecute and punish' school discovered in a couple of high-profile court cases just how difficult it would be to secure convictions of even the most prominent perpetrators.[401] Post-1994 our wounded country needed all its resources to build newness rather than chase the chimera of retribution. On the other hand, the call by people of the previous regime to "take hands and forgive and forget" was an outrageous presumption. Having lived in the American South, which was built on the 246-year-long atrocity of slavery, I am acutely aware of how that buried past still lies like toxic waste beneath everything achieved since, and how it continues to seep to the surface, poisoning their present.[402] For me the genius of the TRC design is that it steered a courageous course between the twin reefs of 'prosecute and punish' and 'forgive and forget', either of which would have wrecked us. Instead of these equally inadequate options it had the courage to ask the question 'Is it possible to both *remember* and *forgive*?' I am biased because the model is one of grace. It has been criticised for being 'religious' but in our context that was not inappropriate. South Africa may rightly be a secular state, but South Africans in the main are not secular people. I mean no disrespect for the law when I say that some wrongs are just too big for law to handle. The travail of our history did more than produce punishable brutalities: it lacerated our souls and corroded our humanity. It is significant that in the most searing TRC hearings when victims broke down while telling their stories the audience sang hymns – not struggle songs – to help them through. Those who brought their pain to the TRC were looking for more than a verdict or even a reward; they wanted healing and this may be why it was more appropriate for a priest with a pastor's heart, rather than a judge, to lead the commission.

Of course, no one can force repentance on anyone else, but the TRC did the next best thing – it created a kind of 'sacred space' in which such repentance would find hospitality rather than rejection. It was up to perpetrators to decide whether they would use the gift of that space to begin the healing of their guilt or simply follow the letter of the law to escape prison. I saw both. When hearings contained expressions of deep contrition and when – amazingly – someone would say, "It is not easy, but I must forgive," the whole nation breathed in the new life set free by those words. Victims who found the magnanimity to forgive – and Desmond Tutu reminds us that they did more often than not[403] – seemed to enlarge the heart of the nation itself. We were witnessing a new kind of South Africa being born.

On the other hand, it was galling to listen to a portly, mustachioed ex-general reciting his misdeeds – including the shooting of women and children in a cross-border raid – in a toneless, almost defiant monotone while the families of some of the dead sat just a few yards away, pain etched into their faces. He didn't once meet their eyes as they heard the details of their loved ones' deaths for the first time and with such lack of shame one was tempted to ask, "What's the point?" Yet even in those circumstances I sensed something happening. As he recited his cruelties this man who once struck fear into others began to look more and more ordinary and banal; he seemed to shrink and become little before our eyes. When the hearing ended without any rapprochement, the family got up and walked past him and one of them said it all: "*Suka wena!*"[404] The hoped for confession and forgiveness may not have occurred, but now he was known he would no longer haunt their nightmares and was feared no more. The importance of that new freedom cannot be overestimated.

Of course the TRC had some design faults. A bad mistake was to grant immediate amnesty to perpetrators who met the required criteria, while leaving reparations and rehabilitation for victims to a slow-moving Parliament increasingly distracted by other priorities.[405] Another failure is that it should have gone deeper into our society. It is said that 'what is not local is not real', and I believe that TRC-type hearings should have been carried through to every town and village and every township in the land. Only the churches could have facilitated such local hearings. They had the trust of the people as well as the infrastructure to ensure it happened in every one of those places, but we were very tired and many were anxious to get back to parish-pump irrelevance. It is sad that we failed to use this remarkable instrument of healing and reconciliation at the level where the people lived. The supreme sadness, however, is not about the TRC but about those of us who should have taken it most seriously. Instead of attending the hearings or at least engaging with the daily TV and radio reports, most white South Africans turned their backs on the TRC and the challenges it posed for their own lives. I am ashamed that they did and if we whites are feeling marginalised now, it is perhaps a deserved consequence of that apathy and denial. The truth is that, contrary to today's conventional wisdom, the TRC never failed South Africa. It was South Africans – especially white South Africans, a weary Church and a callous Parliament – that failed the Truth Commission.

36

Something New

By 1996 I was sure that my tenure as Bishop of the Central District should end. Ten years earlier I had made an effort to give way to a black successor. It seemed right at the time but it flopped. I had assumed that my deputy, Reverend Sizwe Mbabane, would easily succeed me but some insisted on punting another white name and, with a degree of ethnic rivalry also operating among blacks in my District, Sizwe's chances dimmed. In the end, the rules being "secret ballot without nominations or discussion", the District opted for the status quo and I was re-elected on the first ballot. Afterward I was accused by some of having been patronising in the first place and by others of changing my mind and clinging to power. If the first is true, it was unintended; the latter simply isn't true. The MCSA voting system doesn't allow for the luxury of changed minds: it can draft people whatever their mind.

Now, at my 1996 Synod, two important votes would take place, the first being to elect a new Presiding Bishop. At the last such election I had come a fairly close second but I had no sense that it would be the right thing for me to return to national leadership. All of the thirteen Synods – some 2 500 people – across Southern Africa voted simultaneously and when the result was announced it was decisive: Reverend Mvume Dandala was elected and I was a much-relieved distant second. Mvume and I had been good friends ever since our first meeting at Obedience '81 and he had also succeeded me at CMM. He was a multi-talented but humble person and I was happy to be the first to congratulate him on becoming Chief Shepherd of Southern Africa's million plus Methodists.

SOMETHING NEW

The ballot for Bishop of the District followed and this time Paul Verryn, who had endured so much during the Winnie Madikizela-Mandela saga, was elected in my place. The Synod clearly rejected her attempts to damage his name. As for me, after thirteen years in the hot-seat, freedom beckoned, but no matter how right one feels about things, moments like this are not without their heartache and a little emptiness of soul. My place in the church that had nurtured me from birth and trusted me with so much had suddenly changed – and it takes an exceptional person not to feel some regret. The Synod was meeting in Potchefstroom so I took Paul for a congratulatory coffee and then wandered the streets of the old town for a while, mulling things over. When I called Elizabeth she had heard the news already and was deeply relieved. "It's been enough," she said. "Come home and we can think about something new."

When I came out of the Episcopacy I was 57, the same age Dad was when he died. I think I had always subconsciously expected an early death too, yet much to my – and even more Elizabeth's – surprise I was alive and fairly well, so it seemed there might be more for us. The "something new" she spoke of had been brewing for a while: over the past three decades there had been a steady flow of international invitations – especially from the USA. I had travelled there two or three times each year, sometimes on SACC or Life Line business but mainly to preach and teach. A couple of American universities had kindly bestowed honorary doctorates on me – something that would have been met with some incredulity by my Rhodes professors of long ago – and there had been approaches from Australia, New Zealand and the USA to take up church appointments, the most tempting being Sydney's CMM and Foundry United Methodist Church in Washington DC. I had always turned away for what seemed obvious reasons but there was no need to any longer: we were a free people at last.

I also believed that the journey we had travelled in South Africa could offer a message to the wider world. Straight after my Synod I had to deliver an address on '*Good News for the Poor*' at the World Methodist Conference in Rio de Janeiro. I told the 2 700 delegates that there was a struggle for the soul of our church. "There is a prosperous Methodism in the developed world, and a 'Methodism with the poor' in the rest of the world, with some places, like South Africa, where both exist in glaring contrast next to each other." The question was: which model would become the true sign of who we were? Would the prosperous learn to let go? "In proclaiming personal salvation, we have been admirable; in campaigning for political liberation, we have been passable; on the issue of economic justice – abysmal." John Wesley had taught that engagement with the poor was as essential to holiness as communion with God. "For him, the two together made a Christian." In the name of Jesus and the poor, would Methodists reject the world's orthodoxy of greed and commit to the search for a compassionate economic order?

Some Americans present were uncomfortable with my message and took open umbrage, but many more said they needed to hear hard words about their comfortable Christianity. As I sat at lunch with two old friends, Drs Maxie Dunham and Ned Dewire, the presidents of Asbury Seminary in Kentucky and the Methodist Theological School in Ohio, a decision was made: Elizabeth and I would come to the US and I would teach on their campuses and also be available to colleges and churches across the USA. It felt right.

In mid-1997 there was the expected round of farewells, some of which we would rather have ducked. On such occasions one discovers who really understood what one was about and who didn't. There were two that meant most to us. I had wanted to establish a chain of pre-schools across the District and a remarkable woman named Sue Pretorius had taken up the vision. By the time I left, we had 39 pre-schools up and running between Bedfordview in the east and Vryburg 250 miles to the west. Most of them were located in very poor areas and we called it the Chain of Hope. Sue had bussed children from all of them to come and say goodbye to us. They sang with all their hearts and presented me with a gold cross on a chain consisting of 39 precious links. It was a heart-warming time.

The other was at Wadela, a black township near Carletonville. Visiting places like this and trying to bring some word of hope was what being a Bishop had been all about, and this group of tough black mineworkers seem to have got it. At the end they walked in bearing three huge blue candles set in a wooden stand, each wrapped in barbed wire like the one on CMM's altar. The message read: "We hail your years of struggle. May the memory of your service light our hearts forever."

Elizabeth's retirement was a moving one, with colleagues identifying themselves as friends and speaking about how she personified what IMSSA was all about: enabling, training and empowering people to be more effective resolvers of disputes. Kolisa Xinunu, who she had encouraged from the day she met her in a menial position at IMSSA, and who was now ready to start her own company managing union elections, thanked her for being her "mother, leader, adviser and most of all a great friend!" Driving home, Elizabeth mused, "I think I have been able to be a friend, bringing love and courage to others."

September 1997 saw us arrive in the United States – at Asbury Seminary, tucked away in Kentucky in the middle of bluegrass country. Elizabeth and I had never lived in a small town before, nor spent so much unbroken time in each other's company, and it was a good spot for us both to begin to depressurise. It took longer than we expected to let go the stresses of our homeland, a process made more difficult because I had left my trusty pipe behind in South Africa. Pipe-smoking had comforted me through all my years of ministry, but the US was ahead of us in making pariahs of smokers so I had decided to go cold turkey. Elizabeth had to put up with some scratchy moments as I grieved my way through nicotine withdrawal but she made up for it with long walks through the outrageously beautiful countryside. "It's amazing to walk without fear," she said.

Asbury was a theologically conservative campus and the way we saw our faith and the world was a little different but we enjoyed our time there and made good friends. We were about to spend our first Thanksgiving in the US when a call came from the Truth and Reconciliation Commission in South Africa. Would I return to give evidence in the Winnie Madikizela-Mandela hearing? It was a hard thing to do and returning from that emotionally draining experience, my rehabilitation had to begin all over. We both realised that perhaps there were no unwounded people in our homeland and that we, too, needed healing. It would come by having time to pray and process – and through the gifts of distance and time and new friendships that weren't dependent on where one stood in 'the struggle'. It would come, too, by the simple joy of talking about other things and not feeling guilty about it.

The weekend of 7 December 1997 found us on the campus of Duke University Divinity School (DDS), a prestige United Methodist Church seminary in Durham, North Carolina. I was there to address some of the DDS students on the Saturday and preach in the cathedral-like university chapel the next day. After my talk some of us went to supper and carried on a robust conversation around the different challenges facing American and South African Christians. Duke's star theologian, Dr Stanley Hauerwas, asked me in his point-blank style what the problem was with the American church. "You're too rich," I said. "Is that all?" he asked. "That's everything," I replied. Someone who had been rather quiet during the meal introduced himself afterwards as Greg Jones, the Divinity School Dean. I was surprised at how young he was and learned later that Greg was one of the whiz-kids of the theological firmament. He then surprised me even more by saying that if I ever wanted to serve on the faculty of DDS, I shouldn't hesitate to make contact. Apart from being very flattered, I thought no more about it because we were anticipating being in the US only eighteen months, so after preaching about John the Baptist in the glorious chapel the next day, we returned to Asbury and a Kentucky Christmas.

At the turn of 1998 we moved on to our second assignment, the Methodist Theological School in Ohio, another beautiful campus, this time on the edge of the town of Delaware. Ned Dewire, the MTSO President, and Shirley were old and dear friends and living on campus and eating each day with the students was a rich experience. I was becoming more confident in the teaching role. My classes were full and Elizabeth, while enjoying being a university level student for the first time in her life, was increasingly looked up to as wise counsellor and spiritual mentor. Moreover, her love for nature nearly burst her heart in this new land. "We experience spring's appearance more tentatively in our northern abode," she wrote. "I searched eagerly for the little signs, swelling buds on dead-appearing branches, the shy greening of deep grass, the rosy haze around the heads of tall trees, an almost impossible emergence of daffodils and jonquils from the brown earth or sometimes snow ... the heart quickens!"

But with the Ohio summer came another call from the TRC: could I return once again, this time to give evidence in the upcoming trial of ex-President PW Botha? It would mean two 24-hour flights inside of one week but the journey needed to be made. Botha had spurned coming before the Truth Commission, claiming that he had nothing to confess, and that Afrikaners "asked forgiveness of nobody but their God," so he had been charged with contempt. My evidence was needed to show that the bombing of Khotso House was a gross human rights violation because of the people it injured and may have killed. Botha's minister of Police and his top Police general had already told the TRC that the SACC headquarters had been bombed on his orders, but the TRC legal team had also called the regime's most infamous assassin, Colonel Eugene de Kock, to clinch their case. The trial was to be held in the town of George, a short distance from where Botha lived. By happenstance our son Chris and Kim lived only 60 km from George and they had just had a second daughter, Frances, born two months before, so I could visit them too.

Just before testifying I had a happy reunion with Desmond Tutu and we shared the sense of wonder at how the wheel had turned since those bruising encounters with Botha in the 1980s. The prophetic warnings of those years, often made at the end of hope's limits with nothing but the promise of a just God to lean on, had come true. This once all-powerful ruler, called Die Groot Krokodil[406] behind his back by fearful cabinet ministers, was now 'the accused' standing in the dock before a black magistrate. He, more than any other apartheid ruler, had tried to crush the witness of the Church, first with the Eloff Commission, and later with the destructive violence of a massive bomb. Now he would have to sit and listen to the consequences of his actions.

In court Alex Boraine and I found ourselves sitting right next to the man whose nickname was 'Prime Evil'. Colonel Eugene de Kock had been brought from jail where he was serving 212 years and two life sentences for numerous state-sponsored murders. The really frightening thing about him was how ordinary he looked with his nerdish thick-lensed spectacles; he was anything but the image of a ruthless assassin. PW Botha, large and still intimidating, occupied the dock just a few yards away. When my turn in the witness box came I testified to the horror, the incredible destruction, the bloodied victims of the explosion and the miracle that nobody had been killed. I called it the most violent act of terrorism by the apartheid state against the Church of God. Then 'Prime Evil' described how he and his team planted and detonated the bomb. He was clear that the orders to "destroy Khotso House so it could never be used again" came from Botha himself. He was scathing about the "cowardly" politicians who ordered men like him to do their dirty work. Desmond Tutu testified to the extraordinary lengths the TRC had gone to in trying to make it as painless as possible for PW to come before them, to no avail. He ended his evidence with an appeal, saying that PW's government had caused "deep, deep anguish and pain and suffering" to many people. "If Mr Botha was able to say: 'I am sorry that the policies of my government caused you pain.' Just that ... that would be a tremendous thing and I appeal to him."[407] Defiant to the last, Botha made no response.

There was a lighter moment. At 3.30 pm that day, both prosecution and defence suddenly indicated to the magistrate that they needed a little more preparation. Court was adjourned and everyone made a hasty exit. The real reason was that the touring Irish rugby team was about to play South Western Districts in the George stadium. I was walking to my car when Desmond's chauffeur-driven Merc stopped next to me: "Jump in, Petros!" Desmond shouted. "We're going to watch the rugby." And we did. The two of us sat in the cramped VIP stand of this rural sports ground – Desmond the only black person in sight – surrounded by burly Afrikaners. They greeted us politely enough when we arrived but as they cheered on their local heroes, I had little doubt who they supported in the other match going on in the magistrate's court down the road. That night I emailed Elizabeth: "Only in South Africa could we be in court one moment with an ex-State President, the world's worst killer and a Nobel Laureate and then go off to watch rugby with a bunch of Afrikaners who could not be more polite when the Arch comes in!" I have no recollection of who won the rugby match.

After the trial it was a relief to spend a night in Mossel Bay with Chris and Kim and their new baby Frances before returning exhausted to the United States. I gave thanks that she and our other grandchildren would grow up in a very different country than the one we and our children had known.

Botha was found guilty and sentenced to a fine of R10 000 or twelve months' imprisonment plus a further twelve months, suspended for five years. A higher court upheld an appeal lodged by his lawyers –

entirely on a small legal technicality.[408] Before the verdict I had written to friends that it really didn't matter because enough of the truth about his deeds had now come out. However, I was discovering how deeply my feelings were affected by encounters like this. To the many friends who had been praying for this trip, I wrote, "I went up to the old man, greeted him with a handshake, gave evidence against him and then sat very near him for three days. There is no desire for retribution but the experience did bring back the feelings of those days. They are quite indescribable and destructive to one's well-being and emotional health. Sleep has been hard to come by since."[409]

On my return from South Africa another invitation awaited. A good friend, Bishop Ken Carder in Nashville, Tennessee, wanted to know if I'd like to take the pulpit of Calvary United Methodist Church[410] in Nashville from July? He needed an interim preacher until mid-1999. Truth to tell I was finding the academic life rather too peaceful and welcomed the call. Ned happily agreed to the six-month overlap and for the balance of our time at MTSO I commuted the 340 miles from Columbus to Nashville each Friday, preaching in Calvary United Methodist Church on the Sunday, meeting with the staff and attending to administration on Monday, before flying back to teach during the midweek. It was the best of both worlds.

At the end of 1998 we packed our few goods and my books into a U-Haul trailer, hitched it onto our venerable Oldsmobile, and drove down to Nashville, where we soon settled in to the parsonage next to the tall-steepled church. In some ways American Methodists 'did church' differently from their South African counterparts, so it was a good learning experience for me. My Associate Minister at Calvary was Pam Hawkins, a deep and remarkable disciple of Jesus. Not only did I learn to trust her with the real leadership of Calvary, but she and her spouse Ray became lifelong friends along the way.[411]

As the time to leave Calvary approached, our future was uncertain. We were hoping that my next task would be back home, using whatever experience and gifts I had to offer without the burdens of office, but nothing of that kind emanated from South Africa. Ross Olivier, who was now the Executive Secretary of MCSA, confided that most of the bishops back home were uncomfortable about having me in their Districts. "They would feel threatened," he wrote. The result was that Elizabeth and I were feeling somewhat adrift until I remembered the offer Greg Jones had made two years before. I asked him if it still held. His response was immediate and welcoming and a complete contrast to the prevarications back home. Subject to some formalities, he hoped I could start in the Fall semester – September 1999 – as Professor of the Practice of Christian Ministry.

37

Professor at Large

For the next seven years Durham, North Carolina and the Duke campus became our American home. They were among the happiest and least stressful years in our life together and I never lost the feeling of contented belonging when I walked onto the campus with its graceful gothic buildings of blue-grey 'Duke' stone. On the main quad at the heart of it all, nestling below the soaring tower of Duke Chapel lay the Divinity School, rooted in the Methodist tradition with around 500 students and some of the best theologians and Wesleyan scholars in the world. Despite my lack of academic prowess, they welcomed me as if I was one of them and it was an immense privilege to be part of it all. Elizabeth received permission to sit in on courses taught by fine scholars like Ellen Davis, Willie Jennings, Stanley Hauerwas, Teresa Berger and Richard Lischer. Off campus we built deep friendships with Greg and Susan Jones, Richard and Judy Hayes, Rick and Tracy Lischer, and numbers of others.

I revelled in the teaching, offering two courses to Master of Divinity students each semester. One was about Church and State, using the South African saga as a lens through which my largely Southern students could see with new eyes the issues of colonialism, racism and exclusion in their own context. We were entering the George W Bush era and under his presidency, especially after the September 11 attacks on the World Trade Centre and Pentagon in 2001, American nationalism and imperialism became more blatant. My students may not have been products of the religious right, but many of them needed to discover how much their Christianity had become wrapped in the nation's flag and captured by American culture. I was hopeful that young pastors would emerge from this course unafraid to liberate their congregations from these bonds. Who knows what exciting action could come from churches when they discovered that God was not an American? The second course was about how local congregations should and could look beyond themselves and become agents of transformation in their communities. I was able to reflect on the decades I had spent in the local church and to share the lessons learned. Both courses were always fully subscribed and each semester brought the joy of seeing aspirant pastors change and grow before my eyes. We seemed to connect well and a signal honour was to be chosen three times by the leaving students to preach the Baccalaureate sermon on the eve of their graduation.

Sometime in May 2000, Ross Olivier called from South Africa saying that Presiding Bishop Dandala wanted to nominate me for General Secretary of the World Methodist Council. It was certainly an honour but it was largely an administrative position and I was not drawn to it. Dandala had also spoken of my possibly taking over the small John Wesley College in Pretoria but I heard no more of that either. It was time to end the dance. That August Greg and Susan visited South Africa and we travelled round the country for a couple of weeks. When we stopped in to introduce them at a meeting of the MCSA's top leadership,[412] I took the opportunity to ask permission to retire from the active ministry of MCSA. Permission was granted.

We returned to Duke with lighter hearts. This was where we would be for some years at least and we were content. I was also finding a widening ministry beyond the campus. On weekends when we weren't listening to Will Willimon's lively preaching in Duke Chapel I was teaching and preaching somewhere across the continent. In the end I visited something like 140 US cities and got to know the heartbeat of this great country and its people as well as most. People of conscience were struggling with the new climate of fear-mongering and war under President Bush and invitations poured in asking for conversations around church/state and war/peace issues. One if the most gut-wrenching was with some 40 pastors in Norfolk, Virginia, an enormous concentration of US military and naval might. It happened in the same week that Bush attacked Iraq and almost all of them were dealing with men and women in their congregations going off to war. Some were in tears as we talked through their fear of challenging the war-machine. Another invitation was to Washington DC where some senior military, CIA and State Department officers who ran war-gaming scenarios for the White House were troubled about directions taken by the Bush Administration. They decided to assemble a group of policy people and theologians in order to see what options "ethical leaders" would come up with for the President instead of simply criticising his actions. So there I was, promoted to the National Security Council for a day and invited to role-play Secretary of State Colin Powell because they wanted "some fresh thinking rooted in the Gospel and courageous experience".[413] The 'Defence Secretary' sitting to my left was Ambassador Joe Wilson, who had exposed Bush's lie about Saddam Hussein buying uranium 'yellowcake' in Niger. On my right was Sidney Blumenthal, author and former aide to President Clinton. Together with other heavyweights around the table, each with our 'policy advisers' sitting behind us, we were confronted with genuine briefs about the Global War on Terror, Iran's nuclear plans and progress, and the role of the poppy crop in the conflict in Afghanistan. I soon had to acknowledge the complexities of the issues and how much harder it was to make decisions than to criticise them, yet the underlying immorality of the Bush/Cheney ideology had to be confronted. Before the end of the scenario, I had reached my limits. "As Secretary of State my job is to sell US policy across the world," I said. "I can't sell damaged goods. I can't promote a policy that exacerbates the problem of terrorism rather than ameliorates it, so I must resign."

One hope was to build a relationship between the richly resourced

Duke Divinity School and MCSA's clergy training regime. Both MCSA General Secretary Ross Olivier and Presiding Bishop Mvume Dandala visited Durham in 2001 and a covenant of mutual engagement and support was signed. However, on ground level the response from our South African educators was disappointing. South Africans often accuse Americans of arrogance and insensitivity, but we need to acknowledge that there is a corresponding arrogance among us which seems to say, "there's nothing the rest of the world can teach us" – an attitude that leaves us content with just "getting by" instead of striving for excellence. It saddened me to watch our tiny college struggling without even the fundamentals of financial resourcing in place, yet neglecting to take advantage of the mentorship Duke could have given about institutional development, also failing to fully utilise some of the best theologians and Biblical scholars in the world. In spite of this, Duke's offer of help remained graciously open, something I was grateful for later.

During the US summer Elizabeth and I began to take Duke faculty and students on 'Pilgrimages of Pain and Hope' in South Africa, visiting people and places that were at the heart of our nation's struggle and transformation. These were rich experiences of encounter, not only with remarkable people but with God. We emphasised that pilgrimage was not primarily about knowing more, but *feeling* more, and many of our pilgrims wrote testifying to deep changes in their lives as a result of their encounters. We also began to place a small number of Duke students in MCSA churches or agencies for ten-week 'Field Education' stints for an even deeper insertion into life here, with similar transformative results.

In January 2001, just before her 89th birthday my mother fell ill and Elizabeth flew back to Cape Town to be with her. While she was there, Chris and Kim, and later Jane and Gilbert took her to see a house in Simon's Town that we had admired on the internet. After a flurry of emails and telephone calls we took the plunge. Elizabeth's hand shook as she signed the deal, but she said she knew it would lift my soul and bring joyful freedom to her too. She was so right: I had always dreamed of retiring to a place where I could wake up and see the ocean. Number 2 Trafalgar Place is perched on the mountainside high above the naval dockyard with magnificent views of the 18-mile wide False Bay embraced by its horseshoe of grey-blue mountains. Alongside the harbour lies the yacht basin and this is where I later moored the other love of my life, my 25ft sailboat named *Flash*. We both felt greatly privileged to live in this home and of course there is no way to describe the sheer ecstasy of steering a lively little boat into the white-caps of a fresh False Bay Sou'Easter.

By March, however, my mother was slipping away and I flew home to join my sister Valmai holding vigil with her. I was there for five days, with Mom sometimes lucid and at other times peacefully sleeping before she died quietly on 13 March. It was a healing time with both mother and sister. I had been in Cape Town by complete coincidence when Valmai lost her husband Paul to pancreatic cancer just seven months before; now it was possible for us to be together again. I am sad that I never ever knew emotional closeness with Mom but I admired her bravery. She had been widowed at 46 years and had returned to teaching to become the beloved Vice-Principal of Greenfields School until retirement. Always more comfortable with little children, she was a loving grandma to our boys and great-grandma to our young granddaughters.

Now that we had a home to return to, I decided to teach only the Spring semester at Duke each year, giving us from June to December in Simon's Town. Our four granddaughters were growing fast and the regular travel back and forth was becoming more burdensome. In 2003 I was named a Distinguished Professor with an endowed chair.[414] The new status involved a fine dinner and an Inaugural Lecture, and as I prepared for this rite of passage I found that I was struggling to marshal my thoughts. I had always been able to structure sermons and lectures with ease and was suddenly in difficulty – so much so that the lecture was still incomplete at 3 am the day it was to be delivered. In the end it went off reasonably well,[415] but I knew something was wrong. I had already been a patient at the magnificent Duke Medical Centre for heart treatment as well as a corneal implant and once more it came to my aid, diagnosing a minor stroke that had damaged the organisational centre of my brain. Words – and the ability to string them together – are of course the tools of any preacher or teacher's trade and this weakness has been sorely felt since.

We remained happily commuting to Duke until June 2006, when Elizabeth and I both felt the pull of home. I calculated that I had done the transatlantic haul 105 times since my first journey in 1966. It was enough. On 13 May I preached the Baccalaureate once more in the great chapel and we said our goodbyes to a place and its people who had become deeply precious to us. In July we led our last Pilgrimage of Pain and Hope and began to settle down in Simon's Town. Duke wasn't quite finished with me, however. In May 2007 the university invited me back to receive an Honorary Doctorate. We returned to wonderful reunions and my dear Duke friend Rick Lischer acted as my sponsor at the Commencement Ceremonies. The real honour, however, was to have been invited into the faculty in the first place. Recalling those years among them – together with the earlier periods at METHESCO and Asbury – brings nothing but thankfulness.

38

A Last Task

I expected my 'second retirement' to be my last, but it was not to be. A new Presiding Bishop, Reverend Ivan Abrahams, named me to a commission to review the training of MCSA's ministers. We had lost both our residential seminaries for different reasons and for some years had been using an in-service model supplemented by a temporary one-year live-in experience at the old Kilnerton campus. Many felt that without the formational disciplines of life in community, the system was turning out a less-than-complete product. Nor could a UNISA correspondence degree replace face-time with teachers over three years. There were exceptions, of course, but they tended to prove the rule.

The commission consulted widely but ran into a theological training regime that had become something of a fiefdom. There were excellent and committed people among them but others were more obstructive than helpful. The commission, however, was mandated to go ahead: we defined the skills and qualities of the 'transformative ministers' MCSA was asking for and worked from there, designing the formation process we believed would be needed. We also investigated what different localities and universities had to offer.

When the time came to present our report to the 2005 Conference we unanimously recommended that a stand-alone residential seminary should be built in Pietermaritzburg and that all desiring to enter our ministry should spend the first three years of their formation there. The seminary would offer its own Bachelor of Theology degree but would be much more than an academic institution, prioritising spiritual formation and vocational readiness just as much. After a long debate, our recommendations were overwhelmingly approved subject to satisfactory financial arrangements being made.

The venture lost eighteen months while committees haggled and in July 2007 a troubled Presiding Bishop sat me down to lunch and asked me to take over the entire project. I looked away and saw a long hard road stretching ahead. This would change everything Elizabeth and I had talked about and dreamed of. Yet the past nine years had given me unique access to different styles of seminary formation and I truly believed that this was MCSA's one best shot at reforming the shape of our ministry: how could I refuse? Our quiet future would have to wait. So I swallowed hard and said, "Yes." But there were conditions: "I'll do it, Ivan, but let me assemble a dedicated team to get it done without a lot of meddling committees slowing us. Secondly, promise me that when the time comes to select faculty, you will not allow any political interference in making the most effective appointments." To his great credit, Ivan Abrahams remained faithful to both. I made two more conditions to myself: to complete the task in three years and to hand MCSA a whole seminary – campus, residences, everything. In my experience uncompleted building schemes tended to remain that way for ever.

The next three years were a whirlwind of dreaming, planning, fundraising, building, staffing and monitoring. On 5 September 2007 the vision was shared with 40 key persons. Dean Greg Jones came all the way from Duke to give a masterly presentation on the possibilities before us. A deeply committed Methodist businessman pledged the first gift of R10m provided MCSA and others came to the party. At a small supper that week the vision statement that still guides the seminary was born: *Forming Transforming Leaders for Church and Nation*.

I set up a Planning Executive and five 'Birthing Teams'[416] to take the project forward. It looked like it would cost between R80m and R100m. The MCSA central finance office agreed to match my fundraising up to R33m. We were able to persuade Epworth Girls' High School – a long-standing Methodist project – to part with a corner of their well-positioned land for the site. With the land secured, MCSA put up R40m to purchase five nearby houses for staff and two blocks of flats for residences. They regarded these as easily disposable assets so they kept them on their own books. That left me to find 50% of the likely R66m balance. It was do-able!

For the next 36 months I rose at 4 am each Tuesday, drove to Cape Town airport and left for either Johannesburg or Pietermaritzburg – Joburg to raise money and Maritzburg to spend it. To beat my three-year deadline I was building on a hand-to-mouth basis and had to keep the donations coming in. Some potential donors were more generous in their promises than in their giving and when a promise was broken my nights became scarily sleepless.

The campus was to be aspirational. Designed by a young black architect named Leon Witbooi in the Pretoria firm of Boogertman, it was handed on to Jon Sanders in their Westville office for the building phase. Trips to KZN usually began with dropping into his office and then moving on to site meetings with the building team. At my side was MCSA General Treasurer Anthony Tibbit who was passionately committed to the project. Jock Seeliger, a Bryanston Methodist with a nation-wide development company, placed his project team at our disposal – a donation worth millions – and we were in excellent hands. All I had to do was stay ahead of them by making the design decisions and keeping the money flowing.

We asked the 2007 MCSA Conference to name the new venture the Seth Mokitimi Methodist Seminary (SMMS) after the first black President of the MCSA, who had modelled the kind of 'transforming leadership' we were hoping to emulate. After a rigorous search we chose Ross Olivier as first President of SMMS. He had the mix of gifts we were looking for: a top-level administrator, an outstanding parish minister and preacher of excellence, a fine theologian and teacher, a person with a strong spirituality steeped in prayer, with a national and international profile. The fact that he didn't have doctoral level academics brought charges of 'anti-intellectualism' from some quarters more impressed with degrees than performance, but we were not limiting the academic challenges, we were adding to them. Our seminarians were to be prepared, not just for Graduation but for Ordination. Each seminarian would be evaluated on rigorous academic performance, but also on a number of other skills and qualities.[417] The Seminary President therefore needed to be a leader with the widest possible vision for and experience of 'transforming ministry'.

My last duty for MCSA had an unfortunate side. While the project excited most Methodists, others seemed willing to do anything to torpedo it. There was also a vicious racial undertone I had never experienced in the church before. The 2008 Conference saw a cynical attempt to limit faculty selection by prescribing not only academic but racial conditions on appointments. The paragraphs recording them slipped into the 2008 Conference Yearbook and I said that they would sicken those who fought for MCSA's historic mission policy as a "one and undivided" church. We would ignore them anyway: the government certifying bodies would never permit such racial constraints. Rumours were stoked about me taking on the SMMS task so that I could appoint my son as its head – a sheer nonsense. A minister sent a scurrilous letter far and wide alleging that the choice of Olivier was a political one "made by white liberals who have been controlling and manipulating the SMMS process". The fact that his brother was an unsuccessful candidate for the position was, I am sure, a coincidence. MCSA's finance body was falsely and repeatedly accused of using the ministers' pension fund to finance the project. I also found that my leadership of the Journey to the New Land process in the early 90s was still resented among more authoritarian clergy who had not forgiven me for introducing new structures empowering the laity. They feared that the new seminary would inculcate more 'democratisation'.[418]

When I reported progress to the Bishops' Meetings I was cheered on but when I travelled around the country seeking support, some Bishops sat on their hands. Our Presiding Bishop was right and the commission was right: there was a deep malaise in our ministry which our training was not addressing and some would go to great lengths not to have it challenged. All of this was unpleasant but it tended to make our team more determined. The Search Committee held firm and did what it believed to be right.[419] While the sniping from the edges continued, we got on with the job.

Ross came on board running. Together with our very first staff appointment, Rowanne Sarojini Marie, Dean of Students Sox Leleke and Professor Neville Richardson, ex-Dean of the UKZN School of Religion and Theology, he enrolled the pioneer class of 38 seminarians in February 2009. Jack and Joan Scholtz came from Johannesburg to help supervise the transformation of our first block of flats. Ross's wife Shayne, herself quite a force of nature, organised and 'mothered' those coming into residence. Temporary classrooms, chapel and library were fashioned out of spare spaces. Ross and his team did a superhuman job actualising the dream and implanted a remarkable family ethos at SMMS. Meanwhile 2008 brought the world-wide economic crash and fundraising became much more difficult. The new stadiums planned for South Africa's 2010 FIFA World Cup created a shortage of steel and building operations slowed.

Somehow we got through: on 4 September 2010, exactly three years after our first planning gathering, we were able to dedicate a fully functioning seminary with a set of outstanding buildings that we believed would speak to incoming seminarians about their sacred vocation. They entered through the 'Life Door' carrying Jesus' promise of 'life in all its fullness' onto a magnificent campus consisting of the administration block, the Nelson Mandela & Robert Sobukwe Library,[420] the Moseneke Lecture Hall building, a Community Life building and the Chapel of Christ the Servant, where hopefully Jesus' servant-model of ministry would be rediscovered and emulated. We unveiled a bas relief of Seth Mokitimi and then opened the great chapel doors, ensuring that the needs of the world outside could not be excluded from this place of worship.[421] In my welcoming words, I affirmed that people were shaped not only by ideas but by the spaces that surround them. "If, when you enter this place, you think of God, we will have done our work," I said, but more: "if, when you walk about here, you are convinced that this God is best served by serving God's world, we will have done our work well." I could also report that the campus was all but paid for. With MCSA matching funds we had raised R58.6m – just short of what we needed. It was the largest amount ever raised by MCSA and every cent had been sourced in South Africa. "This is up there with the big miracles," I said and indeed it was, worth every ounce of effort and all the long days of travel, the nights away from home and the countless meetings and setbacks. The Presiding Bishop announced that an annual Peter Storey Lecture would be established in my honour and an award in my name would be given annually to the exiting seminarian who had "exhibited the highest calibre of devotion to duty, diligence, moral character, courage, and leadership potential." It was a kind gesture.

Yet the day was not without its controversy. We held a luncheon to thank the wonderful mix of people – architects, builders, donors, clergy and laity, rich and poor – who had cared enough to work and sacrifice for this vision. It was celebration time for those who together had pulled off a miracle and to each one we presented a small model of the tower and cross that looked over the campus. Unfortunately, for some people protocol trumps performance and I had apparently committed a serious breach by not inviting *all* of the Bishops. Later, at the MCSA Conference I was subjected to a public drubbing for 'disrespecting' them. Over my long ministry I have not found it difficult to be corrected, but this was petty nonsense. I have always been firm that being a Methodist Bishop was a function, not a status – which is why we do not retain the title when we retire from the job. The Bishops who had organised support for the project were invited and honoured; why should others be there because of a mere title? I assured the Conference as graciously as I could that no insult was intended, but I could not apologise. As we left the hall the Presiding Bishop came alongside me, saying that "it was not supposed to go that way". I wrote to him later that on my last appearance on the floor of the Conference after 52 years of service to MCSA, being lectured like a delinquent schoolboy was hard to stomach and that the complaining Bishops reminded me more than anything of "Pharisees swatting at gnats while happily swallowing a camel – in this case a whole new Seminary".[422]

Following the opening the team had to get the SMMS family bedded down in its new surroundings. The Planning Executive had been dissolved and we now had a Governing Council, of which I was elected chairperson. The pace for me was no longer as hectic, although I was still winding up the building project. It was a joy to see how warmly the seminarian community responded to Ross's grace-filled leadership. He and Rowanne ensured that the Bachelor of Theology programme was accredited in record time with the Council for Higher Education and the SA Qualifications Authority. A Diploma in Practical Ministry was added soon after. Soon faculty members – with adjunct faculty – numbered fourteen, with a score of other staff. By 2011 two dedicated United Methodists from the US came and assisted in the establishment of a Field Education and Ministry programme linking all 90 seminarians weekly with eighteen non-profit agencies, hospitals and prisons around Pietermartizburg.

Then came tragedy. Early in 2012, Ross Olivier fell into a deep depression. The Governing Council sent him on a two-month 'mid-term leave', watched over by medical experts, but it was soon evident that things were much more serious and that he would not be returning soon. Visits to Ross during these months were deeply worrying.

A LAST TASK

He had gone into a faraway place inside himself and was difficult to reach. Shayne took leave to be with him and we needed to shore up the management of SMMS. For me this meant more frequent trips to the seminary again, supporting the small management group. Ross never returned to his task and on 2 May 2012, just a fortnight before the graduation of his pioneer class, he took his own life. I had just arrived from Cape Town to see him and Shayne slipped home from SMMS to see if he was awake. I followed her a few minutes later and found her with her son Peter, nursing his body.

Seven days later a massive crowd spilled out onto the lawns around the Chapel of Christ the Servant. Once more I found myself preaching the eulogy for a beloved friend. "The story of Ross is a story of Jesus," I said, "Jesus and his love." I recalled Ross's amazing testimony of having encountered the embracing love of God years before in a prison cell in Pretoria, and how this had led him into a new life as a Christ-follower. How this white Afrikaner had found himself to be part of a new, non-racial community and how he had become one of MCSA's most remarkable preachers, pastors and teachers. Three times his gifting had led him to be plucked out of the local church to serve on the MCSA's national stage: first as Co-ordinator of the Journey to a New Land, then as Executive Secretary of MCSA, and finally as first President of SMMS. "Despite the carping of small-minded critics who saw no further than academic degrees and skin-colour," I said, "... nobody else could have done it." We had chosen him above all to carve out "a new Gospel-shaped ministerial formation combining academic excellence with spiritual growth and skill training", and to be the guardian of what he called "Seth Mokitimi Seminary's DNA". I addressed Ross's suicide head on: "Let me cut through all the pious perplexity and hushed discussion and let me dare to say what Jesus might say today: *'Please understand that my friend Ross fell ill to a terminal disease. It is like cancer. Not all people die from it but many do. It puzzles us because we cannot see its wounds ... but sometimes people see no escape ... it is called Depression and when it strikes it can take the best of us.'"*

Ross's tragic death stunned the SMMS family but in the next days we had to prepare them for their first graduation – a strange mix of the joy of achievement and the stabbing pain of loss. The night before graduation Professor Jonathan Jansen was the first Peter Storey Lecturer and he handled the special circumstances with great sensitivity. Then, as chair of the Governing Council, it was my privilege to cap SMMS's first BTh graduates – a proud yet heartbreaking moment.

In this weekend marking the graduation of our pioneer seminarian class, I planned to finish my work with SMMS. I had resigned as chair of the Governing Council but in the light of the tragedy we had all suffered, I was immediately asked to take over as an interim President until a replacement for Ross could be found. My heart sank. Elizabeth was simply angry. She knew that the SMMS project had wrung every drop out of my limited reserves of strength and it had inevitably impacted on our life together. She had a tough talk with our Presiding Bishop but in the end we both reconciled to the logic of it. I took the job provided she could join me in Maritzburg and a tiny cottage was found for us. Somehow another seven months' energy would need to be found too.

I couldn't have done it without Elizabeth by my side. It was extremely difficult to pull a broken community back out of despondency. Some faculty and staff were magnificent in their support; others acted out their struggles with tragedy and change, making it harder for themselves and for me. But we saw it through until a successor – again the many-gifted Mvume Dandala – was appointed by the Council and we could go home, leaving behind this legacy project that had cost so much in the life of Ross and the lives of Shayne and their family.

It had cost us too.

The full story of the conception and birth of Seth Mokitimi Methodist Seminary has yet to be told, and we will see whether the vision it was born to express can survive the changes Ross's death brought about. The danger is ever present that the seminary will lose its unique DNA and slip back into the outworn shape of just another 'Theological College', but I pray it will not. I hope the bold new campus will always invite its occupants into newness. The possibilities of SMMS are limited only by the imaginations of those privileged to lead it. I hope that the God who inspired us to birth SMMS will give our successors great and holy imaginations!

Epilogue

In 2013 Nelson Mandela died. I attended the rain-soaked state memorial in Johannesburg, but the truly moving experience for Elizabeth and me was visiting Robben Island on the eve of his Qunu funeral. We joined our local Bishop and a group of ex-political prisoners to spend the night in a prayer vigil outside Madiba's old cell – having sailed there in the very same ferry that had brought me to the Island just over 50 years before.

That night I pondered how the years had unfolded for me since I first stepped ashore there in 1962. I wouldn't have been there at all had it not been for that inner voice calling me away from the sea six years before that. The voice had never lost its resonance: many times I had doubted both my worthiness and effectiveness, but there was never any doubt about that call. My lifelong fate was to be a teller of the Jesus story and to stand – however inadequately – for his truths.

I said in a sermon once: "If you want to know whether God is alive, don't go to the places of comfort and ease; inquire rather in those places where the fire of testing burns most fiercely."[423] Those who look for the real Jesus will find that he's no meek and mild Saviour, but a fermenting and disturbing presence confronting humanity. So it was with me.

Long before any adult engagement with faith, I had been conscious of nations clashing in terrible conflict because some things were right and others wrong, and of the voice of my preacher-dad speaking of a different, peaceable kingdom where people lived justly and kindly with one another, a kingdom within reach if we were willing to become different persons.

The youthful years at Kilnerton had planted further seeds: what could be right about the uncrossable lines that lay between the lives of those students and my own? The inner voice was there again urging me never to stop asking such questions.

After that, it seemed that the one who had called me thrust me repeatedly into disturbing places and situations for which I was seldom qualified, but which challenged and grew me.

This very Robben Island: I was young for the job but my encounters with Sobukwe, Mandela and the other moral giants incarcerated here made neutrality about my homeland impossible. Saying "Yes" to Jesus had to involve saying a clear "No" to the pervasive evil that held these remarkable men prisoner.

Then the strong sense of call towards Sydney's CMM had sealed yet another commitment, this time to the cities of the world and the hidden lives of pain to be found in their anonymous streets. Surely, the inner voice said, it is possible to make a difference, to give cities a more caring heart, a more human face? The years that followed enabled me to make a small difference to life in the cities of South Africa each time someone in distress dialled Life Line.

Sydney was also the place where the inner voice asked what I was going to do about the compromises my faith had made with violence and war, inviting me to take a different road.

Being offered the chance to build a national church newspaper and later be a columnist in a Sunday paper was yet another privilege; could the pen sometimes make a difference?

In District Six I found Jesus in the courage and suffering of a community cast out of their homes and exiled beyond the city. Being permitted the privilege of carrying a tiny corner of their pain and joining their cries of protest was an intense gift.

Then to Johannesburg to different people and congregations ensnared by privilege and living comfortably with injustice, working with them to become "contrast people" instead, fashioning a new inclusive community called CMM, offering hospitality to all, care to children, the street people and the infirm, and sanctuary to the politically persecuted – expressing in multiple ways God's solidarity with the "least of these".[424]

Ministering amidst the smell of teargas and being invited beyond the confines of one denomination and faith into the wider ecumenism of all God's people of faith – and no faith – and witnessing together to another way of being South Africans. Standing with some of South Africa's great souls and taking on the might of the state together, saying to the oppressive darkness: "We beg to differ!"

The inner voice also took me to some exposed and lonely places, especially in leadership positions where "begging to differ" drew unwanted battle lines. In such times it was hard to cling to one's truth – and even harder when knowing that it might hurt or alienate friends.

Then joining those seeking to do the impossible: saying to the violence-mongers bent on tearing our nation to pieces for the sake of power: "We will differ and we will stop you," and telling those who thought reconciliation to be impossible, that to both remember *and* forgive was the only way, and that we South Africans could be the first in history to make it happen.

Finally there had come the incredible privilege of helping to form young women and men, both in the USA and South Africa, into servant-leaders and pastors of the people – and maybe even prophets – searching for deeper ways of being faithful and modelling a different way of being human and being Church.

Throughout this personal journey the nation was passing through the most climactic years of its painful history. When I arrived at my first church in 1960, our land was a prison. The horror of Sharpeville was turning the future toward confrontation, tumult and war. When I discharged my last duty 53 years later, it was in a South Africa free and finding peace. The cost of the years between was immense, not least for the man called to lead us, yet Nelson Mandela lived and led in a way that made all of us want to be better human beings. For a brief, glorious epoch we showed the world what a nation with that kind of spirit looks like. Only those privileged to have lived in both South Africas can testify to the almost intoxicating difference we felt in those first years following 1994.

But freedom also brings with it the liberty to be selfish and unwise. Under Mandela's successors we chose a lower road. We frittered away the moral capital and world-wide admiration that he and people like Desmond Tutu had garnered for the new South Africa. We permitted cynicism to replace the uniting vision of a Rainbow Nation. Instead of defending it, the chattering classes scratched delightedly at scabs scarcely healed and vied with each other to pronounce the vision dead. Whites went on ignoring the generous grace of those they had oppressed, choosing rather to snipe from the sidelines. Politicians with small souls exploited the nation's wounds instead of working to heal them. Someone like Jacob Zuma was an inevitable consequence, a grubby progeny of the new cynicism. As he and his venal colleagues set about ransacking the state and turning governance into thievery, only a dogged defence of the Constitution by some parliamentarians, a brave Public Defender, those "uncaptured" elements of the media and a thin line of judges saved us from complete implosion. Civil society rallied strongly and the churches, disappointingly silent since 1994, finally began to find their voice again. I celebrated seeing a renewed SACC emerge once more to hold this corrupt Caesar accountable.

Now he is gone, and as I write we have been promised that the corrupted 'ruling party' will try to become a 'serving party'. The ghost of Madiba is being evoked once more and self-seeking is to be replaced by the spirit of *Thuma mina ... Send me, Lord!* We need to work and pray that this new spirit finds a foothold in a battered and unbelieving citizenry. Those who got rich on thievery have not gone away; many are still in place while Zuma and his friends prowl in the wings looking for ways to return. Others, in the name of being 'radical' have tied their fortunes to fomenting hatred and division. I fear that together they could win once more unless all South Africans, black and white, women and men, rich and poor, make a supreme effort to find one another, hear one another and join one another in a common quest for true equity and justice. That is the challenge for those to whom we bequeath our legacy.

As for me and my generation, looking back I cannot think of a more privileged time to have been a South African, nor will I ever cease to be grateful for having been permitted to play a tiny part in the story.

Elizabeth died in January 2015.

The precious two years after handing over the seminary were spent very much together. She gave up volunteering with mothers in the Red Hill informal settlement above Simon's Town and journeying with the group of intellectually challenged young adults in their workshop at the local church. We were both free.

International invitations still came, and we visited Mississippi to engage with courageous people confronting the stubborn demons of racism there. A week with them convinced us that progress in South Africa was not as bad as some made out. At least in our homeland animosities were not wrapped in genteel denial but were on the table for all to see. The US summer of 2013 saw us spending seven carefree weeks in Washington DC, with me preaching and teaching at Mount Vernon Place UMC – a church led by Donna Claycomb-Sokol just a few blocks from the White House. Donna was one of my most exciting Duke students. On the Fourth of July Elizabeth got to see her heartthrob Neil Diamond performing live on the lawns of the Capitol.

In 2014 she began to experience worrying *petit mal* seizures but they were brought under control and by mid-year we were able to make a nostalgic road-trip to the Eastern Cape, spending a reflective day in the quiet village of Salem where our forbears had first settled on African soil in 1820. There, in the little Methodist chapel, we gave thanks for their lives and the sturdy faith they had bequeathed us. We also gave thanks for the Reverend William Shaw and other missionaries and educators who went out from this humble place. Because of them millions of black voices rise in Christian worship across the land. Both Nelson Mandela and Robert Sobukwe were impacted by their spiritual descendants at Healdtown College. One of history's ironies is that a faith spread under the shadow of Empire contained within it the seeds of colonialism's demise. Almost as proof of this we learned that South Africa's land restitution programme is returning much of the land the 1820 Settlers occupied to the Khoi and San people who roamed it even before the Xhosa ancestors of Mandela. This is a difficult prospect for families who have farmed there for 198 years, but the correction of past wrongs is not a painless process.

A day at Rhodes University completed one sentimental journey before we set out on another. In July we returned to the US for wonderful reunions with many precious friends. Elizabeth suffered no more seizures but she was a little unsure on her feet, speaking sometimes of "feeling fragile". This made her anxious but she met these challenges with determination.

December 2014 brought a providential gift. John, our first-born, was marrying again and his wedding to lovely Michelle brought the whole family together on the 13th. Chris and Dave and Alan joined their brother, plus Chris's Kim and David's Alex and our granddaughters Simone, Jessica, Frances, Sarah and Adrienne – and new grandson, Scott. Elizabeth looked lovely in black and silver and was showered with love. The wedding was followed by a gentle Christmas, first worshipping at Cape Town's CMM and then lunching with family at the home of Chris, Kim and their girls in Somerset West.

We shared a quiet 54th anniversary on 31 December, and enjoyed guests from Canada and the UK in the early weeks of 2015. Then on Monday, 26 January I woke at 5.30 am to find Elizabeth terribly distressed and struggling to get out of bed. She had suffered a stroke, immobilising her left side. We ambulanced her to hospital and Alan met her there. The next hours consisted of scans and other diagnostics and by mid-afternoon she was in a ward and more at peace, and we could sit together while she smiled at staff and learned their names. Chris and Simone came, as did Elizabeth's brother Allan and his wife Jo and a couple of other close friends. Her speech, while slurred, was intelligible and we could converse. She spoke by phone with John and David and later Kim and Frances. The last visitors that night were Gilbert and Jane, our deep friends from District Six days, and Gilbert led an evening prayer. Elizabeth was serene and beautiful, her smile all-embracing, her eyes bright. Around 9.30 pm I left with a smiling "Goodnight" and a promise that we would see each other in the morning.

Death came with a heart attack at 5.10 am. She called the nurses for some help and as they lifted her upright she suddenly paled and stopped breathing. Twenty minutes' work by the Resuscitation Team could not bring her back. By the time I got there the hospital had laid her gently in a private room and because it took time for family from far away to gather, we were with her for most of the hours of that day. She lay utterly serene as we took our turns to spend time with her, to reflect and pray and say our own thank yous. I left her at about 5 pm.

It was a hard leaving.

Messages came from all over the world. This woman who always said she felt most comfortable in one-on-one relationships had reached a multitude. Most of them wanted to tell of some transforming encounter with her. One ex-Duke student said simply, "I always felt more sure of myself when I had walked with Elizabeth ... she was my spiritual mother."[425]

A great congregation gathered in Rosebank Church under the shadow of the mountain, where her family had worshipped for generations, where she was baptised, where she met Jesus, where we first met and later married, and where we said goodbye to all four of our parents. It was a place soaked in generations of prayer and God had used it well to feed us, form us and tie us together. Her simple pine coffin with its rope handles had a single pink rose laid upon it, for our love, and standing behind it was a gift from her dear friend Janet Vercoe – a gloriously free arrangement of her favourite flowers, roses, daisies and her beloved roadside cosmos amongst them. I asked Alan to do the costly work of praying us into the service. Addressing Elizabeth's closest friend, he said:

> "Jesus, we have your name on our lips today for many reasons – not least because Mom carried your name in her heart for the longest time. From you she learned that she was carved on the palm of God's hand, always to be treasured, never to be forgotten; from you she learned that to be gentle is the greatest strength; from you she learned that no grave can hold a life lived lovingly and truthfully …"

The great and the good spoke. A visibly frail Desmond Tutu said beautiful things of his friend and former PA, and Jane and our sons each paid tribute. Eldest grandchild Simone spoke for Jessica, Frances, Sarah, Adrienne and Scott. My friend Reverend Peter Witbooi held it all together. Then the liturgy took us to the inevitable parting:

> O God, all that you have given us is yours.
> As first you gave Elizabeth to us,
> so now we give Elizabeth back to you.
> Receive her into the arms of your mercy.

We were married for 54 years and knew each other for 62. Carving a life after such loss is not easy, but our sons and the special people in their lives were all amazingly caring. When there is so much to be thankful for, gratitude brings a balm that slowly overwhelms one's sorrow. As for death, each year Elizabeth would purchase a little diary into which she entered various dates. After she died I paged through the one she had bought for 2015. It had the usual dental and haircut appointments and such, but against Easter Sunday she had written in bold letters: "Resurrection Day!" None of us knows exactly what happens after death but I do know this: our lives in all their totality – from birth to death and beyond – are held in loving hands. I've never needed more detail than that.

Much, much later, when the time seemed right, I took Elizabeth's ashes to Knysna, the beautiful estuary town some 500 km from our home. It was where we first fell in love. Whenever we holidayed there on Leisure Isle, Elizabeth used to take her cup of coffee every morning to a bench that looked out across the lagoon toward the Knysna Heads. It was her special, sacred spot. Now, just below it, in the warm embrace of a January evening, David and I waded out into the water and I quietly released her ashes into the ebbing tide, to be borne out through the Heads into the ocean beyond.

And what of that other love, the Church? I am deeply grateful to have spent my active life serving this amazing community which introduced me to Jesus of Nazareth, nurtured my spirituality, helped me want to be different and put me in places where I could be of some small service. However, I do know this: there is the Church of Jesus and there is this other thing that we keep thinking we can construct ourselves. The first is a community of hope and love that excites and challenges me; the second is a boring institution made for fuddy-duddies. I have a deep pride in the Wesleyan heritage that shaped my thinking and believe that it has much to give to a needful world. At its simplest it is about three priorities: introducing us to the life-changing, disturbing love of Jesus of Galilee, declaring what kind of world God wants, and birthing the kind of transformed people whose lives and actions make such a world possible. It sounds clear enough, but I know that given half a chance, we Christians lose the plot and slip comfortably into a cosy, irrelevant pietism. That is why I am grateful for the anti-apartheid struggle. It galvanised us and called us out into relevance. The Church is only the Church when it cares more about the world than about itself and it was because we forgot about ourselves for a while that our contribution had significance.

Since 1994 I'm not so sure. Judging by the headlines in our church newspaper[426] these days it seems that at a time when the world's trust in institutions is at an all-time low, that is where our focus lies. The institution – the comings and goings of its Bishops and endless reports of organisations meeting to talk to themselves – seems to obsess us. The world we are called to love and serve has little interest in these things; its concerns are light-years away. I venture to believe that Jesus has little interest in them either but continues to implore us to focus rather on "setting your mind on God's Kin-dom and God's justice above all else …"[427] Maybe that is why, for most of 2017 I found myself in yet another struggle, this time within my Church. The MCSA had dismissed a lesbian minister from our clergy ranks because she dared to marry the person she loved instead of hiding in a secret partnership. Many of us saw this as an unjust and loveless act – a form of apartheid based not on skin colour but sexual orientation – with the church now the oppressor. She asked me to represent her in the last of a long series of hearings of her case. It was a painful privilege to do so. In the end, we failed to move MCSA to a more enlightened position, which was very hurtful to her and to others like her in our ranks. I wrote to *New Dimension*: "I have no doubt that the church we love will one day look back on their treatment of this remarkable woman with sorrow and contrition."[428]

And so, the struggle continues, whether for the hearts and minds of men and women, or in religious or national institutions. Always it is about bringing our individual or corporate consciences into conformity with God's dream of a world of compassion and justice. The single life-span given to each of is our one chance to play a bit-part in God's long love-story with the world. If we hold back for fear that our effort can make no difference, we rob God. Playing our part offers no guarantees and we don't have the last word, but …

> You say the little efforts that I make
> will do no good: they never will prevail
> to tip the hovering scale
> where justice hangs in balance.
> I don't think
> I ever thought they would.
> But I am prejudiced beyond debate
> in favour of my right to choose which side
> shall feel the stubborn ounces of my weight.[429]

Endnotes

Chapter 1: The South African English
1 GH Calpin, *There Are No South Africans*, Thomas Nelson & Sons, London, 1941, p 189
2 shoes of animal hide (Afrik); goatee beard

Chapter 2: Homes and Schools
3 Manse is the name some Protestant denominations use to describe church-provided ministers' homes.

Chapter 3: Kilnerton
4 Other churches: Anglican 19.2%, Roman Catholic 13.4%, Lutheran 7.6%, London Missionary Society (Congregational) 5.6%, Bantu Presbyterian 3.3%, Dutch Reformed 2.5%, Church of Scotland 1%
5 Statistics from a 1950 letter by CK Storey to Dr Kimber, Richmond College, Surrey
6 Ibid
7 Morley Nkosi, *Memories of KTI, 1952-On* (private memoir)
8 Struggle stalwart JB Marks later became prominent in the Communist Party of South Africa, was forced into exile and died in Moscow. His remains were brought home in 2015 and buried in Tshing township outside Ventersdorp.
9 Stanley Mutlanyane Mogoba was an Alumnus of KTI and a teacher there at the time. He was active in the PAC and was imprisoned on Robben Island from 1964 to 1966. In prison he discerned a call to the ordained ministry and ultimately became Presiding Bishop of the Methodist Church of Southern Africa. In 1996 he resigned that position to become leader of the PAC in Parliament for a brief period.

Chapter 4: Then There Was Elizabeth
10 Neil Veitch, *Altius et Latius – Rondebosch Boys' High and Preparatory Schools 1897-1997*, published by the Centenary Committee, 1996
11 Two of Elizabeth's favourite hymns were Charles Wesley's *Jesu, Lover of my soul* ... and George Matheson's *O Love that wilt not let me go*...
12 Mr John Rees, Reverend John Thorne, Bishop Desmond Tutu
13 At IMSSA: Mr Charles Nupen, Ms Thandi Orleyne. At Wits/Vaal Peace Secretariat: Mr Peter Harris.

Chapter 5: The Sea
14 Asdic (named after the Royal Navy's Anti-Submarine Detection Investigation Committee) was an early form of sonar, using soundwaves in WWII to detect submerged U-boats.

Chapter 6: The God Thing
15 Kagawa (1888-1960) was a Christian preacher, pacifist and labour activist.
16 2 Corinthians 5:19
17 *When I Survey the Wondrous Cross*, Hymn & Psalms, 180, Methodist Publishing House, London, 1983
18 Scottish preacher Thomas Chalmers had a great influence on William Wilberforce. He preached a famous sermon under this title arguing that unless "a greater power grips our hearts, we remain powerless to change."
19 Title of a poem by Geoffrey Studdert-Kennedy, Anglican priest, beloved WWI chaplain and social reformer
20 John Wesley was a philosophy don and Fellow of Lincoln College who led the renewal. Younger brother Charles was a poet and prolific hymn writer who "set it to music."

ENDNOTES

21. John Wesley's Journal, 24 May 1738. For John it happened two days after Charles experienced it, in a meeting house in Aldersgate Street, London.
22. Quoted in JW Bready, *England Before and After Wesley*, Hodder & Stoughton, London, 1939, p 252
23. The 'Tolpuddle Martyrs' led by Methodist lay preacher George Loveless were farm labourers. Half of them were members of the local Tolpuddle Methodist Chapel. In 1834, in response to local farmers colluding to depress their wages, they formed a union, binding their members with a secret oath. For this they were sentenced to seven years' transportation to Australia. Within weeks, 30 000 people marched on Parliament demanding their release and two years later, Prime Minister Lord Melbourne, who as Home Secretary had sanctioned their sentence, had to authorise their release. They are seen as fathers of British trades unionism. Labour Prime Minister Harold Wilson once reminded the Party that "Labour owes more to Methodism than to Marx." Keir Hardie was a founder and first leader of the Labour Party in the House of Commons. He stood for peace, temperance, education, justice and social equity based firmly on Christian principles.
24. John Wesley, Journal, 9 February 1753
25. John Wesley, *Thoughts on Slavery*
26. John Wesley, sermon *On the Use of Money*
27. Based on Peter Storey, *And Are We Yet Alive? – Revisioning our Wesleyan Heritage in the New Southern Africa*, Methodist Publishing House, Cape Town, 2004, p 46
28. Barbara Brown Taylor, *Leaving Church: A Memoir of Faith*, Harper One, 2012, pp xiii, xiv, 219, 229-230
29. John 10:10.
30. Matthew 5:1 – 7:29
31. Matthew 5:1-16
32. Daniel W Erlander, *Manna & Mercy – A Brief History of God's Unfolding Promise to Mend the Whole Universe*, The Order of Saints Martin and Teresa, Mercer Island, Washington, 1992, p 45
33. Acts 10:34
34. A Franciscan blessing, author unknown

Chapter 7: Reluctant Scholar

35. 2 Timothy 1:12
36. Declaration on Missionary Policy, Conference of the Methodist Church of South Africa, Pietermaritzburg, October 1958
37. The International Defence and Aid Fund (IDAF) was set up by Canon John Collins in London to assist with legal and family support costs during the 1956 Treason Trial in Johannesburg. It went on to provide help in many other political trials. When it was banned in South Africa in 1966 it continued to operate through 'fronts' set up for the purpose. My father was Vice-Chair of IDAF in the Cape.
38. Letter from the Minister of Justice to Messrs PJ Storey and Others dated 16 September 1959 (author's papers)

Chapter 8: Stumbling into Ministry

39. Some church traditions hold Watch-Night services, typically beginning at 11.15 pm on New Year's Eve, to commit themselves to God for the coming year.
40. South Africa's currency went metric in February 1961 with the rand (R1.00) equalling ten former sterling shillings.
41. Alan Walker, *The Whole Gospel for the Whole World*, Marshall, Morgan & Scott, London, 1958
42. Reverend Theo Kotze was minister at Sea Point Methodist Church and a friend and mentor to me in the Camps Bay years. He later became prominent as Cape Town Director of the Christian Institute, fled into exile to escape arrest, and worked tirelessly against apartheid while in exile. Theo and Helen Kotze's lives have been celebrated in *Beyond Fear* by Jean Knighton-Fitt, Pre Text Publishers, Claremont, 2003.

Chapter 9: The Island

43. Quoted in J Whiteside, *History of the Wesleyan Methodist Church of South Africa*, Juta & Co, 1906, Cape Town, p 70. Apart from his work in Cape Town, Shaw trekked north. The first indigenous Methodist converts were a result of his preaching and he established the first Methodist Mission Station in South Africa at Lelyfountain, Namaqualand.
44. Nelson Mandela, *Long Walk to Freedom*, Macdonald Purnell, 1994, p 336. *Umkhonto we Sizwe* means 'Spear of the Nation'.

45 'Work sets you free', the slogan greeting prisoners arriving at Auschwitz and other Nazi camps
46 It was only later that Sobukwe was relocated to the house now displayed to tourists as his prison residence.
47 Told to the author
48 Daniels, from District Six in Cape Town, had joined the small Armed Resistance Movement after the multi-racial Liberal Party to which he belonged dissolved rather than submit to laws prohibiting multi-racial political parties. He and others had committed some small acts of sabotage before being betrayed by one of their own number.
49 John 8:36

Chapter 10: Life Line in the Lucky Country
50 Alan Walker, *Life Line – Help is as Close as the Telephone*, Collins Fontana Books, London, 1967, p 18
51 Psychotherapist Carl Rogers' client-centred counselling theory emphasising an approach of 'Unconditional Positive Regard' toward the client and 'Non-directive Counselling'. This approach was central to the training of lay Life Line counsellors.
52 The Gap was the ocean entrance to Sydney harbour. Its steep cliffs were a favourite suicide spot.
53 Donald Soper, minister at the West London Mission, famous for his 70 years of open-air preaching at Tower Hill on Wednesdays and Hyde Park Corner on Sundays. Later he became a Labour Peer, Lord Soper of Kingsway.
54 Harold R Henderson, *Reach for the World – The Alan Walker Story*, Collins, London, 1981, p 111
55 Lesbian, Gay, Bisexual, Transgender, Queer, Intersex. Variations of the acronym reflect the fluidity and ongoing debate around issues of sexual identity.

Chapter 11: District Six
56 On 11 February 1966, the then Minister of Community Development, PW Botha, had declared District Six to be a 'White Group Area'.
57 MCSA Circuits were still designated by race. There was also a 'European' Circuit known as the 'Metropolitan Circuit' and an 'African Circuit'. Being 'One and Undivided' might have been a declared ideal, but MCSA was a long way from it in practice.
58 'Cape Flats' was the name given to the low sand-flats stretching some 24 km south-eastward of Cape Town, used as a dumping ground for people of colour removed from their homes in areas declared 'white' under the Group Areas Act. New arrivals found mile after mile of two-room, breeze-block houses with asbestos roofs, no ceilings or internal doors, perched on the white sea-sand.
59 MCSA only adopted the Episcopal title 'Bishop' for its regional leaders in 1989. Previously they were known as 'Chairmen of the District'. To avoid confusion in this book I use the later titles throughout.
60 The Khoi were fairly light-skinned aboriginal hunter-gatherers, the first indigenous Southern Africans encountered by the seventeenth-century Dutch colonists.
61 Television was resisted by the apartheid regime for fear that reliance on foreign content would spread 'liberal' ideas. It was only introduced unwillingly to South Africa in 1976.
62 The Nuremburg-like Population Registration Act of 1950 provided the foundation for the entire apartheid edifice, requiring all South Africans to be classified by race. The initial categories of White, Coloured and Bantu were later expanded to include Cape Coloured, Malay, Griqua, Chinese, Indian and – just in case any person of colour had been missed – Other Coloured.
63 Television interview: Bill Moyers talks with Archbishop Desmond Tutu, PBS, 27 April 1999
64 The Race Classification Court, where 'borderline' race cases were adjudicated, was in Victoria Street, diagonally opposite the Anglican cathedral.
65 In Methodism the Leaders' Meeting is the body that gives direction to a congregation. It is chaired by the minister and consists of lay members with any kind of leadership responsibility in that congregation.
66 Various versions of this prayer are attributed to St Basil of Caesarea; this version found in my father's collection of prayers.

Chapter 12: The Ocean in a Single Drop
67 'Kerem' was similar to billiards but played on a smaller board with puck-shaped discs instead of balls.
68 Section 6 of the Immorality Act and the Mixed Marriages Act prohibited any sexual contact or marriages between persons of different races.
69 Tomb of a Muslim holy man, in this case Sheikh Mohamed Hassen Ghaibie Shah
70 In 1965 a 'Commission for the Renewal of the Church' was set up by the MCSA to undertake a wide-ranging revision of Methodist structures and practices in order to make them more relevant and effective.

ENDNOTES

71 Ibid, p 36
72 PJ Storey, *Towards Racially Inclusive Congregations*, 1970
73 Ibid
74 We were not yet sensitised to sexist language. My Brother and Me courses involved both women and men.
75 A small 'coloured' village abutting on the white suburb of Pinelands
76 Dr James Leatt was later to become a professor at the University of Cape Town, then Vice-Chancellor of Natal University and widely respected as a consultant in the world of mediation and conflict resolution.
77 In all our projects, The Carpenter's House, Nuwedorp Church in Darling, Gateway Children's Centre and The Christian Leadership Centre, we were mightily assisted by Henk Koolhaas, a Dutch-born senior architect in the Cape Town City Council. In his spare time and without charging fees, he produced the designs we needed.
78 One of the spin-offs from the MLK Memorial Service was a request by spouses of US embassy staff to get involved in one of our ministries, so they formed Friends of Gateway, pledged to raise our annual deficit. Gateway still functions 50 years later.
79 Dr Gilbert Lawrence later studied Community Medicine, became superintendent of major hospitals in Cape Town, including the Red Cross Children's Hospital and Groote Schuur, rose to become Director-General of Health in the Western Cape and ultimately Director-General of the province itself, retiring in 2016. Jane Lawrence later returned to education, earning a number of degrees, including an MEd. She was detained without trial for two weeks in 1985 and has spent the rest of her life helping form better teachers. They are both still active in the Central Methodist Mission in Cape Town.

Chapter 13: Then Came the Bulldozers
80 GG (Government Garage) licence plates identified government vehicles.
81 Donald W Shriver Jr, *Honest Patriots – Loving a Country Enough to Remember its Misdeeds*, Oxford, 2005, p 75
82 Alan Walker, Ed, *See How They Grow,* Collins Fount Paperbacks, 1979, p 86
83 See Ch 14
84 *The Holy City,* 1892. Music: Michael Maybrick (alias Stephen Adams), lyrics based on Revelation 21:25: *The gates of the city shall never be shut by day – and there will be no night*: Frederic E Weatherly
85 *History of the Central Methodist Mission (CMM)*, cmm.org.za

Chapter 14: Amateur Journo
86 Boraine would rise to be President of MCSA in 1971 before being seconded to industry to lead the transformation programme in the Anglo American Corporation. He then became the Progressive Party MP who walked out of Parliament with Dr Van Zyl Slabbert to launch the Institute for Democratic Alternatives in South Africa (IDASA); later he was Vice-Chairperson of the Truth and Reconciliation Commission.
87 Of the 'mainline' churches at the time, only the United Congregational Church of Southern Africa ordained women ministers.
88 *Dimension*, Vol 1, No 4, June 1970, p 4
89 Bona fide religious bodies in SA do not pay rates on those parts of their properties used exclusively for religious purposes.
90 NYLTP was the National Youth Leadership Training Programme set up by Alex Boraine. It consisted of three months of multi-racial, residential training, after which the participants were appointed to youth leadership positions across South Africa. Because of its multi-racial and progressive character, NYLTP and its instructors were closely watched and often harassed by Security Police. One ex-participant died at their hands in Kimberley.
91 Inkatha was the increasingly violent Zulu-based movement in KwaZulu-Natal used by Buthelezi to propel his political ambitions. In the late 80s and early 90s it was armed by the apartheid regime to destabilise the advance to democracy. An impi is a Zulu military formation.
92 *Dimension*, Vol VII, No 6, July 1976, p 1
93 Ibid, Vol V, No 2, March 1974, p 2
94 Ibid, Vol V, No 3, April 1974, p 2
95 Ibid, Vol VI, No 9, October 1975, p 2
96 Ibid, Vol VII, No 8, September 1976, p 2
97 Ibid, Vol VII, No 11, December 1976, p 2

98   Ibid, Vol VIII, No 7, August 1977, p 2
99   Ibid, Vol VIII, No 10, November 1977, p 8
100 Ibid, Vol IX, No 5, July 1978, p 1
101 Conversation with Reverend Sizwe Mbabane, the most senior black minister to defy Matanzima
102 *Dimension*, Vol VIII, No 11, December 1977, p 7
103 Ibid
104 Ibid
105 Ibid
106 Ibid
107 Ibid, Vol VIII, No 11, December 1977, p 6
108 Ibid, p 7
109 Minutes of Conference, Methodist Church of Southern Africa, 1977, pp 201-202

Chapter 15: Young Church
110 Initially an apartment building known as Civic Hill, the structure later became the Protea Hotel by Marriott.
111 Referencing the radical statement by Jesus in Matthew 25:31ff, that when we reach out in healing ways to the hungry and thirsty, the stranger, the naked, the sick and the prisoner, we are doing these things to him.
112 The issue was whether a church congregation was a club obsessed with numerical growth and preoccupied with entertaining its members, or whether it existed primarily for those outside its membership. It is my conviction that a congregation is only truly a Church when engaging with the needs of the world. When congregations commit to caring about these needs – "doing justly and loving mercy" – their members become less obsessed with getting to heaven and more passionate about bringing heaven to earth, which is what Jesus taught us to pray and work for. Only then do they find new life themselves.
113 The concept of 'call' rather than institutional 'programming' deciding the shape of a congregation's ministries belongs primarily to the famous Church of the Savior in Washington DC. I visited this remarkable community in November 1966, and a number of times thereafter. It was the most authentic church community I had ever known. The New Testament principles inspiring its life are described in *Call to Commitment: The Story of the Church of the Saviour*, by Elizabeth O'Connor, Harper & Row, New York, 1963.
114 Matthew 13: 31 – 32
115 The name change denoted our location immediately below the new Johannesburg Civic Centre as well as our commitment to serve the city.
116 "If of thy mortal goods, thou art bereft, and from thy slender store two loaves alone to thee are left, sell one and from the dole, buy hyacinths to feed the soul." – Muslihuddin Sadi, thirteenth century Persian poet
117 *Hymns & Psalms*, No 431, Methodist Publishing House, London, 1986
118 Forty-five years later, with demographic and other changes, the ex-Braamfontein congregation now has sole use of the CCMC building.
119 Genesis 1:1 – 27, Acts 10:34, Galatians 3:28
120 The United Party, now defunct, was the official opposition in the white Parliament at that time, opposed to the worst excesses of the apartheid regime, but only a shade less white supremacist.

Chapter 16: Spreading Wings
121 Paper presented at a conference on Human Genetics, Johannesburg, September 1978, *South African Medical Journal*, 26 October 1980
122 Seminar on Communicating with the Dying Patient, Wits Medical School, 1978
123 See Chapters 22 – 25
124 African Enterprise was a para-Church team based in Pietermaritzburg and headed by Cassidy. A dynamic but politically cautious evangelical Anglican, he had credibility in conservative-evangelical and some Dutch Reformed circles.
125 Very soon after, as church-state relations became much more strained, the notion of churches seeking government permission for such a gathering would have been rejected outright.
126 'Congress Touches Heart of God's Cross in SA', in *Dimension*, April 1973, p 1
127 'Split was Misunderstood', ibid, p 2
128 *Prisoners of Hope – The Story of Christians at the Crossroads*, African Enterprise, Pietermaritzburg, 1974, p 79

ENDNOTES

129 Lewis V Baldwin, *Toward the Beloved Community*, Pilgrim Press, Cleveland, Ohio, 1995, p 83
130 Two Keys to Crisis Care – the Layman and the Telephone. Address to second Life Line International Conference, Chicago, 1969
131 Carl Rogers' 'client-centred counselling' discouraged any directive advice by counsellors.
132 Beyers Naudé confided that it was based on a fear of losing Jewish financial support.
133 In the late 60s there were approximately 600 telephone subscribers in the whole of Soweto.
134 Coincidentally, all were prominent Methodist ministers. Life Line Southern Africa owes an enormous debt to them for their leadership.
135 Life Line Southern Africa Directory of Centres, 22 April 1996
136 Rev Sir Alan Walker was knighted in 1981 for his services to the Australian people. He died in 2003 in Sydney at age 91.
137 *Counselling and Christian Faith* – The Sir Alan Walker Lectures, 10th Conference and 30th Anniversary of Life Line International, Sydney, Australia, October 1996
138 "In accepting the violence of the cross, God, in Jesus Christ, sanctified violence into a redemptive instrument for bringing into being a fuller human life." Address by Canon Burgess Carr at WCC Assembly, Nairobi, 1975
139 In October 1975 disguised South African troops, initially with the support of the American CIA, mounted a secret invasion of Angola called Operation Savannah. By mid-December they were nearing Luanda when news of it began to leak out. The CIA abandoned the South Africans and international pressure forced Prime Minister Vorster to order a retreat. The South African public had been kept in the dark.

Chapter 17: No Soft Landing

140 Hymn No 669, *The Methodist Hymn Book*, Methodist Conference Office, London, 1933
141 Deaconesses – from the Greek *Diakonia*, meaning humble service – were women ordained primarily to serve the poor.
142 The famous rambling old Methodist Central Hall had been replaced in 1966 by a new Central Methodist Church with its 900-seat sanctuary, numerous halls, offices and accommodation spaces.
143 The Johannesburg Central Circuit, as it was then named, consisted of CMC, CCMC (my previous congregation in Braamfontein) and two congregations in Jeppe and Bertrams served by one minister.
144 Motlalepula Chabaku served in various positions with the United Methodist Church in the US before returning to South Africa, where she ultimately became the Speaker of the Free State Legislature. She died in 2012.
145 Rev David Newby, letter written 31 December 1991
146 Jeremiah 1: 18–19
147 Matthew 5:9
148 Letter from John C Rees, 23 June 1976
149 SACC headquarters in Braamfontein at that time
150 After a carefully orchestrated diplomatic effort, Vorster's 'outward policy' had been rewarded by a meeting with Henry Kissinger, planned for 23 June in Bodenmais, West Germany.
151 Jeremiah 9:1
152 Later founder-leader of the National Union of Mineworkers, chief ANC negotiator of the Constitution, and currently President of SA
153 Helen Muller, *Thlokomelong* – document describing Aims, December 1980
154 Johannesburg Central Circuit: *Superintendent's Report for year January to December 1977*

Chapter 18: Broken Open Church

155 The Tenebrae is a candle-light service in which the record of Christ's last days in Jerusalem is read, with the candles being gradually extinguished until the people, anticipating Good Friday, leave in total darkness.
156 State President PW Botha
157 From *Celebrate with me!* – preached to the 15th World Methodist Council gathering, Kenyatta Centre, Nairobi, 1986
158 Rhema Bible Church now claims 40 000 members and is based on a massive campus in Randburg. At the Rustenburg Conference between the Dutch Reformed, SACC-linked and Pentecostal churches in 1990, McCauley publicly confessed that Pentecostals had been silent through a revolution.
159 *What a Family*, November 1991

160 The candle surrounded by barbed wire is the official logo of Amnesty International. I must now confess that in introducing it to our altar I failed to ask the appropriate permission. Ours was made by staff member Wendy Young and I trust that its rapid spread across South African churches provided Amnesty with sufficient free publicity to earn me their forgiveness.
161 John 1:5
162 This widely used prayer is attributed to Bishop Trevor Huddleston, Community of the Resurrection. At CMM we sang it to a tune composed by our young choirmaster, Craig Tocher.
163 Mandela refers in his prison diary to one such broadcast sermon titled *Forgiveness* on 20 August 1986. Dennis Cruywagen, *The Spiritual Mandela: The Role of Religion in the Life of Nelson Mandela*, 2016
164 Statement by Peter Storey in *What a Family*, February 1990, p 2
165 *What a Family*, June 1979, p 9
166 *Sunday Star*, March 1993
167 Certain luxury 'international' hotels received permission to host foreign business people of colour in their restaurants, but ordinary South Africans were not permitted to take advantage of this.
168 *Sunday Star*, March 1993. The People Centre operated for fifteen years until it was closed in March 1993 "due to the present economic climate," two years after I had left CMM.
169 Wesley preached in the open air, welcoming all, but those who responded to the Gospel were immediately placed into disciplined 'Classes' under a lay leader to enable their spiritual growth.
170 GIFT (Growing in Faith Together) groups met in people's homes around the city and suburbs.
171 The Fort prison was very near CCMC and inmates from other prisons were also sent there to be 'processed out'. After 1994 the new Constitutional Court was built on the site, constructed partly out of the bricks of the old prison.
172 While she was with us Lindi Myeza was named the *Star* newspaper's 'Woman of the Year' for her sterling work after the June 16 uprising. Years later the President of South Africa invested her with the Order of the Baobab for her services to nation-building.
173 Enabling landlords to 'unbundle' apartment blocks and sell off each apartment separately, making enormous profits
174 *What a Family*, August 1989, p 3
175 We had fought for this classification to be established in MCSA to encourage city ministries across the land to become multi-racial and enable them to retain a viable witness in the face of much heavier costs than those in the suburbs and townships.
176 Alan had declared himself a Conscientious Objector. See Ch 21: *Shadows of War*
177 Helen went on to complete her training as a psychotherapist at the famous Tavistock Clinic in London. She recently retired from long years of practice with the UK National Health Service.
178 *CMM Superintendent's Report*, 1988, p 1

Chapter 19: Ministry With a Whiff of Teargas
179 For the full story of CMM's unique history as a sanctuary and especially its recent care for refugees, read Christa Kuljian, *Sanctuary: How an Inner-City Church Spilled onto a Sidewalk*, Jacana, 2013.
180 Psalms 46:1, 31:3 & 20, 91:2
181 Matthew 2:13-15
182 See Ch 21: *Shadows of War*. The Conscription Advice Bureau was a front for the banned End Conscription Campaign.
183 Action Committee to Stop Evictions
184 The South African Railways and Harbour Workers' Union strike involved seven workers being killed by police and 16 000 dismissed. Some workers themselves committed horrific acts. Their meetings were repeatedly broken up by police. Ultimately the strikers prevailed and the sacked workers were reinstated.
185 *Knobkierie:* wooden stick with a knotty or carved club head at one end, claimed by some rural Africans as a 'cultural weapon'
186 We now know that the bomb was organised by notorious secret police operative Craig Williamson, who confessed to it at the TRC. For his arrogance and lack of remorse I have found him the most difficult to forgive. The bomb-maker was one Roger (Jerry) Raven. Both were amnestied by the TRC.
187 The CCB (Civil Cooperation Bureau) was a secret Military Intelligence hit-squad operated by Military Intelligence.
188 We also banned the national flag, but not only because it had come to represent the hated apartheid regime. The post-1994 South African flag is also not permitted in Methodist churches, not out of disrespect, but simply because Caesar's banner has no place in the house of God.

ENDNOTES

189 *Sunday Star*, March 1993
190 'Red Russian' Swanepoel was notorious for ordering the police to shoot protesting schoolchildren on 16 June 1976, and headed up a task force in the following days that was responsible for killing many more. He later became the much-feared chief interrogator of the Security Branch, overseeing the torture of many detainees.
191 Acts 16:16–34
192 *"Look, you're priests. Please promise me you won't come out of here."*
193 Acts 16:28
194 John 16:3
195 Psalm 79:1
196 *Sentence them to Church! – With God in the Crucible – Preaching Costly Discipleship*, Abingdon Press, 2001, p 118
197 *The Citizen*, 1 September 1988, p 2
198 See Chapters 24 and 36
199 White Wolves
200 The Delmas Treason Trial was the prosecution of 22 UDF activists. It lasted from 1985-1988. Eleven were found guilty, but this verdict was later overturned by the Supreme Court.
201 "We have a problem ... the priest says they're in the church itself."
202 "Move!"
203 "Finish off, priest, finish off!"
204 The Afrikaner Broederbond was a secret society of Afrikaans political, academic, religious, military and business elite, dedicated first to establishing an Afrikaner republic outside of the British Commonwealth, and then ensuring the hegemony of Afrikaner culture and political power. It is widely regarded as the invisible hand behind the policies and actions of the apartheid regime.
205 See Chapters 20 – 27 especially.

Chapter 20: Encounters in the Public Square

206 *Sunday Times*, 10 August 1980
207 "Oh, you two are speaking sh-t!"
208 Bold for a ten-year-old and definitely learned outside our home.
209 JHP Serfontein, *Sunday Times*, 19 July 1981
210 Obedience Charter, 1981
211 Serfontein, op cit
212 Ever since 1981 small prayer and discussion groups had gathered in the Nicolaikirche in Leipzig and by 1989 they had become a nation-wide movement. On 9 October between 80 000 and 100 000 people marched from the church, defying the Stasi secret police and claiming "We are the People." The Wall fell just over a month later.
213 The Baader-Meinhof Group, also known as the Red Army Faction, was a ruthless West German far-left militant organisation responsible for numerous terrorist acts over three decades. Some of its members were later imprisoned in West Germany and there remain questions about the supposed suicide of Baader himself and others.
214 Now Polokwane in Limpopo province
215 The Tonton Macoute were a special operations paramilitary unit under Haitian President 'Papa Doc' Duvalier's personal control, used to terrorise the populace and keep him in power.
216 *The Citizen*, 26 March 1985
217 Ermelo, where Tutu's father was a teacher for some time
218 The 'Total Strategy' was PW Botha's response to what he called the 'Total Onslaught' against South Africa by 'Communist-inspired terrorism' and the international community. Bypassing the usual parliamentary and administrative channels, Botha assembled a militarised Security Council, which wielded the real power in the land.
219 Emmanuel Lafont's outspoken support for the liberation struggle was not always approved by his superiors and consequently he used to wryly call me 'my Methodist Bishop'. He served in Soweto for fourteen years and I was saddened when his Order recalled him to France after the 1994 election. He later became Catholic Bishop of Cayenne in French Guiana.
220 The Rustenburg Declaration, November 1991
221 The Afrikaanse Protestante Kerk

Chapter 21: Shadows of War
222 Nicholas Monsarrat, *The Cruel Sea*, Cassell & Co, London, 1952, p 200
223 Clause 10(c) of the Defence Further Amendment Bill made it an offence to "encourage, aid, incite, instigate, suggest or otherwise cause any person to refuse to do military service."
224 Rev Don Williams, who with his colleague Rev Fred Celliers suffered for their faithfulness to the Gospel within the SADF. The encounter took place on 23 September 1985.
225 *The Star*, 19 February 1982
226 *Beeld*, 20 February 1982
227 *Cape Argus*, 25 February 1982
228 Book of set prayers for morning and evening of each day, and other prayers
229 Afrikaner Resistance Movement – a Nazi-like ultra-right-wing movement dedicated to maintaining white supremacy in South Africa
230 The battle of Cuito Cuanavale was fought in south-east Angola from November 1987 to March 1988 between UNITA/SADF forces on one side and FAPLA/Cuban forces on the other. The outcome is still a matter of contention, with each side claiming a victory of sorts. What is certain, however, is that the intensive fighting there and the stalemate that followed signalled an imminent end to South Africa's Border War and the withdrawal of SADF and Cuban troops from Angola.
231 Margaret Williams, *The Velveteen Rabbit; or How Toys Become Real*, David R Godine, 1983, Boston, pp 4-6
232 Theresa Edlmann, 'The Scars of Conscription' in *The Natal Mercury*, 3 September 2015

Chapter 22: A Blow Falls
233 The United Democratic Front was the major internal anti-apartheid movement of the 1980s. Formed in 1983, it was a non-racial coalition of more than 400 civic, church, students', workers' and other organisations.
234 Message of the 4th Assembly of the World Council of Churches, Uppsala, Sweden, 1968
235 Circuit Stewards were the lay leaders of a Circuit, responsible with the Superintendent Minister for its proper administration and for the care, housing etc of all the ministers in the Circuit.
236 John Rees interview with Linda W Keister, 5 May 1987
237 *Councils in the Ecumenical Movement – South Africa 1904-75*, David Thomas, SACC Johannesburg, 1979, p 57
238 Ibid, p 64
239 Roelofse had been appointed by John to open an Ombudsman office protecting consumers from abuse in the marketplace, but showed an abnormal interest in the lives of his colleagues. The fact that he was white made it more sensitive. While he did expose some issues relating to SACC funds, his numerous accusations did much damage. During the Eloff Commission hearings, Adv Sydney Kentridge demolished much of his evidence and virtually established that he had set out deliberately to undermine the Council.
240 Mokoena turned out to be a pliant government stooge. After leaving SACC and with government help, he set up an organisation that majored in vilifying the SACC. He was decorated by the regime for his work.
241 Handwritten letter from SACC Senior Vice-President to General Secretary, SACC, 9 June 1979
242 Minutes of Presidium meeting, office of the General Secretary, 10 April 1981
243 The Asingeni Relief Fund had been set up initially to assist victims and families arising out of the 1976 youth uprising. It evolved into much wider use for victims of the regime. Seventy per cent went to defence costs and legal expenses (eg for the Steve Biko inquest). It was always at the complete discretion of the General Secretary.
244 Minutes of Presidium meeting, 13 April 1981, President's Office, Khotso House, 12.00 noon
245 Minutes of Presidium meeting, 14 April 1981, CMM Board Room, 2.00 pm
246 Letter from Bishop Philip Russell, dated 15 April 1981
247 ffrench-Beytagh was initially held without trial and brutally interrogated, then charged with furthering the objectives of the ANC and SACP and found guilty. His appeal, however, was upheld and he left South Africa the same day.
248 Letter from John Rees to the Presidium, dated 21 April 1981

Chapter 23: Perfect Storm
249 Notes on SACC Executive meeting of 22 April 1981, Khotso House
250 Letter from President of SACC to Mr Tim Potter, Alex, Aiken & Carter, Accountants, 1 September 1981

ENDNOTES

251 'SACC Cleared Rees of Theft and Fraud Allegations', *The Star*, 13 October 1981
252 'SACC President Hits at Remark from Bench', *The Star*, 10 October 1981
253 *Cape Times*, 15 October 1981; *Rand Daily Mail*, 28 October 1981
254 Minutes of SACC Executive of 27/28 October 1981
255 Letter from Mr ML Marais, Secretary to the Commission of Inquiry into the SACC, dated 3 December 1981
256 Letter from Bishop Desmond Tutu to Peter Storey, 17 November 1981
257 'Second New Year', a uniquely Cape Province holiday celebrated on 2 January
258 Luke 21:28
259 *Stand Upright – Your Liberation is Near!* Presidential Address, Reverend Peter Storey, SACC National Conference, June 1982
260 Meeting of the 'Expanded Presidium', 13 July 1982
261 Later to be Desmond Tutu's successor as Archbishop of Cape Town

Chapter 24: Bearing Witness
262 Evidence-in-Chief of Bishop Desmond Tutu, General Secretary of the SACC, presented to the Eloff Commission of Inquiry on 1 September 1982, published as *The Divine Intention* (SACC publication)
263 The CLSA was exposed as having been secretly funded by the apartheid regime as part of the Information Department's propaganda war against South Africa's 'enemies'.
264 Luke 12:11-12: "When they bring you before the synagogues and the rulers and the authorities, do not worry about how or what you are to speak in your defence, or what you are to say; for the Holy Spirit will teach you in that very hour what you ought to say." (NIV)
265 Evidence-in-Chief of Rev Peter John Storey, President of the SACC, presented to the Eloff Commission of Inquiry on 9 March 1983, published as *Here we Stand* (SACC publication)
266 Matthew 25:31-46
267 Record of the Commission of Inquiry into the SACC, 9-11 March 1983, Vols 41-45, Lubbe Recordings, Pretoria
268 Such a declaration would have crippled the SACC by preventing it from receiving any monies from outside of South Africa. At the time 96% of the Council's R4 300 000 budget was sourced internationally.
269 Shirley Du Boulay, *Tutu – Voice of the Voiceless,* Hodder & Stoughton, 1988, p 178

Chapter 25: Trial by Friendship
270 Rees "is meticulous, self-denying," *Cape Times*, 21 April 1983
271 Joseph Lelyveld, 'Fraud Case Splits South Africa Church Group' in *The New York Times*, 21 June 1983
272 Jo-Ann Collings, 'John Rees has Racially Divided the SACC', in *Rand Daily Mail*, 22 June 1983
273 Ibid
274 Wilmar Utting, 'Churchmen meet to decide on action over Rees', in *Sunday Express*, 22 May 1983
275 Shirley Du Boulay, op cit, p 180

Chapter 26: National Leadership
276 The position of Presiding Bishop of MCSA is now a full-time appointment at Methodist House in Johannesburg, carrying no other responsibilities. The incumbent is elected for a five-year term, renewable once.
277 A clear majority, ie 51% of the votes cast, was required to be elected.
278 *Relocation: the Churches' Report on Forced Removals*, produced by the SA Catholic Bishops' Conference & South African Council of Churches in co-operation with the Surplus People's Project, 1984
279 (Resistência Nacional Moçambicana) RENAMO and Machel's ruling FRELIMO party fought a sixteen-year civil war from 1976, in which a million people died before a peace accord ended the fighting.
280 Scandalous (Afrik)
281 Johannesburg *Star*, 3 April 1984
282 *Sunday Times*, 22 April 1984
283 James M Markham, 'Europeans Give Botha a Frosty Visit' in *New York Times*, 10 June 1984
284 Handwritten letter from Nelson Mandela, dated 11 June 1984
285 *The Wellsprings of our Hope*, President's Induction Address, MCSA Conference, Pretoria, October 1984
286 *Ministers as Messengers of Hope*, President's address to the Ministerial Session, ibid
287 *Finding Hope for South Africa*, President's address to the Representative Session, ibid
288 *Sunday Star*, 21 October 1984

289 Editorial, *Rand Daily Mail*, 24 October 1984
290 *Sunday Star*, ibid

Chapter 27: Among God's People
291 See Ch 29: Hostage Crisis
292 *Statement by the President of the Methodist Church of Southern Africa on the Langa Shootings and other Violence in SA*, issued 25 March 1985
293 MCSA was divided into eleven Districts at that time. In each District the annual Synod of clergy and lay leaders, presided over by the Bishop, usually assembled in June. The call for additional one-day 'crisis' Synods in April 1985 was unprecedented.
294 A Message to the Methodist People, Signed by Rev Peter Storey, President of the Conference, Rev Stanley Mogoba, Secretary of the Conference, and ten District Bishops, 7 May 1985
295 See Ch 21 Shadows of War
296 We were later able to bring Rev Matussi to South Africa for further surgery and the fitting of a prosthetic leg.
297 Methodist Relief was at that time a sophisticated aid operation run by MCSA.
298 Luke 3:11-22
299 See Ch 9 The Island
300 Wesley's Chapel in City Road, London is the spiritual home of world Methodism. It was built under Rev John Wesley's supervision and opened in 1778. The house he lived in for the last eleven years of his life stands in the chapel precincts, as does his grave. Wesley died in 1791.
301 In those years, every return from an international trip involved being held by authorities until all other passengers had gone, with elaborate searches of luggage and clothing, and lengthy questioning about my travels.
302 Alan Cowell, 'Defiance in South Africa', *New York Times* Johannesburg bureau, 14 April 1985
303 Barbecue (Afrik)
304 'Storey Hits at Falwell', *The Citizen*, 20 August 1985
305 Philippe Denis and Graham Duncan, *The Native School that Caused all the Trouble – A History of the Federal Theological Seminary of South Africa*, Cluster Publications, Pietermaritzburg, 2011, p 184
306 Ibid, pp 182, 183
307 By this time Nelson Mandela had been moved from Robben Island to Pollsmoor Prison, located in the Southern Suburbs of Cape Town.
308 Joshua 3: 13-17
309 Michael Cassidy, *The Passing Summer – A South African Pilgrimage in the Politics of Love*, Hodder & Stoughton, London, 1989, p 302
310 'Conference Hears of Year of Crisis', in *Dimension*, Mid-October, 1985, p 1
311 Matthew 25:31-46

Chapter 28: Stress Fractures
312 Conflict between brothers (Afrik)
313 Until 1990 membership of the ANC, PAC and SACP was illegal, so such membership would have been secret.
314 Interview with LW Keister, 1985
315 Allan A Boesak & Charles Villa-Vicencio, editors, *When Prayer Makes News*, Westminster Press, 1986, p 16
316 Archbishop Philip Russell, Pastoral Letter to be Read from all Pulpits on Sunday, 16th June 1985
317 Rev Peter Storey, President's Update sent to all Methodist leaders, 14 June 1985
318 John Allen, *Rabble-Rouser for Peace: Authorised Biography of Desmond Tutu*, Random House, 2006, p 331
319 *When Prayer Makes News*, p 18
320 Known simply as 'The Kairos Document', its full title was *Challenge to the Church, A Theological Comment on the Political Crisis in South Africa*.
321 Bernard Spong with Cedric Mayson, *Come Celebrate! Twenty-Five Years of the South African Council of Churches*, SACC Communications, 1993, p 121
322 Interview with the author at UNISA, Pretoria, 1990
323 Ibid
324 *Challenge to the Church, A Theological Comment on the Political Crisis in South Africa*, p 29

ENDNOTES

325 See 'Conscripts to their Age – ANC Operational Strategy 1976-1986', Howard Barrell's DPhil thesis, quoted in Padraig O'Malley, *Shades of Difference: Mac Maharaj and the Struggle for South Africa*, Viking, 2007, p 202
326 Quoted by H Paul Santmire in *The Christian Century*, 30 October 1985, p 965
327 Peter Storey, *Kairos – A Response*, Symposium on Kairos Document, CCMC, Braamfontein, 24 August 1986
328 Allister Sparks, *Tomorrow is Another Country*, Struik, 1994, p 26
329 Ibid

Chapter 29: Hostage Crisis
330 Letter from Nelson Mandela to the author, 11 June 1984
331 Emma Gilbey, *The Lady: The Life and Times of Winnie Mandela,* Jonathan Cape, 1993, p 159. Ms Gilbey spent many hours with me and many others when researching her book and in my view hers remains the most thorough and accurate reconstruction of events in print.
332 Emma Gilbey, op cit, p 186
333 Aubrey Mokoena was head of the Release Mandela Campaign and was living under certain restrictions at the time.
334 It turned out that the killer, Jerry Richardson, worked at times as an *agent provocateur* for the Security Police. Other Football Team members are suspected of having done the same.

Chapter 30: Confronting Expediency
335 The story was broken by *Weekly Mail* reporter Thandeka Gqubule, daughter of Dr Simon Gqubule, a prominent Methodist Church leader. Following Winnie's death, those attempting to rewrite the story falsely accused Thandeka and another journalist of being Security Branch spies.
336 Later to become Minister of Police in the Mandela government

Chapter 31: Soul Wounds
337 From contemporaneous verbatim notes made by the author
338 Full text of this Eulogy in Peter Storey, *With God in the Crucible – Preaching Costly Discipleship*, Abingdon Press, 2002, Ch 16: *I'm so Sorry, Mama*, p 121
339 Emma Gilbey, op cit, p 229
340 Capital punishment was still part of the South African legal system at the time. In its very first ruling, the Constitutional Court of the new dispensation struck it down. Jerry Richardson was not executed but died in prison in 2009.
341 Emma Gilbey, op cit, p 261
342 George Bizos, *Odyssey to Freedom,* Random House, 2007
343 The witnesses who helped construct this 'alibi' have all since retracted their statements. Moreover, a security policeman named Daniel Bosman, who was in charge of tapping Winnie's Diepkloof telephone, has said that she was recorded speaking on it during the weekend 29 to 31 December, when she claimed to be in Brandfort http//www.justice.gov.za/trc/media%5C1998%5C9801/s980128g.htm
344 Emma Gilbey, op cit, p 261
345 Martin Williams, *The Citizen*, 29 November 1997
346 At the time of Winnie's death retired Police General George Fivaz claimed to have reopened the investigation into Stompie's murder at the request of Sydney Mufamadi, Minister of Police in the post-1994 administration, and that no connection between Winnie and the murder could be established. I was neither approached nor interviewed.
347 *Mail & Guardian*, 5 December 1997
348 Walter Wink, 'On Not Becoming What We Hate' in *Sojourners Magazine*, 16 November 1986, p 15
349 Truth & Reconciliation Commission of South Africa Report, Vol 2, p 581, October 1998, Juta, Cape Town
350 Ibid, p 568
351 Ibid
352 Ibid, p 569
353 Ibid, p 570
354 Ibid

Chapter 32: The Thin Orange Line

355 Peace Monitors wore an orange vest with two superimposed doves on the front. The original design had one dove but at the last minute it was learned that a single dove was apparently a bad omen in Zulu culture.
356 Bishop's Address to the Annual Synod of the Central District, MCSA, June 1990
357 The National Peace Accord structure was sketched out by Dr Theuns Eloff, a theologically trained Afrikaner who ran the Consultative Business Movement at the time. His original rough organograms, sketched out on newsprint, are virtually the only acknowledgement of the NPA to be found in the Apartheid Museum in Johannesburg.
358 The 33-page accord was signed on 14 September 1991 by all the parties except the white right wing, the PAC and the Azanian People's Organisation (AZAPO) and was established by Parliament in the National Peace Institutions Act.
359 Seminar on Violence, Yeoville, 29 October 1991
360 Ibid, p 27
361 The Wits/Vaal RPC ran eighteen LPCs covering all of Johannesburg and Soweto, the East and West Rand and areas south of Johannesburg like Sebokeng, Sharpeville and Boipatong.
362 Peter Harris was so effective as leader of the Wits/Vaal RPC that he was later seconded to the Independent Electoral Commission to set up the entire 1994 election monitoring process. David had by that time taken up a Fulbright scholarship at Harvard, but was called back to assist him once more as his deputy. Harris later recorded the story of this period in *Birth: The Conspiracy to Stop the 1994 Election*, published by Umuzi, Cape Town, 2010. In it he describes Dave as someone with "an exceptional ability to plan and organise ... combined with an inspiring energy" (p 14).
363 Matthew 5:9
364 The JOC was manned by senior decision-makers from each party so that decisions could be made immediately without having to refer them. As sometimes happened in these surreal days, the person whom the ANC appointed to the JOC found himself working with a Security Branch officer who had once tortured him in prison.

Chapter 33: Taking on the Guns

365 Reconciliation Day was formerly known as The Day of the Covenant, a remembrance of the Boer victory over a Zulu army at Blood River in KwaZulu-Natal on 16 December 1838. Gatherings on that date had been occasions to whip up Afrikaner Nationalism and sense of manifest destiny.
366 Now regarded as commonplace, the idea of South African police officers sitting down with community members could not have been more foreign in 1993, but with the help of the humble but unstoppable activist Phiroshaw Camay and David Storey and an inter-party committee we were making slow progress, creating a template for Police-Community relations across the land.
367 George had served as a US diplomat in South Africa, Kenya and Nigeria and been Ambassador to Malawi. Sharon was a passionate South African activist with expertise in social housing programmes and many other areas of concern.
368 The Black Sash was a women's human rights group begun in the early days of the apartheid regime. Sheena's mother had been a founder and she had followed in her footsteps to become President. She was also a prominent Anglican, respected and sometimes feared for her incisive mind and uncompromising honesty.
369 These varied from arguments engaging us such as Ian Lehr's *Random Shots: The Bishop's Story*, in the November 1994 issue of *Man Magnum* magazine, p 6, warning that GFSA was seeking an end to civilian firearm ownership, to irrational rants accusing us of being agents of communist plans to disarm whites.
370 the Boer from his gun
371 *The Star*, 17 December 1994
372 GFSA statement, *Gun campaign nets variety of weapons – and will continue*, released 20 December 1994
373 Adele Kirsten, *A Nation Without Guns? The Story of Gun Free South Africa*, UKZN Press, 2008, p 34
374 Ibid, p 35
375 Ibid, p 43
376 *Why the New Constitution Should Exclude any Reference to the 'Right to Bear Arms.'* Submission to Theme Committee 6 (Sub-Committee on Security Apparatus) of the Constituent Assembly by GFSA
377 The Firearms Control Act of 2000
378 Adele Kirsten, op cit, p 184

ENDNOTES

Chapter 34: Days of Grace

379 John 1:16: "Out of his full store we have all received grace upon grace, for while the law was given by Moses, grace and truth came through Jesus Christ."
380 Mvume Dandala was my successor at CMM and its first black Superintendent Minister. He came from the Eastern Cape but because he had been appointed in his younger days to a church in KwaZulu-Natal he was uniquely placed to be a bridge between his own Xhosa people and Zulu culture and concerns. Mvume's Hostel Peace Initiative was one of the unsung peace-making triumphs of the early 90s. I recall watching a soccer match with him, the players being hostel-dwellers who just months before had been killing each other.
381 The detailed story of how this deeply devout Christian was brought into the mediation in the first place and the series of miraculous events that kept him engaged and enabled him to succeed is told in Michael Cassidy's *A Witness Forever*, Hodder & Stoughton, 1995. When Washington Okumo died the *Sunday Times* of 27 November 2016 called him "the Professor who saved South Africa from war in 1994."
382 For an insider's minute-by-minute record of that race, read Peter Harris, *Birth – the Conspiracy to Stop the '94 Election*, Umuzi, 2010
383 Now Mbombela
384 *Churches Mount Election Rescue*, Wits Vaal Peace Secretariat Press Release, 3 May 1994
385 Ibid
386 Portions of Isaiah 54:7-10
387 President Mandela's Inaugural Speech, 10 May 1994
388 Trevor Huddleston, *Naught for Your Comfort*, William Collins & Co, 1955
389 Formerly Libertas
390 The post-1994 National Anthem of South Africa is an amalgam of *Nkosi Sikelel' iAfrika* and *Die Stem*, anthem of the previous order.
391 Speech by President Nelson Mandela to the 1994 Conference of the Methodist Church of Southern Africa
392 Susan Collin Marks, *Watching the Wind – Conflict Resolution During South Africa's Transition to Democracy*, Endowment of the US Institute of Peace, Washington DC, 2000, p 196
393 Matthew 20:16
394 *Statement and Resolution on Abortion*, MCSA Annual Conference, 1995

Chapter 35: Search for Healing

395 Dullah Omar, speech in Parliament, 17 May 1995, quoted in Alex Boraine, *A Country Unmasked*, Oxford University Press, 2000, p 69
396 The politicians were the ANC's Baleka Kgositsile-Mbete (now Speaker of Parliament), Senator Ray Radue (NP), Professor Harriet Ngubane (IFP MP), and Senator Rosier de Ville (FF). Civil society was represented by Jayandrah Naidoo of the National Economic Development and Labour Council (NEDLAC) and Jody Kollapen from Lawyers for Human Rights (LHR). SACC General Secretary Brigalia Bam and myself brought the church presence.
397 Promotion of National Unity and Reconciliation Act, No 34 of 1995
398 *Thoughts on Additional Criteria*, 30 October 1995
399 Dr Mgojo had originally been nominated but had withdrawn his name in deference to his Presiding Bishop (Stanley Mogoba) when Mogoba became a candidate too.
400 For two years – 1996/97 – I authored a regular op-ed column called *Faith and Life* for the *Sunday Independent* newspaper.
401 Trials of former Defence Minister Magnus Malan and Dr Wouter Basson ('Dr Death'), neither of which secured a conviction.
402 In 2008 an apology for the institution of slavery was issued by the US House of Representatives and the National Museum of African American History and Culture now stands on the Mall in Washington DC as witness to that part of US history. In spite of these positive developments there remains a stubborn spirit of denial in many places in the American South. I was privileged to be an adviser to the first Truth & Reconciliation Commission in the USA – in Greensboro, North Carolina.
403 Desmond Tutu, *No Future Without Forgiveness*, Doubleday, 1999, p 271
404 Get lost (isiXhosa)
405 Once Thabo Mbeki became President I feared that reparations and rehabilitation for victims of apartheid would take a back seat. In my interchanges with returned exiles I had found little interest in the suffering of their compatriots during their absence. They preferred to perpetuate the myth that

it was primarily their work on the outside that had brought about the end of apartheid. The failure adequately to follow through the TRC's recommendations in this regard is a moral disgrace.

Chapter 36: Something New
406 The Big Crocodile (Afrik)
407 John Allen, *Rabble-Rouser for Peace: Authorised Biography of Desmond Tutu*, Random House, 2006, p 357
408 Dr Alex Boraine's *A Country Unmasked – Inside South Africa's Truth and Reconciliation Commission* (Oxford University Press) has the full story of what led up to Botha's subpoena and of the trial and aftermath (pp 188-220).
409 *Confronting the Crocodile,* Circular letter dated 14 June 1998
410 The Methodist Church in the United States is known as the United Methodist Church (UMC), stemming from the mid-twentieth century union of three major US denominations of Wesleyan origin. The UMC, which has work in many countries other than the USA, is 12.8 million strong.
411 Pam taught me much about stillness of heart and has authored a number of deeply devotional books. Ray taught me about humility and service and remained an example of it until his untimely death in 2014.

Chapter 37: Professor at Large
412 Known as the 'Connexional Executive' and consisting of all the bishops, departmental heads and top lay officials of MCSA
413 Letter from Dave McMakin, USAID (retd), re *Mock Security Council Meeting – An Examination of Security Policy Questions from a Faith-Based Perspective,* 29 January 2004
414 Endowed by Ruth W and A Morris Williams Jr. I got to know both Ruth and Morris as highly principled and generous Christian people. Morris's father had been a country pastor in North Carolina who owed his theological education to the generosity of Duke Divinity School. In recognition of this Morris returned that generosity to the university many times over.
415 *Rules of Engagement: Faithful Congregations in a Dangerous World,* Inaugural Lecture by Peter Storey, Ruth W and A Morris Williams Jr, Professor of the Practice of Christian Ministry, 10 February 2004

Chapter 38: A Last Task
416 Land/Buildings, Governance/Administration, Academics/Faculty/Staff, Student Life, Funding
417 The 'sevenfold' evaluation criteria at SMMS were: Spiritual Development, Vocational Readiness, Academic Progress, Attitudinal Maturity, Interpersonal Skills, Discipline & Responsibility, Personal Bearing and Conduct. It was possible for a seminarian to achieve an excellent first-class BTh degree and still not be advanced to Ordination because of failing to satisfy some of the other requirements.
418 I certainly hoped it would. In parts of MCSA the spirit of domination rather than servanthood still tends to permeate the ministry.
419 The Search Committee that recommended Olivier and the Planning Executive that approved his name both had black majorities. The Presiding Bishop who confirmed his appointment was also a person of colour. The Search Committee had previously invited two outstanding and well-qualified black ministers to apply but they declined. The final two candidates each underwent a seven-hour external Psychometric Competencies Assessment, which placed Olivier well ahead. None of these facts, nor that MCSA was a non-racial church, appeared to disturb our detractors.
420 The Nelson Mandela & Robert Sobukwe Library is unique in bringing together these two names. Because both leaders were members of the MCSA, the foundations established to honour them each gave permission for the joint use of their names. Other buildings on the site include the Samuel Moseneke Lecture Hall building, donated by ex-Deputy Chief Justice Dikgang Moseneke and his brother in memory of their grandfather who was a Methodist preacher, and the McAllister Administration building, donated by Roy McAllister in memory of his father, another Methodist preacher.
421 One end of the Chapel consists of two great doors that open it entirely to the world. The SMMS campus was awarded the KZN Institute of Architects' Merit Award for 2011 and reached the final 40 in the World Architectural News design competition for public spaces anywhere in the world.
422 Letter to Presiding Bishop Ivan Abrahams. The quote is from Matthew 23:24, "You blind guides! You strain out a gnat but swallow a camel."

ENDNOTES

Epilogue
423 Peter Storey, *With God in the Crucible,* Abingdon Press, 2002, p 66
424 Matthew 25:40
425 Letter from Rev Jaylynn Byasee, now ministering in Canada
426 Now known as *The New Dimension*, it has been published for 48 years.
427 Matthew 5:33. The use of 'Kin' instead of 'King' is a non-sexist preference to the word 'kingdom'.
428 Letter to *New Dimension,* July 2017, p 13
429 Bonaro Overstreet, *To One Who Doubts the Worth of Doing Anything If You Can't Do Everything*

Author's Notes and Acknowledgements

This book had a long history in my head but for many years it simply refused to be born. In 1997 I retired as Bishop in Johannesburg/Soweto and began a second career teaching on seminary campuses in the United States. A good friend generously arranged for my papers to be couriered to Duke University so that I could begin to put together a memoir of the years I had lived through. This was not because my life was particularly extraordinary, but because those years certainly were, and anyone who lived through them and made a modest contribution has a story to tell, and should do so.

Throughout the nine years we were in the USA, the boxes of diaries, clippings and files stared at me and I stared back, unable to open them. It was all too close and too raw. When we returned to South Africa in 2006, my friend couriered them all back with more grace than I deserved. For ten more years, the boxes and I stared at each other until I spoke at an event at my old school, resulting in a reporter profiling me in his newspaper. Soon after that an editor at Tafelberg Publishers called, urging me to write a memoir. The boxes were opened at last.

Writing anything like this is lonely, scary and enriching: lonely because there is no alternative but to put everything aside for many months and sit down quite alone each day with only a laptop for company. Scary, because memories that one has often suppressed invite themselves back with the challenge of recording them as truthfully as possible. And enriching, because as I wrote, I found that the overwhelming emotion accompanying me was *gratitude*.

AUTHOR'S NOTES AND ACKNOWLEDGEMENTS

I have so much and so many to be thankful for. My parental home and family, my rich years with Elizabeth my life-partner, our four remarkable sons and those precious to them, and seven wonderful grandchildren all contribute to my gratitude. I also thank the Methodist Church in whose bosom I was nurtured and with whom I have enjoyed a 'lover's quarrel'[1] for fifty-eight years. Then there is a God whose relentless patience with me is proof that none are ever rejected. I am indeed fortunate.

This book is about ministry and ministry is always about people. I deliberately mention many names because without them, very little I've written about would have happened. Throughout my ministry I have been blessed by remarkably gifted, loyal and loving colleagues who appear all over these pages. If we achieved anything significant together, it was most often they who made it happen. I want them all to know how much I honour them and how privileged I feel to have walked with them.

The book would likely not have happened had Annie Olivier not invited me to coffee and asked me to write it. It would certainly not have been completed had Commissioning Editor Gill Moodie not expended nearly three years of meetings, coffees and calls ensuring that I kept at it. Her gentle yet firm commitment to the project and her ready advice overcame my hesitations and made it happen. My appreciation too, to Alison Lowry, who edited the manuscript with a deft and caring touch, and to Thuli Madonsela and Jonathan Jansen for their undeservedly generous commendations. Finally, my deep thanks to Di Conradie for being alongside me with encouragement, wisdom and love all the way.

Peter Storey
Simon's Town, July 2018

---

1 The phrase belongs to great preacher William Sloane Coffin – former Pastor of Riverside Church, New York City.

Index

A Garland of Flowers for Soweto 232
Abrahams family, District Six 152
Abrahams, Jane 137, 151, 153
Abrahams, Jane
   Pastoral Assistant 137-138
Abrahams, Janie, *see* Abrahams, Jane
Abrahams, Rev Ivan 446, 447
Academy for Christian Living 208, 218
Acheson, Donald 229
Act of Union 21
ACTIPAX 284, 287, 305
Actstop 224, 227
African Enterprise 188, 257, 335
African National Congress (ANC) 41, 96, 108, 164,
   339-340, 343, 347, 349-350, 358, 366, 371,
   375-376, 386, 389-390, 395, 397, 411
African Old Age Pensioners Scheme 278
Afrikaans Dutch Reformed family, *see* Dutch
   Reformed Church
Afrikaans Hoërskool 13, 33
Afrikaans, language instruction forced on black
   scholars 44, 201
Afrikaner Party 24
Afrikaner Weerstandsbeweging (AWB) 268, 386
Afrikaners, in SA Navy during 1956, 56-57
after-school care centres 178
Alan Walker Mission 103
Albertus Street Primary School 141
alcoholism 125
Aldersgate Street experience 71-72
Algoa Bay 16
Alice 81
all-male ministry 160
Alty, Tom 90-91
Andrews, Colin 193
Andy's Cash Store 35
Anglican Cathedral of St Michael, Grahamstown 80
anti-pass-book campaigns 96
apartheid 36, 37, 39, 47, 73, 86, 87, 102-104,
   112-115, 130-131, 134, 138, 146-148, 150-151,
   153, 156, 169, 185, 198, 204, 214, 228,
   233-234, 243-244, 253, 255, 257-258, 261,
   273, 299, 302, 304, 310, 314, 319, 332, 340,
   352, 375, 381-382, 436, 466
   1948-1994, 15
   Afrikaans language instruction forced on black
      scholars 44, 201

Bantustans 248, 418
church resistance 87, 162, 171, 173, 191,
   291-292, 296-297, 345, 352
CMC and 205, 212-213
Daantjie Oosthuizen and 83
Dr Billy Graham 189
forced removals 315
form of slavery 86
government policy 47, 75
ideologues 43, 167, 239
injustice 185
John Wesley on 75
Kairos 346
legislation 42-43, 217
military service during 209, 270, 274, 264,
   270, 377
opposition to 186, 339, 417
petty 138
post-apartheid TRC 226, 423-424
prime minister BJ Vorster 28
Robben Island, symbol of 102
SABC as propagandist of 196
shaped by Calvinist exclusionism 73
social sin of 103
Arcadia Primary School 29
Asabi, Rabbi Adi 233
Asingeni Relief Fund 204, 284
Assegai Bush River 16
Asvat, Abu-Baker 355, 365, 372
Atamelang, Western Transvaal 323
Attwell, Rev Arthur 62, 119
Australia 119-132
Australian Methodist Church, Sydney 130
aversion therapy 128-129
Avril Elizabeth Home 309
Ayob, Ishmael 358, 359, 368, 372, 375

Baader-Meinhof Group 248
Baartman, Rev Ernest 170, 319, 337
Baker, Herbert 110
Bam, Rev Tranquil 38
Bantu Education 41-44, 170
   Act 43
Bantustans 248, 313
Baragwanath Hospital, Soweto 233
Barayi, Elijah 369
Barnard, Chris 186-187

INDEX

Barnard, Dr Niel 332
Barrett, Oliver Prof 83, 275, 281-283, 285, 287, 293, 298, 305
Bassingthwaite, Judy 222
Battis, Walter 33
Battle of Bloedriver 25
Battle of the Atlantic 56, 61
Baumann, Len 155
Bax, Rev Douglas 260
Beckett, Denis 217, 230
Beetge, Bp David 399
Behrens, Kevin 398
Bellville Methodist Church, Cape Town 93
  Peter Storey appointed Probationer Minister 92-106
Belville 97
Benevolent Loan Fund 73
Benyon, John 90
Berea Methodist Church, Yeoville 232
Berger, Teresa 440
Bethesda Methodist Mission Hospital 151
Bevan, Aneurin 20
Biko, Steve 168, 212, 228
Bird, Ann 213
black congregations 181-182
Black Consciousness Movement 168
Black December 64
Black Methodist Consultation (BMC) 170
Blomkamp, Paul 181
Blumel, Barbara 247-248
Boesak, Dr Allan 237, 322, 334, 341, 384
Boichoko 36
Bonteheuwel 152
Boraine, Jenny 161
Boraine, Rev Alex 155, 160, 166, 312, 426, 436
Border War 259, 266, 267, 324
Bosch, David 336, 344
Bosch, Prof David 336, 344
Botha, Louis 22
Botha, Min MC 170
Botha, Pres PW 236, 241, 313, 315, 316, 328, 332, 336, 340, 435, 436
Braamfontein Methodist Church 181-182
Brakpan 28
  25 Muir Avenue, birthplace of Peter Storey 26
Brandfort 324, 347, 349, 376, 378, 380
Brews, Rev Alan 146, 334
British Labour Party 19
Brown, Brian 168
Brown, Kate 149
Brown, Robert J 351
Brutus, Dennis 111
Buchanan, Bp Duncan 385
Buchman, Dr Frank 47
Budlender, Geoff 358, 371
Buitenkant Street Methodist Church 133, 158
Burnett, Bp Bill 277
Buthelezi, Bp Manas 263, 293
Buthelezi, Chief Min Mangosuthu 168, 334

Buti, Ds Sam 279, 285

Cachalia, Azhar 369
Calata, Fort 30
Calvinism 339
Calvinist exclusionism 73
Calvinistic religiosity 141
  in District Six 141
Cameron, Adv Edwin 273
Camps Bay
  Peter Storey Probationer Minister in 97, 102-103
  Peter Storey's probation ended and ordained 105-106
Candle of Peace, Hope and Justice 213
Cape Colony 16
Cape Flats 134, 152-154, 334
  evictions/dispossesions 152
Cape Flats Methodist Mission 154
Cape Town Coloured Circuit 134
Caprivi 259, 266
Carder, Bp Ken 438
Careways Children's Centre, May 1973, 178-179
Carmichael, Canon Michael 287
Carmichael, Rev Liz 390
Carpenter's House
  District Six 141-142
  lunch club for workers 144
  Seekers 143-144
  Youth Cabaret 143-144
Carr, Canon Burgess 196
Casbah 89-90
Cassidy, Michael 188, 335
Catholic Bishops' Conference (CBC) 275
Cebekhulu, Katiza 354- 355
Central Methodist Church (CMC), Johannesburg 172, 183-185
Central Methodist Mission (CMM)
  Alan Storey Superintendent Minister 158
  Johannesburg 158, 200, 222, 277, 372
  Sydney 105, 120, 190-191
Central News Agency 216
Chabaku, Motlalepula 199
Chain of Hope 433
Chikane, Frank 235, 237, 255, 342, 352, 353, 379, 385, 393
Ching, David 218, 224
Christian Impact 104, 159, 163
Christian Institute (CI) 115, 145, 168, 199, 275, 338
Christian journalism 159-174
Christian Leadership Centre (CLC) 150-151
Christian League of South Africa (CLSA) 169, 242, 297
Christian pacifism 127-128, 259
Christian pacifists 126
Christian Union, Rondebosch Boys' High School (RBHS) 45
Christianity 66, 68, 71, 100, 141, 159, 250, 276, 432, 440

Church of England 72
Church of the Good Shepherd, see Leper Church
church, defined by Peter Storey 78
Churchill, Winston 35
circuit ministry 133, 240
City Care 219
city ministry 105
Civic Centre Methodist Church (CCMC),
    Rissik Street, Jun 1973, 180
Claremont Mosque 146
Clarke, 'Nobby' 45
Clarkebury 35
Class Leaders 72, 136-137
Class Meetings 136-137
Clifton Methodist Church, Braamfontein
    Johannesburg 166, 175-186
    survey 177
Coetzee, Gen Johan 207, 297
Coggin, Theo 328
Colbyn 37
Coleyn, Piet 413-414
coloureds 134
Commemoration Methodist Church,
    Grahamstown 80
Commission for the Renewal of the Church
    147-148, 160
Commonwealth of Nations 99
Communist Manifesto 332
Conscientious Objection resolution 261
Conscientious Objectors 227, 261, 262, 272
    Support Group (COSG) 272-273
Conscription Advice Bureau 227
Constitutional Court 273, 304
Contact Teleministries 132
Cook, Rev Jack 175-176
Cornerstone House 220-221, 235, 278
Cowell, Alan 330
Cradock 330, 331
Cripps, Sir Stafford 20
Crisis Committee 352, 357-359, 364, 366-368,
    370, 377, 382
Crisis Synods 324
Crocker, Dr Chester 314
Cuito Cuanavale 269

Dandala, Mvume 226, 244, 328, 340, 399, 410,
    430, 441, 443, 454
Daniel, Arch George 313
Daniels, Eddie 116
Darling 136
    declared white Group Area 167
Davis, Ellen 440
De Beers Diamonds 222
De Bruyn, Rev Trevour 218
De Cuéllar, Dr Pérez 313
De Klerk, FW 375, 384, 417
De Kock, Col Eugene 234, 264, 435, 436
De Korte Street 120, Braamfontein,
    Johannesburg 175

De Villiers Graaff, Sir 147
De Villiers, Dr Bruckner 155
Deaconess Society 198
deaths, in detention 170-171
Defence Further Amendment Bill 169, 261
Delmas Treason Trial 237
Detainees' Parents Support Committee (DPSC) 227
detention, deaths in 170-171
Dewire, Dr Ned 432, 435
Dhlomo, Jacob 410
Diakonia House 203
Die Groot Krokodil 436
Dimension
    assistant editor Rev Stanley Mogoba 163-164
    editorial assistant Helen Muller 166
    first issue of 161-162
    MCSA monthly newspaper 155
    naming of 160-161
    Peter Storey editor of 155
    reporting on apartheid 169
    reporting on deaths in detention 170-171
    use in Clifton Methodist Church 177
discernment process 178
District Six 133-142
    apartheid in 157
    dispossessions 152-158
    Museum 158
    return to 157-158
diversity training 148-149
    coloureds 149
    whites 148-149
Donald Cragg, 244, 330
dormitory accommodations 40
Driscoll's Scouts 20
Drostdy Wall, Grahamstown 80
Dugard, Prof John 305
Dugmore, Rev Deryck 42
Duncan, Sheena 270, 399, 405, 407
Dunham, Dr Maxie 432
Dutch East India Company 33, 134
Dutch Reformed Church 87, 176, 182, 231, 239,
    257-258, 261, 292, 333, 336, 339-340, 343, 401

Eddie, Ken 89-90
Edendale Ecumenical Centre, Pietermaritzburg 168
Edlmann, Theresa 274
Edwards, Kathleen 150
Eglin, Colin 146
El Alamein 18
electric shock treatment 128-129
Eloff Commission 236, 290, 294, 303, 306, 308,
    319, 436
Eloff, Justice CF 290
End Conscription Campaign (ECC) 272
England, Evangelical Revival 73
Epworth Girls' High School 448
Erasmus, FC 63, 96
Erlander, Daniel 77
Ermelo 28

INDEX

Eskom 254
Evangelical Revival, England 73
evictions, District Six 152-158
Extension of University Education Act 87

faith and believe, Peter Storey 66-79
Falati, Xoliswa 354
Falwell, Rev Jerry 333
family discipline 135
Federal Theological Seminary, Alice 81, 167
ffrench-Beytagh, Very Rev Gonville 284
Firearms Act 407
Flying Doctor Service 120
Flynn, John 120
food protests 40
For Love of Children (FLOC) 223
forced removal
  Mamelodi, Pretoria 43
  Soweto, Johannesburg 43
Fry, Elizabeth 74

gamblers 125
Gamblers' Liberty Group 125
Gandhi, Christian pacifist 128
Gardener, John 104, 163
Geneva Conventions 266
GIFT groups 218
Gilbey, 350, 355, 375
Goldstone Commission's Committee on Children and Violence 309-310
Goldstone, Richard 304
Gongo, Mita 30
Goniwe, Matthew 330
Good Friday 174, 211
Gordon, Alec 150
Gqubule, Dr Simon 228, 286, 333
Graham, Billy 189-190
Graham, Paul 407
Grahamstown 80-92
Great Trek 24
Greenmarket Square 158
Gribble, Rev James 334
Group Areas Act 133, 150, 181-182
Gruber, Rudolph 88-89
Gumede, Archie 369
Gun Control Alliance (GCA) 406
Gun Free Election Campaign 397
Gun Free South Africa (GFSA) Campaign 396, 398, 405
Gun Free Zones 406
gun-rights cultism 406

Hall, John 387, 396
Hammanskraal Resolution 265
Hani, Chris 228, 395, 409
Hanmer, Tom 148
Hanover Park, evictions 152
Hardie, Allan 46, 142, 155, 193, 244
Hardie, Elizabeth 95
  see also Storey, Elizabeth
  and Peter Storey 45-55
  marriage to Peter Storey 98-100
Hardie, Flo 48
Hardie, Graeme 233
Hardie, Tom 46, 48, 99
Haron, Imam Abdullah 146
Harris, Chief Rabbi Cyril 399
Harris, Peter 389, 395, 409, 411
Hartshorne, Kenneth 41
Hatfield 37
Hatfield Primary School 29
Hatfield, Mark 314
Hauerwas, Stanley 434, 440
Hayes, Judy 440
Hayes, Richard 440
Haysom, Fink 230, 358, 368, 423
Healdtown 35
Healdtown Institution 168
Heard, Tony 104, 159
Heidelberg Military Base 272
Hendricks, Abel 154, 172, 334
Hendricks, Freda 154
Hewson, Prof 85, 90-91
Hillbrow House 183, 218
Hind, Errol 252
Holomisa, Gen Bantu 172
Holy Club 71, 74
homosexuality 128-129
hostel accommodation 40
Hostel Peace Initiative 399, 410
Howard, John 74
Hudson, Rev Janet 218, 223, 419
Hudson, Rev Trevor 218
Hurley, Arch Denis 332

IEC Monitoring Directorate 411
Ikageng, Potchefstroom 252, 359
Ikaneng, Lerotodi 356, 362, 375
Indaleni 36
Independent Electoral Commission 411
Independent Mediation Service of South Africa (IMSSA) 53, 388
injustice, and apartheid 185
inner cities 159-160
Inner City Mission 144
Institute for Democracy in South Africa 407
Inter-Church Committee on Military Chaplaincy (ICCM) 265
Irvine, George 193
Irving, Prof 84
Islam 250

Jackson, Charles 40
Jansen, Prof Jonathan 454
Jenkins, Prof Trefor 186, 212
Jennings, Willie 440
Jews 77, 191
Johannesburg Sun 221

Johannesburg, Peter Storey moved to 156
John Dickinson Stationery Company 50
John Vorster Square 288, 385
Johnson, Commander 'Flam' 62
Johnson, Shaun 399
Joint Operational Centre (JOC) 395
Jones, Dean Greg 447
Jones, Greg 440
Jones, Susan 440
Jonker, Prof Willie 257
Jordan, Clarence 145
Joubert, Maj-Gen Jaap 371
Joza, Grah
Judaism 250
Justice and Reconciliation task groups 166

Kagawa, Toyohiko 69
Kairos – Challenge to the Church 343
Kairos Document 335
Kalksteenfontein 154
Kasteel de Goede Hoop 33
Katane, Rev Dan 207
Kathrada, Ahmed 116
Keister, Linda 252
Keister, Paul 252
Kensington 150
Kgase, Kenny 352, 355-357, 376
Kgosana, Philip 96
Khoi roots 134
Khotso House 221, 234-236, 286, 435-436
Kidger, Peter Storey's mother's forbears 20
Kilnerton 'Normal College' 41
Kilnerton 35-44
Kilnerton Mission House I 29
Kilnerton Training Institution (KTI) 29, 42, 111
Kimberley, siege of 21
Kirsten, Adele 274, 399, 405-407
Kissinger, Dr Henry 203, 410
Kistner, Dr Wolfram 208, 297
Koedoespoort
  railway works, land expropriation 42
  Station 12, 25
  train to 11-14
Koevoet police 264
Kohl, Chan Helmut 315-316
Koornhof, Piet 242
Kotze, Rev Theo 104, 115, 155, 168
Kramer, Reid 167
Kramer, Tammy 167
Kriegler, Johann 304
Krugersdorp 268
Kuzwayo, Ellen 255

Lafont, Father Emmanuel 256
Lageson, Les 178
land expropriation, Koedoespoort railway works 42
Landlords' Act 219
Langa 96
latchkey children, Hillbrow 178

Lavender Hill, evictions/dispossesions 152
Lawrence, Gilbert 151, 290
Lawrence, Jane 290
Leatt, Rev James 150
Leleke, Sox 450
Leper Church, Robben Island 110
Lewin, Hugh 89, 159
LGBTQI community 128-129
liberation movements, grants to 164
Lichtenburg 269
Life Line, telephone-based counselling 120
Life Line Centre Australia 121
  Gamblers' Liberty Group 125
  Trouble Team 124-125
Life Line Centre Cape Town 155
Life Line centres 131, 190, 193
Life Line Durban 155
Life Line East Rand 155
Life Line International 131, 155, 191, 193
  see Contact Teleministries
Life Line Kimberley 155
Life Line Pietermaritzburg 155
Life Line Southern Africa 192-193
Life Line Welkom 155
Life Line Witwatersrand 155
Life Line USA, *see* Contact Teleministries
Ligh, Ray 193
Lischer, Richard 440
Lischer, Rick 445
Lischer, Tracy 440
Livingstone House 85-86, 90
  Rhodes University 81
Local Peace Committees (LPCs) 387-388
Logan, Beth 227
Lorimer, Rupert 389
Loyal Church of England 70-71
Lubowski, Anton 229
Lugar, Richard 314
Luthuli, Albert
  banned for another five years 87-88
  church education 43

Mabuza, Rev Wesley 244
MacDonald Ramsay 19-20
Machel, Pres Samora 313
Macmillan, Harold, 'Wind of Change' speech 96
Macoute, Tonton 249
Madikiza, Rev Victor 328
Madikizela-Mandela, Winnie, 317, 324, 347-359, 361-362, 364-369, 371-383, 431, 434
Madikizela-Mandela, Zinzi 350-351, 356-357, 368
Mahabane, Rev Ezekiel 87, 182
Mahlabegoane, Rev 181-183
Mahlalela, Rev Isaac 326
Mahlamba Ndlopfu 37, 417
Mahlasela, Rev De Waal 171-172
Maitland Garden Village 149
Majwemasweu 324, 347-348
Makeba, Miriam 41

INDEX

Maker, Alan 385
Makgatho, Rev Sefako Mapogo 41
Makhubu, Mbuyisa 168
Makletha family, Klipspruit 206
Malan Dr DF 24-25
Malta 18
Mandela United Football Club 350, 364, 368, 382
Mandela, Nelson 113, 116, 214, 316, 332, 346, 349, 352, 358, 372, 376, 398, 409, 419-420, 450, 457, 459, 462
   arrived in 1963, 108
   church education 43
   detained 97
   pastoral care on Robben Island 109
   Peter Storey first chaplain to 115
Mandela, Winnie, *see* Madikizela-Mandela, Winnie
Manna and Mercy 77
Manenberg, evictions/dispossesions 153
Manthatha, Tom 203, 207
Marais, Jacques 106
Margate Bay battle 64-65
Marion Island 59
Marks, JB 40
Marks, Susan Collin 420
Martin Luther King 145, 159-160
   Christian pacifist 128
   public memorial service 145
Mashabane family 206
Mashabane, Jackie 206
Mashinini, Tsietsi 201-202, 206-207
Mass Democratic Movement (MDM) 354, 369
Massey, Austen 214
Matanzima, Kaiser 164, 167
   banning of MCSA from Transkei Bantustan 171
   declaring MCSA undesirable organisation 171
Matthews, Rev Ric 218
Matussi, Rev Chikona 326
Maximum Security B Section 115
Maxwell, Prof 85
Mbabane, Rev Sizwe 218, 328, 430
Mbatha, 280, 287-288
Mbeki, Govan 116
Mbete, Rev Andile 328
McCauley, Pastor Ray 257
McCrae, Ian 254
MCSA 147
   churches 174
   churches, declared 'white' Group Areas 167
   Publishing House 155
   Renewal Commission 278
Meals on Wheels 278
Meara, William 183, 199
Mekgwe, Pelo 352, 355, 371, 372
Message of Obedience Charter 245
Methodism 71
   and Probationer Ministers 93-106
   probation 93-106
Methodist Bookshops 155
Methodist Central Hall 28, 31, 184, 198, 317

Methodist Church
   and Peter Storey 70-71
   Robben Island, pastoral care by 109
Methodist Church of Southern Africa (MCSA) 52, 72, 100
   Peter Storey's dad became the leader of 86-87
Methodist Church of Transkei 171-172
Methodist Churchman 160-161
Methodist Conferences of 1976, 169-170
Methodist Conferences of 1977, 171
Methodist missionary education 36
Methodist Order of Peacemakers (MOP) 271
Methodist Relief 278, 326
Methodist Society (METHSOC)
   Wits University 179-180
Methodist Youth Centre, Jabavu 207-208
Metropolitan Church, Greenmarket Square 175
Mgojo, Khoza 220, 242, 333, 426
Mhlauli, Sicelo 330
military chaplaincy 259, 263, 265
Military Intelligence 250, 264
Mills, Allan 281
Milnerton, Peter Storey Probationer Minister in 97, 102-103
Miss Mickey's Kindergarten, Arcadia 29
Mission House 37, 40
mixed restaurants 217
Mkhonto, Sparrow 330
Mlhele family 206
Mogoba, Rev Stanley 42, 111, 118, 163-164, 244, 247, 293, 298, 305, 328, 372, 373, 379, 387, 426
Mokitimi, Rev Seth 87, 113
Mokoena, Aubrey 352, 356, 368
Mokoena, Isaac 280
Moloabi, Rev Ike 252
Mono, Thabiso 352, 355, 371
Monte Cassino 18
Montgomery, Field Marshall Bernard 29
Moral Majority 333
Moral Rearmament (MTA) 47-48
Morobe, Murphy 269, 275
Moroka 35
Mosala, Bernadette 207
Moseneke, Dikgang 41
Moshage, Dan 369
Motlana, Dr Nthato 41, 356, 365
Motlana, Sally 242, 275, 286, 289
Motor Union Insurance 50
Moufhe, Rev Tshifiwa 248
Mouille Point foghorn 110
Mowbray Maternity Home, Cape Town 101
Moyes, Gordon 209
Mozambique 35, 313, 326-327
Mufamadi, 3 Sydney 52, 368, 403
Muller, Helen 166, 177, 199, 223
Muller, Michelle 183
multi-racial in-service training courses 167
Muslims 134, 153, 191

491

Mvunyiswa, Philip 215, 224
Mvusi, Jotham 87
My Brother and Me courses 148-149, 183
Myeza, Lindi 199, 206, 216, 219
Mzizi, Gertrude 409

Naidoo, Krish 359, 361, 368
Namibia 222, 229, 250, 264, 266, 321, 325, 340
Napier, Bp Wilfred 385
National Initiative for Reconciliation (NIR) 335
National Intelligence Service 332
National Party (NP) 24, 41
National Peace Accord (NPA) 258, 384, 387, 396, 419, 492
Naudé, Beyers 115, 145, 155, 168, 199, 208, 231, 275, 319, 338, 352, 367, 368
Naval Reserve Base, Port Elizabeth 82
Ncube, Bernard 255, 352, 361
Ndungane, Arch Njongonkulu 118
Ndungane, Winston 293
New Life Group 218
New South Wales, compulsive gamblers 125
Newby, David 200, 218, 224, 405-406
Newby, Rev David 200, 218, 224, 405, 406
Ngakane, Barney 41, 207
Ngoyi, Lillian 41
Ngwenya, Steward 259, 361
Nightingale, Florence 74
Nkomati Accord 313, 326
Nkomo, Dr William 145, 165
Nkosi Sikelel' iAfrika 39
Nkosi, Morley 38
Nobel Peace Prize 319
Nolan, Father Albert 343
Normandy 18
Northern Star 119
Ntumba, Welcome 235
Nupen, Charles 54, 388
Nussbaum, Barbara 409
Nyanga 96
NYLTO delegates 170
NYLTP workers, deported 167

Oates, Elizabeth 16
Oates, Ivy, Peter Storey's grandmother 21
Oates, John 21
Oates, John, great-great-great-grandfather of Peter Storey 16
Obedience '81, 243-245, 278, 344, 430
Obedience Charter 245, 332
Okumo, Prof Washington 411
Omar, Dullah 401, 423
Oosthuizen, Daantjie 83-84
Oosthuizen, Rev Connie 167
Operation Hunger 222
Oppenheimer, Bridget 222
Oppenheimer, Harry 222
Orator's Cup 63
ordination 106

Peter Storey's 105-106
Orlando East 352, 354
Orlando West 203, 289, 367
Ostrogorski 73

Paballo ya Batho 223
Palermo 18
Pan-Africanist Congress (PAC) 96-97, 111-112, 164, 339-340, 428
 anti-pass-book campaigns 96
 banning 96
Parker, Tom 161
pass-burning campaign 112
Paton, Alan 315, 335
Pawson, Alec 95
Peace Church 268-269
Pendlebury, Jim 209
People Centre 215-218, 224, 227, 230
Phelps House 85-86
Pietermaritzburg Life Line 155
Pietersen, Hector 168
Pilgrim's Progress 39
Pitts, Rev Stanley 183-184
Plaque of Conscience' 156-157
Polley, James 93
Pollsmoor Maximum Prison 316
Portuguese East Africa 35
Potgieter, Dr Pieter 258
poverty 130-140
 District Six 139
Pray-Away 336
Prayers for the Downfall of the Government controversy 325, 340
press freedom, to MCSA Conference 166
Pretoria Boys' High School (PBHS) 28, 41
 Peter Storey in 1951, 33
Pretoria Castle 29
Pretoria Central Prison 230
Pretoria Girls' High School 45
Pretorius, Sue 432
prevenient grace 73
privilege, and racism 148
Probationer Ministers, Methodism 93-106
Programme to Combat Racism (PCR) 277
prophetic evangelism 320
protests
 90-Day Detention Act 145-146
 District Six removals 145-146
 Wits University 179-180
Public Interest Advertising Committee 402

Qambela, Hamilton 168
Queen Bess Club 144
Queenswood 37

Race Classification Board 138
 racial criteria 138
racial reconciliation 148-149
racial separation 204

INDEX

racism 139
  Alan Walker on 104
  and privilege 148
  deeply rooted 182-183
  food quality 40
  living conditions 40
Raikes, Robert 74
Ramaphosa, Cyril 43, 206, 255, 352
Randera, Dr Fazel 226
Rasmeni family 206
Raven, Margaret 93
Raven, Rob 93
Rayan, Samuel 7, 213
RBHS Centenary 48
Reconciliation Day 398, 401
Rees, Dulcie 04
Rees, John 114, 164, 187, 189, 195, 202-203, 207, 220-221, 235, 243, 275-276, 278-280, 288, 290, 292-293, 304, 306-308, 312, 328
Referendum (Oct 1960) 99
Regional Peace Committees (RPCs) 388
Release Mandela Campaign 350
Religious Bodies Sub-Committee 397
RENAMO 314, 36, 327
Rhema Bible Church 212, 414
Rhodeo 159
  Peter Storey appointed assistant editor 89
Rhodes University
  Divinity Department 80-92
  Peter Storey at 80-92
Richardson, Jerry 355, 360, 365, 371, 375
Richardson, Prof Neville 450
Richmond College 36
Rivonia trialists
  Peter Storey first chaplain to 115
  Robben Island 109
Robben Island 107-118
  pastoral care by Methodist Church 109
  Peter Storey appointed Chaplain in 1962, 102-103
Roberts, Ken 184-185, 216, 238, 262
Robertson, Rob 147
Roelofse, Eugene 279
Roestoff, Mrs 220
Rogers, Carl 51, 192
Rondebosch Boys' High School (RBHS) 45
  Christian Union 45
Rosebank Methodist Church, Cape Town 45
  Peter Storey's father's funeral 91
  wedding of Peter Storey and Elizabeth Hardie 99-100
Roseneath Primary School 179
Rotunda 102
Rudolph, Joan 216, 217, 220, 227
Rundu, Angola 266, 324
Russell, Michael 28
Russell, Philip 265, 282, 332, 341
Rustenburg Declaration 258
Rustenburg Girls' High School 46

SA Institute of Race Relations 182, 278, 281
SA Native National Congress 41
SA Navy 62, 270
SABC 112, 196, 197, 214, 319, 398, 402
SACC Accounting Service (SACCAS) 279
Saldanha Bay, life in the navy 56-61
Salem 17
Salerno 18
Salisbury Island, Durban 61
sanctuaries 180
Sangster, William 84
Sarojini Marie, Rowanne 450
Schlebusch Commission 168
Schnehage, Alfie 95
School for Christian Living 178, 180
Schoon, Katryn 228
Schoon, Jeanette 228
Schreiner, Olive 81, 83
Second World War, *see* World War Two
Sectional Title Act 219
Security Council 254, 255, 442
Security Police 83, 108, 114, 146, 156, 170-171, 206, 207, 230, 231, 234, 236, 252, 270, 275-276, 280, 302, 310, 330-331, 348, 350, 353-354, 361, 385, 389
Seekers, in Carpenter's House 143, 145
Seeliger, 448
segregation 160
  Alan Walker on 104
Seipei, Joyce 366, 380, 382
Seipei, Stompie 352, 354, 371, 373, 381
Sekano-Ntoane High School 206
self-defence units (SDUs) 256
Separate Amenities legislation 217
Sephton, Hezekiah 16
Seremane, Joe 114
service delivery 40
Service of the Tenebrae 211
Seth Mokitimi Methodist Seminary (SMMS) 448, 454
Setiloane, Gabriel 87
Settler Country, Grahamstown 80
Sexwale, Tokyo 397
Sharpeville massacre 96, 112
Shaw, Rev Barnabas 72, 107
Shaw, Rev William 35
Shriver, Donald 153
Sifrin, Geoff 232
Sisulu, Albertina 255, 366, 380
Sisulu, Walter 43, 109, 116
Sithole, Sizwe 256
Slade, Don 137
Slade, Sergeant George 334
Smith, Lawrence 398
Smuts, Field Marshal 32-33
Smuts, Jan 22, 24
Sobukwe, Robert 108, 112, 115, 118
  church education 43
  detained 97

meeting Peter Storey 112
 pastoral care on Robben Island 109
social justice 47, 103, 329
Social Welfare Department 191
Socialism 19, 247
solitariness, habitual 37-38, 92
Sontonga, Enoch 39
South African Broadcasting Corporation (SABC) 169
South African Council of Churches (SACC) 53, 114, 172
South African Defence Force (SADF) 259
South African English 15-25
South African Foundation 88
South African Gun-owners' Association (SAGA) 400
South African Navy 56
South African War 17, 23
South Western Townships, *see* Soweto
South-West Africa 229
Soweto Murder and Robbery Squad 371
Sparks, Allister 346
St George Trinity Presbyterian Church, Grahamstown 80
St Mary's Cathedral 204, 219, 255, 385
Stalingrad 18
State of Emergency 96, 328
Statesmanship 321
Stead, Rev Bob 312
Steele, Ron 385
Stellenbosch, declared white Group Areas 167
Stevenson, Matt 275, 280-281, 287, 289, 293
stipends, inequality in ministers' 167
Storey, Alan, fourth son of Peter Storey 51-52, 154, 158, 206, 223, 256, 269, 271-273, 377, 399, 411, 420, 462-464
Storey, Christopher, second son of Peter Storey 51-52, 65, 101-102, 265, 269-271
Storey, David, third son of Peter Storey 51-52, 154, 269-270, 291, 380, 389, 409, 411, 420, 462-463, 465
Storey, Elizabeth 46-55, 80, 95-96, 98-99, 101-102, 111, 117, 122-123, 133, 136, 140, 151, 154-156, 175, 190, 193, 206-207, 209, 213, 218, 232, 253, 268, 272, 277, 286, 288, 302, 304-305, 308-309, 311-312, 323-328, 330, 337, 348, 388, 405, 409, 411-412, 417, 420-421, 431-433, 435, 437, 439-440, 443, 445, 447, 454, 457
 see also Hardie, Elizabeth
 Christian pacifist 130-131
 in District Six 142
 of 461-465
 parenting 52-55
 passage back to South Africa 131
 passage to Sydney, Australia 119
Storey, John, eldest son of Peter Storey 51-52, 101 265, 269-271, 290, 420, 462-463
Storey, John, Peter Storey's paternal grandfather 21

Storey, Peter
 and Elizabeth Hardie 45-55
 appointed assistant editor of *Rhodeo* 89
 appointed Probationer Minister at Bellville Methodist Church, Cape Town 92-106
 at Rhodes University 80-92
 aunt Beattie and spouse Harry 32
 birth of 26
 Dad became the leader of MCSA 86
 definition of church 78
 Director of the Australian Life Line Centre 121, 123-124
 District Bishop 172
 editor of *Dimension* 155
 faith and believe 66-79
 father died on 21 Aug 1959, 91
 first act of public protest (1959) 87-88
 first trip to USA 131-132
 health breakdown (1971) 155
 homes and schools 26-34, 41
 John Oates, great-great-great-grandfather of 16
 marriage to Elizabeth Hardie 98-100
 move to Johannesburg 156
 naval career 56-65
 reluctant scholar 80-92
 request to move to Central Methodist House 183-185
 solitariness 37-38
 Stationing Committee move to Johannesburg 156
 stumbling into ministry 93-106
 Vice-President of SACC 172
Storey, Valmai, sister of Peter Storey 19, 28, 45
Stoutt, Rupert 31, 173, 198
Strangers' Friend Society 73
Stretton, Peter Storey's mother's forbears 20
Strijdom Square, Pretoria 236
Strydom, Barend 236
student uprisings, 1976, 231
Students' Representative Council (SRC) 88-90
Sudbury, Dr Stanley 165-166
Suzman, Helen 146
Swanepoel, Col 'Rooi Rus' 231
SWAPO 229, 259, 264, 265
Swart, CR 87

Tambo, Oliver 43, 358-359
Taylor, Barbara Brown 76
Taylor, Most Rev Selby 285
Tebbutt, Peter 09
telephone counselling 120, 132
Terrorism Act 169
Thatcher, Margaret 315
The Alan Walker Mission (1963), 103-104
The Death of a Man 161
The Excursion 27
The Strategic Importance of the City 188
The Whole Gospel for the Whole World 103
Thlokomelong pre-school centres 201

INDEX

Thomson, Rob 149-150
Thorne, Hector 28
Thorne, John 203, 230, 278-279
Thorne, Peter Storey's mother's forbears 20
Thorne, Rev John 390
Thorne, Stretton 31
Thuillier, Christine 178
Tivane, Americo 328
Tobruk 18
Tollman Towers Hotel 219, 221
Transkei Bantustan 164, 168
Transvaal, SAS frigate 58
Treurnicht, Min 170
Trouble Team 124
Truth and Reconciliation Commission (TRC) 194, 226, 235, 258, 274, 379, 422, 434, 492
Tsotsetsi, Charity 219
Tucker, Bob 399
Tunyiswa, Margaret 330
Tunyiswa, Rev Gladwell 330
Tutu, Desmond 43, 51, 54, 138, 173, 195, 203, 208, 231, 242, 248-249, 253, 257, 263, 265, 275, 278, 279, 280, 285, 288, 290, 292, 301, 303, 306, 312, 319, 321, 336, 340, 342, 345, 380, 384, 393, 425, 428, 436, 460, 464, 492
Twelve Club 46
Tyson, Harvey 399

Ubombo, KwaZulu-Natal 151
Umkhonto we Sizwe (MK) 108, 266, 346
Undesirable Organisation Act 171
United Party 31
urban ministry 75

Valmai, Welsh 155
   see also Storey, Valmai
Van Riebeeck, Jan 33
Venda 248-250
Ventersdorp 268
Verryn, Paul 352, 355, 356, 359, 360, 366, 367, 368, 376, 380, 382, 383, 431
Verwoerd, Hendrik 28, 130
   death of 130
   Referendum for Oct 1960, 99
Villa-Vicencio, Charles 146, 334, 342
virtues 27
Von Lieres und Wilkau, Adv Klaus 297
Voortrekker Monument 24
   anniversary of Blood River 25
Vorster, BJ 28, 108, 130, 146-147, 164, 170, 196, 203, 277
Vryburg Children's Centre 323
Vrystaat, SAS 63-64

Walker, Alan 102-103, 120-121, 123, 126, 159, 190-194, 209, 259, 330

1963 preaching campaign in SA 113
1963 preaching mission 113, 119-120
Australian evangelist 102-104
Walmer Estate, Cape Town 134
war crimes 23
Waterkloof Air Force Base 268
Webb, Rev JB 28, 30-31, 183
Welsh, Rev Paul 155
Wesley Methodist Church, Pretoria 66
Wesley Teachers' Training College, Cape Town 148
Wesley, Charles 70-71
Wesley, Rev John 47, 70-71, 82, 136, 217-218, 299, 318, 329, 432
   activism 75
   Aldersgate Street experience 71-72
   on apartheid 75
Wesleyan Class Meetings 47
Wessels, John 400
Western Province Council of Churches (WPCC) 341
Westminster Abbey 22, 315
white evangelical Christians 192
white tribes 22, 25
Wilberforce, William 74
Wilkinson, Rev Dr C Edgar 160-161
Williams, PD 139
Windermere Methodist Primary School 150
Wing, Rev Joe 287
Wit Wolwe 236
Witbooi, Leon 448
Wits University, leaders banned 179-180
Wits-Vaal Peace Accord 53
Wood, Jack, Peter Storey's, maternal grandfather 20
Wood, Mabel 20
Wood, Noel 155, 193
Woodington, Alfred 389, 403
Woods, D 164
Workers' Worship 219
World Council of Churches (WCC) 164, 194, 212, 276
   Central Committee 398
World Methodist Peace Conference 328
World War One 17
World War Two 17, 24, 28, 56
Wrankmore, Bernie 146-147
Wrankmore, Valerie 146-147

Xakane, Mary 41
Xhosa chiefs 35
Xhosa people 16
Xinunu, Kolisa 433

Young Turks 160, 165
Young, Wendy 224, 227
Youth Cabaret, Carpenter's House 143-144

Zeelie, Lt Charles 235

About the Author

Peter Storey is a former bishop of the Methodist Church of Southern Africa and a Distinguished Professor Emeritus of Duke University in North Carolina. Once chaplain to Nelson Mandela and others on Robben Island, he spent most of his 40-year ministry in inner cities, including District Six and central Johannesburg. He led the South African Council of Churches with Bishop Desmond Tutu when it was a fierce opponent of the apartheid state, chaired the National Peace Accord body intervening in pre-election violence in the Witwatersrand and served as a member of the panel that selected the Truth and Reconciliation Commission.

Storey founded Life Line SA and Gun Free SA and has preached and lectured in more than 160 cities around the world. He lives in retirement in Simon's Town and sails on False Bay. He and his late wife Elizabeth had four sons and seven grandchildren.

Picture: Brenda Veldtman